The Ultimate Ninja Foodi 2-Basket Air Fryer Cookbook

500
Super Easy, Delicious & Healthy and Affordable Recipes for Beginners and Advanced Users.

Susan Pena

All Rights Reserved:

The content contained within this book may not be reproduced, duplicated, or transmitted without direct written permission from the author or the publisher. Under no circumstances will any blame or legal responsibility be held against the publisher, or author, for any damages, reparation, or monetary loss due to the information contained within this book, either directly or indirectly.

Legal Notice:
This book is copyright protected. It is only for personal use. You cannot amend, distribute, sell, use, quote or paraphrase any part, or the content within this book, without the consent of the author or publisher.

Disclaimer Notice:

Please note the information contained within this document is for educational and entertainment purposes only. All effort has been executed to present accurate, up to date, reliable, complete information. No warranties of any kind are declared or implied. Readers acknowledge that the author is not engaged in the rendering of legal, financial, medical, or professional advice. The content within this book has been derived from various sources. Please consult a licensed professional before attempting any techniques outlined in this book. By reading this document, the reader agrees that under no circumstances is the author responsible for any losses, direct or indirect, that are incurred as a result of the use of the information contained within this document, including, but not limited to, errors, omissions, or inaccuracies.

Table of Contents

Table of Contents 3
Introduction 8
Getting Started with the Ninja Foodi Dual Zone Air Fryer 8
What the Ninja Foodi Dual Zone Air Fryer is 8
The Features and Benefits of the Ninja Foodi Dual Zone Air Fryers 9
Maintaining and Cleaning the Appliance 9
Main Functions of the Ninja Foodi Dual Zone Air Fryers .. 10
Tips for Cooking Success 10

Appetizers And Snacks 12

Crispy Chicken Bites With Gorgonzola Sauce 12
Classic Potato Chips 12
Beer-battered Onion Rings 12
Wrapped Shrimp Bites 12
Avocado Fries 12
Bbq Chips 12
Fiery Sweet Chicken Wings 13
Antipasto-stuffed Cherry Tomatoes 13
Vegetable Spring Rolls 13
Spicy Chicken And Pepper Jack Cheese Bites 13
Russian Pierogi With Cheese Dip 14
Buffalo Wings 14
Home-style Buffalo Chicken Wings 14
Panko-breaded Onion Rings 14
Tasty Roasted Black Olives&Tomatoes 15
Chicken Shawarma Bites 15
Shrimp Toasts 15
Blooming Onion 15
Zucchini Boats With Bacon 16
Dill Fried Pickles With Light Ranch Dip 16
Classic Chicken Wings 16
Mediterranean Potato Skins 16
Bagel Chips 17
Fried Green Tomatoes 17
Spanish Fried Baby Squid 17
Oyster Spring Rolls 17
Dijon Chicken Wings 17
Green Olive And Mushroom Tapenade 18
Nicoise Deviled Eggs 18
Popcorn Chicken Bites 18
Spiced Parsnip Chips 18
Turkey Burger Sliders 18
Prosciutto Polenta Rounds 18
Beer Battered Onion Rings 19
Spanakopita Spinach,Feta And Pine Nut Phyllo Bites 19
Sweet Potato Chips 19
Cheesy Green Wonton Triangles 19
Indian Cauliflower Tikka Bites 20
Veggie Chips 20
Hot Avocado Fries 20
Cheese Arancini 20
Garlic Wings 21
Tempura Fried Veggies 21
Spiced Nuts 21
Curried Veggie Samosas 21
Stuffed Baby Bella Caps 22
Crunchy Parmesan Edamame 22
Fried Cheese Ravioli With Marinara Sauce 22
Fried Bananas 22
Baba Ghanouj 22
Korean Brussels Sprouts 23
Sweet Apple Fries 23
Hot Cheese Bites 23
Stuffed Prunes In Bacon 23
Salty Pita Crackers 23
String Bean Fries 23
Fried Gyoza 24
Honey Tater Tots With Bacon 24
Tomato&Halloumi Bruschetta 24
Jalapeño Poppers 24

Bread And Breakfast 25

Hush Puffins 25
Country Gravy 25
Bacon Puff Pastry Pinwheels 25
Tuscan Toast 25
Shakshuka Cups 25
Lemon Monkey Bread 26
Cherry-apple Oatmeal Cups 26
Matcha Granola 26
Christmas Eggnog Bread 26
Blueberry Applesauce Oat Cake 26
Pumpkin Bread With Walnuts 26
Cinnamon Biscuit Rolls 27
Sweet Potato-cinnamon Toast 27
Spinach-bacon Rollups 27
Wild Blueberry Lemon Chia Bread 27
Morning Loaded Potato Skins 28
Chili Hash Browns 28
Aromatic Mushroom Omelet 28
Apple&Turkey Breakfast Sausages 28
Farmers Market Quiche 28
Oat&Nut Granola 29
Morning Apple Biscuits 29
Breakfast Chimichangas 29
Blueberry Pannenkoek(dutch Pancake) 29
Bagels With Avocado&Tomatoes 29
Cheddar&Sausage Tater Tots 29
Banana Bread 30
Pesto Egg&Ham Sandwiches 30
Garlic Bread Knots 30
Fluffy Vegetable Strata 30
Western Omelet 30
Coffee Cake 31
Smoked Salmon Croissant Sandwich 31
Effortless Toffee Zucchini Bread 31
Morning Burrito 31
Peppered Maple Bacon Knots 31
Fry Bread 31
Breakfast Sausage Bites 32

Breakfast Burrito With Sausage 32
Veggie&Feta Scramble Bowls 32
Egg&Bacon Toasts 32
Honey Donuts 32
English Breakfast 33
Ham And Cheddar Gritters 33
Nutty Whole Wheat Muffins 33
Mini Everything Bagels 33
Pumpkin Empanadas 34
Chicken Scotch Eggs 34
Chocolate Chip Banana Muffins 34
Cinnamon Banana Bread With Pecans 34

Vegetable Side Dishes Recipes 35

Speedy Baked Caprese With Avocado 35
Stunning Apples&Onions 35
Perfect French Fries 35
Sriracha Green Beans 35
Roasted Broccoli And Red Bean Salad 35
Tuna Platter 36
Hasselback Garlic-and-butter Potatoes 36
Cheesy Breaded Eggplants 36
Crispy Herbed Potatoes 36
Almond-crusted Zucchini Fries 36
Parsnip Fries With Romesco Sauce 37
Dilly Sesame Roasted Asparagus 37
French Fries 37
Roasted Ratatouille Vegetables 37
Tomato Candy 37
Fried Pearl Onions With Balsamic Vinegar And Basil 38
Honey-roasted Parsnips 38
Yellow Squash 38
Sage&Thyme Potatoes 38
Dijon Artichoke Hearts 38
Honey-mustard Asparagus Puffs 39
Roasted Fennel Salad 39
Buttery Stuffed Tomatoes 39
Hawaiian Brown Rice 39
Honey-mustard Roasted Cabbage 39
Cauliflower 39
Bacon-wrapped Asparagus 40
Herbed Baby Red Potato Hasselback 40
Roasted Brussels Sprouts With Bacon 40
Panko-crusted Zucchini Fries 40
Sea Salt Radishes 40
Green Dip With Pine Nuts 40
Almond Green Beans 40
Steak Fries 41
Crispy Brussels Sprouts 41
Asparagus 41
Grits Casserole 41
Roasted Thyme Asparagus 41
Succulent Roasted Peppers 41
Honey Brussels Sprouts 42
Curried Cauliflower With Cashews And Yogurt 42
Simple Green Bake 42
Corn On The Cob 42
Mushrooms 42
Charred Radicchio Salad 42
Citrusy Brussels Sprouts 43
Simple Peppered Carrot Chips 43
Polenta 43
Sticky Broccoli Florets 43
Moroccan Cauliflower 43
Tofu&Broccoli Salad 43
Green Beans 43
Teriyaki Tofu With Spicy Mayo 44
Sweet Potato Fries 44
Steamboat Shrimp Salad 44
Roasted Belgian Endive With Pistachios And Lemon 44
Cheese&Bacon Pasta Bake 44
Homemade Potato Puffs 45
Patatas Bravas 45
Mouth-watering Provençal Mushrooms 45

Beef, pork&Lamb Recipes 46

Zesty London Broil 46
Rib Eye Bites With Mushrooms 46
Country-style Pork Ribs(2) 46
Peachy Pork Chops 46
Crispy Smoked Pork Chops 46
Smokehouse-style Beef Ribs 47
Spicy Hoisin Bbq Pork Chops 47
French-style Pork Medallions 47
Golden Pork Quesadillas 47
Balsamic Beef&Veggie Skewers 47
Lamb Koftas Meatballs 48
Vietnamese Shaking Beef 48
Coffee-rubbed Pork Tenderloin 48
Teriyaki Country-style Pork Ribs 48
Bbq Back Ribs 48
Beef Brazilian Empanadas 49
Sage Pork With Potatoes 49
Suwon Pork Meatballs 49
Traditional Moo Shu Pork Lettuce Wraps 49
Beef Meatballs With Herbs 49
Delicious Juicy Pork Meatballs 50
Original Köttbullar 50
Tuscan Chimichangas 50
Oktoberfest Bratwursts 50
Sloppy Joes 50
Chicken Fried Steak 51
Crispy Lamb Shoulder Chops 51
Boneless Ribeyes 51
Pepperoni Pockets 51
Easy Carnitas 51
Barbecue-style London Broil 52
Chinese-style Lamb Chops 52
Mushroom&Quinoa-stuffed Pork Loins 52
Kentucky-style Pork Tenderloin 52
Traditional Italian Beef Meatballs 52
Almond And Sun-dried Tomato Crusted Pork Chops 53
Baby Back Ribs 53
Bourbon Bacon Burgers 53
Natchitoches Meat Pies 53
Argentinian Steak Asado Salad 54
Tonkatsu 54
Lamb Meatballs With Quick Tomato Sauce 54
Tasty Filet Mignon 55
Balsamic Short Ribs 55
Balsamic London Broil 55
Crunchy Veal Cutlets 55
Sirloin Steak Bites With Gravy 55
Wasabi Pork Medallions 56

Beef Short Ribs 56	Pepperoni Bagel Pizzas 59
Broccoli&Mushroom Beef 56	Cheeseburger Sliders With Pickle Sauce 59
Better-than-chinese-take-out Sesame Beef 56	Fusion Tender Flank Steak 59
Wasabi-coated Pork Loin Chops 57	Peppered Steak Bites 60
Sriracha Pork Strips With Rice 57	Pork Loin 60
Mini Meatloaves With Pancetta 57	Easy-peasy Beef Sliders 60
Homemade Pork Gyoza 57	Honey Mesquite Pork Chops 60
Greek Pork Chops 57	Calzones South Of The Border 60
Chile Con Carne Galette 58	Beef And Spinach Braciole 61
Tamari-seasoned Pork Strips 58	Basil Cheese&Ham Stromboli 61
Friendly Bbq Baby Back Ribs 58	Garlic And Oregano Lamb Chops 61
Tacos Norteños 58	Aromatic Pork Tenderloin 62
Paprika Fried Beef 58	T-bone Steak With Roasted Tomato,Corn And Asparagus Salsa 62
Skirt Steak Fajitas 59	

Fish And Seafood Recipes 63

Shrimp-jalapeño Poppers In Prosciutto 63	Old Bay Fish`n´Chips 70
Basil Crab Cakes With Fresh Salad 63	Chinese Fish Noodle Bowls 70
Hot Calamari Rings 63	Five Spice Red Snapper With Green Onions And Orange Salsa 70
Old Bay Lobster Tails 63	
Speedy Shrimp Paella 63	Fish Sticks With Tartar Sauce 71
Autenthic Greek Fish Pitas 64	Catalan Sardines With Romesco Sauce 71
Tuna Nuggets In Hoisin Sauce 64	Salmon Croquettes 71
Cheese&Crab Stuffed Mushrooms 64	Fish Nuggets With Broccoli Dip 71
Masala Fish`n´Chips 64	Fish Tacos With Jalapeño-lime Sauce 71
Sweet Potato–wrapped Shrimp 64	Sinaloa Fish Fajitas 72
Lime Halibut Parcels 65	Crab Cakes On A Budget 72
Popcorn Crawfish 65	Herb-crusted Sole 72
Maple Balsamic Glazed Salmon 65	Coconut-shrimp Po'Boys 72
Mediterranean Salmon Cakes 65	Restaurant-style Breaded Shrimp 73
Coconut Shrimp With Plum Sauce 65	Sea Bass With Fruit Salsa 73
Mojito Fish Tacos 66	Flounder Fillets 73
Salty German-style Shrimp Pancakes 66	Rich Salmon Burgers With Broccoli Slaw 73
Perfect Soft-shelled Crabs 66	Easy-peasy Shrimp 73
Crispy Smelts 66	Salmon Puttanesca En Papillotte With Zucchini 74
Curried Sweet-and-spicy Scallops 66	Caribbean Jerk Cod Fillets 74
Black Olive&Shrimp Salad 67	Blackened Red Snapper 74
Sweet&Spicy Swordfish Kebabs 67	Yummy Salmon Burgers With Salsa Rosa 74
Oyster Shrimp With Fried Rice 67	Salmon 75
Catfish Nuggets 67	Family Fish Nuggets With Tartar Sauce 75
Mojo Sea Bass 67	Shrimp Patties 75
Almond-crusted Fish 67	Fish Goujons With Tartar Sauce 75
Lemon-dill Salmon Burgers 68	Easy Scallops With Lemon Butter 75
Dilly Red Snapper 68	Old Bay Crab Cake Burgers 76
Fish Piccata With Crispy Potatoes 68	Saucy Shrimp 76
Southeast Asian-style Tuna Steaks 68	Shrimp,Chorizo And Fingerling Potatoes 76
Easy Asian-style Tuna 68	Nutty Shrimp With Amaretto Glaze 76
Horseradish Tuna Croquettes 69	Shrimp Al Pesto 77
Tex-mex Fish Tacos 69	Fish Cakes 77
Piña Colada Shrimp 69	Butternut Squash–wrapped Halibut Fillets 77
King Prawns Al Ajillo 69	Quick Tuna Tacos 77
Holiday Shrimp Scampi 69	Lemon&Herb Crusted Salmon 77
Catalan-style Crab Samfaina 70	Korean-style Fried Calamari 78
British Fish&Chips 70	Horseradish-crusted Salmon Fillets 78

Poultry Recipes 79

Crispy Cordon Bleu 79	Popcorn Chicken Tenders With Vegetables 80
Smoky Chicken Fajita Bowl 79	Satay Chicken Skewers 80
Asian-style Orange Chicken 79	Maple Bacon Wrapped Chicken Breasts 81
Super-simple Herby Turkey 79	Turkey&Rice Frittata 81
Asian Meatball Tacos 79	Mushroom&Turkey Bread Pizza 81
Buttered Turkey Breasts 80	Chicken Pinchos Morunos 81
Simple Salsa Chicken Thighs 80	Italian Roasted Chicken Thighs 81
Indian-inspired Chicken Skewers 80	Sunday Chicken Skewers 82

Buttery Chicken Legs 82	Garlic Chicken 86
Cornflake Chicken Nuggets 82	Parmesan Crusted Chicken Cordon Bleu 87
Crispy Chicken Parmesan 82	Chicken&Rice Sautée 87
Katsu Chicken Thighs 82	Chicken Nuggets 87
Cajun Fried Chicken 82	Cajun Chicken Kebabs 87
Mustardy Chicken Bites 83	Ranch Chicken Tortillas 88
Lemon Sage Roast Chicken 83	Poblano Bake 88
Gluten-free Nutty Chicken Fingers 83	Chicken Rochambeau 88
Teriyaki Chicken Legs 83	Saucy Chicken Thighs 88
Boss Chicken Cobb Salad 83	Farmer's Fried Chicken 89
Vip's Club Sandwiches 84	Windsor's Chicken Salad 89
Masala Chicken With Charred Vegetables 84	Maewoon Chicken Legs 89
Spinach And Feta Stuffed Chicken Breasts 84	German Chicken Frikadellen 89
Teriyaki Chicken Drumsticks 84	Paprika Chicken Drumettes 89
Sweet-and-sour Chicken 85	Fiesta Chicken Plate 89
Daadi Chicken Salad 85	Jerk Chicken Drumsticks 90
Sage&Paprika Turkey Cutlets 85	The Ultimate Chicken Bulgogi 90
Southern-fried Chicken Livers 85	Irresistible Cheesy Chicken Sticks 90
Pecan Turkey Cutlets 86	Turkey Scotch Eggs 90
Chicken Skewers 86	Peanut Butter-barbeque Chicken 91
Rich Turkey Burgers 86	Chicken Parmesan 91
Fancy Chicken Piccata 86	Apricot Glazed Chicken Thighs 91

Vegetarians Recipes 92

Authentic Mexican Esquites 92	Easy Cheese&Spinach Lasagna 98
Curried Potato,Cauliflower And Pea Turnovers 92	Spicy Vegetable And Tofu Shake Fry 99
Vegetable Couscous 92	Tomato&Squash Stuffed Mushrooms 99
Veggie Fried Rice 93	Falafels 99
Effortless Mac`n´Cheese 93	Crunchy Rice Paper Samosas 99
Zucchini Tamale Pie 93	Roasted Vegetable,Brown Rice And Black Bean Burrito .100
Pine Nut Eggplant Dip 93	Spinach And Cheese Calzone 100
Cheesy Eggplant Rounds 93	Zucchini Tacos 100
Sushi-style Deviled Eggs 94	Roasted Vegetable Pita Pizza 100
Hellenic Zucchini Bites 94	Roasted Vegetable Thai Green Curry 101
Berbere Eggplant Dip 94	Vietnamese Gingered Tofu 101
Vegan Buddha Bowls(2) 94	Balsamic Caprese Hasselback 101
Harissa Veggie Fries 94	General Tso's Cauliflower 101
Thyme Lentil Patties 95	Thai Peanut Veggie Burgers 102
Bell Pepper&Lentil Tacos 95	Quinoa&Black Bean Stuffed Peppers 102
Garlicky Brussel Sprouts With Saffron Aioli 95	Vegetarian Shepherd's Pie 102
Vegetable Hand Pies 95	Quinoa Burgers With Feta Cheese And Dill 102
Vegetarian Paella 95	Chicano Rice Bowls 103
Sweet Corn Bread 95	Cheddar-bean Flautas 103
Lentil Burritos With Cilantro Chutney 96	Pineapple&Veggie Souvlaki 103
Tropical Salsa 96	Smoked Paprika Sweet Potato Fries 103
Bite-sized Blooming Onions 96	Honey Pear Chips 104
Pizza Portobello Mushrooms 96	Cheesy Enchilada Stuffed Baked Potatoes 104
Cheese&Bean Burgers 97	Spicy Bean Patties 104
Stuffed Portobellos 97	Asparagus,Mushroom And Cheese Soufflés 104
Stuffed Zucchini Boats 97	Quinoa Green Pizza 105
Easy Zucchini Lasagna Roll-ups 97	Powerful Jackfruit Fritters 105
Vegetarian Eggplant"pizzas" 98	Corn And Pepper Jack Chile Rellenos With Roasted Tomato Sauce 105
Caprese-style Sandwiches 98	
Ricotta Veggie Potpie 98	Rice&Bean Burritos 106
Mexican Twice Air-fried Sweet Potatoes 98	

Sandwiches And Burgers Recipes 107

Philly Cheesesteak Sandwiches 107	Chicken Club Sandwiches 108
Inside Out Cheeseburgers 107	Crunchy Falafel Balls 109
Asian Glazed Meatballs 107	Chicken Saltimbocca Sandwiches 109
Thanksgiving Turkey Sandwiches 107	Eggplant Parmesan Subs 109
Chicken Spiedies 108	Chili Cheese Dogs 109
Best-ever Roast Beef Sandwiches 108	Thai-style Pork Sliders 110
Perfect Burgers 108	Dijon Thyme Burgers 110

White Bean Veggie Burgers 110	Mexican Cheeseburgers 111
Inside-out Cheeseburgers 110	Chicken Gyros 111
Black Bean Veggie Burgers 111	Chicken Apple Brie Melt 112

Desserts And Sweets 113

Gingerbread 113	Fruity Oatmeal Crisp 118
Strawberry Pastry Rolls 113	Nutty Banana Bread 118
Wild Blueberry Sweet Empanadas 113	Home-style Pumpkin Pie Pudding 118
Mango Cobbler With Raspberries 114	British Bread Pudding 118
Strawberry Donuts 114	Carrot-oat Cake Muffins 119
Puff Pastry Apples 114	Fried Cannoli Wontons 119
Baked Stuffed Pears 114	Fall Pumpkin Cake 119
Peach Cobbler 115	Pumpkin Brownies 119
Apple-carrot Cupcakes 115	Chewy Coconut Cake 119
S'mores Pockets 115	Mixed Berry Hand Pies 120
Raspberry Empanada 115	Honeyed Tortilla Fritters 120
Fast Brownies 115	Baked Apple 120
Coconut-custard Pie 116	Banana Bread Cake 120
Cherry Cheesecake Rolls 116	Roasted Pears 121
Ricotta Stuffed Apples 116	Dark Chokolate Cookies 121
Sea-salted Caramel Cookie Cups 116	Apple&Blueberry Crumble 121
Oreo-coated Peanut Butter Cups 116	Cheesecake Wontons 121
Black And Blue Clafoutis 116	Cheese&Honey Stuffed Figs 122
Nutty Cookies 117	Giant Buttery Oatmeal Cookie 122
Mixed Berry Pie 117	Carrot Cake With Cream Cheese Icing 122
Spiced Fruit Skewers 117	Vanilla-strawberry Muffins 122
Banana-almond Delights 117	Orange-chocolate Cake 123
Cinnamon Canned Biscuit Donuts 117	Honey-roasted Mixed Nuts 123
Cheese Blintzes 117	Giant Vegan Chocolate Chip Cookie 123
Tortilla Fried Pies 118	Fluffy Orange Cake 124

RECIPE INDEX 125

Introduction

Life is too busy today, and there is no time to cook for a long day. If you want to eat delicious and healthy meals, the Ninja Foodi Dual Zone Air Fryer solves your problem. The Ninja Foodi Dual Zone Air Fryer is a new arrival amongst diversified air fryers. Now, you can cook a large amount of food because it has two baskets. You can cook two different food items with two same or different settings. It is different from a single basket air fryer. This appliance targets people who want to enjoy delicious and healthy but less fatty meals with a crispy texture. The Ninja Foodi Dual Zone Air Fryer is an excellent appliance to fulfill all the cooking needs. You can create excellent restaurant-style meals in your kitchen with the Ninja Foodi Dual Zone Air Fryer.

No doubt, the Ninja Foodi Dual Zone Air Fryer plays a vital role in making healthy and delicious foods. You don't need to stand in your kitchen cooking food for a long time. The benefits of this appliance are that it is easily washable and requires less oil to cook food. The Ninja Foodi Dual Zone Air Fryer works on dual zone technology. It allows you to prepare double dishes at the same time with two different cooking baskets and temperatures. If you have a big family, then you can cook food for them at the same time. The cooking zones have a separate temperature controller and cyclonic fan that spread heat evenly into the cooking baskets. The Ninja Foodi Dual Zone Air Fryer cooks your favorite food in less oil. It gives you crispy food without changing the taste and texture.

You can create different dishes for any occasion or picnic. The Ninja Foodi Dual Zone Air Fryer has useful cooking functions, such as max crisp, air fry, roast, reheat, dehydrate, and bake. All valuable functions are present in one appliance. You don't need to purchase separate appliances for baking or dehydrating food. You can roast chicken, beef, and fish using this appliance. Bake the cake, muffins, cupcakes, pancakes using bake cooking functions.

This Ninja Foodi Dual Zone Air Fryer cookbook will introduce you to the features and benefits of this revolutionary appliance. Apart from that, the functions of the Ninja Foodi Dual Zone Air Fryer are discussed in this cookbook, helping you unleash its full potential. And, of course, I'll introduce you to a wide variety of recipes so you can use it every day. The air fryer is pretty simple to use. Once you understand the Ninja Foodi Dual Zone Air Fryer, you can prepare delicious food for your family and friends without any hesitation. Cook food with the Ninja Foodi Dual Zone Air Fryer!

Getting Started with the Ninja Foodi Dual Zone Air Fryer

What the Ninja Foodi Dual Zone Air Fryer is

The new Ninja Foodi Dual Zone Air Fryer has a DUAL-ZONE technology that includes a smart finish button that cooks two food items in two different ways at the same time. It has a MATCH button that cooks food by copying the setting across both zones.

The 8 –quart air fryer has a capacity that can cook full family meals up to 4 pounds. The two zones have their separate baskets that cook food using cyclonic fans that heat food rapidly with circulating hot air all-around. The baskets are very easy to clean and dishwasher safe. The Ninja Foodi Dual Zone Air Fryer has a range of 105-450 °F temperature. The Ninja Foodie Dual Zone Air Fryer is easily available at an affordable price online and at local stores.

If you are always worried about the lack of time to prepare two different meals or a large number of meals in a single go, then this appliance is a must to have. It can hold plenty of food that can feed a large family.

The Features and Benefits of the Ninja Foodi Dual Zone Air Fryers

The Ninja Foodi Dual Zone Air Fryer is one of the innovative product designs manufactured. If you are looking for a perfect air fryer for your family, then the Ninja Foodi Dual Zone Air Fryer is one of the best options available for you. Some of the important features and benefits of the Ninja Foodi Dual Zone Air Fryer are mentioned as follows.

1. 8-Quart Capacity XL
The enormous 8-quart capacity, which can be divided into two sections, provides ample area for cooking both large and small amounts of food. This oven can cook 2 pounds of fries and 2 pounds of wings and drumettes.

2. Multifunctional Air Fryer
The Ninja Foodi Dual Zone Air Fryer comes with 6 preset functions. These easily customizable functions include max crisp, air fry, roast, bake, reheat and dehydrate. You never need to buy separate appliances for a single cooking function.

3. Safer Than Deep Fryer
Traditional deep frying method involves a large container full of sizzling oil. This can increase the safety risk of splashing hot oil over the skin. While the Ninja Foodi Dual Zone Air Fryer is close from all the sides when getting hot, there is no risk of splashing, spilling or accidental burn during the cooking process.

4. Smart Finish
This culinary marvel can intelligently sync the cook timings of both cooking zones, allowing you to prepare multiple items at the same time while maintaining the same finish time. So, here's how it's done! When you put various foods in the baskets, each one takes a different amount of time to cook. When you use the smart cooking feature and start the operation, the basket with the longer cooking time will run first, while the other basket will remain on hold until the other chamber reaches the same cooking duration. Both sides finish cooking at the same time in this manner.

5. Match Cook
This air fryer's total 8 quartz capacity is divided into two 4-quart air fryer baskets, allowing you to cook various foods and the same dish in both baskets at the same time. You can utilize the same cooking mode for both baskets and utilize the XL capacity with the match cook technology.

6. Reduce the Risk of Acrylamide Formation
Deep frying is one of the high heat cooking methods in which harmful acrylamide is formed. It is one of the causes of developing some cancer like ovarian, endometrial, oesophageal and breast cancer. On the other side, this air fryer cooks your food into very little oil and fat by circulating hot air around the food. This process lowers the risk of acrylamide formation.

7. Use Less Oil and Fats
The cooking basket of the oven comes with ceramic non-stick coatings and allows you to prepare your favorite food using up to 75 to 80 % less fat and oils than the traditional deep frying method.

8. Wide Temperature Range
The Ninja Foodi Dual Zone Air Fryer offers a range of 105 °F to 400 °F temperature. The lower temperature range is suitable for dehydrating your favorite fruits, vegetable, and meat slices, and the higher temperature range allows you to cook thick cuts of meat.

9. Easy to Clean
The interior of this air fryer is made up of a non-stick coating so that you can clean it easily. The cooking tray comes in metallic and dishwasher safe, but you can easily clean it by hand if you want to.

Maintaining and Cleaning the Appliance

1. Maintaining
- It is very important to check that the voltage indication is corresponding to the main voltage from the switch.
- Do not immerse the appliance in water.
- Keep the cord away from the hot area.
- Do not touch the outer surface of the air fryer hen using for cooking purposes.
- Put the appliance on a horizontal and flat surface.
- Unplug the appliance after use.

2. Cleaning
- First, unplug the power cord of the air fryer.
- Make sure the appliance is cooled before cleaning.
- The air fryer should be cleaning after every use.

Ninja Foodi 2-Basket Air Fryer

- To clean the outer surface, use a damp towel.
- Clean the inside of the air fryer with a nonabrasive sponge.
- The accessories of the air fryer are dishwasher safe, but to extend the life of the drawers, it's recommended to wash them manually.

Main Functions of the Ninja Foodi Dual Zone Air Fryers

The Ninja Foodi Dual Zone Air Fryer has six cooking functions: max crisp, air fry, roast, reheat, dehydrate and bake. This appliance has a large capacity. You can prepare food for your big family. If you want to bake a cake with the Ninja Foodi Dual Zone Air Fryer, you can select "bake" cooking mode.

1. Max Crisp
This cooking function is perfect for frozen foods such as chicken nuggets and French fries etc. Using this function, you will get crispy and tender food. With less time, you will get crispy and tender food.

2. Air Fry
This cooking function will allow you to cook food with less oil and fat than other cooking methods. Using this function, you will get crunchy and crispy food from the outside and juicy and tender food from the inside. You can prepare chicken, beef, lamb, pork, and seafood using this cooking option.

3. Roast
Now, you didn't need an oven to roast food. The Ninja Foodi Dual Zone Air Fryer has useful cooking function, "roast". With this function, you can roast chicken, lamb, seafood, and vegetable dishes. It is one of the dry cooking methods that give you a nice brown texture to the food and increase the flavor of your foods.

4. Reheat
The reheat function can quickly warm your food without changing its texture and flavor if you have leftover food. Now, you didn't need to place food onto the stovetop for reheating.

5. Dehydrate
This cooking function is used to dehydrate fruits, meat, and vegetables. Using this cooking method, you can preserve food for a long time. It takes hours to dehydrate the food but gives you a delicious and crispy texture.

6. Bake
This cooking method allows you to bake cakes, muffins, cupcakes, and any other dessert on any occasion or regular day. You didn't need an oven to bake the food. The Ninja Foodi Dual Zone Air Fryer has a baking option for baking your food with delicious texture.

Tips for Cooking Success

Remember these nifty tips whenever you are cooking with your new air fryer.

1. Pressing the Start/Pause button while using the Smart Finish will pause the cooking process on both zones. Press the same button to resume cooking.
2. If at any time you need to pause the cooking process in one of the baskets, first select the zone, then the Start/Pause button.
3. To stop or end the cooking process, select the zone, then set the time to zero using the arrow down button. The display should show End after a few seconds, and the cooking process in this zone will stop.
4. You can adjust the temperature and time in each zone at any time during the cooking process. Select the zone, then adjust the setting using the arrow buttons.
5. Place a single layer of food and avoid stacking whenever possible.
6. To get the best results, toss or shake the food at least twice within the cooking cycle, especially for foods that overlap, like French fries. This will produce a more even cooking throughout.
7. When cooking fresh vegetables, add at least one tablespoon of cooking oil. More oil can be added to create a crispier texture.
8. Use the crisper plates when you want your food to become crunchy. Note that the crisper plates will slightly elevate your food to allow hot air to permeate the bottom

and result in a crispier texture.

9. Follow the correct breading technique for wet battered food. Coat the food with flour first, then with egg, and finally with bread crumbs. Press the crumbs into the food to avoid it from flying around when air frying.

10. It is best to regularly check the progress to avoid overcooking.

11. A food-safe temperature must be reached to avoid any foodborne illness. Use a thermometer to check for doneness, especially when cooking raw meat. Instant-read thermometers are your best choice for this. Once cooking time is up or when the desired browning is achieved, promptly remove the food from the unit.

12. Do not use metal cutleries or tools that can damage the non-stick coating. Dump the food directly on a plate or use silicon-tipped tongs.

13. Small bits of food may be blown away while cooking. You can avoid this by securing pieces of food with toothpicks.

14. To cook recipes intended for traditional ovens, simply reduce the temperature by 25 °F and regularly check for doneness.

15. Do not let food touch the heating elements.

16. Never overload the baskets. Not only will this result in uneven cooking, but it may also cause the appliance to malfunction as well.

Ninja Foodi 2-Basket Air Fryer

Appetizers And Snacks

Crispy Chicken Bites With Gorgonzola Sauce

Servings: 4
Cooking Time: 30 Minutes
Ingredients:
- ¼ cup crumbled Gorgonzola cheese
- ¼ cup creamy blue cheese salad dressing
- 1 lb chicken tenders, cut into thirds crosswise
- ½ cup sour cream
- 1 celery stalk, chopped
- 3 tbsp buffalo chicken sauce
- 1 cup panko bread crumbs
- 2 tbsp olive oil

Directions:
1. Preheat air fryer to 350°F. Blend together sour cream, salad dressing, Gorgonzola cheese, and celery in a bowl. Set aside. Combine chicken pieces and Buffalo wing sauce in another bowl until the chicken is coated.
2. In a shallow bowl or pie plate, mix the bread crumbs and olive oil. Dip the chicken into the bread crumb mixture, patting the crumbs to keep them in place. Arrange the chicken in the greased frying basket and Air Fry for 8-9 minutes, shaking once halfway through cooking until the chicken is golden. Serve with the blue cheese sauce.

Classic Potato Chips

Servings: 4
Cooking Time: 8 Minutes
Ingredients:
- 2 medium russet potatoes, washed
- 2 cups filtered water
- 1 tablespoon avocado oil
- ½ teaspoon salt

Directions:
1. Using a mandolin, slice the potatoes into ⅛-inch-thick pieces.
2. Pour the water into a large bowl. Place the potatoes in the bowl and soak for at least 30 minutes.
3. Preheat the air fryer to 350°F.
4. Drain the water and pat the potatoes dry with a paper towel or kitchen cloth. Toss with avocado oil and salt. Liberally spray the air fryer basket with olive oil mist.
5. Set the potatoes inside the air fryer basket, separating them so they're not on top of each other. Cook for 5 minutes, shake the basket, and cook another 5 minutes, or until browned.
6. Remove and let cool a few minutes prior to serving. Repeat until all the chips are cooked.

Beer-battered Onion Rings

Servings: 4
Cooking Time: 25 Minutes
Ingredients:
- 2 sliced onions, rings separated
- 1 cup flour
- Salt and pepper to taste
- 1 tsp garlic powder
- 1 cup beer

Directions:
1. Preheat air fryer to 350°F. In a mixing bowl, combine the flour, garlic powder, beer, salt, and black pepper. Dip the onion rings into the bowl and lay the coated rings in the frying basket. Air Fry for 15 minutes, shaking the basket several times during cooking to jostle the onion rings and ensure a good even fry. Once ready, the onions should be crispy and golden brown. Serve hot.

Wrapped Shrimp Bites

Servings: 4
Cooking Time: 15 Minutes
Ingredients:
- 2 jumbo shrimp, peeled
- 2 bacon strips, sliced
- 2 tbsp lemon juice
- ½ tsp chipotle powder
- ½ tsp garlic salt

Directions:
1. Preheat air fryer to 350°F. Wrap the bacon around the shrimp and place the shrimp in the foil-lined frying basket, seam side down. Drizzle with lemon juice, chipotle powder and garlic salt. Air Fry for 10 minutes, turning the shrimp once until cooked through and bacon is crispy. Serve hot.

Avocado Fries

Servings: 8
Cooking Time: 8 Minutes
Ingredients:
- 2 medium avocados, firm but ripe
- 1 large egg
- ½ teaspoon garlic powder
- ¼ teaspoon cayenne pepper
- ¼ teaspoon salt
- ¾ cup almond flour
- ½ cup finely grated Parmesan cheese
- ½ cup gluten-free breadcrumbs

Directions:
1. Preheat the air fryer to 370°F.
2. Rinse the outside of the avocado with water. Slice the avocado in half, slice it in half again, and then slice it in half once more to get 8 slices. Remove the outer skin. Repeat for the other avocado. Set the avocado slices aside.
3. In a small bowl, whisk the egg, garlic powder, cayenne pepper, and salt in a small bowl. Set aside.
4. In a separate bowl, pour the almond flour.
5. In a third bowl, mix the Parmesan cheese and breadcrumbs.
6. Carefully roll the avocado slices in the almond flour, then dip them in the egg wash, and coat them in the cheese and breadcrumb topping. Repeat until all 16 fries are coated.
7. Liberally spray the air fryer basket with olive oil spray and place the avocado fries into the basket, leaving a little space around the sides between fries. Depending on the size of your air fryer, you may need to cook these in batches.
8. Cook fries for 8 minutes, or until the outer coating turns light brown.
9. Carefully remove, repeat with remaining slices, and then serve warm.

Bbq Chips

Servings: 2
Cooking Time: 30 Minutes
Ingredients:
- 1 scrubbed russet potato, sliced
- ½ tsp smoked paprika
- ¼ tsp chili powder
- ¼ tsp garlic powder
- 1/8 tsp onion powder
- ¼ tbsp smoked paprika

Ninja Foodi 2-Basket Air Fryer

- 1/8 tsp light brown sugar
- Salt and pepper to taste
- 2 tsp olive oil

Directions:
1. Preheat air fryer at 400°F. Combine all seasoning in a bowl. Set aside. In another bowl, mix potato chips, olive oil, black pepper, and salt until coated. Place potato chips in the frying basket and Air Fry for 17 minutes, shaking 3 times. Transfer it into a bowl. Sprinkle with the bbq mixture and let sit for 15 minutes. Serve immediately.

Fiery Sweet Chicken Wings

Servings: 4
Cooking Time: 30 Minutes
Ingredients:
- 8 chicken wings
- 1 tbsp olive oil
- 3 tbsp brown sugar
- 2 tbsp maple syrup
- ½ cup apple cider vinegar
- ½ tsp Aleppo pepper flakes
- Salt to taste

Directions:
1. Preheat air fryer to 390°F. Toss the wings with olive oil in a bowl. Bake in the air fryer for 20 minutes, shaking the basket twice. While the chicken is cooking, whisk together sugar, maple syrup, vinegar, Aleppo pepper flakes, and salt in a small bowl. Transfer the wings to a baking pan, then pour the sauce over the wings. Toss well to coat. Cook in the air fryer until the wings are glazed, or for another 5 minutes. Serve hot.

Antipasto-stuffed Cherry Tomatoes

Servings: 12
Cooking Time: 9 Minutes
Ingredients:
- 12 Large cherry tomatoes, preferably Campari tomatoes (about 1½ ounces each and the size of golf balls)
- ½ cup Seasoned Italian-style dried bread crumbs (gluten-free, if a concern)
- ¼ cup (about ¾ ounce) Finely grated Parmesan cheese
- ¼ cup Finely chopped pitted black olives
- ¼ cup Finely chopped marinated artichoke hearts
- 2 tablespoons Marinade from the artichokes
- 4 Sun-dried tomatoes (dry, not packed in oil), finely chopped
- Olive oil spray

Directions:
1. Preheat the air fryer to 400°F.
2. Cut the top off of each fresh tomato, exposing the seeds and pulp. (The tops can be saved for a snack, sprinkled with some kosher salt, to tide you over while the stuffed tomatoes cook.) Cut a very small slice off the bottom of each tomato (no cutting into the pulp) so it will stand up flat on your work surface. Use a melon baller to remove and discard the seeds and pulp from each tomato.
3. Mix the bread crumbs, cheese, olives, artichoke hearts, marinade, and sun-dried tomatoes in a bowl until well combined. Stuff this mixture into each prepared tomato, about 1½ tablespoons in each. Generously coat the tops of the tomatoes with olive oil spray.
4. Set the tomatoes stuffing side up in the basket. Air-fry undisturbed for 9 minutes, or until the stuffing has browned a bit and the tomatoes are blistered in places.
5. Remove the basket and cool the tomatoes in it for 5 minutes. Then use kitchen tongs to gently transfer the tomatoes to a serving platter.

Vegetable Spring Rolls

Servings: 6
Cooking Time: 8 Minutes
Ingredients:
- ¾ cup (a little more than 2½ ounces) Fresh bean sprouts
- 6 tablespoons Shredded carrots
- 6 tablespoons Slivered, drained, sliced canned bamboo shoots
- 1½ tablespoons Regular or low-sodium soy sauce or gluten-free tamari sauce
- 1½ teaspoons Granulated white sugar
- 1½ teaspoons Toasted sesame oil
- 6 Spring roll wrappers (gluten-free, if a concern)
- 1 Large egg, well beaten
- Vegetable oil spray

Directions:
1. Gently stir the bean sprouts, carrots, bamboo shoots, soy or tamari sauce, sugar, and oil in a large bowl until the vegetables are evenly coated. Set aside at room temperature for 10 to 15 minutes.
2. Preheat the air fryer to 400°F.
3. Set a spring roll wrapper on a clean, dry work surface. Pick up about ¼ cup of the vegetable mixture and gently squeeze it in your clean hand to release most of the liquid. Set this bundle of vegetables along one edge of the wrapper.
4. Fold two opposing sides (at right angles to the filling) up and over the filling, concealing part of it and making a folded-over border down two sides of the wrapper. Brush the top half of the wrapper (including the folded parts) with beaten egg so it will seal when you roll it closed.
5. Starting with the side nearest the filling, roll the wrapper closed, working to make a tight fit, eliminating as much air as possible from inside the wrapper. Set it aside seam side down and continue making more filled rolls using the same techniques.
6. Lightly coat all the sealed rolls with vegetable oil spray on all sides. Set them seam side down in the basket and air-fry undisturbed for 8 minutes, or until golden brown and very crisp.
7. Use a nonstick-safe spatula and a flatware fork for balance to transfer the rolls to a wire rack. Cool for at least 5 minutes or up to 15 minutes before serving.

Spicy Chicken And Pepper Jack Cheese Bites

Servings: 8
Cooking Time: 8 Minutes
Ingredients:
- 8 ounces cream cheese, softened
- 2 cups grated pepper jack cheese
- 1 Jalapeño pepper, diced
- 2 scallions, minced
- 1 teaspoon paprika
- 2 teaspoons salt, divided
- 3 cups shredded cooked chicken
- ¼ cup all-purpose flour*
- 2 eggs, lightly beaten
- 1 cup panko breadcrumbs*
- olive oil, in a spray bottle
- salsa

Directions:
1. Beat the cream cheese in a bowl until it is smooth and easy to stir. Add the pepper jack cheese, Jalapeño pepper, scallions, paprika and 1 teaspoon of salt. Fold in the shredded cooked chicken and combine well. Roll this mixture into 1-inch balls.

2. Set up a dredging station with three shallow dishes. Place the flour into one shallow dish. Place the eggs into a second shallow dish. Finally, combine the panko breadcrumbs and remaining teaspoon of salt in a third dish.
3. Coat the chicken cheese balls by rolling each ball in the flour first, then dip them into the eggs and finally roll them in the panko breadcrumbs to coat all sides. Refrigerate for at least 30 minutes.
4. Preheat the air fryer to 400°F.
5. Spray the chicken cheese balls with oil and air-fry in batches for 8 minutes. Shake the basket a few times throughout the cooking process to help the balls brown evenly.
6. Serve hot with salsa on the side.

Russian Pierogi With Cheese Dip

Servings: 6
Cooking Time: 20 Minutes
Ingredients:
- 1 package frozen pierogi
- 1 cup sour cream
- 1 tbsp fresh lemon juice
- ½ chopped red bell pepper
- 3 spring onions, chopped
- ½ cup shredded carrot
- 1 tsp dried rosemary

Directions:
1. Preheat the air fryer to 400°F. Mix the sour cream and lemon juice in a bowl, then add the bell pepper, spring onions, carrot, and rosemary and mix well. Set the dip aside. Put as many frozen pierogi as will fit in the frying basket in a single layer and spray with cooking oil. Air Fry for 11-14 minutes, rotating pierogis once until golden. Repeat with the remaining pierogi. Serve with the dip.

Buffalo Wings

Servings: 2
Cooking Time: 12 Minutes Per Batch
Ingredients:
- 2 pounds chicken wings
- 3 tablespoons butter, melted
- ¼ cup hot sauce (like Crystal® or Frank's®)
- Finishing Sauce:
- 3 tablespoons butter, melted
- ¼ cup hot sauce (like Crystal® or Frank's®)
- 1 teaspoon Worcestershire sauce

Directions:
1. Prepare the chicken wings by cutting off the wing tips and discarding (or freezing for chicken stock). Divide the drumettes from the wingettes by cutting through the joint. Place the chicken wing pieces in a large bowl.
2. Combine the melted butter and the hot sauce and stir to blend well. Pour the marinade over the chicken wings, cover and let the wings marinate for 2 hours or up to overnight in the refrigerator.
3. Preheat the air fryer to 400°F.
4. Air-fry the wings in two batches for 10 minutes per batch, shaking the basket halfway through the cooking process. When both batches are done, toss all the wings back into the basket for another 2 minutes to heat through and finish cooking.
5. While the wings are air-frying, combine the remaining 3 tablespoons of butter, ¼ cup of hot sauce and the Worcestershire sauce. Remove the wings from the air fryer, toss them in the finishing sauce and serve with some cooling blue cheese dip and celery sticks.

Home-style Buffalo Chicken Wings

Servings: 4
Cooking Time: 35 Minutes
Ingredients:
- 2 lb chicken wing portions
- 6 tbsp chili sauce
- 1 tsp dried oregano
- 1 tsp smoked paprika
- 1 tsp garlic powder
- ½ tsp salt
- ¼ cup crumbled blue cheese
- 1/3 cup low-fat yogurt
- ½ tbsp lemon juice
- ½ tbsp white wine vinegar
- 2 celery stalks, cut into sticks
- 2 carrots, cut into sticks

Directions:
1. Add chicken with 1 tbsp of chili sauce, oregano, garlic, paprika, and salt to a large bowl. Toss to coat well, then set aside. In a small bowl, mash blue cheese and yogurt with a fork. Stir lemon juice and vinegar until smooth and blended. Refrigerate covered until it is time to serve.
2. Preheat air fryer to 300°F. Place the chicken in the greased frying basket and Air Fry for 22 minutes, flipping the chicken once until crispy and browned. Set aside in a clean bowl. Coat with the remaining tbsp of chili sauce. Serve with celery, carrot sticks and the blue cheese dip.

Panko-breaded Onion Rings

Servings: 4
Cooking Time: 12 Minutes
Ingredients:
- 1 large sweet onion, cut into ½-inch slices and rings separated
- 2 cups ice water
- ½ cup all-purpose flour
- 1 teaspoon paprika
- 1 teaspoon salt
- ½ teaspoon black pepper
- ½ teaspoon garlic powder
- ¼ teaspoon onion powder
- 1 egg, whisked
- 2 tablespoons milk
- 1 cup breadcrumbs

Directions:
1. Preheat the air fryer to 400°F.
2. In a large bowl, soak the onion rings in the water for 5 minutes. Drain and pat dry with a towel.
3. In a medium bowl, place the flour, paprika, salt, pepper, garlic powder, and onion powder.
4. In a second bowl, whisk together the egg and milk.
5. In a third bowl, place the breadcrumbs.
6. To bread the onion rings, dip them first into the flour mixture, then into the egg mixture (shaking off the excess), and then into the breadcrumbs. Place the coated onion rings onto a plate while you bread all the rings.
7. Place the onion rings into the air fryer basket in a single layer, sometimes nesting smaller rings into larger rings. Spray with cooking spray. Cook for 3 minutes, turn the rings over, and spray with more cooking spray. Cook for another 3 to 5 minutes. Cook the rings in batches; you may need to do 2 or 3 batches, depending on the size of your air fryer.

Tasty Roasted Black Olives & Tomatoes

Servings: 6
Cooking Time: 25 Minutes
Ingredients:
- 2 cups grape tomatoes
- 4 garlic cloves, chopped
- ½ red onion, chopped
- 1 cup black olives
- 1 cup green olives
- 1 tbsp thyme, minced
- 1 tbsp oregano, minced
- 2 tbsp olive oil
- ½ tsp salt

Directions:
1. Preheat air fryer to 380°F. Add all ingredients to a bowl and toss well to coat. Pour the mixture into the frying basket and Roast for 10 minutes. Stir the mixture, then Roast for an additional 10 minutes. Serve and enjoy!

Chicken Shawarma Bites

Servings: 6
Cooking Time: 22 Minutes
Ingredients:
- 1½ pounds Boneless skinless chicken thighs, trimmed of any fat and cut into 1-inch pieces
- 1½ tablespoons Olive oil
- Up to 1½ tablespoons Minced garlic
- ½ teaspoon Table salt
- ¼ teaspoon Ground cardamom
- ¼ teaspoon Ground cinnamon
- ¼ teaspoon Ground cumin
- ¼ teaspoon Mild paprika
- Up to a ¼ teaspoon Grated nutmeg
- ¼ teaspoon Ground black pepper

Directions:
1. Preheat the air fryer to 400°F.
2. Mix all the ingredients in a large bowl until the chicken is thoroughly and evenly coated in the oil and spices.
3. When the machine is at temperature, scrape the coated chicken pieces into the basket and spread them out into one layer as much as you can. Air-fry for 22 minutes, shaking the basket at least three times during cooking to rearrange the pieces, until well browned and crisp.
4. Pour the chicken pieces onto a wire rack. Cool for 5 minutes before serving.

Shrimp Toasts

Servings: 4
Cooking Time: 8 Minutes
Ingredients:
- ½ pound raw shrimp, peeled and de-veined
- 1 egg (or 2 egg whites)
- 2 scallions, plus more for garnish
- 2 teaspoons grated fresh ginger
- 1 teaspoon soy sauce
- ½ teaspoon toasted sesame oil
- 2 tablespoons chopped fresh cilantro or parsley
- 1 to 2 teaspoons sriracha sauce
- 6 slices thinly-sliced white sandwich bread (Pepperidge Farm®)
- ½ cup sesame seeds
- Thai chili sauce

Directions:
1. Combine the shrimp, egg, scallions, fresh ginger, soy sauce, sesame oil, cilantro (or parsley) and sriracha sauce in a food processor and process into a chunky paste, scraping down the sides of the food processor bowl as necessary.
2. Cut the crusts off the sandwich bread and generously spread the shrimp paste onto each slice of bread. Place the sesame seeds on a plate and invert each shrimp toast into the sesame seeds to coat, pressing down gently. Cut each slice of bread into 4 triangles.
3. Preheat the air fryer to 400°F.
4. Transfer one layer of shrimp toast triangles to the air fryer and air-fry at 400°F for 8 minutes, or until the sesame seeds are toasted on top.
5. Serve warm with a little Thai chili sauce and some sliced scallions as garnish.

Blooming Onion

Servings: 4
Cooking Time: 25 Minutes
Ingredients:
- 1 large Vidalia onion, peeled
- 2 eggs
- ½ cup milk
- 1 cup flour
- 1 teaspoon salt
- ½ teaspoon freshly ground black pepper
- ¼ teaspoon ground cayenne pepper
- ½ teaspoon paprika
- ½ teaspoon garlic powder
- Dipping Sauce:
- ½ cup mayonnaise
- ½ cup ketchup
- 1 teaspoon Worcestershire sauce
- ½ teaspoon ground cayenne pepper
- ½ teaspoon paprika
- ½ teaspoon onion powder

Directions:
1. Cut off the top inch of the onion, leaving the root end of the onion intact. Place the now flat, stem end of the onion down on a cutting board with the root end facing up. Make 16 slices around the onion, starting with your knife tip ½-inch away from the root so that you never slice through the root. Begin by making slices at 12, 3, 6 and 9 o'clock around the onion. Then make three slices down the onion in between each of the original four slices. Turn the onion over, gently separate the onion petals, and remove the loose pieces of onion in the center.
2. Combine the eggs and milk in a bowl. In a second bowl, combine the flour, salt, black pepper, cayenne pepper, paprika, and garlic powder.
3. Preheat the air fryer to 350°F.
4. Place the onion cut side up into a third empty bowl. Sprinkle the flour mixture all over the onion to cover it and get in between the onion petals. Turn the onion over to carefully shake off the excess flour and then transfer the onion to the empty flour bowl, again cut side up.
5. Pour the egg mixture all over the onion to cover all the flour. Let it soak for a minute in the mixture. Carefully remove the onion, tipping it upside down to drain off any excess egg, and transfer it to the empty egg bowl, again cut side up.
6. Finally, sprinkle the flour mixture over the onion a second time, making sure the onion is well coated and all the petals have the seasoned flour mixture on them. Carefully turn the onion over, shake off any excess flour and transfer it to a plate or baking sheet. Spray the onion generously with vegetable oil.
7. Transfer the onion, cut side up to the air fryer basket and air-fry for 25 minutes. The onion petals will open more fully as

it cooks,so spray with more vegetable oil at least twice during the cooking time.
8. While the onion is cooking,make the dipping sauce by combining all the dip ingredients and mixing well.Serve the Blooming Onion as soon as it comes out of the air fryer with dipping sauce on the side.

Zucchini Boats With Bacon

Servings:4
Cooking Time:35 Minutes
Ingredients:
- 1¼cups shredded Havarti cheese
- 3 bacon slices
- 2 large zucchini
- Salt and pepper to taste
- ¼tsp garlic powder
- ¼tsp sweet paprika
- 8 tsp buttermilk
- 2 tbsp chives,chopped

Directions:
1. Preheat air fryer to 350°F.Place the bacon in the frying basket and Air Fry it for 10 minutes,flipping once until crisp.Chop the bacon and set aside.Cut zucchini in half lengthwise and then crosswise so that you have 8 pieces.Scoop out the pulp.Sprinkle with salt,garlic,paprika,and black pepper.Place the zucchini skins in the greased frying basket.Air Fry until crisp-tender,8-10 minutes.Remove the basket and add the Havarti inside each boat and top with bacon.Return stuffed boats to the air fryer and fry for 2 minutes or until the cheese has melted.Top with buttermilk and chives before serving immediately.

Dill Fried Pickles With Light Ranch Dip

Servings:4
Cooking Time:8 Minutes
Ingredients:
- 4 to 6 large dill pickles,sliced in half or quartered lengthwise
- ½cup all-purpose flour*
- 2 eggs,lightly beaten
- 1 cup plain breadcrumbs*
- 1 teaspoon salt
- ⅛teaspoon cayenne pepper
- 2 tablespoons fresh dill leaves,dried well
- vegetable oil,in a spray bottle
- Light Ranch Dip
- ¼cup reduced-fat mayonnaise
- ¼cup buttermilk
- ¼cup non-fat Greek yogurt
- 1 tablespoon chopped fresh chives
- 1 tablespoon chopped fresh parsley
- 1 tablespoon lemon juice
- salt and freshly ground black pepper

Directions:
1. Dry the dill pickle spears very well with a clean kitchen towel.
2. Set up a dredging station using three shallow dishes.Place the flour in the first shallow dish.Place the eggs into the second dish.Combine the breadcrumbs,salt,cayenne and fresh dill in a food processor and process until everything is combined and the crumbs are very fine.Place the crumb mixture in the third dish.
3. Preheat the air fryer to 400°F.
4. Coat the pickles by dredging them first in the flour,then the egg,and then the breadcrumbs,pressing the crumbs on gently with your hands.Set the coated pickles on a tray and spray them on all sides with vegetable oil.
5. Air-fry one layer of pickles at a time at 400°F for 8 minutes,turning them over halfway through the cooking process and spraying lightly again if necessary.The crumbs should be nicely browned on all sides.
6. While the pickles are air-frying,make the light ranch dip by mixing everything together in a bowl.Serve the pickles warm with the dip on the side.

Classic Chicken Wings

Servings:8
Cooking Time:20 Minutes
Ingredients:
- 16 chicken wings
- ¼cup all-purpose flour
- ¼teaspoon garlic powder
- ¼teaspoon paprika
- ½teaspoon salt
- ½teaspoon black pepper
- ¼cup butter
- ½cup hot sauce
- ½teaspoon Worcestershire sauce
- 2 ounces crumbled blue cheese,for garnish

Directions:
1. Preheat the air fryer to 380°F.
2. Pat the chicken wings dry with paper towels.
3. In a medium bowl,mix together the flour,garlic powder,paprika,salt,and pepper.Toss the chicken wings with the flour mixture,dusting off any excess.
4. Place the chicken wings in the air fryer basket,making sure that the chicken wings aren't touching.Cook the chicken wings for 10 minutes,turn over,and cook another 5 minutes.Raise the temperature to 400°F and continue crisping the chicken wings for an additional 3 to 5 minutes.
5. Meanwhile,in a microwave-safe bowl,melt the butter and hot sauce for 1 to 2 minutes in the microwave.Remove from the microwave and stir in the Worcestershire sauce.
6. When the chicken wings have cooked,immediately transfer the chicken wings into the hot sauce mixture.Serve the coated chicken wings on a plate,and top with crumbled blue cheese.

Mediterranean Potato Skins

Servings:4
Cooking Time:50 Minutes
Ingredients:
- 2 russet potatoes
- 3 tbsp olive oil
- Salt and pepper to taste
- 2 tbsp rosemary,chopped
- 10 Kalamata olives,diced
- ¼cup crumbled feta
- 2 tbsp chopped dill

Directions:
1. Preheat air fryer to 380°F.Poke 2-3 holes in the potatoes with a fork.Drizzle them with some olive oil and sprinkle with salt.Put the potatoes into the frying basket and Bake for 30 minutes.When the potatoes are ready,remove them from the fryer and slice in half.Scoop out the flesh of the potatoes with a spoon,leaving a½-inch layer of potato inside the skins,and set the skins aside.
2. Combine the scooped potato middles with the remaining olive oil,salt,black pepper,and rosemary in a medium bowl.Mix until well combined.Spoon the potato filling into the potato skins,spreading it evenly over them.Top with olives,dill and feta.Put the loaded potato skins back into the air fryer and Bake for 15 minutes.Enjoy!

Bagel Chips

Servings: 2
Cooking Time: 4 Minutes
Ingredients:
- Sweet
- 1 large plain bagel
- 2 teaspoons sugar
- 1 teaspoon ground cinnamon
- butter-flavored cooking spray
- Savory
- 1 large plain bagel
- 1 teaspoon Italian seasoning
- ½ teaspoon garlic powder
- oil for misting or cooking spray

Directions:
1. Preheat air fryer to 390°F.
2. Cut bagel into ¼-inch slices or thinner.
3. Mix the seasonings together.
4. Spread out the slices, mist with oil or cooking spray, and sprinkle with half of the seasonings.
5. Turn over and repeat to coat the other side with oil or cooking spray and seasonings.
6. Place in air fryer basket and cook for 2 minutes. Shake basket or stir a little and continue cooking for 2 minutes or until toasty brown and crispy.

Fried Green Tomatoes

Servings: 4
Cooking Time: 15 Minutes
Ingredients:
- 2 eggs
- ¼ cup buttermilk
- ½ cup cornmeal
- ½ cup breadcrumbs
- ¼ teaspoon salt
- 1½ pounds firm green tomatoes, cut in ¼-inch slices
- oil for misting or cooking spray
- Horseradish Drizzle
- ¼ cup mayonnaise
- ¼ cup sour cream
- 2 teaspoons prepared horseradish
- ½ teaspoon Worcestershire sauce
- ½ teaspoon lemon juice
- ⅛ teaspoon black pepper

Directions:
1. Mix all ingredients for Horseradish Drizzle together and chill while you prepare the green tomatoes.
2. Preheat air fryer to 390°F.
3. Beat the eggs and buttermilk together in a shallow bowl.
4. Mix cornmeal, breadcrumbs, and salt together in a plate or shallow dish.
5. Dip 4 tomato slices in the egg mixture, then roll in the breadcrumb mixture.
6. Mist one side with oil and place in air fryer basket, oil-side down, in a single layer.
7. Mist the top with oil.
8. Cook for 15 minutes, turning once, until brown and crispy.
9. Repeat steps 5 through 8 to cook remaining tomatoes.
10. Drizzle horseradish sauce over tomatoes just before serving.

Spanish Fried Baby Squid

Servings: 2
Cooking Time: 30 Minutes
Ingredients:
- 1 cup baby squid
- ½ cup semolina flour
- ½ tsp Spanish paprika
- ½ tsp garlic powder
- 2 eggs
- Salt and pepper to taste
- 2 tbsp lemon juice
- 1 tsp Old Bay seasoning

Directions:
1. Preheat air fryer to 350°F. Beat the eggs in a bowl. Stir in lemon juice and set aside. Mix flour, Old Bay seasoning, garlic powder, paprika, salt, and pepper in another bowl. Dip each piece of squid into the flour, then into the eggs, and then again. Transfer them to the greased frying basket and Air Fry for 18-20 minutes, shaking the basket occasionally until crispy and golden brown. Serve hot.

Oyster Spring Rolls

Servings: 4
Cooking Time: 20 Minutes
Ingredients:
- ¼ cup button mushrooms, diced
- ¼ cup bean sprouts
- 1 celery stalk, julienned
- 1 carrot, grated
- 1 tsp fresh ginger, minced
- 1 tsp sugar
- 1 tsp vegeta seasoning
- ½ tsp oyster sauce
- 1 egg
- 1 tsp corn starch
- 6 spring roll wrappers

Directions:
1. Preheat the air fryer to 360°F. Combine the mushrooms, bean sprouts, celery, carrot, ginger, sugar, oyster sauce and stock powder in a mixing bowl. In a second bowl, beat the egg, and stir in the cornstarch.
2. On a clean surface, spoon vegetable filling into each roll, roll up and seal the seams with the egg-cornstarch mixture. Put the rolls in the greased frying basket and Air Fry for 7-8 minutes, flipping once until golden brown. Serve hot.

Dijon Chicken Wings

Servings: 6
Cooking Time: 60 Minutes
Ingredients:
- 2 lb chicken wings, split at the joint
- 1 tbsp water
- 1 tbs salt
- 1 tsp black pepper
- 1 tsp red chili powder
- 1 tbsp butter, melted
- 1 tbsp Dijon mustard
- 2 tbsp yellow mustard
- ¼ cup honey
- 1 tsp apple cider vinegar
- Salt to taste

Directions:
1. Preheat air fryer at 250°F. Pour water in the bottom of the frying basket to ensure minimum smoke from fat drippings. Sprinkle the chicken wings with salt, pepper, and red chili powder. Place chicken wings in the greased frying basket and Air Fry for 12 minutes, tossing once. Whisk the remaining ingredients in a bowl. Add in chicken wings and toss to coat. Serve immediately.

Green Olive And Mushroom Tapenade

Servings: 1
Cooking Time: 10 Minutes
Ingredients:
- ¾ pound Brown or Baby Bella mushrooms, sliced
- 1½ cups (about ½ pound) Pitted green olives
- 3 tablespoons Olive oil
- 1½ tablespoons Fresh oregano leaves, loosely packed
- ¼ teaspoon Ground black pepper

Directions:
1. Preheat the air fryer to 400°F.
2. When the machine is at temperature, arrange the mushroom slices in as close to an even layer as possible in the basket. They will overlap and even stack on top of each other.
3. Air-fry for 10 minutes, tossing the basket and rearranging the mushrooms every 2 minutes, until shriveled but with still-noticeable moisture.
4. Pour the mushrooms into a food processor. Add the olives, olive oil, oregano leaves, and pepper. Cover and process until grainy, not too much, just not fully smooth for better texture, stopping the machine at least once to scrape down the inside of the canister. Scrape the tapenade into a bowl and serve warm, or cover and refrigerate for up to 4 days. (The tapenade will taste better if it comes back to room temperature before serving.)

Nicoise Deviled Eggs

Servings: 4
Cooking Time: 20 Minutes
Ingredients:
- 4 eggs
- 2 tbsp mayonnaise
- 10 chopped Nicoise olives
- 2 tbsp goat cheese crumbles
- Salt and pepper to taste
- 2 tbsp chopped parsley

Directions:
1. Preheat air fryer to 260ºF. Place the eggs in silicone muffin cups to avoid bumping around and cracking during the cooking process. Add silicone cups to the frying basket and Air Fry for 15 minutes. Remove and run the eggs under cold water. When cool, remove the shells and halve them lengthwise.
2. Spoon yolks into a separate medium bowl and arrange white halves on a large plate. Mash the yolks with a fork. Stir in the remaining ingredients. Spoon mixture into white halves and scatter with mint to serve.

Popcorn Chicken Bites

Servings: 2
Cooking Time: 8 Minutes
Ingredients:
- 1 pound chicken breasts, cutlets or tenders
- 1 cup buttermilk
- 3 to 6 dashes hot sauce (optional)
- 8 cups cornflakes (or 2 cups cornflake crumbs)
- ½ teaspoon salt
- 1 tablespoon butter, melted
- 2 tablespoons chopped fresh parsley

Directions:
1. Cut the chicken into bite-sized pieces (about 1-inch) and place them in a bowl with the buttermilk and hot sauce (if using). Cover and let the chicken marinate in the buttermilk for 1 to 3 hours in the refrigerator.
2. Preheat the air fryer to 380°F.
3. Crush the cornflakes into fine crumbs by either crushing them with your hands in a bowl, rolling them with a rolling pin in a plastic bag or processing them in a food processor. Place the crumbs in a bowl, add the salt, melted butter and parsley and mix well. Working in batches, remove the chicken from the buttermilk marinade, letting any excess drip off and transfer the chicken to the cornflakes. Toss the chicken pieces in the cornflake mixture to coat evenly, pressing the crumbs onto the chicken.
4. Air-fry the chicken in two batches for 8 minutes per batch, shaking the basket halfway through the cooking process. Re-heat the first batch with the second batch for a couple of minutes if desired.
5. Serve the popcorn chicken bites warm with BBQ sauce or honey mustard for dipping.

Spiced Parsnip Chips

Servings: 2
Cooking Time: 35 Minutes
Ingredients:
- ½ tsp smoked paprika
- ¼ tsp chili powder
- ¼ tsp garlic powder
- ⅛ tsp onion powder
- ⅛ tsp cayenne pepper
- ⅛ tsp granulated sugar
- 1 tsp salt
- 1 parsnip, cut into chips
- 2 tsp olive oil

Directions:
1. Preheat air fryer to 400ºF. Mix all spices in a bowl and reserve. In another bowl, combine parsnip chips, olive oil, and salt. Place parsnip chips in the lightly greased frying basket and Air Fry for 12 minutes, shaking once. Transfer the chips to a bowl, toss in seasoning mix, and let sit for 15 minutes before serving.

Turkey Burger Sliders

Servings: 8
Cooking Time: 7 Minutes
Ingredients:
- 1 pound ground turkey
- ¼ teaspoon curry powder
- 1 teaspoon Hoisin sauce
- ½ teaspoon salt
- 8 slider buns
- ½ cup slivered red onions
- ½ cup slivered green or red bell pepper
- ½ cup fresh chopped pineapple (or pineapple tidbits from kids' fruit cups, drained)
- light cream cheese, softened

Directions:
1. Combine turkey, curry powder, Hoisin sauce, and salt and mix together well.
2. Shape turkey mixture into 8 small patties.
3. Place patties in air fryer basket and cook at 360°F for 7 minutes, until patties are well done and juices run clear.
4. Place each patty on the bottom half of a slider bun and top with onions, peppers, and pineapple. Spread the remaining bun halves with cream cheese to taste, place on top, and serve.

Prosciutto Polenta Rounds

Servings: 6
Cooking Time: 40 Minutes + 10 Minutes To Cool
Ingredients:
- 1 tube precooked polenta
- 1 tbsp garlic oil

- 4 oz cream cheese, softened
- 3 tbsp mayonnaise
- 2 scallions, sliced
- 1 tbsp minced fresh chives
- 6 prosciutto slices, chopped

Directions:
1. Preheat the air fryer to 400°F. Slice the polenta crosswise into 12 rounds. Brush both sides of each round with garlic oil and put 6 of them in the frying basket. Put a rack in the basket over the polenta and add the other 6 rounds. Bake for 15 minutes, flip, and cook for 10-15 more minutes or until the polenta is crispy and golden. While the polenta is cooking, beat the cream cheese and mayo and stir in the scallions, chives, and prosciutto. When the polenta is cooked, lay out on a wire rack to cool for 15 minutes. Top with the cream cheese mix and serve.

Beer Battered Onion Rings

Servings: 2
Cooking Time: 16 Minutes
Ingredients:
- ⅔ cup flour
- ½ teaspoon baking soda
- 1 teaspoon paprika
- 1 teaspoon salt
- ½ teaspoon freshly ground black pepper
- ¾ cup beer
- 1 egg, beaten
- 1½ cups fine breadcrumbs
- 1 large Vidalia onion, peeled and sliced into ½-inch rings
- vegetable oil

Directions:
1. Set up a dredging station. Mix the flour, baking soda, paprika, salt and pepper together in a bowl. Pour in the beer, add the egg and whisk until smooth. Place the breadcrumbs in a cake pan or shallow dish.
2. Separate the onion slices into individual rings. Dip each onion ring into the batter with a fork. Lift the onion ring out of the batter and let any excess batter drip off. Then place the onion ring in the breadcrumbs and shake the cake pan back and forth to coat the battered onion ring. Pat the ring gently with your hands to make sure the breadcrumbs stick and that both sides of the ring are covered. Place the coated onion ring on a sheet pan and repeat with the rest of the onion rings.
3. Preheat the air fryer to 360°F.
4. Lightly spray the onion rings with oil, coating both sides. Layer the onion rings in the air fryer basket, stacking them on top of each other in a haphazard manner.
5. Air-fry for 10 minutes at 360°F. Flip the onion rings over and rotate the onion rings from the bottom of the basket to the top. Air-fry for an additional 6 minutes.
6. Serve immediately with your favorite dipping sauce.

Spanakopita Spinach, Feta And Pine Nut Phyllo Bites

Servings: 8
Cooking Time: 10 Minutes
Ingredients:
- ½ (10-ounce) package frozen spinach, thawed and squeezed dry (about 1 cup)
- ¾ cup crumbled feta cheese
- ¼ cup grated Parmesan cheese
- ¼ cup pine nuts, toasted
- ⅛ teaspoon ground nutmeg
- 1 egg, lightly beaten
- ½ teaspoon salt
- freshly ground black pepper
- 6 sheets phyllo dough
- ½ cup butter, melted

Directions:
1. Combine the spinach, cheeses, pine nuts, nutmeg and egg in a bowl. Season with salt and freshly ground black pepper.
2. While building the phyllo triangles, always keep the dough sheets you are not working with covered with plastic wrap and a damp clean kitchen towel. Remove one sheet of the phyllo and place it on a flat surface. Brush the phyllo sheet with melted butter and then layer another sheet of phyllo on top. Brush the second sheet of phyllo with butter. Cut the layered phyllo sheets into 6 strips, about 2½-to 3-inches wide.
3. Place a heaping tablespoon of the spinach filling at the end of each strip of dough. Fold the bottom right corner of the strip over the filling towards the left edge of the strip to make a triangle. Continue to fold the phyllo dough around the spinach as you would fold a flag, making triangle after triangle. Brush the outside of the phyllo triangle with more melted butter and set it aside until you've finished the 6 strips of dough, making 6 triangles.
4. Preheat the air fryer to 350°F.
5. Transfer the first six phyllo triangles to the air fryer basket and air-fry for 5 minutes. Turn the triangles over and air-fry for another 5 minutes.
6. While the first batch of triangles is air-frying, build another set of triangles and air-fry in the same manner. You should do three batches total. These can be warmed in the air fryer for a minute or two just before serving if you like.

Sweet Potato Chips

Servings: 4
Cooking Time: 10 Minutes
Ingredients:
- 2 medium sweet potatoes, washed
- 2 cups filtered water
- 1 tablespoon avocado oil
- 2 teaspoons brown sugar
- ½ teaspoon salt

Directions:
1. Using a mandolin, slice the potatoes into ⅛-inch pieces.
2. Add the water to a large bowl. Place the potatoes in the bowl, and soak for at least 30 minutes.
3. Preheat the air fryer to 350°F.
4. Drain the water and pat the chips dry with a paper towel or kitchen cloth. Toss the chips with the avocado oil, brown sugar, and salt. Liberally spray the air fryer basket with olive oil mist.
5. Set the chips inside the air fryer, separating them so they're not on top of each other. Cook for 5 minutes, shake the basket, and cook another 5 minutes, or until browned.
6. Remove and let cool a few minutes prior to serving. Repeat until all the chips are cooked.

Cheesy Green Wonton Triangles

Servings: 20 Wontons
Cooking Time: 55 Minutes
Ingredients:
- 6 oz marinated artichoke hearts
- 6 oz cream cheese
- ¼ cup sour cream
- ¼ cup grated Parmesan
- ¼ cup grated cheddar
- 5 oz chopped kale
- 2 garlic cloves, chopped
- Salt and pepper to taste
- 20 wonton wrappers

Directions:
1. Microwave cream cheese in a bowl for 20 seconds.Combine with sour cream,Parmesan,cheddar,kale,artichoke hearts,garlic,salt,and pepper.Lay out the wrappers on a cutting board.Scoop 1½tsp of cream cheese mixture on top of the wrapper.Fold up diagonally to form a triangle.Bring together the two bottom corners.Squeeze out any air and press together to seal the edges.
2. Preheat air fryer to 375°F.Place a batch of wonton in the greased frying basket and Bake for 10 minutes.Flip them and cook for 5-8 minutes until crisp and golden.Serve.

Indian Cauliflower Tikka Bites

Servings:6
Cooking Time:20 Minutes
Ingredients:
- 1 cup plain Greek yogurt
- 1 teaspoon fresh ginger
- 1 teaspoon minced garlic
- 1 teaspoon vindaloo
- ½teaspoon cardamom
- ½teaspoon paprika
- ½teaspoon turmeric powder
- ½teaspoon cumin powder
- 1 large head of cauliflower,washed and cut into medium-size florets
- ½cup panko breadcrumbs
- 1 lemon,quartered

Directions:
1. Preheat the air fryer to 350°F.
2. In a large bowl,mix the yogurt,ginger,garlic,vindaloo,cardamom,paprika,turmeric,and cumin.Add the cauliflower florets to the bowl,and coat them with the yogurt.
3. Remove the cauliflower florets from the bowl and place them on a baking sheet.Sprinkle the panko breadcrumbs over the top.Place the cauliflower bites into the air fryer basket,leaving space between the florets.Depending on the size of your air fryer,you may need to make more than one batch.
4. Cook the cauliflower for 10 minutes,shake the basket,and continue cooking another 10 minutes(or until the florets are lightly browned).
5. Remove from the air fryer and keep warm.Continue to cook until all the florets are done.
6. Before serving,lightly squeeze lemon over the top.Serve warm.

Veggie Chips

Servings:X
Cooking Time:X
Ingredients:
- sweet potato
- large parsnip
- large carrot
- turnip
- large beet
- vegetable or canola oil,in a spray bottle
- salt

Directions:
1. You can do a medley of vegetable chips,or just select from the vegetables listed.Whatever you choose to do,scrub the vegetables well and then slice them paper-thin using a mandolin(about-1/16 inch thick).
2. Preheat the air fryer to 400°F.
3. Air-fry the chips in batches,one type of vegetable at a time.Spray the chips lightly with oil and transfer them to the air fryer basket.The key is to NOT over-load the basket.You can overlap the chips a little,but don't pile them on top of each other.Doing so will make it much harder to get evenly browned and crispy chips.Air-fry at 400°F for the time indicated below,shaking the basket several times during the cooking process for even cooking.
4. Sweet Potato–8 to 9 minutes
5. Parsnips–5 minutes
6. Carrot–7 minutes
7. Turnips–8 minutes
8. Beets–9 minutes
9. Season the chips with salt during the last couple of minutes of air-frying.Check the chips as they cook until they are done to your liking.Some will start to brown sooner than others.
10. You can enjoy the chips warm out of the air fryer or cool them to room temperature for crispier chips.

Hot Avocado Fries

Servings:2
Cooking Time:20 Minutes
Ingredients:
- 1 egg
- 2 tbsp milk
- Salt and pepper to taste
- 1 cup crushed chili corn chips
- 2 tbsp Parmesan cheese
- 1 avocado,sliced into fries

Directions:
1. Preheat air fryer at 375ºF.In a bowl,beat egg and milk.In another bowl,add crushed chips,Parmesan cheese,salt and pepper.Dip avocado fries into the egg mixture,then dredge into crushed chips mixture to coat.Place avocado fries in the greased frying basket and Air Fry for 5 minutes.Serve immediately.

Cheese Arancini

Servings:8
Cooking Time:12 Minutes
Ingredients:
- 1 cup Water
- ½cup Raw white Arborio rice
- 1½teaspoons Butter
- ¼teaspoon Table salt
- 8¾-inch semi-firm mozzarella cubes(not fresh mozzarella)
- 2 Large egg(s),well beaten
- 1 cup Seasoned Italian-style dried bread crumbs(gluten-free,if a concern)
- Olive oil spray

Directions:
1. Combine the water,rice,butter,and salt in a small saucepan.Bring to a boil over medium-high heat,stirring occasionally.Cover,reduce the heat to very low,and simmer very slowly for 20 minutes.
2. Take the saucepan off the heat and let it stand,covered,for 10 minutes.Uncover it and fluff the rice.Cool for 20 minutes.(The rice can be made up to 1 hour in advance;keep it covered in its saucepan.)
3. Preheat the air fryer to 375°F.
4. Set up and fill two shallow soup plates or small bowls on your counter:one with the beaten egg(s)and one with the bread crumbs.
5. With clean but wet hands,scoop up about 2 tablespoons of the cooked rice and form it into a ball.Push a cube of mozzarella into the middle of the ball and seal the cheese inside.Dip the ball in the egg(s)to coat completely,letting any excess egg slip back into the rest.Roll the ball in the bread

crumbs to coat evenly but lightly. Set aside and continue making more rice balls.
6. Generously spray the balls with olive oil spray, then set them in the basket in one layer. They must not touch. Air-fry undisturbed for 10 minutes, or until crunchy and golden brown. If the machine is at 360°F, you may need to add 2 minutes to the cooking time.
7. Use a nonstick-safe spatula, and maybe a flatware spoon for balance, to gently transfer the balls to a wire rack. Cool for at least 5 minutes or up to 20 minutes before serving.

Garlic Wings

Servings: 4
Cooking Time: 15 Minutes
Ingredients:
- 2 pounds chicken wings
- oil for misting
- cooking spray
- Marinade
- 1 cup buttermilk
- 2 cloves garlic, mashed flat
- 1 teaspoon Worcestershire sauce
- 1 bay leaf
- Coating
- 1½ cups grated Parmesan cheese
- ¾ cup breadcrumbs
- 1½ tablespoons garlic powder
- ½ teaspoon salt

Directions:
1. Mix all marinade ingredients together.
2. Remove wing tips (the third joint) and discard or freeze for stock. Cut the remaining wings at the joint and toss them into the marinade, stirring to coat well. Refrigerate for at least an hour but no more than 8 hours.
3. When ready to cook, combine all coating ingredients in a shallow dish.
4. Remove wings from marinade, shaking off excess, and roll in coating mixture. Press coating into wings so that it sticks well. Spray wings with oil.
5. Spray air fryer basket with cooking spray. Place wings in basket in single layer, close but not touching.
6. Cook at 360°F for 15 minutes or until chicken is done and juices run clear.
7. Repeat previous step to cook remaining wings.

Tempura Fried Veggies

Servings: 4
Cooking Time: 6 Minutes
Ingredients:
- ½ cup all-purpose flour
- ½ teaspoon black pepper
- ¼ teaspoon salt
- 2 large eggs
- 1¼ cups panko breadcrumbs
- 1 tablespoon extra-virgin olive oil
- 1 cup white button mushrooms, cleaned
- 1 medium zucchini, skinned and sliced
- 1 medium carrot, skinned sliced

Directions:
1. Preheat the air fryer to 400°F.
2. In a small bowl, mix the flour, pepper, and salt.
3. In a separate bowl, whisk the eggs.
4. In a third bowl, mix together the breadcrumbs and olive oil.
5. Begin to batter the vegetables by placing them one at a time into the flour, then dipping them in the eggs, and coating them in breadcrumbs. When you've prepared enough to begin air frying, liberally spray the air fryer basket with olive oil and place the vegetables inside.
6. Cook for 6 minutes, or until the breadcrumb coating on the outside appears golden brown. Repeat coating the other vegetables while the first batch is cooking.
7. When the cooking completes, carefully remove the vegetables and keep them warm. Repeat cooking for the remaining vegetables until all are cooked.
8. Serve warm.

Spiced Nuts

Servings: 3
Cooking Time: 25 Minutes
Ingredients:
- 1 egg white, lightly beaten
- ¼ cup sugar
- 1 teaspoon salt
- ½ teaspoon ground cinnamon
- ¼ teaspoon ground cloves
- ¼ teaspoon ground allspice
- pinch ground cayenne pepper
- 1 cup pecan halves
- 1 cup cashews
- 1 cup almonds

Directions:
1. Combine the egg white with the sugar and spices in a bowl.
2. Preheat the air fryer to 300°F.
3. Spray or brush the air fryer basket with vegetable oil. Toss the nuts together in the spiced egg white and transfer the nuts to the air fryer basket.
4. Air-fry for 25 minutes, stirring the nuts in the basket a few times during the cooking process. Taste the nuts to see if they are crunchy and nicely toasted. Air-fry for a few more minutes if necessary.
5. Serve warm or cool to room temperature and store in an airtight container for up to two weeks.

Curried Veggie Samosas

Servings: 4
Cooking Time: 30 Minutes
Ingredients:
- 4 cooked potatoes, mashed
- ¼ cup peas
- 2 tsp coconut oil
- 3 garlic cloves, minced
- 1½ tbsp lemon juice
- 1½ tsp cumin powder
- 1 tsp onion powder
- 1 tsp ground coriander
- Salt to taste
- ½ tsp curry powder
- ¼ tsp cayenne powder
- 10 rice paper wrappers
- 1 cup cilantro chutney

Directions:
1. Preheat air fryer to 390°F. In a bowl, place the mashed potatoes, peas, oil, garlic, lemon juice, cumin, onion powder, coriander, salt, curry powder, and cayenne. Stir.
2. Fill a bowl with water. Soak a rice paper wrapper in the water for a few seconds. Lay it on a flat surface. Place ¼ cup of the potato filling in the center of the wrapper and roll like a burrito or spring roll. Repeat the process until you run out of ingredients. Place the "samosas" inside in the greased frying basket, separating them. Air Fry for 8-10 minutes or until hot and crispy around the edges. Let cool for a few minutes. Enjoy with the cilantro chutney.

Stuffed Baby Bella Caps

Servings: 16
Cooking Time: 12 Minutes
Ingredients:
- 16 fresh, small Baby Bella mushrooms
- 2 green onions
- 4 ounces mozzarella cheese
- ½ cup diced ham
- 2 tablespoons breadcrumbs
- ½ teaspoon garlic powder
- ¼ teaspoon ground oregano
- ¼ teaspoon ground black pepper
- 1 to 2 teaspoons olive oil

Directions:
1. Remove stems and wash mushroom caps.
2. Cut green onions and cheese in small pieces and place in food processor.
3. Add ham, breadcrumbs, garlic powder, oregano, and pepper and mince ingredients.
4. With food processor running, dribble in just enough olive oil to make a thick paste.
5. Divide stuffing among mushroom caps and pack down lightly.
6. Place stuffed mushrooms in air fryer basket in single layer and cook at 390°F for 12 minutes or until tops are golden brown and mushrooms are tender.
7. Repeat step 6 to cook remaining mushrooms.

Crunchy Parmesan Edamame

Servings: 4
Cooking Time: 25 Minutes + Cooling Time
Ingredients:
- 1 cup edamame, shelled
- 1 tbsp sesame oil
- 1 tsp five-spice powder
- ½ tsp salt
- ½ tsp garlic powder
- ¼ cup grated Parmesan

Directions:
1. Cook the edamame in boiling salted water until crisp-tender, about 10 minutes. Drain and leave to cool. Preheat air fryer to 350ºF. Combine edamame, garlic, and sesame oil in a bowl. Place them in the frying basket and Air Fry for 16 minutes, shaking twice. Transfer to a small bowl and toss with five-spice powder and salt. Serve chilled topped with Parmesan cheese. Enjoy!

Fried Cheese Ravioli With Marinara Sauce

Servings: 4
Cooking Time: 7 Minutes
Ingredients:
- 1 pound cheese ravioli, fresh or frozen
- 2 eggs, lightly beaten
- 1 cup plain breadcrumbs
- ½ teaspoon paprika
- ½ teaspoon dried oregano
- ½ teaspoon salt
- grated Parmesan cheese
- chopped fresh parsley
- 1 to 2 cups marinara sauce (jarred or homemade)

Directions:
1. Bring a stockpot of salted water to a boil. Boil the ravioli according to the package directions and then drain. Let the cooked ravioli cool to a temperature where you can comfortably handle them.
2. While the pasta is cooking, set up a dredging station with two shallow dishes. Place the eggs into one dish. Combine the breadcrumbs, paprika, dried oregano and salt in the other dish.
3. Preheat the air fryer to 380°F.
4. Working with one at a time, dip the cooked ravioli into the egg, coating all sides. Then press the ravioli into the breadcrumbs, making sure that all sides are covered. Transfer the ravioli to the air fryer basket, cooking in batches, one layer at a time. Air-fry at 380°F for 7 minutes.
5. While the ravioli is air-frying, bring the marinara sauce to a simmer on the stovetop. Transfer to a small bowl.
6. Sprinkle a little Parmesan cheese and chopped parsley on top of the fried ravioli and serve warm with the marinara sauce on the side for dipping.

Fried Bananas

Servings: 4
Cooking Time: 8 Minutes
Ingredients:
- ½ cup panko breadcrumbs
- ½ cup sweetened coconut flakes
- ¼ cup sliced almonds
- ½ cup cornstarch
- 2 egg whites
- 1 tablespoon water
- 2 firm bananas
- oil for misting or cooking spray

Directions:
1. In food processor, combine panko, coconut, and almonds. Process to make small crumbs.
2. Place cornstarch in a shallow dish. In another shallow dish, beat together the egg whites and water until slightly foamy.
3. Preheat air fryer to 390°F.
4. Cut bananas in half crosswise. Cut each half in quarters lengthwise so you have 16 "sticks."
5. Dip banana sticks in cornstarch and tap to shake off excess. Then dip bananas in egg wash and roll in crumb mixture. Spray with oil.
6. Place bananas in air fryer basket in single layer and cook for 4 minutes. If any spots have not browned, spritz with oil. Cook for 4 more minutes, until golden brown and crispy.
7. Repeat step 6 to cook remaining bananas.

Baba Ghanouj

Servings: 2
Cooking Time: 40 Minutes
Ingredients:
- 2 Small (12-ounce) purple Italian eggplant(s)
- ¼ cup Olive oil
- ¼ cup Tahini
- ½ teaspoon Ground black pepper
- ¼ teaspoon Onion powder
- ¼ teaspoon Mild smoked paprika (optional)
- Up to 1 teaspoon Table salt

Directions:
1. Preheat the air fryer to 400°F.
2. Prick the eggplant(s) on all sides with a fork. When the machine is at temperature, set the eggplant(s) in the basket in one layer. Air-fry undisturbed for 40 minutes, or until blackened and soft.
3. Remove the basket from the machine. Cool the eggplant(s) in the basket for 20 minutes.
4. Use a nonstick-safe spatula, and perhaps a flatware tablespoon for balance, to gently transfer the eggplant(s) to a bowl. The juices will run out. Make sure the bowl is close to the basket. Split the eggplant(s) open.

5. Scrape the soft insides of half an eggplant into a food processor. Repeat with the remaining piece(s). Add any juices from the bowl to the eggplant in the food processor, but discard the skins and stems.
6. Add the olive oil, tahini, pepper, onion powder, and smoked paprika (if using). Add about half the salt, then cover and process until smooth, stopping the machine at least once to scrape down the inside of the canister. Check the spread for salt and add more as needed. Scrape the baba ghanouj into a bowl and serve warm, or set aside at room temperature for up to 2 hours, or cover and store in the refrigerator for up to 4 days.

Korean Brussels Sprouts

Servings: 4
Cooking Time: 20 Minutes
Ingredients:
- 1 lb Brussels sprouts
- 1½ tbsp maple syrup
- 1½ tsp white miso
- 1 tsp toasted sesame oil
- 1½ tsp soy sauce
- 2 garlic cloves, minced
- 1 tsp grated fresh ginger
- ½ tsp Gochugaru chili flakes

Directions:
1. Preheat air fryer to 390°F. Place the Brussels sprouts in the greased basket, spray with oil and Air Fry for 10-14 minutes, tossing once until crispy, tender, and golden.
2. In a bowl, combine maple syrup and miso. Whisk until smooth. Add the sesame oil, soy sauce, garlic, ginger, and Gochugaru flakes. Stir well. When the Brussels sprouts are done, add them to the bowl and toss with the sauce. Serve immediately.

Sweet Apple Fries

Servings: 3
Cooking Time: 8 Minutes
Ingredients:
- 2 Medium-size sweet apple(s), such as Gala or Fuji
- 1 Large egg white(s)
- 2 tablespoons Water
- 1½ cups Finely ground gingersnap crumbs (gluten-free, if a concern)
- Vegetable oil spray

Directions:
1. Preheat the air fryer to 375°F.
2. Peel and core an apple, then cut it into 12 slices (see the headnote for more information). Repeat with more apples as necessary.
3. Whisk the egg white(s) and water in a medium bowl until foamy. Add the apple slices and toss well to coat.
4. Spread the gingersnap crumbs across a dinner plate. Using clean hands, pick up an apple slice, let any excess egg white mixture slip back into the rest, and dredge the slice in the crumbs, coating it lightly but evenly on all sides. Set it aside and continue coating the remaining apple slices.
5. Lightly coat the slices on all sides with vegetable oil spray, then set them curved side down in the basket in one layer. Air-fry undisturbed for 6 minutes, or until browned and crisp. You may need to air-fry the slices for 2 minutes longer if the temperature is at 360°F.
6. Use kitchen tongs to transfer the slices to a wire rack. Cool for 2 to 3 minutes before serving.

Hot Cheese Bites

Servings: 6
Cooking Time: 30 Minutes + Cooling Time

Ingredients:
- 1/3 cup grated Velveeta cheese
- 1/3 cup shredded American cheese
- 4 oz cream cheese
- 2 jalapeños, finely chopped
- ½ cup bread crumbs
- 2 egg whites
- ½ cup all-purpose flour

Directions:
1. Preheat air fryer to 400°F. Blend the cream cheese, Velveeta, American cheese, and jalapeños in a bowl. Form the mixture into 1-inch balls. Arrange them on a sheet pan and freeze for 15 minutes.
2. Spread the flour, egg, and bread crumbs in 3 separate bowls. Once the cheese balls are removed from the freezer, dip them first in flour, then in the egg and finally in the crumbs. Air Fry for 8 minutes in the previously greased frying basket. Flip the balls and cook for another 4 minutes until crispy. Serve warm.

Stuffed Prunes In Bacon

Servings: 6
Cooking Time: 20 Minutes
Ingredients:
- 12 bacon slices, halved
- 24 pitted prunes
- 3 tbsp crumbled blue cheese
- 1 tbsp cream cheese

Directions:
1. Cut prunes in half lengthwise, but do not cut all the way through. Add ½ tsp of blue cheese and cream cheese to the center of each prune. Wrap each prune with a slice of bacon and seal with a toothpick.
2. Preheat air fryer to 400°F. Place the prunes on the bottom of the greased frying basket in a single layer. Bake for 6-8 minutes, flipping the prunes once until the bacon is cooked and crispy. Allow to cool and serve warm.

Salty Pita Crackers

Servings: 2
Cooking Time: 15 Minutes
Ingredients:
- 2 pitas, cut into wedges
- 1 tbsp olive oil
- ½ tsp garlic salt
- ¼ tsp paprika

Directions:
1. Preheat air fryer to 360°F. Coat the pita wedges with olive oil, paprika and garlic salt in a bowl. Put them into the frying basket and Air Fry for 6-8 minutes. Serve warm.

String Bean Fries

Servings: 4
Cooking Time: 6 Minutes
Ingredients:
- ½ pound fresh string beans
- 2 eggs
- 4 teaspoons water
- ½ cup white flour
- ½ cup breadcrumbs
- ¼ teaspoon salt
- ¼ teaspoon ground black pepper
- ¼ teaspoon dry mustard (optional)
- oil for misting or cooking spray

Directions:
1. Preheat air fryer to 360°F.

2. Trim stem ends from string beans,wash,and pat dry.
3. In a shallow dish,beat eggs and water together until well blended.
4. Place flour in a second shallow dish.
5. In a third shallow dish,stir together the breadcrumbs,salt,pepper,and dry mustard if using.
6. Dip each string bean in egg mixture,flour,egg mixture again,then breadcrumbs.
7. When you finish coating all the string beans,open air fryer and place them in basket.
8. Cook for 3minutes.
9. Stop and mist string beans with oil or cooking spray.
10. Cook for 3 moreminutes or until string beans are crispy and nicely browned.

Fried Gyoza

Servings:18
Cooking Time:6 Minutes
Ingredients:
- 5 ounces Lean ground pork
- 2½tablespoons Very thinly sliced scallion
- 1 tablespoon plus 2 teaspoons Minced peeled fresh ginger
- 1¼teaspoons Toasted sesame oil
- ⅛teaspoon Table salt
- ⅛teaspoon Ground black pepper
- 18 Round gyoza or square wonton wrappers(thawed,if necessary)
- Vegetable oil spray

Directions:
1. Preheat the air fryer to 350°F.
2. Mix the ground pork,scallion,ginger,sesame oil,salt,and pepper in a bowl until well combined.
3. Set a bowl of water on a clean,dry surface or next to a clean,dry cutting board.Set one gyoza or wonton wrapper on that surface.Dip your clean finger in the water and run it around the perimeter of the gyoza wrapper or the edge of the wonton wrapper.Put about 1½teaspoons of the meat mixture in the center of the wrapper.
4. For the gyoza wrapper,fold the wrapper in half to close,pressing the edge to seal,then wet the outside of the edge of both sides of the seam and pleat it into little ridges to seal.
5. For the wonton wrapper,fold it in half lengthwise to make a rectangle,then seal the sides together,flattening the packet a bit as you do.
6. Set the filled wrapper aside and continue making more in the same way.When done,generously coat them on all sides with vegetable oil spray.
7. Place the gyoza in the basket in one layer and air-fry undisturbed for 6 minutes,or until browned and crisp at the edges.
8. Use kitchen tongs or a nonstick-safe spatula to gently transfer the gyoza to a wire rack.Cool for only 2 or 3 minutes before serving hot.

Honey Tater Tots With Bacon

Servings:4
Cooking Time:25 Minutes
Ingredients:
- 24 frozen tater tots
- 6 bacon slices
- 1 tbsp honey
- 1 cup grated cheddar

Directions:
1. Preheat air fryer to 400°F.Air Fry the tater tots for 10 minutes,shaking the basket once halfway through cooking.Cut the bacon into pieces.When the tater tots are done,remove them from the fryer to a baking pan.Top them with bacon and drizzle with honey.Air Fry for 5 minutes to crisp up the bacon.Top the tater tots with cheese and cook for 2 minutes to melt the cheese.Serve.

Tomato&Halloumi Bruschetta

Servings:4
Cooking Time:20 Minutes
Ingredients:
- 2 tbsp softened butter
- 8 French bread slices
- 1 cup grated halloumi cheese
- ½cup basil pesto
- 12 chopped cherry tomatoes
- 2 green onions,thinly sliced

Directions:
1. Preheat air fryer to 350°F.Spread butter on one side of the bread.Place butter-side up in the frying basket.Bake until the bread is slightly brown,3-5 minutes.Remove the bread and top it with halloumi cheese.Melt the cheese on the bread in the air fryer for another 1-3 minutes.
2. Meanwhile,mix pesto,cherry tomatoes,and green onions in a small bowl.When the cheese has melted,take the bread out of the fryer and arrange on a plate.Top with pesto mix and serve.

Jalapeño Poppers

Servings:18
Cooking Time:5 Minutes
Ingredients:
- ½pound jalapeño peppers
- ¼cup cornstarch
- 1 egg
- 1 tablespoon lime juice
- ¼cup plain breadcrumbs
- ¼cup panko breadcrumbs
- ½teaspoon salt
- oil for misting or cooking spray
- Filling
- 4 ounces cream cheese
- 1 teaspoon grated lime zest
- ¼teaspoon chile powder
- ⅛teaspoon garlic powder
- ¼teaspoon salt

Directions:
1. Combine all filling ingredients in small bowl and mix well.Refrigerate while preparing peppers.
2. Cut jalapeños into½-inch lengthwise slices.Use a small,sharp knife to remove seeds and veins.
3. a.For mild appetizers,discard seeds and veins.
4. b.For hot appetizers,finely chop seeds and veins.Stir a small amount into filling,taste,and continue adding a little at a time until filling is as hot as you like.
5. Stuff each pepper slice with filling.
6. Place cornstarch in a shallow dish.
7. In another shallow dish,beat together egg and lime juice.
8. Place breadcrumbs and salt in a third shallow dish and stir together.
9. Dip each pepper slice in cornstarch,shake off excess,then dip in egg mixture.
10. Roll in breadcrumbs,pressing to make coating stick.
11. Place pepper slices on a plate in single layer and freeze them for 30minutes.
12. Preheat air fryer to 390°F.
13. Spray frozen peppers with oil or cooking spray.Place in air fryer basket in a single layer and cook for 5minutes.

Bread And Breakfast

Hush Puffins

Servings:20
Cooking Time:8 Minutes
Ingredients:
- 1 cup buttermilk
- ¼cup butter,melted
- 2 eggs
- 1½cups all-purpose flour
- 1½cups cornmeal
- ⅓cup sugar
- 1 teaspoon baking soda
- 1 teaspoon salt
- 4 scallions,minced
- vegetable oil

Directions:
1. Combine the buttermilk,butter and eggs in a large mixing bowl.In a second bowl combine the flour,cornmeal,sugar,baking soda and salt.Add the dry ingredients to the wet ingredients,stirring just to combine.Stir in the minced scallions and refrigerate the batter for 30 minutes.
2. Shape the batter into 2-inch balls.Brush or spray the balls with oil.
3. Preheat the air fryer to 360°F.
4. Air-fry the hush puffins in two batches at 360°F for 8 minutes,turning them over after 6 minutes of the cooking process.
5. Serve warm with butter.

Country Gravy

Servings:2
Cooking Time:7 Minutes
Ingredients:
- ¼pound pork sausage,casings removed
- 1 tablespoon butter
- 2 tablespoons flour
- 2 cups whole milk
- ½teaspoon salt
- freshly ground black pepper
- 1 teaspoon fresh thyme leaves

Directions:
1. Preheat a saucepan over medium heat.Add and brown the sausage,crumbling it into small pieces as it cooks.Add the butter and flour,stirring well to combine.Continue to cook for 2 minutes,stirring constantly.
2. Slowly pour in the milk,whisking as you do,and bring the mixture to a boil to thicken.Season with salt and freshly ground black pepper,lower the heat and simmer until the sauce has thickened to your desired consistency–about 5 minutes.Stir in the fresh thyme,season to taste and serve hot.

Bacon Puff Pastry Pinwheels

Servings:8
Cooking Time:10 Minutes
Ingredients:
- 1 sheet of puff pastry
- 2 tablespoons maple syrup
- ¼cup brown sugar
- 8 slices bacon(not thick cut)
- coarsely cracked black pepper
- vegetable oil

Directions:
1. On a lightly floured surface,roll the puff pastry out into a square that measures roughly 10 inches wide by however long your bacon strips are(usually about 11 inches).Cut the pastry into eight even strips.
2. Brush the strips of pastry with the maple syrup and sprinkle the brown sugar on top,leaving 1 inch of dough exposed at the far end of each strip.Place a slice of bacon on each strip of puff pastry,letting 1/8-inch of the length of bacon hang over the edge of the pastry.Season generously with coarsely ground black pepper.
3. With the exposed end of the pastry strips away from you,roll the bacon and pastry strips up into pinwheels.Dab a little water on the exposed end of the pastry and pinch it to the pinwheel to seal the pastry shut.
4. Preheat the air fryer to 360°F.
5. Brush or spray the air fryer basket with a little vegetable oil.Place the pinwheels into the basket and air-fry at 360°F for 8 minutes.Turn the pinwheels over and air-fry for another 2 minutes to brown the bottom.Serve warm.

Tuscan Toast

Servings:4
Cooking Time:5 Minutes
Ingredients:
- ¼cup butter
- ½teaspoon lemon juice
- ½clove garlic
- ½teaspoon dried parsley flakes
- 4 slices Italian bread,1-inch thick

Directions:
1. Place butter,lemon juice,garlic,and parsley in a food processor.Process about 1 minute,or until garlic is pulverized and ingredients are well blended.
2. Spread garlic butter on both sides of bread slices.
3. Place bread slices upright in air fryer basket.(They can lie flat but cook better standing on end.)
4. Cook at 390°F for 5minutes or until toasty brown.

Shakshuka Cups

Servings:4
Cooking Time:25 Minutes
Ingredients:
- 2 tbsp tomato paste
- ½cup chicken broth
- 4 tomatoes,diced
- 2 garlic cloves,minced
- ½tsp dried oregano
- ½tsp dried coriander
- ½tsp dried basil
- ¼tsp red pepper flakes
- ¼tsp paprika
- 4 eggs
- Salt and pepper to taste
- 2 scallions,diced
- ½cup grated cheddar cheese
- ½cup Parmesan cheese
- 4 bread slices,toasted

Directions:
1. Preheat air fryer to 350°F.Combine the tomato paste,chicken broth,tomatoes,garlic,oregano,coriander,basil,red pepper flakes,and paprika.Pour the mixture evenly into greased ramekins.Bake in the air fryer for 5 minutes.Carefully remove the ramekins and crack one egg in each ramekin,then season with salt and pepper.Top with scallions,grated cheese,and Parmesan cheese.Return the ramekins to the frying basket and bake for 3-5 minutes until the eggs are set,and the cheese is melted.Serve with toasted bread immediately.

Lemon Monkey Bread

Servings: 4
Cooking Time: 15 Minutes
Ingredients:
- 1 can refrigerated biscuits
- ¼ cup white sugar
- 3 tbsp brown sugar
- ½ tsp ground cinnamon
- 1 lemon, zested
- ¼ tsp ground nutmeg
- 3 tbsp melted butter

Directions:
1. Preheat air fryer to 350°F. Take the biscuits out of the can and separate them. Cut each biscuit into 4 equal pieces. In a bowl, mix white sugar, brown sugar, lemon zest, cinnamon, and nutmeg. Have the melted butter nearby. Dip each biscuit piece into the butter, then roll into the cinnamon sugar until coated. Place in a baking pan. Bake in the air fryer until golden brown, 6-9 minutes. Let cool for 5 minutes before serving as the sugar will be hot.

Cherry-apple Oatmeal Cups

Servings: 2
Cooking Time: 20 Minutes
Ingredients:
- 2/3 cup rolled oats
- 1 cored apple, diced
- 4 pitted cherries, diced
- ½ tsp ground cinnamon
- ¾ cup milk

Directions:
1. Preheat air fryer to 350°F. Mix the oats, apple, cherries, and cinnamon in a heatproof bowl. Add in milk and Bake for 6 minutes, stir well and Bake for 6 more minutes until the fruit are soft. Serve cooled.

Matcha Granola

Servings: 4
Cooking Time: 15 Minutes
Ingredients:
- 2 tsp matcha green tea
- ½ cup slivered almonds
- ½ cup pecan pieces
- ½ cup sunflower seeds
- ½ cup pumpkin seeds
- 1 cup coconut flakes
- ¼ cup coconut sugar
- ⅛ cup flour
- ⅛ cup almond flour
- 1 tsp vanilla extract
- 2 tbsp melted butter
- 2 tbsp almond butter
- ⅛ tsp salt

Directions:
1. Preheat air fryer to 300°F. Mix the green tea, almonds, pecan, sunflower seeds, pumpkin seeds, coconut flakes, sugar, and flour, almond flour, vanilla extract, butter, almond butter, and salt in a bowl. Spoon the mixture into an ungreased round 4-cup baking dish. Place it in the fryer and Bake for 6 minutes, stirring once. Transfer to an airtight container, let cool for 10 minutes, then cover and store at room temperature until ready to serve.

Christmas Eggnog Bread

Servings: 6
Cooking Time: 18 Minutes
Ingredients:
- 1 cup flour, plus more for dusting
- ¼ cup sugar
- 1 teaspoon baking powder
- ¼ teaspoon salt
- ¼ teaspoon nutmeg
- ½ cup eggnog
- 1 egg yolk
- 1 tablespoon butter, plus 1 teaspoon, melted
- ¼ cup pecans
- ¼ cup chopped candied fruit (cherries, pineapple, or mixed fruits)
- cooking spray

Directions:
1. Preheat air fryer to 360°F.
2. In a medium bowl, stir together the flour, sugar, baking powder, salt, and nutmeg.
3. Add eggnog, egg yolk, and butter. Mix well but do not beat.
4. Stir in nuts and fruit.
5. Spray a 6 x 6-inch baking pan with cooking spray and dust with flour.
6. Spread batter into prepared pan and cook at 360°F for 18 minutes or until top is dark golden brown and bread starts to pull away from sides of pan.

Blueberry Applesauce Oat Cake

Servings: 4
Cooking Time: 65 Minutes
Ingredients:
- 1 cup applesauce
- 2/3 cup quick-cooking oats
- ½ tsp baking powder
- A pinch of salt
- ½ cup almond milk
- 5 tbsp almond flour
- 1 tbsp honey
- 1 egg
- 1 tsp vanilla extract
- ½ cup blueberries
- 4 tbsp grape preserves

Directions:
1. In a bowl, combine oats, baking powder, and salt. In a larger bowl, combine milk, almond flour, honey, egg, and vanilla with a whisk until well mixed. Add the applesauce until combined, then add the oat mixture. Gently fold in blueberries. Pour the mixture into a greased baking dish. Spoon jelly over the top, but do not stir it in.
2. Preheat air fryer to 300°F. Put the baking dish into the air fryer. Bake until the top is golden and the oatmeal is set, 25 minutes. Remove and allow to cool for 10-15 minutes. Slice four ways and serve warm.

Pumpkin Bread With Walnuts

Servings: 6
Cooking Time: 30 Minutes
Ingredients:
- ½ cup canned pumpkin purée
- 1 cup flour
- ½ tsp baking soda
- ½ cup granulated sugar
- 1 tsp pumpkin pie spice
- ¼ tsp nutmeg
- ¼ tsp salt
- 1 egg
- 1 tbsp vegetable oil

- 1 tbsp orange juice
- 1 tsp orange zest
- ¼ cup crushed walnuts

Directions:
1. Preheat air fryer at 375ºF. Combine flour, baking soda, sugar, nutmeg, pumpkin pie spice, salt, pumpkin purée, egg, oil, orange juice, orange zest, and walnuts in a bowl. Pour the mixture into a greased cake pan. Place cake pan in the frying basket and Bake for 20 minutes. Let sit for 10 minutes until slightly cooled before slicing. Serve.

Cinnamon Biscuit Rolls

Servings: 12
Cooking Time: 5 Minutes

Ingredients:
- Dough
- ¼ cup warm water (105–115°F)
- 1 teaspoon active dry yeast
- 1 tablespoon sugar
- ½ cup buttermilk, lukewarm
- 2 cups flour, plus more for dusting
- 1 teaspoon baking powder
- ½ teaspoon salt
- 3 tablespoons cold butter
- Filling
- 1 tablespoon butter, melted
- 1 teaspoon cinnamon
- 2 tablespoons sugar
- Icing
- ⅔ cup powdered sugar
- ¼ teaspoon vanilla
- 2–3 teaspoons milk

Directions:
1. Dissolve yeast and sugar in warm water. Add buttermilk, stir, and set aside.
2. In a large bowl, sift together flour, baking powder, and salt. Using knives or a pastry blender, cut in butter until mixture is well combined and crumbly.
3. Pour in buttermilk mixture and stir with fork until a ball of dough forms.
4. Knead dough on a lightly floured surface for 5 minutes. Roll into an 8 x 11-inch rectangle.
5. For the filling, spread the melted butter over the dough.
6. In a small bowl, stir together the cinnamon and sugar, then sprinkle over dough.
7. Starting on a long side, roll up dough so that you have a roll about 11 inches long. Cut into 12 slices with a serrated knife and sawing motion so slices remain round.
8. Place rolls on a plate or cookie sheet about an inch apart and let rise for 30 minutes.
9. For icing, mix the powdered sugar, vanilla, and milk. Stir and add additional milk until icing reaches a good spreading consistency.
10. Preheat air fryer to 360°F.
11. Place 6 cinnamon rolls in basket and cook 5 minutes or until top springs back when lightly touched. Repeat to cook remaining 6 rolls.
12. Spread icing over warm rolls and serve.

Sweet Potato-cinnamon Toast

Servings: 6
Cooking Time: 8 Minutes

Ingredients:
- 1 small sweet potato, cut into ⅜-inch slices
- oil for misting
- ground cinnamon

Directions:
1. Preheat air fryer to 390°F.
2. Spray both sides of sweet potato slices with oil. Sprinkle both sides with cinnamon to taste.
3. Place potato slices in air fryer basket in a single layer.
4. Cook for 4 minutes, turn, and cook for 4 more minutes or until potato slices are barely fork tender.

Spinach-bacon Rollups

Servings: 4
Cooking Time: 9 Minutes

Ingredients:
- 4 flour tortillas (6- or 7-inch size)
- 4 slices Swiss cheese
- 1 cup baby spinach leaves
- 4 slices turkey bacon

Directions:
1. Preheat air fryer to 390°F.
2. On each tortilla, place one slice of cheese and ¼ cup of spinach.
3. Roll up tortillas and wrap each with a strip of bacon. Secure each end with a toothpick.
4. Place rollups in air fryer basket, leaving a little space in between them.
5. Cook for 4 minutes. Turn and rearrange rollups (for more even cooking) and cook for 5 minutes longer, until bacon is crisp.

Wild Blueberry Lemon Chia Bread

Servings: 6
Cooking Time: 27 Minutes

Ingredients:
- ¼ cup extra-virgin olive oil
- ⅓ cup plus 1 tablespoon cane sugar
- 1 large egg
- 3 tablespoons fresh lemon juice
- 1 tablespoon lemon zest
- ⅔ cup milk
- 1 cup all-purpose flour
- ¾ teaspoon baking powder
- ⅛ teaspoon salt
- 2 tablespoons chia seeds
- 1 cup frozen wild blueberries
- ⅓ cup powdered sugar
- 2 teaspoons milk

Directions:
1. Preheat the air fryer to 310°F.
2. In a medium bowl, mix the olive oil with the sugar. Whisk in the egg, lemon juice, lemon zest, and milk; set aside.
3. In a small bowl, combine the all-purpose flour, baking powder, and salt.
4. Slowly mix the dry ingredients into the wet ingredients. Stir in the chia seeds and wild blueberries.
5. Liberally spray a 7-inch springform pan with olive-oil spray. Pour the batter into the pan and place the pan in the air fryer. Bake for 25 to 27 minutes, or until a toothpick inserted in the center comes out clean.
6. Remove and let cool on a wire rack for 10 minutes prior to removing from the pan.
7. Meanwhile, in a small bowl, mix the powdered sugar with the milk to create the glaze.
8. Slice and serve with a drizzle of the powdered sugar glaze.

Morning Loaded Potato Skins

Servings: 4
Cooking Time: 55 Minutes
Ingredients:
- 2 large potatoes
- 1 fried bacon slice, chopped
- Salt and pepper to taste
- 1 tbsp chopped dill
- 1½ tbsp butter
- 2 tbsp milk
- 4 eggs
- 1 scallion, sliced
- ¼ cup grated fontina cheese
- 2 tbsp chopped parsley

Directions:
1. Preheat air fryer to 400°F. Wash each potato and poke with fork 3 or 4 times. Place in the frying basket and bake for 40-45 minutes. Remove the potatoes and let cool until they can be handled. Cut each potato in half lengthwise. Scoop out potato flesh but leave enough to maintain the structure of the potato. Transfer the potato flesh to a medium bowl and stir in salt, pepper, dill, bacon, butter, and milk until mashed with some chunky pieces.
2. Fill the potato skin halves with the potato mixture and press the center of the filling with a spoon about ½-inch deep. Crack an egg in the center of each potato, then top with scallions and cheese. Return the potatoes to the air fryer and bake for 3 to 5 minutes until the egg is cooked to preferred doneness and cheese is melted. Serve immediately sprinkled with parsley.

Chili Hash Browns

Servings: 4
Cooking Time: 45 Minutes
Ingredients:
- 1 tbsp ancho chili powder
- 1 tbsp chipotle powder
- 2 tsp ground cumin
- 2 tsp smoked paprika
- 1 tsp garlic powder
- 1 tsp cayenne pepper
- Salt and pepper to taste
- 2 peeled russet potatoes, grated
- 2 tbsp olive oil
- 1/3 cup chopped onion
- 3 garlic cloves, minced

Directions:
1. Preheat the air fryer to 400°F. Combine chili powder, cumin, paprika, garlic powder, chipotle, cayenne, and black pepper in a small bowl, then pour into a glass jar with a lid and store in a cool, dry place. Add the olive oil, onion, and garlic to a cake pan, put it in the air fryer, and Bake for 3 minutes. Put the grated potatoes in a bowl and sprinkle with 2 tsp of the spice mixture, toss and add them to the cake pan along with the onion mix. Bake for 20-23 minutes, stirring once or until the potatoes are crispy and golden. Season with salt and serve.

Aromatic Mushroom Omelet

Servings: 4
Cooking Time: 30 Minutes
Ingredients:
- 6 eggs
- 2 tbsp milk
- ½ yellow onion, diced
- ½ cup diced mushrooms
- 2 tbsp chopped parsley
- 1 tsp dried oregano
- 1 tbsp chopped chives
- ½ tbsp chopped dill
- ½ cup grated Gruyère cheese

Directions:
1. Preheat air fryer to 350°F. Beat eggs in a medium bowl, then add the rest of the ingredients, except for the parsley. Stir until completely combined. Pour the mixture into a greased pan and bake in the air fryer for 18-20 minutes until the eggs are set. Top with parsley and serve.

Apple & Turkey Breakfast Sausages

Servings: 4
Cooking Time: 15 Minutes
Ingredients:
- ½ tsp coriander seeds, crushed
- 1 tbsp chopped rosemary
- 1 tbsp chopped thyme
- Salt and pepper to taste
- 1 tsp fennel seeds, crushed
- ¾ tsp smoked paprika
- ½ tsp garlic powder
- ½ tsp shallot powder
- ⅛ tsp red pepper flakes
- 1 pound ground turkey
- ½ cup minced apples

Directions:
1. Combine all of the seasonings in a bowl. Add turkey and apple and blend seasonings in well with your hands. Form patties about 3 inches in diameter and ¼ inch thick.
2. Preheat air fryer to 400°F. Arrange patties in a single layer on the greased frying basket. Air Fry for 10 minutes, flipping once until brown and cooked through. Serve.

Farmers Market Quiche

Servings: 4
Cooking Time: 35 Minutes
Ingredients:
- 4 button mushrooms
- ¼ medium red bell pepper
- 1 teaspoon extra-virgin olive oil
- One 9-inch pie crust, at room temperature
- ¼ cup grated carrot
- ¼ cup chopped, fresh baby spinach leaves
- 3 eggs, whisked
- ¼ cup half-and-half
- ½ teaspoon thyme
- ½ teaspoon sea salt
- 2 ounces crumbled goat cheese or feta

Directions:
1. In a medium bowl, toss the mushrooms and bell pepper with extra-virgin olive oil; place into the air fryer basket. Set the temperature to 400°F for 8 minutes, stirring after 4 minutes. Remove from the air fryer, and roughly chop the mushrooms and bell peppers. Wipe the air fryer clean.
2. Prep a 7-inch oven-safe baking dish by spraying the bottom of the pan with cooking spray.
3. Place the pie crust into the baking dish; fold over and crimp the edges or use a fork to press to give the edges some shape.
4. In a medium bowl, mix together the mushrooms, bell peppers, carrots, spinach, and eggs. Stir in the half-and-half, thyme, and salt.
5. Pour the quiche mixture into the base of the pie shell. Top with crumbled cheese.

6. Place the quiche into the air fryer basket. Set the temperature to 325°F for 30 minutes.
7. When complete, turn the quiche halfway and cook an additional 5 minutes. Allow the quiche to rest 20 minutes prior to slicing and serving.

Oat & Nut Granola

Servings: 6
Cooking Time: 25 Minutes
Ingredients:
- 2 cups rolled oats
- ¼ cup pistachios
- ¼ cup chopped almonds
- ¼ cup chopped cashews
- ¼ cup honey
- 2 tbsp light brown sugar
- 3 tbsp butter
- ½ tsp ground cinnamon
- ½ cup dried figs

Directions:
1. Preheat the air fryer to 325°F. Combine the oats, pistachios, almonds, and cashews in a bowl and toss, then set aside. In a saucepan, cook the honey, brown sugar, butter, and cinnamon and over low heat, stirring frequently, 4 minutes. Melt the butter completely and make sure the mixture is smooth, then pour over the oat mix and stir.
2. Scoop the granola mixture in a greased baking pan. Put the pan in the frying basket and Bake for 7 minutes, then remove the pan and stir. Cook for another 6-9 minutes or until the granola is golden, then add the dried figs and stir. Remove the pan and let cool. Store in a covered container at room temperature for up to 3 days.

Morning Apple Biscuits

Servings: 6
Cooking Time: 15 Minutes
Ingredients:
- 1 apple, grated
- 1 cup oat flour
- 2 tbsp honey
- ¼ cup peanut butter
- 1/3 cup raisins
- ½ tsp ground cinnamon

Directions:
1. Preheat air fryer to 350°F. Combine the apple, flour, honey, peanut butter, raisins, and cinnamon in a bowl until combined. Make balls out of the mixture. Place them onto parchment paper and flatten them. Bake for 9 minutes until slightly brown. Serve warm.

Breakfast Chimichangas

Servings: 4
Cooking Time: 8 Minutes
Ingredients:
- Four 8-inch flour tortillas
- ½ cup canned refried beans
- 1 cup scrambled eggs
- ½ cup grated cheddar or Monterey jack cheese
- 1 tablespoon vegetable oil
- 1 cup salsa

Directions:
1. Lay the flour tortillas out flat on a cutting board. In the center of each tortilla, spread 2 tablespoons refried beans. Next, add ¼ cup eggs and 2 tablespoons cheese to each tortilla.
2. To fold the tortillas, begin on the left side and fold to the center. Then fold the right side into the center. Next fold the bottom and top down and roll over to completely seal the chimichanga. Using a pastry brush or oil mister, brush the tops of the tortilla packages with oil.
3. Preheat the air fryer to 400°F for 4 minutes. Place the chimichangas into the air fryer basket, seam side down, and air fry for 4 minutes. Using tongs, turn over the chimichangas and cook for an additional 2 to 3 minutes or until light golden brown.

Blueberry Pannenkoek (dutch Pancake)

Servings: 4
Cooking Time: 30 Minutes
Ingredients:
- 3 eggs, beaten
- ½ cup buckwheat flour
- ½ cup milk
- ½ tsp vanilla
- 1½ cups blueberries, crushed
- 2 tbsp powdered sugar

Directions:
1. Preheat air fryer to 330°F. Mix together eggs, buckwheat flour, milk, and vanilla in a bowl. Pour the batter into a greased baking pan and add it to the fryer. Bake until the pancake is puffed and golden, 12-16 minutes. Remove the pan and flip the pancake over onto a plate. Add blueberries and powdered sugar as a topping and serve.

Bagels With Avocado & Tomatoes

Servings: 2
Cooking Time: 35 Minutes
Ingredients:
- 2/3 cup all-purpose flour
- ½ tsp active dry yeast
- 1/3 cup Greek yogurt
- 8 cherry tomatoes
- 1 ripe avocado
- 1 tbsp lemon juice
- 2 tbsp chopped red onions
- Black pepper to taste

Directions:
1. Preheat air fryer to 400°F. Beat the flour, dry yeast, and Greek yogurt until you get a smooth dough, adding more flour if necessary. Make 2 equal balls out of the mixture.
2. Using a rolling pin, roll each ball into a 9-inch long strip. Form a ring with each strip and press the ends together to create 2 bagels. In a bowl with hot water, soak the bagels for 1 minute. Shake excess water and let rise for 15 minutes in the fryer. Bake for 5 minutes, turn the bagels, top with tomatoes, and Bake for another 5 minutes.
3. Cut avocado in half, discard the pit and remove the flesh into a bowl. Mash with a fork and stir in lemon juice and onions. Once the bagels are ready, let cool slightly and cut them in half. Spread on each half some guacamole, top with 2 slices of Baked tomatoes, and sprinkle with pepper. Serve immediately.

Cheddar & Sausage Tater Tots

Servings: 4
Cooking Time: 25 Minutes
Ingredients:
- 12 oz ground chicken sausage
- 4 eggs
- 1 cup sour cream
- 1 tsp Worcestershire sauce
- 1 tsp shallot powder

- Salt and pepper to taste
- 1 lb frozen tater tots
- ¾ cup grated cheddar

Directions:
1. Whisk eggs, sour cream, Worcestershire sauce and shallot in a bowl. Add salt and pepper to taste. Coat a skillet with cooking spray. Over medium heat, brown the ground sausage for 3-4 minutes. Break larger pieces with a spoon or spatula. Set aside.
2. Preheat air fryer to 330°F. Prepare a baking pan with a light spray of cooking oil. Layer the bottom of the pan with tater tots, then place in the air fryer. Bake for 6 minutes, then shake the pan. Cover tater tots with cooked sausage and egg mixture. Continue cooking for 6 minutes. Top with cheese, then cook for another 2-3 minutes or until cheese is melted. Serve warm.

Banana Bread

Servings: 6
Cooking Time: 20 Minutes
Ingredients:
- cooking spray
- 1 cup white wheat flour
- ½ teaspoon baking powder
- ¼ teaspoon salt
- ¼ teaspoon baking soda
- 1 egg
- ½ cup mashed ripe banana
- ¼ cup plain yogurt
- ¼ cup pure maple syrup
- 2 tablespoons coconut oil
- ½ teaspoon pure vanilla extract

Directions:
1. Preheat air fryer to 330°F.
2. Lightly spray 6 x 6-inch baking dish with cooking spray.
3. In a medium bowl, mix together the flour, baking powder, salt, and soda.
4. In a separate bowl, beat the egg and add the mashed banana, yogurt, syrup, oil, and vanilla. Mix until well combined.
5. Pour liquid mixture into dry ingredients and stir gently to blend. Do not beat. Batter may be slightly lumpy.
6. Pour batter into baking dish and cook at 330°F for 20 minutes or until toothpick inserted in center of loaf comes out clean.

Pesto Egg & Ham Sandwiches

Servings: 2
Cooking Time: 20 Minutes
Ingredients:
- 4 sandwich bread slices
- 2 tbsp butter, melted
- 4 eggs, scrambled
- 4 deli ham slices
- 2 Colby cheese slices
- 4 tsp basil pesto sauce
- ¼ tsp red chili flakes
- ¼ sliced avocado

Directions:
1. Preheat air fryer at 370°F. Brush 2 pieces of bread with half of the butter and place them, butter side down, into the frying basket. Divide eggs, chili flakes, sliced avocado, ham, and cheese on each bread slice.
2. Spread pesto on the remaining bread slices and place them, pesto side-down, onto the sandwiches. Brush the remaining butter on the tops of the sandwiches and Bake for 6 minutes, flipping once. Serve immediately.

Garlic Bread Knots

Servings: 8
Cooking Time: 5 Minutes
Ingredients:
- ¼ cup melted butter
- 2 teaspoons garlic powder
- 1 teaspoon dried parsley
- 1 (11-ounce) tube of refrigerated French bread dough

Directions:
1. Mix the melted butter, garlic powder and dried parsley in a small bowl and set it aside.
2. To make smaller knots, cut the long tube of bread dough into 16 slices. If you want to make bigger knots, slice the dough into 8 slices. Shape each slice into a long rope about 6 inches long by rolling it on a flat surface with the palm of your hands. Tie each rope into a knot and place them on a plate.
3. Preheat the air fryer to 350°F.
4. Transfer half of the bread knots into the air fryer basket, leaving space in between each knot. Brush each knot with the butter mixture using a pastry brush.
5. Air-fry for 5 minutes. Remove the baked knots and brush a little more of the garlic butter mixture on each. Repeat with the remaining bread knots and serve warm.

Fluffy Vegetable Strata

Servings: 4
Cooking Time: 30 Minutes
Ingredients:
- ½ red onion, thickly sliced
- 8 asparagus, sliced
- 1 baby carrot, shredded
- 4 cup mushrooms, sliced
- ½ red bell pepper, chopped
- 2 bread slices, cubed
- 3 eggs
- 3 tbsp milk
- ½ cup mozzarella cheese
- 2 tsp chives, chopped

Directions:
1. Preheat air fryer to 330°F. Add the red onion, asparagus, carrots, mushrooms, red bell pepper, mushrooms, and 1 tbsp of water to a baking pan. Put it in the air fryer and Bake for 3-5 minutes, until crispy. Remove the pan, add the bread cubes, and shake to mix. Combine the eggs, milk, and chives and pour them over the veggies. Cover with mozzarella cheese. Bake for 12-15 minutes. The strata should puff up and set, while the top should be brown. Serve hot.

Western Omelet

Servings: 2
Cooking Time: 22 Minutes
Ingredients:
- ¼ cup chopped onion
- ¼ cup chopped bell pepper, green or red
- ¼ cup diced ham
- 1 teaspoon butter
- 4 large eggs
- 2 tablespoons milk
- ⅛ teaspoon salt
- ¾ cup grated sharp Cheddar cheese

Directions:
1. Place onion, bell pepper, ham, and butter in air fryer baking pan. Cook at 390°F for 1 minute and stir. Continue cooking 5 minutes, until vegetables are tender.
2. Beat together eggs, milk, and salt. Pour over vegetables and ham in baking pan. Cook at 360°F for 15 minutes or until eggs set and top has browned slightly.
3. Sprinkle grated cheese on top of omelet. Cook 1 minute or just long enough to melt the cheese.

Coffee Cake

Servings: 8
Cooking Time: 35 Minutes
Ingredients:
- 4 tablespoons butter, melted and divided
- ⅓ cup cane sugar
- ¼ cup brown sugar
- 1 large egg
- 1 cup plus 6 teaspoons milk, divided
- 1 teaspoon vanilla extract
- 2 cups all-purpose flour
- 1½ teaspoons baking powder
- ¼ teaspoon salt
- 2 teaspoons ground cinnamon
- ⅓ cup chopped pecans
- ⅓ cup powdered sugar

Directions:
1. Preheat the air fryer to 325°F.
2. Using a hand mixer or stand mixer, in a medium bowl, cream together the butter, cane sugar, brown sugar, the egg, 1 cup of the milk, and the vanilla. Set aside.
3. In a small bowl, mix together the flour, baking powder, salt, and cinnamon. Slowly combine the dry ingredients into the wet. Fold in the pecans.
4. Liberally spray a 7-inch springform pan with cooking spray. Pour the batter into the pan and place in the air fryer basket.
5. Bake for 30 to 35 minutes. While the cake is baking, in a small bowl, add the powdered sugar and whisk together with the remaining 6 teaspoons of milk. Set aside.
6. When the cake is done baking, remove the pan from the basket and let cool on a wire rack. After 10 minutes, remove and invert the cake from pan. Drizzle with the powdered sugar glaze and serve.

Smoked Salmon Croissant Sandwich

Servings: 1
Cooking Time: 30 Minutes
Ingredients:
- 1 croissant, halved
- 2 eggs
- 1 tbsp guacamole
- 1 smoked salmon slice
- Salt and pepper to taste

Directions:
1. Preheat air fryer to 360°F. Place the croissant, crusty side up, in the frying basket side by side. Whisk the eggs in a small ceramic dish until fluffy. Place in the air fryer. Bake for 10 minutes. Gently scramble the half-cooked egg in the baking dish with a fork. Flip the croissant and cook for another 10 minutes until the scrambled eggs are cooked, but still fluffy, and the croissant is toasted.
2. Place one croissant on a serving plate, then spread the guacamole on top. Scoop the scrambled eggs onto guacamole, then top with smoked salmon. Sprinkle with salt and pepper. Top with the second slice of toasted croissant, close sandwich, and serve hot.

Effortless Toffee Zucchini Bread

Servings: 6
Cooking Time: 30 Minutes
Ingredients:
- 1 cup flour
- ½ tsp baking soda
- ½ cup granulated sugar
- ¼ tsp ground cinnamon
- ¼ tsp nutmeg
- ¼ tsp salt
- 1/3 cup grated zucchini
- 1 egg
- 1 tbsp olive oil
- 1 tsp vanilla extract
- 2 tbsp English toffee bits
- 2 tbsp mini chocolate chips
- 1/2 cup chopped walnuts

Directions:
1. Preheat air fryer at 375ºF. Combine the flour, baking soda, toffee bits, sugar, cinnamon, nutmeg, salt, zucchini, egg, olive oil, vanilla and chocolate chips in a bowl. Add the walnuts to the batter and mix until evenly distributed.
2. Pour the mixture into a greased cake pan. Place the pan in the fryer and Bake for 20 minutes. Let sit for 10 minutes until slightly cooled before slicing. Serve immediately.

Morning Burrito

Servings: 4
Cooking Time: 15 Minutes
Ingredients:
- 2 oz cheddar cheese, torn into pieces
- 2 hard-boiled eggs, chopped
- 1 avocado, chopped
- 1 red bell pepper, chopped
- 3 tbsp salsa
- 4 flour tortillas

Directions:
1. Whisk the eggs, avocado, red bell pepper, salsa, and cheese. Pout the tortillas on a clean surface and divide the egg mix between them. Fold the edges and roll up; poke a toothpick through so they hold. Preheat air fryer to 390°F. Place the burritos in the frying basket and Air Fry for 3-5 minutes until crispy and golden. Serve hot.

Peppered Maple Bacon Knots

Servings: 6
Cooking Time: 8 Minutes
Ingredients:
- 1 pound maple smoked center-cut bacon
- ¼ cup maple syrup
- ¼ cup brown sugar
- coarsely cracked black peppercorns

Directions:
1. Tie each bacon strip in a loose knot and place them on a baking sheet.
2. Combine the maple syrup and brown sugar in a bowl. Brush each knot generously with this mixture and sprinkle with coarsely cracked black pepper.
3. Preheat the air fryer to 390°F.
4. Air-fry the bacon knots in batches. Place one layer of knots in the air fryer basket and air-fry for 5 minutes. Turn the bacon knots over and air-fry for an additional 3 minutes.
5. Serve warm.

Fry Bread

Servings: 4
Cooking Time: 5 Minutes
Ingredients:
- 1 cup flour
- 2 teaspoons baking powder
- ¼ teaspoon salt
- ¼ cup lukewarm milk

Ninja Foodi 2-Basket Air Fryer

- 1 teaspoon oil
- 2–3 tablespoons water
- oil for misting or cooking spray

Directions:
1. Stir together flour, baking powder, and salt. Gently mix in the milk and oil. Stir in 1 tablespoon water. If needed, add more water 1 tablespoon at a time until stiff dough forms. Dough shouldn't be sticky, so use only as much as you need.
2. Divide dough into 4 portions and shape into balls. Cover with a towel and let rest for 10 minutes.
3. Preheat air fryer to 390°F.
4. Shape dough as desired:
5. a. Pat into 3-inch circles. This will make a thicker bread to eat plain or with a sprinkle of cinnamon or honey butter. You can cook all 4 at once.
6. b. Pat thinner into rectangles about 3 x 6 inches. This will create a thinner bread to serve as a base for dishes such as Indian tacos. The circular shape is more traditional, but rectangles allow you to cook 2 at a time in your air fryer basket.
7. Spray both sides of dough pieces with oil or cooking spray.
8. Place the 4 circles or 2 of the dough rectangles in the air fryer basket and cook at 390°F for 3 minutes. Spray tops, turn, spray other side, and cook for 2 more minutes. If necessary, repeat to cook remaining bread.
9. Serve piping hot as is or allow to cool slightly and add toppings to create your own Native American tacos.

Breakfast Sausage Bites

Servings: 4
Cooking Time: 30 Minutes
Ingredients:
- 1 lb ground pork sausages
- ¼ cup diced onions
- 1 tsp rubbed sage
- ¼ tsp ground nutmeg
- ½ tsp fennel
- ¼ tsp garlic powder
- 2 tbsp parsley, chopped
- Salt and pepper to taste

Directions:
1. Preheat air fryer at 350ºF. Combine all ingredients, except the parsley, in a bowl. Form mixture into balls. Place them in the greased frying basket and Air Fry for 10 minutes, flipping once. Sprinkle with parsley and serve immediately.

Breakfast Burrito With Sausage

Servings: 6
Cooking Time: 35 Minutes
Ingredients:
- 2 tbsp olive oil
- Salt and pepper to taste
- 6 eggs, beaten
- ½ chopped red bell pepper
- ½ chopped green bell pepper
- 1 onion, finely chopped
- 8 oz chicken sausage
- ½ cup salsa
- 6 flour tortillas
- ½ cup grated cheddar

Directions:
1. Warm the olive oil in a skillet over medium heat. Add the eggs and stir-fry them for 2-3 minutes until scrambled. Season with salt and pepper and set aside.
2. Sauté the bell peppers and onion in the same skillet for 2-3 minutes until tender. Add and brown the chicken sausage, breaking into small pieces with a wooden spoon, about 4 minutes. Return the scrambled eggs and stir in the salsa. Remove the skillet from heat. Divide the mixture between the tortillas. Fold up the top and bottom edges, then roll to fully enclose the filling. Secure with toothpicks. Spritz with cooking spray.
3. Preheat air fryer to 400°F. Bake the burritos in the air fryer for 10 minutes, turning them once halfway through cooking until crisp. Garnish with cheddar cheese. Serve.

Veggie & Feta Scramble Bowls

Servings: 2
Cooking Time: 25 Minutes
Ingredients:
- 1 russet potato, cubed
- 1 bell pepper, cut into strips
- ½ feta, cubed
- 1 tbsp nutritional yeast
- ½ tsp garlic powder
- ½ tsp onion powder
- ¼ tsp ground turmeric
- 1 tbsp apple cider vinegar

Directions:
1. Preheat air fryer to 400°F. Put in potato cubes and bell pepper strips and Air Fry for 10 minutes. Combine the feta, nutritional yeast, garlic, onion, turmeric, and apple vinegar in a small pan. Fit a trivet in the fryer, lay the pan on top, and Air Fry for 5 more minutes until potatoes are tender and feta cheese cooked. Share potatoes and bell peppers into 2 bowls and top with feta scramble. Serve.

Egg & Bacon Toasts

Servings: 4
Cooking Time: 25 Minutes
Ingredients:
- 4 French bread slices, cut diagonally
- 1+ tsp butter
- 4 eggs
- 2 tbsp milk
- ½ tsp dried thyme
- Salt and pepper to taste
- 4 oz cooked bacon, crumbled
- 2/3 cup grated Colby cheese

Directions:
1. Preheat the air fryer to 350°F. Spray each slice of bread with oil and Bake in the frying basket for 2-3 minutes until light brown; set aside. Beat together the eggs, milk, thyme, salt, and pepper in a bowl and add the melted butter. Transfer to a 6-inch cake pan and place the pan into the fryer. Bake for 7-8 minutes, stirring once or until the eggs are set. Transfer the egg mixture into a bowl.
2. Top the bread slices with egg mixture, bacon, and cheese. Return to the fryer and Bake for 4-8 minutes or until the cheese melts and browns in spots. Serve.

Honey Donuts

Servings: 6
Cooking Time: 25 Minutes + Chilling Time
Ingredients:
- 1 refrigerated puff pastry sheet
- 2 tsp flour
- 2½ cups powdered sugar
- 3 tbsp honey
- 2 tbsp milk
- 2 tbsp butter, melted
- ½ tsp vanilla extract

- ½ tsp ground cinnamon
- Pinch of salt

Directions:
1. Preheat the air fryer to 325°F. Dust a clean work surface with flour and lay the puff pastry on it, then cut crosswise into five 3-inch wide strips. Cut each strip into thirds for 15 squares. Lay round parchment paper in the bottom of the basket, then add the pastry squares in a single layer.
2. Make sure none are touching. Bake for 13-18 minutes or until brown, then leave on a rack to cool. Repeat for all dough. Combine the sugar, honey, milk, butter, vanilla, cinnamon, and salt in a small bowl and mix with a wire whisk until combined. Dip the top half of each donut in the glaze, turn the donut glaze side up, and return to the wire rack. Let cool until the glaze sets, then serve.

English Breakfast

Servings: 2
Cooking Time: 30 Minutes
Ingredients:
- 6 bacon strips
- 1 cup cooked white beans
- 1 tbsp melted butter
- ½ tbsp flour
- Salt and pepper to taste
- 2 eggs

Directions:
1. Preheat air fryer to 360°F. In a second bowl, combine the beans, butter, flour, salt, and pepper. Mix well. Put the bacon in the frying basket and Air Fry for 10 minutes, flipping once. Remove the bacon and stir in the beans. Crack the eggs on top and cook for 10-12 minutes until the eggs are set. Serve with bacon.

Ham And Cheddar Gritters

Servings: 6
Cooking Time: 12 Minutes
Ingredients:
- 4 cups water
- 1 cup quick-cooking grits
- ¼ teaspoon salt
- 2 tablespoons butter
- 2 cups grated Cheddar cheese, divided
- 1 cup finely diced ham
- 1 tablespoon chopped chives
- salt and freshly ground black pepper
- 1 egg, beaten
- 2 cups panko breadcrumbs
- vegetable oil

Directions:
1. Bring the water to a boil in a saucepan. Whisk in the grits and ¼ teaspoon of salt, and cook for 7 minutes until the grits are soft. Remove the pan from the heat and stir in the butter and 1 cup of the grated Cheddar cheese. Transfer the grits to a bowl and let them cool for just 10 to 15 minutes.
2. Stir the ham, chives and the rest of the cheese into the grits and season with salt and pepper to taste. Add the beaten egg and refrigerate the mixture for 30 minutes. (Try not to chill the grits much longer than 30 minutes, or the mixture will be too firm to shape into patties.)
3. While the grit mixture is chilling, make the country gravy and set it aside.
4. Place the panko breadcrumbs in a shallow dish. Measure out ¼-cup portions of the grits mixture and shape them into patties. Coat all sides of the patties with the panko breadcrumbs, patting them with your hands so the crumbs adhere to the patties. You should have about 16 patties. Spray both sides of the patties with oil.
5. Preheat the air fryer to 400°F.
6. In batches of 5 or 6, air-fry the fritters for 8 minutes. Using a flat spatula, flip the fritters over and air-fry for another 4 minutes.
7. Serve hot with country gravy.

Nutty Whole Wheat Muffins

Servings: 8
Cooking Time: 11 Minutes
Ingredients:
- ½ cup whole-wheat flour, plus 2 tablespoons
- ¼ cup oat bran
- 2 tablespoons flaxseed meal
- ¼ cup brown sugar
- ½ teaspoon baking soda
- ½ teaspoon baking powder
- ¼ teaspoon salt
- ½ teaspoon cinnamon
- ½ cup buttermilk
- 2 tablespoons melted butter
- 1 egg
- ½ teaspoon pure vanilla extract
- ½ cup grated carrots
- ¼ cup chopped pecans
- ¼ cup chopped walnuts
- 1 tablespoon pumpkin seeds
- 1 tablespoon sunflower seeds
- 16 foil muffin cups, paper liners removed
- cooking spray

Directions:
1. Preheat air fryer to 330°F.
2. In a large bowl, stir together the flour, bran, flaxseed meal, sugar, baking soda, baking powder, salt, and cinnamon.
3. In a medium bowl, beat together the buttermilk, butter, egg, and vanilla. Pour into flour mixture and stir just until dry ingredients moisten. Do not beat.
4. Gently stir in carrots, nuts, and seeds.
5. Double up the foil cups so you have 8 total and spray with cooking spray.
6. Place 4 foil cups in air fryer basket and divide half the batter among them.
7. Cook at 330°F for 11 minutes or until toothpick inserted in center comes out clean.
8. Repeat step 7 to cook remaining 4 muffins.

Mini Everything Bagels

Servings: 4
Cooking Time: 6 Minutes
Ingredients:
- 1 cup all-purpose flour
- 2 teaspoons baking powder
- ½ teaspoon salt
- 1 cup plain Greek yogurt
- 1 egg, whisked
- 1 teaspoon sesame seeds
- 1 teaspoon dehydrated onions
- ½ teaspoon poppy seeds
- ½ teaspoon garlic powder
- ½ teaspoon sea salt flakes

Directions:
1. In a large bowl, mix together the flour, baking powder, and salt. Make a well in the dough and add in the Greek yogurt. Mix with a spoon until a dough forms.
2. Place the dough onto a heavily floured surface and knead for 3 minutes. You may use up to 1 cup of additional flour as you knead the dough, if necessary.

3. Cut the dough into 8 pieces and roll each piece into a 6-inch, snakelike piece. Touch the ends of each piece together so it closes the circle and forms a bagel shape. Brush the tops of the bagels with the whisked egg.
4. In a small bowl, combine the sesame seeds, dehydrated onions, poppy seeds, garlic powder, and sea salt flakes. Sprinkle the seasoning on top of the bagels.
5. Preheat the air fryer to 360°F. Using a bench scraper or flat-edged spatula, carefully place the bagels into the air fryer basket. Spray the bagel tops with cooking spray. Air-fry the bagels for 6 minutes or until golden brown. Allow the bread to cool at least 10 minutes before slicing for serving.

Pumpkin Empanadas

Servings: 4
Cooking Time: 30 Minutes
Ingredients:
- 1 can pumpkin purée
- ¼ cup white sugar
- 2 tsp cinnamon
- 1 tbsp brown sugar
- ½ tbsp cornstarch
- ¼ tsp vanilla extract
- 2 tbsp butter
- 4 empanada dough shells

Directions:
1. Place the puree in a pot and top with white and brown sugar, cinnamon, cornstarch, vanilla extract, 1 tbsp of water and butter and stir thoroughly. Bring to a boil over medium heat. Simmer for 4-5 minutes. Allow to cool.
2. Preheat air fryer to 360°F. Lay empanada shells flat on a clean counter. Spoon the pumpkin mixture into each of the shells. Fold the empanada shells over to cover completely. Seal the edges with water and press down with a fork to secure. Place the empanadas on the greased frying basket and Bake for 15 minutes, flipping once halfway through until golden. Serve hot.

Chicken Scotch Eggs

Servings: 4
Cooking Time: 25 Minutes
Ingredients:
- 1 lb ground chicken
- 2 tsp Dijon mustard
- 2 tsp grated yellow onion
- 1 tbsp chopped chives
- 1 tbsp chopped parsley
- ⅛ tsp ground nutmeg
- 1 lemon, zested
- Salt and pepper to taste
- 4 hard-boiled eggs, peeled
- 1 egg, beaten
- 1 cup bread crumbs
- 2 tsp olive oil

Directions:
1. Preheat air fryer to 350°F. In a bowl, mix the ground chicken, mustard, onion, chives, parsley, nutmeg, salt, lemon zest and pepper. Shape into 4 oval balls and form the balls evenly around the boiled eggs. Submerge them in the beaten egg and dip in the crumbs. Brush with olive oil. Place the scotch eggs in the frying basket and Air Fry for 14 minutes, flipping once. Serve hot.

Chocolate Chip Banana Muffins

Servings: 12
Cooking Time: 14 Minutes
Ingredients:
- 2 medium bananas, mashed
- ¼ cup brown sugar
- 1½ teaspoons vanilla extract
- ⅔ cup milk
- 2 tablespoons butter
- 1 large egg
- 1 cup white whole-wheat flour
- ½ cup old-fashioned oats
- 1 teaspoon baking soda
- ⅓ teaspoon baking powder
- ⅛ teaspoon sea salt
- ¼ cup mini chocolate chips

Directions:
1. Preheat the air fryer to 330°F.
2. In a large bowl, combine the bananas, brown sugar, vanilla extract, milk, butter, and egg; set aside.
3. In a separate bowl, combine the flour, oats, baking soda, baking powder, and salt.
4. Slowly add the dry ingredients into the wet ingredients, folding in the flour mixture ⅓ cup at a time.
5. Mix in the chocolate chips and set aside.
6. Using silicone muffin liners, fill 6 muffin liners two-thirds full. Carefully place the muffin liners in the air fryer basket and bake for 20 minutes (or until the tops are browned and a toothpick inserted in the center comes out clean). Carefully remove the muffins from the basket and repeat with the remaining batter.
7. Serve warm.

Cinnamon Banana Bread With Pecans

Servings: 6
Cooking Time: 35 Minutes
Ingredients:
- 2 ripe bananas, mashed
- 1 egg
- ¼ cup Greek yogurt
- ¼ cup olive oil
- ½ tsp peppermint extract
- 2 tbsp honey
- 1 cup flour
- ¼ tsp salt
- ¼ tsp baking soda
- ½ tsp ground cinnamon
- ¼ cup chopped pecans

Directions:
1. Preheat air fryer to 360°F. Add the bananas, egg, yogurt, olive oil, peppermint, and honey in a large bowl and mix until combined and mostly smooth.
2. Sift the flour, salt, baking soda, and cinnamon into the wet mixture, then stir until just combined. Gently fold in the pecans. Spread to distribute evenly into a greased loaf pan. Place the loaf pan in the frying basket and Bake for 23 minutes or until golden brown on top and a toothpick inserted into the center comes out clean. Allow to cool for 5 minutes. Serve.

Vegetable Side Dishes Recipes

Speedy Baked Caprese With Avocado

Servings:4
Cooking Time:15 Minutes
Ingredients:
- 4 oz fresh mozzarella
- 8 cherry tomatoes
- 2 tsp olive oil
- 2 halved avocados,pitted
- ¼tsp salt
- 2 tbsp basil,torn

Directions:
1. Preheat air fryer to 375ºF.In a bowl,combine tomatoes and olive oil.Set aside.Add avocado halves,cut sides up,in the frying basket,scatter tomatoes around halves,and Bake for 7 minutes.Divide avocado halves between 4 small plates,top each with 2 tomatoes and sprinkle with salt.Cut mozzarella cheese and evenly distribute over tomatoes.Scatter with the basil to serve.

Stunning Apples&Onions

Servings:4
Cooking Time:30 Minutes
Ingredients:
- 2 peeled McIntosh apples,sliced
- 1 shallot,sliced
- 2 tsp canola oil
- 2 tbsp brown sugar
- 1 tbsp honey
- 1 tbsp butter,melted
- ½tsp sea salt

Directions:
1. Preheat the air fryer to 325°F.Toss the shallot slices with oil in a bowl until coated.Put the bowl in the fryer and Bake for 5 minutes.Remove the bowl and add the apples,brown sugar,honey,melted butter,and sea salt and stir.Put the bowl back into the fryer and Bake for 10-12 more minutes or until the onions and apples are tender.Stir again and serve.

Perfect French Fries

Servings:3
Cooking Time:37 Minutes
Ingredients:
- 1 pound Large russet potato(es)
- Vegetable oil or olive oil spray
- ½teaspoon Table salt

Directions:
1. Cut each potato lengthwise into¼-inch-thick slices.Cut each of these lengthwise into¼-inch-thick matchsticks.
2. Set the potato matchsticks in a big bowl of cool water and soak for 5 minutes.Drain in a colander set in the sink,then spread the matchsticks out on paper towels and dry them very well.
3. Preheat the air fryer to 225°F(or 230°F,if that's the closest setting).
4. When the machine is at temperature,arrange the matchsticks in an even layer(if overlapping but not compact)in the basket.Air-fry for 20 minutes,tossing and rearranging the fries twice.
5. Pour the contents of the basket into a big bowl.Increase the air fryer's temperature to 325°F(or 330°F,if that's the closest setting).
6. Generously coat the fries with vegetable or olive oil spray.Toss well,then coat them again to make sure they're covered on all sides,tossing(and maybe spraying)a couple of times to make sure.
7. When the machine is at temperature,pour the fries into the basket and air-fry for 12 minutes,tossing and rearranging the fries at least twice.
8. Increase the machine's temperature to 375°F(or 380°F or 390°F,if one of these is the closest setting).Air-fry for 5 minutes more(from the moment you raise the temperature),tossing and rearranging the fries at least twice to keep them from burning and to make sure they all get an even measure of the heat,until brown and crisp.
9. Pour the contents of the basket into a serving bowl.Toss the fries with the salt and serve hot.

Sriracha Green Beans

Servings:4
Cooking Time:30 Minutes
Ingredients:
- ½tbsp toasted sesame seeds
- 1 tbsp tamari
- ½tbsp Sriracha sauce
- 4 tsp canola oil
- 12 oz trimmed green beans
- 1 tbsp cilantro,chopped

Directions:
1. Mix the tamari,sriracha,and 1 tsp of canola oil in a small bowl.In a large bowl,toss green beans with the remaining oil.Preheat air fryer to 375°F.Place the green beans in the frying basket and Air Fry for 8 minutes,shaking the basket once until the beans are charred and tender.Toss the beans with sauce,cilantro,and sesame seeds.Serve.

Roasted Broccoli And Red Bean Salad

Servings:3
Cooking Time:14 Minutes
Ingredients:
- 3 cups(about 1 pound)1-to 1½-inch fresh broccoli florets(not frozen)
- 1½tablespoons Olive oil spray
- 1¼cups Canned red kidney beans,drained and rinsed
- 3 tablespoons Minced yellow or white onion
- 2 tablespoons plus 1 teaspoon Red wine vinegar
- ¾teaspoon Dried oregano
- ¼teaspoon Table salt
- ¼teaspoon Ground black pepper

Directions:
1. Preheat the air fryer to 375°F.
2. Put the broccoli florets in a big bowl,coat them generously with olive oil spray,then toss to coat all surfaces,even down into the crannies,spraying them a couple of times more.
3. Pour the florets into the basket,spreading them into as close to one layer as you can.Air-fry for 12 minutes,tossing and rearranging the florets twice so that any touching or covered parts are eventually exposed to the air currents,until light browned but still a bit firm.(If the machine is at 360°F,you may need to add 2 minutes to the cooking time.)
4. Dump the contents of the basket onto a large cutting board.Cool for a minute or two,then chop the florets into small bits.Scrape these into a bowl and add the kidney beans,onion,vinegar,oregano,salt,and pepper.Toss well and serve warm or at room temperature.

Tuna Platter

Servings: 4
Cooking Time: 9 Minutes
Ingredients:
- 4 new potatoes, boiled in their jackets
- ½ cup vinaigrette dressing, plus 2 tablespoons
- ½ pound fresh green beans, cut in half-inch pieces and steamed
- 1 tablespoon Herbes de Provence
- 1 tablespoon minced shallots
- 1½ tablespoons tarragon vinegar
- 4 tuna steaks, each ¾-inch thick, about 1 pound
- salt and pepper
- Salad
- 8 cups chopped romaine lettuce
- 12 grape tomatoes, halved lengthwise
- ½ cup pitted olives (black, green, nicoise, or combination)
- 2 boiled eggs, peeled and halved lengthwise

Directions:
1. Quarter potatoes and toss with 1 tablespoon salad dressing.
2. Toss the warm beans with the other tablespoon of salad dressing. Set both aside while you prepare the tuna.
3. Mix together the herbs, shallots, and vinegar and rub into all sides of tuna. Season fish to taste with salt and pepper.
4. Cook tuna at 390°F for 7 minutes and check. If needed, cook 2 minutes longer, until tuna is barely pink in the center.
5. Spread the lettuce over a large platter.
6. Slice the tuna steaks in ½-inch pieces and arrange them in the center of the lettuce.
7. Place the remaining ingredients around the tuna. Diners create their own plates by selecting what they want from the platter. Pass remainder of salad dressing at the table.

Hasselback Garlic-and-butter Potatoes

Servings: 3
Cooking Time: 48 Minutes
Ingredients:
- 3 8-ounce russet potatoes
- 6 Brown button or Baby Bella mushrooms, very thinly sliced
- Olive oil spray
- 3 tablespoons Butter, melted and cooled
- 1 tablespoon Minced garlic
- ¾ teaspoon Table salt
- 3 tablespoons (about ½ ounce) Finely grated Parmesan cheese

Directions:
1. Preheat the air fryer to 350°F.
2. Cut slits down the length of each potato, about three-quarters down into the potato and spaced about ¼ inch apart. Wedge a thin mushroom slice in each slit. Generously coat the potatoes on all sides with olive oil spray.
3. When the machine is at temperature, set the potatoes mushroom side up in the basket with as much air space between them as possible. Air-fry undisturbed for 45 minutes, or tender when pricked with a fork.
4. Increase the machine's temperature to 400°F. Use kitchen tongs, and perhaps a flatware fork for balance, to gently transfer the potatoes to a cutting board. Brush each evenly with butter, then sprinkle the minced garlic and salt over them. Sprinkle the cheese evenly over the potatoes.
5. Use those same tongs to gently transfer the potatoes cheese side up to the basket in one layer with some space for air flow between them. Air-fry undisturbed for 3 minutes, or until the cheese has melted and begun to brown.
6. Use those same tongs to gently transfer the potatoes back to the wire rack. Cool for 5 minutes before serving.

Cheesy Breaded Eggplants

Servings: 2
Cooking Time: 35 Minutes
Ingredients:
- 4 eggplant slices
- 1 cup breadcrumbs
- ½ tsp garlic powder
- 2 eggs, beaten
- Salt and pepper to taste
- 1 tbsp dried oregano
- 1 cup marinara sauce
- 2 provolone cheese slices
- 1 tbsp Parmesan cheese
- 6 basil leaves

Directions:
1. Preheat air fryer to 350°F. Mix the breadcrumbs, oregano, garlic powder, salt, and pepper in a bowl. Dip the eggplant slices into the beaten eggs, then coat in the dry ingredients. Arrange the coated eggplant slices on the greased frying basket. Air Fry for 14-16 minutes, turning once. Spread half of the marinara sauce onto a baking pan. Lay the cooked eggplant on top of the sauce. Pour the remaining marinara sauce over the eggplant and top with the provolone cheese slices and grated Parmesan cheese. Bake in the air fryer for 5 minutes or until the cheese is melted. Serve topped with basil leaves.

Crispy Herbed Potatoes

Servings: 6
Cooking Time: 20 Minutes
Ingredients:
- 3 medium baking potatoes, washed and cubed
- ½ teaspoon dried thyme
- 1 teaspoon minced dried rosemary
- ½ teaspoon garlic powder
- 1 teaspoon sea salt
- ½ teaspoon black pepper
- 2 tablespoons extra-virgin olive oil
- ¼ cup chopped parsley

Directions:
1. Preheat the air fryer to 390°F.
2. Pat the potatoes dry. In a large bowl, mix together the cubed potatoes, thyme, rosemary, garlic powder, sea salt, and pepper. Drizzle and toss with olive oil.
3. Pour the herbed potatoes into the air fryer basket. Cook for 20 minutes, stirring every 5 minutes.
4. Toss the cooked potatoes with chopped parsley and serve immediately.
5. VARY IT! Potatoes are versatile—add any spice or seasoning mixture you prefer and create your own favorite side dish.

Almond-crusted Zucchini Fries

Servings: 2
Cooking Time: 30 Minutes
Ingredients:
- ½ cup grated Pecorino cheese
- 1 zucchini, cut into fries
- 1 tsp salt
- 1 egg
- 1 tbsp almond milk
- ½ cup almond flour

Directions:
1. Preheat air fryer to 370ºF. Distribute zucchini fries evenly over a paper towel, sprinkle with salt, and let sit for 10 minutes to pull out moisture. Pat them dry with paper towels. In a bowl, beat egg and almond milk. In another bowl, combine almond flour and Pecorino cheese. Dip fries in egg mixture and then dredge them in flour mixture. Place zucchini fries in the lightly greased frying basket and Air Fry for 10 minutes, flipping once. Serve.

Parsnip Fries With Romesco Sauce

Servings: 2
Cooking Time: 24 Minutes
Ingredients:
- Romesco Sauce:
- 1 red bell pepper, halved and seeded
- 1 (1-inch) thick slice of Italian bread, torn into pieces (about 1 to 1½ cups)
- 1 cup almonds, toasted
- olive oil
- ½ Jalapeño pepper, seeded
- 1 tablespoon fresh parsley leaves
- 1 clove garlic
- 2 Roma tomatoes, peeled and seeded (or ⅓ cup canned crushed tomatoes)
- 1 tablespoon red wine vinegar
- ¼ teaspoon smoked paprika
- ½ teaspoon salt
- ¾ cup olive oil
- 3 parsnips, peeled and cut into long strips
- 2 teaspoons olive oil
- salt and freshly ground black pepper

Directions:
1. Preheat the air fryer to 400°F.
2. Place the red pepper halves, cut side down, in the air fryer basket and air-fry for 10 minutes, or until the skin turns black all over. Remove the pepper from the air fryer and let it cool. When it is cool enough to handle, peel the pepper.
3. Toss the torn bread and almonds with a little olive oil and air-fry for 4 minutes, shaking the basket a couple times throughout the cooking time. When the bread and almonds are nicely toasted, remove them from the air fryer and let them cool for just a minute or two.
4. Combine the toasted bread, almonds, roasted red pepper, Jalapeño pepper, parsley, garlic, tomatoes, vinegar, smoked paprika and salt in a food processor or blender. Process until smooth. With the processor running, add the olive oil through the feed tube until the sauce comes together in a smooth paste that is barely pourable.
5. Toss the parsnip strips with the olive oil, salt and freshly ground black pepper and air-fry at 400°F for 10 minutes, shaking the basket a couple times during the cooking process so they brown and cook evenly. Serve the parsnip fries warm with the Romesco sauce to dip into.

Dilly Sesame Roasted Asparagus

Servings: 6
Cooking Time: 15 Minutes
Ingredients:
- 1 lb asparagus, trimmed
- 1 tbsp butter, melted
- ¼ tsp salt
- 1 clove garlic, minced
- 2 tsp chopped dill
- 3 tbsp sesame seeds

Directions:
1. Preheat air fryer to 370ºF. Combine asparagus and butter in a bowl. Place asparagus mixture in the frying basket and Roast for 9 minutes, tossing once. Transfer it to a serving dish and stir in salt, garlic, sesame seeds and dill until coated. Serve immediately.

French Fries

Servings: 4
Cooking Time: 25 Minutes
Ingredients:
- 2 cups fresh potatoes
- 2 teaspoons oil
- ½ teaspoon salt

Directions:
1. Cut potatoes into ½-inch-wide slices, then lay slices flat and cut into ½-inch sticks.
2. Rinse potato sticks and blot dry with a clean towel.
3. In a bowl or sealable plastic bag, mix the potatoes, oil, and salt together.
4. Pour into air fryer basket.
5. Cook at 390°F for 10 minutes. Shake basket to redistribute fries and continue cooking for approximately 15 minutes, until fries are golden brown.

Roasted Ratatouille Vegetables

Cooking Time: 15 Minutes
Servings: 2
Ingredients:
- 1 baby or Japanese eggplant, cut into 1½-inch cubes
- 1 red pepper, cut into 1-inch chunks
- 1 yellow pepper, cut into 1-inch chunks
- 1 zucchini, cut into 1-inch chunks
- 1 clove garlic, minced
- ½ teaspoon dried basil
- 1 tablespoon olive oil
- salt and freshly ground black pepper
- ¼ cup sliced sun-dried tomatoes in oil
- 2 tablespoons chopped fresh basil

Directions:
1. Preheat the air fryer to 400°F.
2. Toss the eggplant, peppers and zucchini with the garlic, dried basil, olive oil, salt and freshly ground black pepper.
3. Air-fry the vegetables at 400°F for 15 minutes, shaking the basket a few times during the cooking process to redistribute the ingredients.
4. As soon as the vegetables are tender, toss them with the sliced sun-dried tomatoes and fresh basil and serve.

Tomato Candy

Servings: 12
Cooking Time: 120 Minutes
Ingredients:
- 6 Small Roma or plum tomatoes, halved lengthwise
- 1½ teaspoons Coarse sea salt or kosher salt

Directions:
1. Before you turn the machine on, set the tomatoes cut side up in a single layer in the basket (or the basket attachment). They can touch each other, but try to leave at least a fraction of an inch between them (depending, of course, on the size of the basket or basket attachment). Sprinkle the cut sides of the tomatoes with the salt.
2. Set the machine to cook at 225°F (or 230°F, if that's the closest setting). Put the basket in the machine and air-fry for 2

hours,or until the tomatoes are dry but pliable,with a little moisture down in their centers.
3. Remove the basket from the machine and cool the tomatoes in it for 10 minutes before gently transferring them to a plate for serving,or to a shallow dish that you can cover and store in the refrigerator for up to 1 week.

Fried Pearl Onions With Balsamic Vinegar And Basil

Servings:2
Cooking Time:10 Minutes
Ingredients:
- 1 pound fresh pearl onions
- 1 tablespoon olive oil
- salt and freshly ground black pepper
- 1 teaspoon high quality aged balsamic vinegar
- 1 tablespoon chopped fresh basil leaves(or mint)

Directions:
1. Preheat the air fryer to 400°F.
2. Decide whether you want to peel the onions before or after they cook.Peeling them ahead of time is a little more laborious.Peeling after they cook is easier,but a little messier since the onions are hot and you may discard more of the onion than you'd like to.If you opt to peel them first,trim the tiny root of the onions off and pinch off any loose papery skins.(It's ok if there are some skins left on the onions.)Toss the pearl onions with the olive oil,salt and freshly ground black pepper.
3. Air-fry for 10 minutes,shaking the basket a couple of times during the cooking process.(If your pearl onions are very large,you may need to add a couple of minutes to this cooking time.)
4. Let the onions cool slightly and then slip off any remaining skins.
5. Toss the onions with the balsamic vinegar and basil and serve.

Honey-roasted Parsnips

Servings:3
Cooking Time:23 Minutes
Ingredients:
- 1½pounds Medium parsnips,peeled
- Olive oil spray
- 1 tablespoon Honey
- 1½teaspoons Water
- ¼teaspoon Table salt

Directions:
1. Preheat the air fryer to 350°F.
2. If the thick end of a parsnip is more than½inch in diameter,cut the parsnip just below where it swells to its large end,then slice the large section in half lengthwise.If the parsnips are larger than the basket(or basket attachment),trim off the thin end so the parsnips will fit.Generously coat the parsnips on all sides with olive oil spray.
3. When the machine is at temperature,set the parsnips in the basket with as much air space between them as possible.Air-fry undisturbed for 20 minutes.
4. Whisk the honey,water,and salt in a small bowl until smooth.Brush this mixture over the parsnips.Air-fry undisturbed for 3 minutes more,or until the glaze is lightly browned.
5. Use kitchen tongs to transfer the parsnips to a wire rack or a serving platter.Cool for a couple of minutes before serving.

Yellow Squash

Servings:4
Cooking Time:10 Minutes
Ingredients:
- 1 large yellow squash(about 1½cups)
- 2 eggs
- ¼cup buttermilk
- 1 cup panko breadcrumbs
- ¼cup white cornmeal
- ½teaspoon salt
- oil for misting or cooking spray

Directions:
1. Preheat air fryer to 390°F.
2. Cut the squash into¼-inch slices.
3. In a shallow dish,beat together eggs and buttermilk.
4. In sealable plastic bag or container with lid,combine¼cup panko crumbs,white cornmeal,and salt.Shake to mix well.
5. Place the remaining¾cup panko crumbs in a separate shallow dish.
6. Dump all the squash slices into the egg/buttermilk mixture.Stir to coat.
7. Remove squash from buttermilk mixture with a slotted spoon,letting excess drip off,and transfer to the panko/cornmeal mixture.Close bag or container and shake well to coat.
8. Remove squash from crumb mixture,letting excess fall off.Return squash to egg/buttermilk mixture,stirring gently to coat.If you need more liquid to coat all the squash,add a little more buttermilk.
9. Remove each squash slice from egg wash and dip in a dish of¾cup panko crumbs.
10. Mist squash slices with oil or cooking spray and place in air fryer basket.Squash should be in a single layer,but it's okay if the slices crowd together and overlap a little.
11. Cook at 390°F for 5minutes.Shake basket to break up any that have stuck together.Mist again with oil or spray.
12. Cook 5minutes longer and check.If necessary,mist again with oil and cook an additional two minutes,until squash slices are golden brown and crisp.

Sage&Thyme Potatoes

Servings:4
Cooking Time:30 Minutes
Ingredients:
- 2 red potatoes,peeled and cubed
- ¼cup olive oil
- 1 tsp dried sage
- ½tsp dried thyme
- ½tsp salt
- 2 tbsp grated Parmesan

Directions:
1. Preheat air fryer to 360°F.Coat the red potatoes with olive oil,sage,thyme and salt in a bowl.Pour the potatoes into the air frying basket and Roast for 10 minutes.Stir the potatoes and sprinkle the Parmesan over the top.Continue roasting for 8 more minutes.Serve hot.

Dijon Artichoke Hearts

Servings:4
Cooking Time:25 Minutes
Ingredients:
- 1 jar artichoke hearts in water,drained
- 1 egg
- 1 tbsp Dijon mustard
- ½cup bread crumbs
- ¼cup flour
- 6 basil leaves

Directions:
1. Preheat air fryer to 350ºF.Beat egg and mustard in a bowl.In another bowl,combine bread crumbs and flour.Dip artichoke hearts in egg mixture,then dredge in crumb mixture.Place artichoke hearts in the greased frying basket and Air Fry for 7-10 minutes until crispy.Serve topped with basil.Enjoy!

Honey-mustard Asparagus Puffs

Servings: 4
Cooking Time: 35 Minutes
Ingredients:
- 8 asparagus spears
- ½ sheet puff pastry
- 2 tbsp honey mustard
- 1 egg, lightly beaten

Directions:
1. Preheat the air fryer to 375°F. Spread the pastry with honey mustard and cut it into 8 strips. Wrap the pastry, honey mustard–side in, around the asparagus. Put a rack in the frying basket and lay the asparagus spears on the rack. Brush all over pastries with beaten egg and Air Fry for 12-17 minutes or until the pastry is golden. Serve.

Roasted Fennel Salad

Servings: 3
Cooking Time: 20 Minutes
Ingredients:
- 3 cups (about ¾ pound) Trimmed fennel (see the headnote), roughly chopped
- 1½ tablespoons Olive oil
- ¼ teaspoon Table salt
- ¼ teaspoon Ground black pepper
- 1½ tablespoons White balsamic vinegar (see here)

Directions:
1. Preheat the air fryer to 400°F.
2. Toss the fennel, olive oil, salt, and pepper in a large bowl until the fennel is well coated in the oil.
3. When the machine is at temperature, pour the fennel into the basket, spreading it out into as close to one layer as possible. Air-fry for 20 minutes, tossing and rearranging the fennel pieces twice so that any covered or touching parts get exposed to the air currents, until golden at the edges and softened.
4. Pour the fennel into a serving bowl. Add the vinegar while hot. Toss well, then cool a couple of minutes before serving. Or serve at room temperature.

Buttery Stuffed Tomatoes

Servings: 6
Cooking Time: 15 Minutes
Ingredients:
- 3 8-ounce round tomatoes
- ½ cup plus 1 tablespoon Plain panko bread crumbs (gluten-free, if a concern)
- 3 tablespoons (about ½ ounce) Finely grated Parmesan cheese
- 3 tablespoons Butter, melted and cooled
- 4 teaspoons Stemmed and chopped fresh parsley leaves
- 1 teaspoon Minced garlic
- ¼ teaspoon Table salt
- Up to ¼ teaspoon Red pepper flakes
- Olive oil spray

Directions:
1. Preheat the air fryer to 375°F.
2. Cut the tomatoes in half through their "equators" (that is, not through the stem ends). One at a time, gently squeeze the tomato halves over a trash can, using a clean finger to gently force out the seeds and most of the juice inside, working carefully so that the tomato doesn't lose its round shape or get crushed.
3. Stir the bread crumbs, cheese, butter, parsley, garlic, salt, and red pepper flakes in a bowl until the bread crumbs are moistened and the parsley is uniform throughout the mixture. Pile this mixture into the spaces left in the tomato halves. Press gently to compact the filling. Coat the tops of the tomatoes with olive oil spray.
4. Place the tomatoes cut side up in the basket. They may touch each other. Air-fry for 15 minutes, or until the filling is lightly browned and crunchy.
5. Use nonstick-safe spatula and kitchen tongs for balance to gently transfer the stuffed tomatoes to a platter or a cutting board. Cool for a couple of minutes before serving.

Hawaiian Brown Rice

Servings: 4
Cooking Time: 12 Minutes
Ingredients:
- ¼ pound ground sausage
- 1 teaspoon butter
- ¼ cup minced onion
- ¼ cup minced bell pepper
- 2 cups cooked brown rice
- 1 8-ounce can crushed pineapple, drained

Directions:
1. Shape sausage into 3 or 4 thin patties. Cook at 390°F for 6 to 8 minutes or until well done. Remove from air fryer, drain, and crumble. Set aside.
2. Place butter, onion, and bell pepper in baking pan. Cook at 390°F for 1 minute and stir. Cook 4 minutes longer or just until vegetables are tender.
3. Add sausage, rice, and pineapple to vegetables and stir together.
4. Cook at 390°F for 2 minutes, until heated through.

Honey-mustard Roasted Cabbage

Servings: 4
Cooking Time: 35 Minutes
Ingredients:
- 4 cups chopped green cabbage
- 1/3 cup honey mustard dressing
- 1 shallot, chopped
- 2 garlic cloves, minced
- 2 tbsp olive oil
- 1 tbsp lemon juice
- 1 tbsp cornstarch
- ½ tsp fennel seeds

Directions:
1. Preheat the air fryer to 370°F. Toss the cabbage, shallot, olive oil and garlic in a cake pan. Bake for 10 minutes or until the cabbage is wilted, then drain the excess liquid. While the cabbage is cooking, combine the salad dressing, lemon juice, cornstarch, and fennel seeds in a bowl. Take cake pan out of the fryer and pour out any excess liquid. Pour the dressing mix over the drained cabbage and mix well. Return the pan to the fryer and Bake for 7-11 minutes more, stirring twice during cooking until the cabbage is tender and the sauce has thickened. Serve warm.

Cauliflower

Servings: 4
Cooking Time: 6 Minutes
Ingredients:
- ½ cup water
- 1 10-ounce package frozen cauliflower (florets)
- 1 teaspoon lemon pepper seasoning

Directions:
1. Pour the water into air fryer drawer.
2. Pour the frozen cauliflower into the air fryer basket and sprinkle with lemon pepper seasoning.
3. Cook at 390°F for approximately 6 minutes.

Ninja Foodi 2-Basket Air Fryer

Bacon-wrapped Asparagus

Servings: 4
Cooking Time: 10 Minutes
Ingredients:
- 1 tablespoon extra-virgin olive oil
- ½ teaspoon sea salt
- ¼ cup grated Parmesan cheese
- 1 pound asparagus, ends trimmed
- 8 slices bacon

Directions:
1. Preheat the air fryer to 380°F.
2. In large bowl, mix together the olive oil, sea salt, and Parmesan cheese. Toss the asparagus in the olive oil mixture.
3. Evenly divide the asparagus into 8 bundles. Wrap 1 piece of bacon around each bundle, not overlapping the bacon but spreading it across the bundle.
4. Place the asparagus bundles into the air fryer basket, not touching. Work in batches as needed.
5. Cook for 8 minutes; check for doneness, and cook another 2 minutes.

Herbed Baby Red Potato Hasselback

Servings: 4
Cooking Time: 35 Minutes
Ingredients:
- 6 baby red potatoes, scrubbed
- 3 tsp shredded cheddar cheese
- 1 tbsp olive oil
- 2 tbsp butter, melted
- 1 tbsp chopped thyme
- Salt and pepper to taste
- 3 tsp sour cream
- ¼ cup chopped parsley

Directions:
1. Preheat air fryer at 350°F. Make slices in the width of each potato about ¼-inch apart without cutting through. Rub potato slices with olive oil, both outside and in between slices. Place potatoes in the frying basket and Air Fry for 20 minutes, tossing once, brush with melted butter, and scatter with thyme. Remove them to a large serving dish. Sprinkle with salt, black pepper and top with a dollop of cheddar cheese, sour cream. Scatter with parsley to serve.

Roasted Brussels Sprouts With Bacon

Cooking Time: 20 Minutes
Servings: 4
Ingredients:
- 4 slices thick-cut bacon, chopped (about ¼ pound)
- 1 pound Brussels sprouts, halved (or quartered if large)
- freshly ground black pepper

Directions:
1. Preheat the air fryer to 380°F.
2. Air-fry the bacon for 5 minutes, shaking the basket once or twice during the cooking time.
3. Add the Brussels sprouts to the basket and drizzle a little bacon fat from the bottom of the air fryer drawer into the basket. Toss the sprouts to coat with the bacon fat. Air-fry for an additional 15 minutes, or until the Brussels sprouts are tender to a knifepoint.
4. Season with freshly ground black pepper.

Panko-crusted Zucchini Fries

Servings: 6
Cooking Time: 8 Minutes
Ingredients:
- 3 medium zucchinis
- ½ cup flour
- 1 teaspoon salt, divided
- ½ teaspoon black pepper, divided
- ¾ teaspoon dried thyme, divided
- 2 large eggs
- 1½ cups whole-wheat or plain panko breadcrumbs
- ½ cup grated Parmesan cheese

Directions:
1. Preheat the air fryer to 380°F.
2. Slice the zucchinis in half lengthwise, then into long strips about ½-inch thick, like thick fries.
3. In a medium bowl, mix the flour, ½ teaspoon of the salt, ¼ teaspoon of the black pepper, and ½ teaspoon of thyme.
4. In a separate bowl, whisk together the eggs, ½ teaspoon of the salt, and ¼ teaspoon of the black pepper.
5. In a third bowl, combine the breadcrumbs, cheese, and the remaining ¼ teaspoon of dried thyme.
6. Working with one zucchini fry at a time, dip the zucchini fry first into the flour mixture, then into the whisked eggs, and finally into the breading. Repeat until all the fries are breaded.
7. Place the zucchini fries into the air fryer basket, spray with cooking spray, and cook for 4 minutes; shake the basket and cook another 4 to 6 minutes or until golden brown and crispy.
8. Remove and serve warm.

Sea Salt Radishes

Servings: 4
Cooking Time: 25 Minutes
Ingredients:
- 1 lb radishes
- 2 tbsp olive oil
- ½ tsp sea salt
- ½ tsp garlic powder

Directions:
1. Preheat air fryer to 360°F. Toss the radishes with olive oil, garlic powder, and salt in a bowl. Pour them into the air fryer. Air Fry for 18 minutes, turning once. Serve.

Green Dip With Pine Nuts

Servings: 3
Cooking Time: 30 Minutes
Ingredients:
- 10 oz canned artichokes, chopped
- 2 tsp grated Parmesan cheese
- 10 oz spinach, chopped
- 2 scallions, finely chopped
- ½ cup pine nuts
- ½ cup milk
- 3 tbsp lemon juice
- 2 tsp tapioca flour
- 1 tsp allspice

Directions:
1. Preheat air fryer to 360°F. Arrange spinach, artichokes, and scallions in a pan. Set aside. In a food processor, blitz the pine nuts, milk, lemon juice, Parmesan cheese, flour, and allspice on high until smooth. Pour it over the veggies and Bake for 20 minutes, stirring every 5 minutes. Serve.

Almond Green Beans

Servings: 4
Cooking Time: 20 Minutes
Ingredients:
- 2 cups green beans, trimmed
- ¼ cup slivered almonds

- 2 tbsp butter, melted
- Salt and pepper to taste
- 2 tsp lemon juice
- Lemon zest and slices

Directions:
1. Preheat air fryer at 375°F. Add almonds to the frying basket and Air Fry for 2 minutes, tossing once. Set aside in a small bowl. Combine the remaining ingredients, except 1 tbsp of butter, in a bowl.
2. Place green beans in the frying basket and Air Fry for 10 minutes, tossing once. Then, transfer them to a large serving dish. Scatter with the melted butter, lemon juice and roasted almonds and toss. Serve immediately garnished with lemon zest and lemon slices.

Steak Fries

Cooking Time: 20 Minutes
Servings: 4

Ingredients:
- 2 russet potatoes, scrubbed and cut into wedges lengthwise
- 1 tablespoon olive oil
- 2 teaspoons seasoning salt (recipe below)

Directions:
1. Preheat the air fryer to 400°F.
2. Toss the potatoes with the olive oil and the seasoning salt.
3. Air-fry for 20 minutes (depending on the size of the wedges), turning the potatoes over gently a few times throughout the cooking process to brown and cook them evenly.

Crispy Brussels Sprouts

Servings: 3
Cooking Time: 12 Minutes

Ingredients:
- 1¼ pounds Medium, 2-inch-in-length Brussels sprouts
- 1½ tablespoons Olive oil
- ¾ teaspoon Table salt

Directions:
1. Preheat the air fryer to 400°F.
2. Halve each Brussels sprout through the stem end, pulling off and discarding any discolored outer leaves. Put the sprout halves in a large bowl, add the oil and salt, and stir well to coat evenly, until the Brussels sprouts are glistening.
3. When the machine is at temperature, scrape the contents of the bowl into the basket, gently spreading the Brussels sprout halves into as close to one layer as possible. Air-fry for 12 minutes, gently tossing and rearranging the vegetables twice to get all covered or touching parts exposed to the air currents, until crisp and browned at the edges.
4. Gently pour the contents of the basket onto a wire rack. Cool for a minute or two before serving.

Asparagus

Servings: 4
Cooking Time: 9 Minutes

Ingredients:
- 1 bunch asparagus (approx. 1 pound), washed and trimmed
- ⅛ teaspoon dried tarragon, crushed
- salt and pepper
- 1 to 2 teaspoons extra-light olive oil

Directions:
1. Spread asparagus spears on cookie sheet or cutting board.
2. Sprinkle with tarragon, salt, and pepper.
3. Drizzle with 1 teaspoon of oil and roll the spears or mix by hand. If needed, add up to 1 more teaspoon of oil and mix again until all spears are lightly coated.
4. Place spears in air fryer basket. If necessary, bend the longer spears to make them fit. It doesn't matter if they don't lie flat.
5. Cook at 390°F for 5 minutes. Shake basket or stir spears with a spoon.
6. Cook for an additional 4 minutes or just until crisp-tender.

Grits Casserole

Servings: 4
Cooking Time: 30 Minutes

Ingredients:
- 10 fresh asparagus spears, cut into 1-inch pieces
- 2 cups cooked grits, cooled to room temperature
- 1 egg, beaten
- 2 teaspoons Worcestershire sauce
- ½ teaspoon garlic powder
- ¼ teaspoon salt
- 2 slices provolone cheese (about 1½ ounces)
- oil for misting or cooking spray

Directions:
1. Mist asparagus spears with oil and cook at 390°F for 5 minutes, until crisp-tender.
2. In a medium bowl, mix together the grits, egg, Worcestershire, garlic powder, and salt.
3. Spoon half of grits mixture into air fryer baking pan and top with asparagus.
4. Tear cheese slices into pieces and layer evenly on top of asparagus.
5. Top with remaining grits.
6. Bake at 360°F for 25 minutes. The casserole will rise a little as it cooks. When done, the top will have browned lightly with just a hint of crispiness.

Roasted Thyme Asparagus

Servings: 4
Cooking Time: 20 Minutes

Ingredients:
- 1 lb asparagus, trimmed
- 2 tsp olive oil
- 3 garlic cloves, minced
- 2 tbsp balsamic vinegar
- ½ tsp dried thyme
- ½ red chili, finely sliced

Directions:
1. Preheat air fryer to 380°F. Put the asparagus and olive oil in a bowl and stir to coat, then put them in the frying basket. Toss some garlic over the asparagus and Roast for 4-8 minutes until crisp-tender. Spritz with balsamic vinegar and toss in some thyme leaves. Top with red chili slices and serve.

Succulent Roasted Peppers

Servings: 2
Cooking Time: 35 Minutes

Ingredients:
- 2 red bell peppers
- 2 tbsp olive oil
- Salt to taste
- 1 tsp dill, chopped

Directions:
1. Preheat air fryer to 400°F. Remove the tops and bottoms of the peppers. Cut along rib sections and discard the seeds. Combine the bell peppers and olive oil in a bowl. Place bell peppers in the frying basket. Roast for 24 minutes, flipping once. Transfer the roasted peppers to a small bowl and cover for 15 minutes. Then, peel and discard the skins. Sprinkle with salt and dill and serve.

Honey Brussels Sprouts

Servings:4
Cooking Time:20 Minutes
Ingredients:
- 1 lb Brussels sprouts,quartered
- 2 tbsp olive oil
- 1 tsp honey
- 1 tbsp balsamic vinegar

Directions:
1. Preheat air fryer to 400°F.Whisk the olive oil,honey,and balsamic vinegar in a bowl.Put in Brussels sprouts and toss to coat.Place them,cut-side up,in a single layer,and Roast for 10 minutes until crispy.Serve warm.

Curried Cauliflower With Cashews And Yogurt

Servings:2
Cooking Time:12 Minutes
Ingredients:
- 4 cups cauliflower florets(about half a large head)
- 1 tablespoon olive oil
- salt
- 1 teaspoon curry powder
- ½cup toasted,chopped cashews
- Cool Yogurt Drizzle
- ¼cup plain yogurt
- 2 tablespoons sour cream
- 1 teaspoon lemon juice
- pinch cayenne pepper
- salt
- 1 teaspoon honey
- 1 tablespoon chopped fresh cilantro,plus leaves for garnish

Directions:
1. Preheat the air fryer to 400°F.
2. Toss the cauliflower florets with the olive oil,salt and curry powder,coating evenly.
3. Transfer the cauliflower to the air fryer basket and air-fry at 400°F for 12 minutes,shaking the basket a couple of times during the cooking process.
4. While the cauliflower is cooking,make the cool yogurt drizzle by combining all ingredients in a bowl.
5. When the cauliflower is cooked to your liking,serve it warm with the cool yogurt either underneath or drizzled over the top.Scatter the cashews and cilantro leaves around.

Simple Green Bake

Servings:4
Cooking Time:15 Minutes
Ingredients:
- 1 cup asparagus,chopped
- 2 cups broccoli florets
- 1 tbsp olive oil
- 1 tbsp lemon juice
- 1 cup green peas
- 2 tbsp honey mustard
- Salt and pepper to taste

Directions:
1. Preheat air fryer to 330°F.Add asparagus and broccoli to the frying basket.Drizzle with olive oil and lemon juice and toss.Bake for 6 minutes.Remove the basket and add peas.Steam for another 3 minutes or until the vegetables are hot and tender.Pour the vegetables into a serving dish.Drizzle with honey mustard and season with salt and pepper.Toss and serve warm.

Corn On The Cob

Servings:4
Cooking Time:12 Minutes
Ingredients:
- 2 large ears fresh corn
- olive oil for misting
- salt(optional)

Directions:
1. Shuck corn,remove silks,and wash.
2. Cut or break each ear in half crosswise.
3. Spray corn with olive oil.
4. Cook at 390°F for 12 minutes or until browned as much as you like.
5. Serve plain or with coarsely ground salt.

Mushrooms

Servings:4
Cooking Time:12 Minutes
Ingredients:
- 8 ounces whole white button mushrooms
- ½teaspoon salt
- ⅛teaspoon pepper
- ¼teaspoon garlic powder
- ¼teaspoon onion powder
- 5 tablespoons potato starch
- 1 egg,beaten
- ¾cup panko breadcrumbs
- oil for misting or cooking spray

Directions:
1. Place mushrooms in a large bowl.Add the salt,pepper,garlic and onion powders,and stir well to distribute seasonings.
2. Add potato starch to mushrooms and toss in bowl until well coated.
3. Dip mushrooms in beaten egg,roll in panko crumbs,and mist with oil or cooking spray.
4. Place mushrooms in air fryer basket.You can cook them all at once,and it's okay if a few are stacked.
5. Cook at 390°F for 5minutes.Shake basket,then continue cooking for 7 more minutes,until golden brown and crispy.

Charred Radicchio Salad

Servings:4
Cooking Time:5 Minutes
Ingredients:
- 2 Small 5-to 6-ounce radicchio head(s)
- 3 tablespoons Olive oil
- ½teaspoon Table salt
- 2 tablespoons Balsamic vinegar
- Up to¼teaspoon Red pepper flakes

Directions:
1. Preheat the air fryer to 375°F.
2. Cut the radicchio head(s)into quarters through the stem end.Brush the oil over the heads,particularly getting it between the leaves along the cut sides.Sprinkle the radicchio quarters with the salt.
3. When the machine is at temperature,set the quarters cut sides up in the basket with as much air space between them as possible.They should not touch.Air-fry undisturbed for 5 minutes,watching carefully because they burn quickly,until blackened in bits and soft.
4. Use a nonstick-safe spatula to transfer the quarters to a cutting board.Cool for a minute or two,then cut out the thick stems inside the heads.Discard these tough bits and chop the remaining heads into bite-size bits.Scrape them into a bowl.Add the vinegar and red pepper flakes.Toss well and serve warm.

Citrusy Brussels Sprouts

Servings: 4
Cooking Time: 15 Minutes
Ingredients:
- 1 lb Brussels sprouts, quartered
- 1 clementine, cut into rings
- 2 garlic cloves, minced
- 1 tbsp olive oil
- 1 tbsp butter, melted
- ½ tsp salt

Directions:
1. Preheat air fryer to 360°F. Add the quartered Brussels sprouts with the garlic, olive oil, butter and salt in a bowl and toss until well coated. Pour the Brussels sprouts into the air fryer, top with the clementine slices, and Roast for 10 minutes. Remove from the air fryer and set the clementines aside. Toss the Brussels sprouts and serve.

Simple Peppered Carrot Chips

Servings: 4
Cooking Time: 15 Minutes
Ingredients:
- 3 carrots, cut into coins
- 1 tbsp sesame oil
- Salt and pepper to taste

Directions:
1. Preheat air fryer at 375°F. Combine all ingredients in a bowl. Place carrots in the frying basket and Roast for 10 minutes, tossing once. Serve right away.

Polenta

Servings: 4
Cooking Time: 15 Minutes
Ingredients:
- 1 pound polenta
- ¼ cup flour
- oil for misting or cooking spray

Directions:
1. Cut polenta into ½-inch slices.
2. Dip slices in flour to coat well. Spray both sides with oil or cooking spray.
3. Cook at 390°F for 5 minutes. Turn polenta and spray both sides again with oil.
4. Cook 10 more minutes or until brown and crispy.

Sticky Broccoli Florets

Servings: 4
Cooking Time: 20 Minutes
Ingredients:
- 4 cups broccoli florets
- 2 tbsp olive oil
- ½ tsp salt
- ½ cup grapefruit juice
- 1 tbsp raw honey
- 4-6 grapefruit wedges

Directions:
1. Preheat air fryer to 360°F. Add the broccoli, olive oil, salt, grapefruit juice, and honey to a bowl. Toss the broccoli in the liquid until well coated. Pour the broccoli mixture into the frying basket and Roast for 12 minutes, stirring once. Serve with grapefruit wedges.

Moroccan Cauliflower

Servings: 6
Cooking Time: 15 Minutes
Ingredients:
- 1 tablespoon curry powder
- 2 teaspoons smoky paprika
- ½ teaspoon ground cumin
- ½ teaspoon salt
- 1 head cauliflower, cut into bite-size pieces
- ¼ cup red wine vinegar
- 2 tablespoons extra-virgin olive oil
- 2 tablespoons chopped parsley

Directions:
1. Preheat the air fryer to 370°F.
2. In a large bowl, mix the curry powder, paprika, cumin, and salt. Add the cauliflower and stir to coat. Pour the red wine vinegar over the top and continue stirring.
3. Place the cauliflower into the air fryer basket; drizzle olive oil over the top.
4. Cook the cauliflower for 5 minutes, toss, and cook another 5 minutes. Raise the temperature to 400°F and continue cooking for 4 to 6 minutes, or until crispy.

Tofu & Broccoli Salad

Servings: 4
Cooking Time: 17 Minutes
Ingredients:
- Broccoli Salad
- 4 cups fresh broccoli, cut into bite-size pieces
- ½ cup red onion, chopped
- ⅓ cup raisins or dried cherries
- ¾ cup sliced almonds
- ½ cup Asian-style salad dressing
- Tofu
- 4 ounces extra firm tofu
- 1 teaspoon smoked paprika
- 1 teaspoon onion powder
- ¼ teaspoon salt
- 2 tablespoons cornstarch
- 1 tablespoon extra virgin olive oil

Directions:
1. Place several folded paper towels on a plate and set tofu on top. Cover tofu with another folded paper towel, put another plate on top, and add heavy items such as canned goods to weigh it down. Press tofu for 30 minutes.
2. While tofu is draining, combine all salad ingredients in a large bowl. Toss together well, cover, and chill until ready to serve.
3. Cut the tofu into small cubes, about ¼-inch thick. Sprinkle the cubes top and bottom with the paprika, onion powder, and salt.
4. Place cornstarch in small plastic bag, add tofu, and shake until cubes are well coated.
5. Place olive oil in another small plastic bag, add coated tofu, and shake to coat well.
6. Cook at 330°F for 17 minutes or until as crispy as you like.
7. To serve, stir chilled salad well, divide among 4 plates, and top with fried tofu.

Green Beans

Servings: 4
Cooking Time: 12 Minutes
Ingredients:
- 1 pound fresh green beans
- 2 tablespoons Italian salad dressing
- salt and pepper

Directions:
1. Wash beans and snap off stem ends.
2. In a large bowl, toss beans with Italian dressing.
3. Cook at 330°F for 5 minutes. Shake basket or stir and cook 5 minutes longer. Shake basket again and, if needed, continue cooking for 2 minutes, until as tender as you like. Beans should shrivel slightly and brown in places.
4. Sprinkle with salt and pepper to taste.

Teriyaki Tofu With Spicy Mayo

Servings: 2
Cooking Time: 35 Minutes + 1 Hour To Marinate
Ingredients:
- 1 scallion, chopped
- 7 oz extra-firm tofu, sliced
- 2 tbsp soy sauce
- 1 tsp toasted sesame oil
- 1 red chili, thinly sliced
- 1 tsp mirin
- 1 tsp light brown sugar
- 1 garlic clove, grated
- ½ tsp grated ginger
- 1/3 cup sesame seeds
- 1 egg
- 4 tsp mayonnaise
- 1 tbsp lime juice
- 1 tsp hot chili powder

Directions:
1. Squeeze most of the water from the tofu by lightly pressing the slices between two towels. Place the tofu in a baking dish. Use a whisk to mix soy sauce, sesame oil, red chili, mirin, brown sugar, garlic and ginger. Pour half of the marinade over the tofu. Using a spatula, carefully flip the tofu down and pour the other half of the marinade over. Refrigerate for 1 hour.
2. Preheat air fryer to 400°F. In a shallow plate, add sesame seeds. In another shallow plate, beat the egg. Remove the tofu from the refrigerator. Let any excess marinade drip off. Dip each piece in the egg mixture and then in the sesame seeds. Transfer to greased frying basket. Air Fry for 10 minutes, flipping once until toasted and crispy. Meanwhile, mix mayonnaise, lime juice, and hot chili powder and in a small bowl. Top with a dollop of hot chili mayo and some scallions. Serve and enjoy!

Sweet Potato Fries

Servings: 4
Cooking Time: 30 Minutes
Ingredients:
- 2 pounds sweet potatoes
- 1 teaspoon dried marjoram
- 2 teaspoons olive oil
- sea salt

Directions:
1. Peel and cut the potatoes into ¼-inch sticks, 4 to 5 inches long.
2. In a sealable plastic bag or bowl with lid, toss sweet potatoes with marjoram and olive oil. Rub seasonings in to coat well.
3. Pour sweet potatoes into air fryer basket and cook at 390°F for approximately 30 minutes, until cooked through with some brown spots on edges.
4. Season to taste with sea salt.

Steamboat Shrimp Salad

Servings: 4
Cooking Time: 4 Minutes
Ingredients:
- Steamboat Dressing
- ½ cup mayonnaise
- ½ cup plain yogurt
- 2 teaspoons freshly squeezed lemon juice (no substitutes)
- 2 teaspoons grated lemon rind
- 1 teaspoon dill weed, slightly crushed
- ½ teaspoon hot sauce
- Steamed Shrimp
- 24 small, raw shrimp, peeled and deveined
- 1 teaspoon lemon juice
- ¼ teaspoon Old Bay Seasoning
- Salad
- 8 cups romaine or Bibb lettuce, chopped or torn
- ¼ cup red onion, cut in thin slivers
- 12 black olives, sliced
- 12 cherry or grape tomatoes, halved
- 1 medium avocado, sliced or cut into large chunks

Directions:
1. Combine all dressing ingredients and mix well. Refrigerate while preparing shrimp and salad.
2. Sprinkle raw shrimp with lemon juice and Old Bay Seasoning. Use more Old Bay if you like your shrimp bold and spicy.
3. Pour 4 tablespoons of water in bottom of air fryer.
4. Place shrimp in air fryer basket in single layer.
5. Cook at 390°F for 4 minutes. Remove shrimp from basket and place in refrigerator to cool.
6. Combine all salad ingredients and mix gently. Divide among 4 salad plates or bowls.
7. Top each salad with 6 shrimp and serve with dressing.

Roasted Belgian Endive With Pistachios And Lemon

Servings: 2
Cooking Time: 7 Minutes
Ingredients:
- 2 Medium 3-ounce Belgian endive head(s)
- 2 tablespoons Olive oil
- ½ teaspoon Table salt
- ¼ cup Finely chopped unsalted shelled pistachios
- Up to 2 teaspoons Lemon juice

Directions:
1. Preheat the air fryer to 325°F (or 330°F, if that's the closest setting).
2. Trim the Belgian endive head(s), removing the little bit of dried-out stem end but keeping the leaves intact. Quarter the head(s) through the stem (which will hold the leaves intact). Brush the endive quarters with oil, getting it down between the leaves. Sprinkle the quarters with salt.
3. When the machine is at temperature, set the endive quarters cut sides up in the basket with as much air space between them as possible. They should not touch. Air-fry undisturbed for 7 minutes, or until lightly browned along the edges.
4. Use kitchen tongs to transfer the endive quarters to serving plates or a platter. Sprinkle with the pistachios and lemon juice. Serve warm or at room temperature.

Cheese & Bacon Pasta Bake

Servings: 4
Cooking Time: 35 Minutes
Ingredients:
- ½ cup shredded sharp cheddar cheese
- ½ cup shredded mozzarella cheese
- 4 oz cooked bacon, crumbled
- 3 tbsp butter, divided
- 1 tbsp flour
- 1 tsp black pepper
- 2 oz crushed feta cheese
- ¼ cup heavy cream
- ½ lb cooked rotini
- ¼ cup bread crumbs

Directions:

1. Melt 2 tbsp of butter in a skillet over medium heat.Stir in flour until the sauce thickens.Stir in all cheeses,black pepper and heavy cream and cook for 2 minutes until creamy.Toss in rotini and bacon until well coated.Spoon rotini mixture into a greased cake pan.
2. Preheat air fryer at 370ºF.Microwave the remaining butter in 10-seconds intervals until melted.Then stir in breadcrumbs.Scatter over pasta mixture.Place cake pan in the frying basket and Bake for 15 minutes.Let sit for 10 minutes before serving.

Homemade Potato Puffs

Servings:4
Cooking Time:15 Minutes
Ingredients:
- 1¾cups Water
- 4 tablespoons(¼cup/½stick)Butter
- 2 cups plus 2 tablespoons Instant mashed potato flakes
- 1½teaspoons Table salt
- ¾teaspoon Ground black pepper
- ¼teaspoon Mild paprika
- ¼teaspoon Dried thyme
- 1¼cups Seasoned Italian-style dried bread crumbs(gluten-free,if a concern)
- Olive oil spray

Directions:
1. Heat the water with the butter in a medium saucepan set over medium-low heat just until the butter melts.Do not bring to a boil.
2. Remove the saucepan from the heat and stir in the potato flakes,salt,pepper,paprika,and thyme until smooth.Set aside to cool for 5 minutes.
3. Preheat the air fryer to 400°F.Spread the bread crumbs on a dinner plate.
4. Scrape up 2 tablespoons of the potato flake mixture and form it into a small,oblong puff,like a little cylinder about 1½inches long.Gently roll the puff in the bread crumbs until coated on all sides.Set it aside and continue making more,about 12 for the small batch,18 for the medium batch,or 24 for the large.
5. Coat the potato cylinders with olive oil spray on all sides,then arrange them in the basket in one layer with some air space between them.Air-fry undisturbed for 15 minutes,or until crisp and brown.
6. Gently dump the contents of the basket onto a wire rack.Cool for 5 minutes before serving.

Patatas Bravas

Servings:4
Cooking Time:35 Minutes
Ingredients:
- 1 lb baby potatoes
- 1 onion,chopped
- 4 garlic cloves,minced
- 2 jalapeño peppers,minced
- 2 tsp olive oil
- 2 tsp Chile deÁrbol,ground
- ½tsp ground cumin
- ½tsp dried oregano

Directions:
1. Preheat air fryer to 370°F.Put the baby potatoes,onion,garlic,and jalapeños in a bowl,stir,then pour in the olive oil and stir again to coat.Season with ground chile deÁrbol,cumin,and oregano,and stir once again.Put the bowl in the air fryer and Air Fry for 22-28 minutes,shake the bowl once.Serve hot.

Mouth-watering Provençal Mushrooms

Servings:4
Cooking Time:35 Minutes
Ingredients:
- 2 lb mushrooms,quartered
- 2-3 tbsp olive oil
- ½tsp garlic powder
- 2 tsp herbs de Provence
- 2 tbsp dry white wine

Directions:
1. Preheat air fryer to 320°F.Beat together the olive oil,garlic powder,herbs de Provence,and white wine in a bowl.Add the mushrooms and toss gently to coat.Spoon the mixture onto the frying basket and Bake for 16-18 minutes,stirring twice.Serve hot and enjoy!

Ninja Foodi 2-Basket Air Fryer

Beef, pork & Lamb Recipes

Zesty London Broil

Servings: 4
Cooking Time: 28 Minutes
Ingredients:
- ⅔ cup ketchup
- ¼ cup honey
- ¼ cup olive oil
- 2 tablespoons apple cider vinegar
- 2 tablespoons Worcestershire sauce
- 2 tablespoons minced onion
- ½ teaspoon paprika
- 1 teaspoon salt
- 1 teaspoon freshly ground black pepper
- 2 pounds London broil, top round or flank steak (about 1-inch thick)

Directions:
1. Combine the ketchup, honey, olive oil, apple cider vinegar, Worcestershire sauce, minced onion, paprika, salt and pepper in a small bowl and whisk together.
2. Generously pierce both sides of the meat with a fork or meat tenderizer and place it in a shallow dish. Pour the marinade mixture over the steak, making sure all sides of the meat get coated with the marinade. Cover and refrigerate overnight.
3. Preheat the air fryer to 400°F.
4. Transfer the London broil to the air fryer basket and air-fry for 28 minutes, depending on how rare or well done you like your steak. Flip the steak over halfway through the cooking time.
5. Remove the London broil from the air fryer and let it rest for five minutes on a cutting board. To serve, thinly slice the meat against the grain and transfer to a serving platter.

Rib Eye Bites With Mushrooms

Servings: 4
Cooking Time: 30 Minutes
Ingredients:
- 1¼ lb boneless rib-eye or sirloin steak, cubed
- 8 oz button mushrooms, halved
- 4 tbsp rapeseed oil
- 1 onion, chopped
- 2 garlic cloves, minced
- Salt and pepper to taste
- 2 tsp lime juice
- 1 tsp dried marjoram
- 2 tbsp chopped parsley

Directions:
1. Preheat the air fryer to 400°F. Combine the rapeseed oil, onion, mushrooms, garlic, steak cubes, salt, pepper, lime juice, marjoram, and parsley in a baking pan. Put it in the frying basket and Bake for 12-15 minutes, stirring once or twice to ensure an even cooking, and until golden brown. The veggies should be tender. Serve hot.

Country-style Pork Ribs(2)

Servings: 4
Cooking Time: 50 Minutes
Ingredients:
- 1 tsp smoked paprika
- 1 tsp ground cumin
- 1 tsp garlic powder
- 1 tsp onion powder
- 1 tbsp honey
- ½ tsp ground mustard
- Salt and pepper to taste
- 2 tbsp olive oil
- 1 tbsp fresh orange juice
- 2 lb country-style pork ribs

Directions:
1. Preheat air fryer to 350°F. Combine all spices and honey in a bowl. In another bowl, whisk olive oil and orange juice and massage onto pork ribs. Sprinkle with the spice mixture. Place the pork ribs in the frying basket and Air Fry for 40 minutes, flipping every 10 minutes. Serve.

Peachy Pork Chops

Servings: 2
Cooking Time: 20 Minutes
Ingredients:
- 2 tbsp peach preserves
- 2 tbsp tomato paste
- 1 tbsp Dijon mustard
- 1 tsp BBQ sauce
- 1 tbsp lime juice
- 1 tbsp olive oil
- 2 cloves garlic, minced
- 2 pork chops

Directions:
1. Whisk all ingredients in a bowl until well mixed and let chill covered in the fridge for 30 minutes. Preheat air fryer to 350°F. Place pork chops in the frying basket and Air Fry for 12 minutes or until cooked through and tender. Transfer the chops to a cutting board and let sit for 5 minutes before serving.

Crispy Smoked Pork Chops

Servings: 3
Cooking Time: 8 Minutes
Ingredients:
- ⅔ cup All-purpose flour or tapioca flour
- 1 Large egg white(s)
- 2 tablespoons Water
- 1½ cups Corn flake crumbs (gluten-free, if a concern)
- 3½-pound, ½-inch-thick bone-in smoked pork chops

Directions:
1. Preheat the air fryer to 375°F.
2. Set up and fill three shallow soup plates or small pie plates on your counter: one for the flour; one for the egg white(s), whisked with the water until foamy; and one for the corn flake crumbs.
3. Set a chop in the flour and turn it several times, coating both sides and the edges. Gently shake off any excess flour, then set it in the beaten egg white mixture. Turn to coat both sides as well as the edges. Let any excess egg white slip back into the rest, then set the chop in the corn flake crumbs. Turn it several times, pressing gently to coat the chop evenly on both sides and around the edge. Set the chop aside and continue coating the remaining chop(s) in the same way.
4. Set the chops in the basket with as much air space between them as possible. Air-fry undisturbed for 8 minutes, or until the coating is crunchy and the chops are heated through.
5. Use kitchen tongs to transfer the chops to a wire rack and cool for a couple of minutes before serving.

Smokehouse-style Beef Ribs

Servings: 3
Cooking Time: 25 Minutes
Ingredients:
- ¼ teaspoon Mild smoked paprika
- ¼ teaspoon Garlic powder
- ¼ teaspoon Onion powder
- ¼ teaspoon Table salt
- ¼ teaspoon Ground black pepper
- 3 10-to 12-ounce beef back ribs (not beef short ribs)

Directions:
1. Preheat the air fryer to 350°F.
2. Mix the smoked paprika, garlic powder, onion powder, salt, and pepper in a small bowl until uniform. Massage and pat this mixture onto the ribs.
3. When the machine is at temperature, set the ribs in the basket in one layer, turning them on their sides if necessary, sort of like they're spooning but with at least ¼ inch air space between them. Air-fry for 25 minutes, turning once, until deep brown and sizzling.
4. Use kitchen tongs to transfer the ribs to a wire rack. Cool for 5 minutes before serving.

Spicy Hoisin Bbq Pork Chops

Servings: 2
Cooking Time: 12 Minutes
Ingredients:
- 3 tablespoons hoisin sauce
- ¼ cup honey
- 1 tablespoon soy sauce
- 3 tablespoons rice vinegar
- 2 tablespoons brown sugar
- 1½ teaspoons grated fresh ginger
- 1 to 2 teaspoons Sriracha sauce, to taste
- 2 to 3 bone-in center cut pork chops, 1-inch thick (about 1¼ pounds)
- chopped scallions, for garnish

Directions:
1. Combine the hoisin sauce, honey, soy sauce, rice vinegar, brown sugar, ginger, and Sriracha sauce in a small saucepan. Whisk the ingredients together and bring the mixture to a boil over medium-high heat on the stovetop. Reduce the heat and simmer the sauce until it has reduced in volume and thickened slightly–about 10 minutes.
2. Preheat the air fryer to 400°F.
3. Place the pork chops into the air fryer basket and pour half the hoisin BBQ sauce over the top. Air-fry for 6 minutes. Then, flip the chops over, pour the remaining hoisin BBQ sauce on top and air-fry for 6 more minutes, depending on the thickness of the pork chops. The internal temperature of the pork chops should be 155°F when tested with an instant read thermometer.
4. Let the pork chops rest for 5 minutes before serving. You can spoon a little of the sauce from the bottom drawer of the air fryer over the top if desired. Sprinkle with chopped scallions and serve.

French-style Pork Medallions

Servings: 4
Cooking Time: 25 Minutes
Ingredients:
- 1 lb pork medallions
- Salt and pepper to taste
- ½ tsp dried marjoram
- 2 tbsp butter
- 1 tbsp olive oil
- 1 tsp garlic powder
- 1 shallot, diced
- 1 cup chicken stock
- 2 tbsp Dijon mustard
- 2 tbsp grainy mustard
- 1/3 cup heavy cream

Directions:
1. Preheat the air fryer to 350°F. Pound the pork medallions with a rolling pin to about ¼ inch thickness. Rub them with salt, pepper, garlic, and marjoram. Place into the greased frying basket and Bake for 7 minutes or until almost done. Remove and wipe the basket clean. Combine the butter, olive oil, shallot, and stock in a baking pan, and set it in the frying basket. Bake for 5 minutes or until the shallot is crispy and tender. Add the mustard and heavy cream and cook for 4 more minutes or until the mix starts to thicken. Then add the pork to the sauce and cook for 5 more minutes, or until the sauce simmers. Remove and serve warm.

Golden Pork Quesadillas

Servings: 2
Cooking Time: 50 Minutes
Ingredients:
- ¼ cup shredded Monterey jack cheese
- 2 tortilla wraps
- 4 oz pork shoulder, sliced
- 1 tsp taco seasoning
- ½ white onion, sliced
- ½ red bell pepper, sliced
- ½ green bell pepper, sliced
- ½ yellow bell pepper, sliced
- 1 tsp chopped cilantro

Directions:
1. Preheat air fryer to 350°F. Place the pork, onion, bell peppers, and taco seasoning in the greased frying basket. Air Fry for 20 minutes, stirring twice; remove.
2. Sprinkle half the shredded Monterey jack cheese over one of the tortilla wraps, cover with the pork mixture, and scatter with the remaining cheese and cilantro. Top with the second tortilla wrap. Place in the frying basket. Bake for 12 minutes, flipping once halfway through cooking until the tortillas are browned and crisp. Let cool for a few minutes before slicing. Serve and enjoy!

Balsamic Beef & Veggie Skewers

Servings: 4
Cooking Time: 25 Minutes
Ingredients:
- 2 tbsp balsamic vinegar
- 2 tsp olive oil
- ½ tsp dried oregano
- Salt and pepper to taste
- ¾ lb round steak, cubed
- 1 red bell pepper, sliced
- 1 yellow bell pepper, sliced
- 1 cup cherry tomatoes

Directions:
1. Preheat air fryer to 390°F. Put the balsamic vinegar, olive oil, oregano, salt, and black pepper in a bowl and stir. Toss the steak in and allow to marinate for 10 minutes. Poke 8 metal skewers through the beef, bell peppers, and cherry tomatoes, alternating ingredients as you go. Place the skewers in the air fryer and Air Fry for 5-7 minutes, turning once until the beef is golden and cooked through and the veggies are tender. Serve and enjoy!

Lamb Koftas Meatballs

Servings: 3
Cooking Time: 8 Minutes
Ingredients:
- 1 pound ground lamb
- 1 teaspoon ground cumin
- 1 teaspoon ground coriander
- 2 tablespoons chopped fresh mint
- 1 egg, beaten
- ½ teaspoon salt
- freshly ground black pepper

Directions:
1. Combine all ingredients in a bowl and mix together well. Divide the mixture into 10 portions. Roll each portion into a ball and then by cupping the meatball in your hand, shape it into an oval.
2. Preheat the air fryer to 400°F.
3. Air-fry the koftas for 8 minutes.
4. Serve warm with the cucumber-yogurt dip.

Vietnamese Shaking Beef

Servings: 3
Cooking Time: 7 Minutes
Ingredients:
- 1 pound Beef tenderloin, cut into 1-inch cubes
- 1 tablespoon Regular or low-sodium soy sauce or gluten-free tamari sauce
- 1 tablespoon Fish sauce (gluten-free, if a concern)
- 1 tablespoon Dark brown sugar
- 1½ teaspoons Ground black pepper
- 3 Medium scallions, trimmed and thinly sliced
- 2 tablespoons Butter
- 1½ teaspoons Minced garlic

Directions:
1. Mix the beef, soy or tamari sauce, fish sauce, and brown sugar in a bowl until well combined. Cover and refrigerate for at least 2 hours or up to 8 hours, tossing the beef at least twice in the marinade.
2. Put a 6-inch round or square cake pan in an air-fryer basket for a small batch, a 7-inch round or square cake pan for a medium batch, or an 8-inch round or square cake pan for a large one. Or put one of these on the rack of a toaster oven–style air fryer. Heat the machine with the pan in it to 400°F. When the machine it at temperature, let the pan sit in the heat for 2 to 3 minutes so that it gets very hot.
3. Use a slotted spoon to transfer the beef to the pan, leaving any marinade behind in the bowl. Spread the meat into as close to an even layer as you can. Air-fry undisturbed for 5 minutes. Meanwhile, discard the marinade, if any.
4. Add the scallions, butter, and garlic to the beef. Air-fry for 2 minutes, tossing and rearranging the beef and scallions repeatedly, perhaps every 20 seconds.
5. Remove the basket from the machine and let the meat cool in the pan for a couple of minutes before serving.

Coffee-rubbed Pork Tenderloin

Servings: 4
Cooking Time: 30 Minutes
Ingredients:
- 1 tbsp packed brown sugar
- 2 tsp espresso powder
- 1 tsp bell pepper powder
- ½ tsp dried parsley
- 1 tbsp honey
- ½ tbsp lemon juice
- 2 tsp olive oil
- 1 pound pork tenderloin

Directions:
1. Preheat air fryer to 400°F. Toss the brown sugar, espresso powder, bell pepper powder, and parsley in a bowl and mix together. Add the honey, lemon juice, and olive oil, then stir well. Smear the pork with the mix, then allow to marinate for 10 minutes before putting it in the air fryer. Roast for 9-11 minutes until the pork is cooked through. Slice before serving.

Teriyaki Country-style Pork Ribs

Servings: 3
Cooking Time: 30 Minutes
Ingredients:
- 3 tablespoons Regular or low-sodium soy sauce or gluten-free tamari sauce
- 3 tablespoons Honey
- ¾ teaspoon Ground dried ginger
- ¾ teaspoon Garlic powder
- 3 8-ounce boneless country-style pork ribs
- Vegetable oil spray

Directions:
1. Preheat the air fryer to 350°F.
2. Mix the soy or tamari sauce, honey, ground ginger, and garlic powder in another bowl until uniform.
3. Smear about half of this teriyaki sauce over all sides of the country-style ribs. Reserve the remainder of the teriyaki sauce. Generously coat the meat with vegetable oil spray.
4. When the machine is at temperature, place the country-style ribs in the basket with as much air space between them as possible. Air-fry undisturbed for 15 minutes. Turn the country-style ribs (but keep the space between them) and brush them all over with the remaining teriyaki sauce. Continue air-frying undisturbed for 15 minutes, or until an instant-read meat thermometer inserted into the center of one rib registers at least 145°F.
5. Use kitchen tongs to transfer the country-style ribs to a wire rack. Cool for 5 minutes before serving.

Bbq Back Ribs

Servings: 4
Cooking Time: 40 Minutes
Ingredients:
- 2 tbsp light brown sugar
- Salt and pepper to taste
- 2 tsp onion powder
- 1 tsp garlic powder
- 1 tsp mustard powder
- 1 tsp dried marjoram
- ½ tsp smoked paprika
- 1 tsp cayenne pepper
- 1½ pounds baby back ribs
- 2 tbsp barbecue sauce

Directions:
1. Preheat the air fryer to 375°F. Combine the brown sugar, salt, pepper, onion and garlic powder, mustard, paprika, cayenne, and marjoram in a bowl and mix. Pour into a small glass jar. Brush the ribs with barbecue sauce and sprinkle 1 tbsp of the seasoning mix. Rub the seasoning all over the meat. Set the ribs in the greased frying basket. Bake for 25 minutes until nicely browned, flipping them once halfway through cooking. Serve hot!

Beef Brazilian Empanadas

Servings: 6
Cooking Time: 40 Minutes
Ingredients:
- 1 cup shredded Pepper Jack cheese
- 1/3 minced green bell pepper
- 1 cup shredded mozzarella
- 2 garlic cloves, chopped
- 1/3 onion, chopped
- 8 oz ground beef
- 1 tsp allspice
- ½ tsp paprika
- ½ teaspoon chili powder
- Salt and pepper to taste
- 15 empanada wrappers
- 1 tbsp butter

Directions:
1. Spray a skillet with cooking oil. Over medium heat, stir-fry garlic, green pepper, and onion for 2 minutes or until aromatic. Add beef, allspice, chili, paprika, salt and pepper. Use a spoon to break up the beef. Cook until brown. Drain the excess fat. On a clean work surface, glaze each empanada wrapper edge with water using a basting brush to soften the crust. Mound 2-3 tbsp of meat onto each wrapper. Top with mozzarella and pepper Jack cheese. Fold one side of the wrapper to the opposite side. Press the edges with the back of a fork to seal.
2. Preheat air fryer to 400°F. Place the empanadas in the air fryer and spray with cooking oil. Bake for 8 minutes, then flip the empanadas. Cook for another 4 minutes. Melt butter in a microwave-safe bowl for 20 seconds. Brush melted butter over the top of each empanada. Serve warm.

Sage Pork With Potatoes

Servings: 4
Cooking Time: 30 Minutes
Ingredients:
- 2 cups potatoes
- 2 tsp olive oil
- 1 lb pork tenderloin, cubed
- 1 onion, chopped
- 1 red bell pepper, chopped
- 2 garlic cloves, minced
- ½ tsp dried sage
- ½ tsp fennel seeds, crushed
- 2 tbsp chicken broth

Directions:
1. Preheat air fryer to 370°F. Add the potatoes and olive oil to a bowl and toss to coat. Transfer them to the frying basket and Air Fry for 15 minutes. Remove the bowl. Add the pork, onion, red bell pepper, garlic, sage, and fennel seeds, to the potatoes, add chicken broth and stir gently. Return the bowl to the frying basket and cook for 10 minutes. Be sure to shake the basket at least once. The pork should be cooked through and the potatoes soft and crispy. Serve immediately.

Suwon Pork Meatballs

Servings: 4
Cooking Time: 30 Minutes
Ingredients:
- 1 lb ground pork
- 1 egg
- 1 tsp cumin
- 1 tbsp gochujang
- 1 tsp tamari
- ¼ tsp ground ginger
- ¼ cup bread crumbs
- 1 scallion, sliced
- 4 tbsp plum jam
- 1 tsp toasted sesame seeds

Directions:
1. Preheat air fryer at 350°F. In a bowl, combine all ingredients, except scallion greens, sesame seeds and plum jam. Form mixture into meatballs. Place meatballs in the greased frying basket and Air Fry for 8 minutes, flipping once. Garnish with scallion greens, plum jam and toasted sesame seeds to serve.

Traditional Moo Shu Pork Lettuce Wraps

Servings: 4
Cooking Time: 40 Minutes
Ingredients:
- ½ cup sliced shiitake mushrooms
- 1 lb boneless pork loin, cubed
- 3 tbsp cornstarch
- 2 tbsp rice vinegar
- 3 tbsp hoisin sauce
- 1 tsp oyster sauce
- 3 tsp sesame oil
- 1 tsp sesame seeds
- ¼ tsp ground ginger
- 1 egg
- 2 tbsp flour
- 1 bag coleslaw mix
- 1 cup chopped baby spinach
- 3 green onions, sliced
- 8 iceberg lettuce leaves

Directions:
1. Preheat air fryer at 350°F. Make a slurry by whisking 1 tbsp of cornstarch and 1 tbsp of water in a bowl. Set aside. Warm a saucepan over heat, add in rice vinegar, hoisin sauce, oyster sauce, 1 tsp of sesame oil, and ginger, and cook for 3 minutes, stirring often. Add in cornstarch slurry and cook for 1 minute. Set aside and let the mixture thicken. Beat the egg, flour, and the remaining cornstarch in a bowl. Set aside.
2. Dredge pork cubes in the egg mixture. Shake off any excess. Place them in the greased frying basket and Air Fry for 8 minutes, shaking once. Warm the remaining sesame oil in a skillet over medium heat. Add in coleslaw mix, baby spinach, green onions, and mushrooms and cook for 5 minutes until the coleslaw wilts. Turn the heat off. Add in cooked pork, pour in oyster sauce mixture, and toss until coated. Divide mixture between lettuce leaves, sprinkle with sesame seed, roll them up, and serve.

Beef Meatballs With Herbs

Servings: 6
Cooking Time: 30 Minutes
Ingredients:
- 1 medium onion, minced
- 2 garlic cloves, minced
- 1 tsp olive oil
- 1 bread slice, crumbled
- 3 tbsp milk
- 1 tsp dried sage
- 1 tsp dried thyme
- 1 lb ground beef

Directions:
1. Preheat air fryer to 380°F. Toss the onion, garlic, and olive oil in a baking pan, place it in the air fryer, and Air Fry for 2-4 minutes. The veggies should be crispy but tender. Transfer the veggies to a bowl and add in the breadcrumbs, milk, thyme, and sage, then toss gently to combine. Add in the ground beef and mix with your hands. Shape the mixture into 24 meatballs. Put them in the frying basket and Air Fry for 12-16 minutes or until the meatballs are browned on all sides. Serve and enjoy!

Delicious Juicy Pork Meatballs

Servings: 4
Cooking Time: 35 Minutes
Ingredients:
- ¼ cup grated cheddar cheese
- 1 lb ground pork
- 1 egg
- 1 tbsp Greek yogurt
- ½ tsp onion powder
- ¼ cup chopped parsley
- 2 tbsp bread crumbs
- ¼ tsp garlic powder
- Salt and pepper to taste

Directions:
1. Preheat air fryer to 350°F. In a bowl, combine the ground pork, egg, yogurt, onion, parsley, cheddar cheese, bread crumbs, garlic, salt, and black pepper. Form mixture into 16 meatballs. Place meatballs in the lightly greased frying basket and Air Fry for 8-10 minutes, flipping once. Serve.

Original Köttbullar

Servings: 4
Cooking Time: 30 Minutes
Ingredients:
- 1 lb ground beef
- 1 small onion, chopped
- 1 clove garlic, minced
- 1/3 cup bread crumbs
- 1 egg, beaten
- Salt and pepper to taste
- 1 cup beef broth
- 1/3 cup heavy cream
- 2 tbsp flour

Directions:
1. Preheat air fryer to 370°F. Combine beef, onion, garlic, crumbs, egg, salt and pepper in a bowl. Scoop 2 tbsp of mixture and form meatballs with hands. Place the meatballs in the greased frying basket. Bake for 14 minutes.
2. Meanwhile, stir-fry beef broth and heavy cream in a saucepan over medium heat for 2 minutes; stir in flour. Cover and simmer for 4 minutes or until the sauce thicken. Transfer meatballs to a serving dish and drizzle with sauce. Serve and enjoy!

Tuscan Chimichangas

Servings: 2
Cooking Time: 8 Minutes
Ingredients:
- ¼ pound Thinly sliced deli ham, chopped
- 1 cup Drained and rinsed canned white beans
- ½ cup (about 2 ounces) Shredded semi-firm mozzarella
- ¼ cup Chopped sun-dried tomatoes
- ¼ cup Bottled Italian salad dressing, vinaigrette type
- 2 Burrito-size (12-inch) flour tortilla(s)
- Olive oil spray

Directions:
1. Preheat the air fryer to 375°F.
2. Mix the ham, beans, cheese, tomatoes, and salad dressing in a bowl.
3. Lay a tortilla on a clean, dry work surface. Put all of the ham mixture in a narrow oval in the middle of the tortilla, if making one burrito; or half of this mixture, if making two. Fold the parts of the tortilla that are closest to the ends of the filling oval up and over the filling, then roll the tortilla tightly closed, but don't press down hard. Generously coat the tortilla with olive oil spray. Make a second filled tortilla, if necessary.
4. Set the filled tortilla(s) seam side down in the basket, with at least ½ inch between them, if making two. Air-fry undisturbed for 8 minutes, or until crisp and lightly browned.
5. Use kitchen tongs and a nonstick-safe spatula to transfer the chimichanga(s) to a wire rack. Cool for 5 minutes before serving.

Oktoberfest Bratwursts

Servings: 4
Cooking Time: 35 Minutes
Ingredients:
- ½ onion, cut into half-moons
- 1 lb pork bratwurst links
- 2 cups beef broth
- 1 cup beer
- 2 cups drained sauerkraut
- 2 tbsp German mustard

Directions:
1. Pierce each bratwurst with a fork twice. Place them along with beef broth, beer, 1 cup of water, and onion in a saucepan over high heat and bring to a boil. Lower the heat and simmer for 15 minutes. Drain.
2. Preheat air fryer to 400°F. Place bratwursts and onion in the frying basket and Air Fry for 3 minutes. Flip bratwursts, add the sauerkraut and cook for 3 more minutes. Serve warm with mustard on the side.

Sloppy Joes

Servings: 4
Cooking Time: 17 Minutes
Ingredients:
- oil for misting or cooking spray
- 1 pound very lean ground beef
- 1 teaspoon onion powder
- ⅓ cup ketchup
- ¼ cup water
- ½ teaspoon celery seed
- 1 tablespoon lemon juice
- 1½ teaspoons brown sugar
- 1¼ teaspoons low-sodium Worcestershire sauce
- ½ teaspoon salt (optional)
- ½ teaspoon vinegar
- ⅛ teaspoon dry mustard
- hamburger or slider buns

Directions:
1. Spray air fryer basket with nonstick cooking spray or olive oil.
2. Break raw ground beef into small chunks and pile into basket.
3. Cook at 390°F for 5 minutes. Stir to break apart and cook 3 minutes. Stir and cook 4 minutes longer or until meat is well done.
4. Remove meat from air fryer, drain, and use a knife and fork to crumble into small pieces.
5. Give your air fryer basket a quick rinse to remove any bits of meat.
6. Place all the remaining ingredients except the buns in a 6 x 6-inch baking pan and mix together.
7. Add meat and stir well.
8. Cook at 330°F for 5 minutes. Stir and cook for 2 minutes.
9. Scoop onto buns.

Chicken Fried Steak

Servings: 4
Cooking Time: 15 Minutes
Ingredients:
- 2 eggs
- ½ cup buttermilk
- 1½ cups flour
- ¾ teaspoon salt
- ½ teaspoon pepper
- 1 pound beef cube steaks
- salt and pepper
- oil for misting or cooking spray

Directions:
1. Beat together eggs and buttermilk in a shallow dish.
2. In another shallow dish, stir together the flour, ½ teaspoon salt, and ¼ teaspoon pepper.
3. Season cube steaks with remaining salt and pepper to taste. Dip in flour, buttermilk egg wash, and then flour again.
4. Spray both sides of steaks with oil or cooking spray.
5. Cooking in 2 batches, place steaks in air fryer basket in single layer. Cook at 360°F for 10 minutes. Spray tops of steaks with oil and cook 5 minutes or until meat is well done.
6. Repeat to cook remaining steaks.

Crispy Lamb Shoulder Chops

Servings: 3
Cooking Time: 28 Minutes
Ingredients:
- ¾ cup All-purpose flour or gluten-free all-purpose flour
- 2 teaspoons Mild paprika
- 2 teaspoons Table salt
- 1½ teaspoons Garlic powder
- 1½ teaspoons Dried sage leaves
- 3 6-ounce bone-in lamb shoulder chops, any excess fat trimmed
- Olive oil spray

Directions:
1. Whisk the flour, paprika, salt, garlic powder, and sage in a large bowl until the mixture is of a uniform color. Add the chops and toss well to coat. Transfer them to a cutting board.
2. Preheat the air fryer to 375°F.
3. When the machine is at temperature, again dredge the chops one by one in the flour mixture. Lightly coat both sides of each chop with olive oil spray before putting it in the basket. Continue on with the remaining chop(s), leaving air space between them in the basket.
4. Air-fry, turning once, for 25 minutes, or until the chops are well browned and tender when pierced with the point of a paring knife. If the machine is at 360°F, you may need to add up to 3 minutes to the cooking time.
5. Use kitchen tongs to transfer the chops to a wire rack. Cool for 5 minutes before serving.

Boneless Ribeyes

Servings: 2
Cooking Time: 10-15 Minutes
Ingredients:
- 2 8-ounce boneless ribeye steaks
- 4 teaspoons Worcestershire sauce
- ½ teaspoon garlic powder
- pepper
- 4 teaspoons extra virgin olive oil
- salt

Directions:
1. Season steaks on both sides with Worcestershire sauce. Use the back of a spoon to spread evenly.
2. Sprinkle both sides of steaks with garlic powder and coarsely ground black pepper to taste.
3. Drizzle both sides of steaks with olive oil, again using the back of a spoon to spread evenly over surfaces.
4. Allow steaks to marinate for 30 minutes.
5. Place both steaks in air fryer basket and cook at 390°F for 5 minutes.
6. Turn steaks over and cook until done:
7. Medium rare: additional 5 minutes
8. Medium: additional 7 minutes
9. Well done: additional 10 minutes
10. Remove steaks from air fryer basket and let sit 5 minutes. Salt to taste and serve.

Pepperoni Pockets

Servings: 4
Cooking Time: 8 Minutes
Ingredients:
- 4 bread slices, 1-inch thick
- olive oil for misting
- 24 slices pepperoni (about 2 ounces)
- 1 ounce roasted red peppers, drained and patted dry
- 1 ounce Pepper Jack cheese cut into 4 slices
- pizza sauce (optional)

Directions:
1. Spray both sides of bread slices with olive oil.
2. Stand slices upright and cut a deep slit in the top to create a pocket—almost to the bottom crust but not all the way through.
3. Stuff each bread pocket with 6 slices of pepperoni, a large strip of roasted red pepper, and a slice of cheese.
4. Place bread pockets in air fryer basket, standing up. Cook at 360°F for 8 minutes, until filling is heated through and bread is lightly browned. Serve while hot as is or with pizza sauce for dipping.

Easy Carnitas

Servings: 3
Cooking Time: 25 Minutes
Ingredients:
- 1½ pounds Boneless country-style pork ribs, cut into 2-inch pieces
- ¼ cup Orange juice
- 2 tablespoons Brine from a jar of pickles, any type, even pickled jalapeño rings (gluten-free, if a concern)
- 2 teaspoons Minced garlic
- 2 teaspoons Minced fresh oregano leaves
- ¾ teaspoon Ground cumin
- ¾ teaspoon Table salt
- ¾ teaspoon Ground black pepper

Directions:
1. Mix the country-style pork rib pieces, orange juice, pickle brine, garlic, oregano, cumin, salt, and pepper in a large bowl. Cover and refrigerate for at least 2 hours or up to 10 hours, stirring the mixture occasionally.
2. Preheat the air fryer to 400°F. Set the rib pieces in their bowl on the counter as the machine heats.
3. Use kitchen tongs to transfer the rib pieces to the basket, arranging them in one layer. Some may touch. Air-fry for 25 minutes, turning and rearranging the pieces at the 10- and 20-minute marks to make sure all surfaces have been exposed to the air currents, until browned and sizzling.
4. Use clean kitchen tongs to transfer the rib pieces to a wire rack. Cool for a couple of minutes before serving.

Barbecue-style London Broil

Servings: 5
Cooking Time: 17 Minutes
Ingredients:
- ¾ teaspoon Mild smoked paprika
- ¾ teaspoon Dried oregano
- ¾ teaspoon Table salt
- ¾ teaspoon Ground black pepper
- ¼ teaspoon Garlic powder
- ¼ teaspoon Onion powder
- 1½ pounds Beef London broil (in one piece)
- Olive oil spray

Directions:
1. Preheat the air fryer to 400°F.
2. Mix the smoked paprika, oregano, salt, pepper, garlic powder, and onion powder in a small bowl until uniform.
3. Pat and rub this mixture across all surfaces of the beef. Lightly coat the beef on all sides with olive oil spray.
4. When the machine is at temperature, lay the London broil flat in the basket and air-fry undisturbed for 8 minutes for the small batch, 10 minutes for the medium batch, or 12 minutes for the large batch for medium-rare, until an instant-read meat thermometer inserted into the center of the meat registers 130°F (not USDA-approved). Add 1, 2, or 3 minutes, respectively (based on the size of the cut) for medium, until an instant-read meat thermometer registers 135°F (not USDA-approved). Or add 3, 4, or 5 minutes respectively for medium, until an instant-read meat thermometer registers 145°F (USDA-approved).
5. Use kitchen tongs to transfer the London broil to a cutting board. Let the meat rest for 10 minutes. It needs a long time for the juices to be reincorporated into the meat's fibers. Carve it against the grain into very thin (less than ¼-inch-thick) slices to serve.

Chinese-style Lamb Chops

Servings: 4
Cooking Time: 25 Minutes
Ingredients:
- 8 lamb chops, trimmed
- 2 tbsp scallions, sliced
- ¼ tsp Chinese five-spice
- 3 garlic cloves, crushed
- ½ tsp ginger powder
- ¼ cup dark soy sauce
- 2 tsp orange juice
- 3 tbsp honey
- ½ tbsp light brown sugar
- ¼ tsp red pepper flakes

Directions:
1. Season the chops with garlic, ginger, soy sauce, five-spice powder, orange juice, and honey in a bowl. Toss to coat. Cover the bowl with plastic wrap and marinate for 2 hours and up to overnight.
2. Preheat air fryer to 400°F. Remove the chops from the bowl but reserve the marinade. Place the chops in the greased frying basket and Bake for 5 minutes. Using tongs, flip the chops. Brush the lamb with the reserved marinade, then sprinkle with brown sugar and pepper flakes. Cook for another 4 minutes until brown and caramelized medium-rare. Serve with scallions on top.

Mushroom & Quinoa-stuffed Pork Loins

Servings: 3
Cooking Time: 25 Minutes
Ingredients:
- 3 boneless center-cut pork loins, pocket cut in each loin
- ½ cup diced white mushrooms
- 1 tsp vegetable oil
- 3 bacon slices, diced
- ½ onion, peeled and diced
- 1 cup baby spinach
- Salt and pepper to taste
- ½ cup cooked quinoa
- ½ cup mozzarella cheese

Directions:
1. Warm the oil in a skillet over medium heat. Add the bacon and cook for 3 minutes until the fat is rendered but not crispy. Add in onion and mushrooms and stir-fry for 3 minutes until the onions are translucent. Stir in spinach, salt, and pepper and cook for 1 minute until the spinach wilts. Set aside and toss in quinoa.
2. Preheat air fryer at 350°F. Stuff quinoa mixture into each pork loin and sprinkle with mozzarella cheese. Place them in the frying basket and Air Fry for 11 minutes. Let rest onto a cutting board for 5 minutes before serving.

Kentucky-style Pork Tenderloin

Servings: 2
Cooking Time: 30 Minutes
Ingredients:
- 1 lb pork tenderloin, halved crosswise
- 1 tbsp smoked paprika
- 2 tsp ground cumin
- 1 tsp garlic powder
- 1 tsp shallot powder
- ¼ tsp chili pepper
- Salt and pepper to taste
- 1 tsp Italian seasoning
- 2 tbsp butter, melted
- 1 tsp Worcestershire sauce

Directions:
1. Preheat air fryer to 350ºF. In a shallow bowl, combine all spices. Set aside. In another bowl, whisk butter and Worcestershire sauce and brush over pork tenderloin. Sprinkle with the seasoning mix. Place pork in the lightly greased frying basket and Air Fry for 16 minutes, flipping once. Let sit onto a cutting board for 5 minutes before slicing. Serve immediately.

Traditional Italian Beef Meatballs

Servings: 4
Cooking Time: 35 Minutes
Ingredients:
- 1/3 cup grated Parmesan
- 1 lb ground beef
- 1 egg, beaten
- 2 tbsp tomato paste
- ½ tsp Italian seasonings
- ¼ cup ricotta cheese
- 3 cloves garlic, minced
- ¼ cup grated yellow onion
- Salt and pepper to taste
- ¼ cup almond flour
- ¼ cup chopped basil
- 2 cups marinara sauce

Directions:
1. Preheat air fryer to 400ºF. In a large bowl, combine ground beef, egg, tomato paste, Italian seasoning, ricotta cheese, Parmesan cheese, garlic, onion, salt, pepper, flour, and basil. Form mixture into 4 meatballs. Add them to the greased frying basket and Air Fry for 20 minutes. Warm the marinara sauce in a skillet over medium heat for 3 minutes. Add in cooked meatballs and roll them around in sauce for 2 minutes. Serve with sauce over the top.

Almond And Sun-dried Tomato Crusted Pork Chops

Servings: 4
Cooking Time: 10 Minutes
Ingredients:
- ½cup oil-packed sun-dried tomatoes
- ½cup toasted almonds
- ¼cup grated Parmesan cheese
- ½cup olive oil
- 2 tablespoons water
- ½teaspoon salt
- freshly ground black pepper
- 4 center-cut boneless pork chops(about 1¼pounds)

Directions:
1. Place the sun-dried tomatoes into a food processor and pulse them until they are coarsely chopped.Add the almonds,Parmesan cheese,olive oil,water,salt and pepper.Process all the ingredients into a smooth paste.Spread most of the paste(leave a little in reserve)onto both sides of the pork chops and then pierce the meat several times with a needle-style meat tenderizer or a fork.Let the pork chops sit and marinate for at least 1 hour(refrigerate if marinating for longer than 1 hour).
2. Preheat the air fryer to 370°F.
3. Brush a little olive oil on the bottom of the air fryer basket.Transfer the pork chops into the air fryer basket,spooning a little more of the sun-dried tomato paste onto the pork chops if there are any gaps where the paste may have been rubbed off.Air-fry the pork chops at 370°F for 10 minutes,turning the chops over halfway through the cooking process.
4. When the pork chops have finished cooking,transfer them to a serving plate and serve with mashed potatoes and vegetables for a hearty meal.

Baby Back Ribs

Servings: 4
Cooking Time: 36 Minutes
Ingredients:
- 2¼pounds Pork baby back rib rack(s)
- 1 tablespoon Dried barbecue seasoning blend or rub(gluten-free,if a concern)
- 1 cup Water
- 3 tablespoons Purchased smooth barbecue sauce(gluten-free,if a concern)

Directions:
1. Preheat the air fryer to 350°F.
2. Cut the racks into 4-to 5-bone sections,about two sections for the small batch,three for the medium,and four for the large.Sprinkle both sides of these sections with the seasoning blend.
3. Pour the water into the bottom of the air-fryer drawer or into a tray placed under the rack.(The rack cannot then sit in water—adjust the amount of water for your machine.)Set the rib sections in the basket so that they're not touching.Air-fry for 30 minutes,turning once.
4. If using a tray with water,check it a couple of times to make sure it still has water in it or hasn't overflowed from the rendered fat.
5. Brush half the barbecue sauce on the exposed side of the ribs.Air-fry undisturbed for 3 minutes.Turn the racks over(but make sure they're still not touching),brush with the remaining sauce,and air-fry undisturbed for 3 minutes more,or until sizzling and brown.
6. Use kitchen tongs to transfer the racks to a cutting board.Let stand for 5 minutes,then slice between the bones to serve.

Bourbon Bacon Burgers

Servings: 2
Cooking Time: 23-28 Minutes
Ingredients:
- 1 tablespoon bourbon
- 2 tablespoons brown sugar
- 3 strips maple bacon,cut in half
- ¾pound ground beef(80%lean)
- 1 tablespoon minced onion
- 2 tablespoons BBQ sauce
- ½teaspoon salt
- freshly ground black pepper
- 2 slices Colby Jack cheese(or Monterey Jack)
- 2 Kaiser rolls
- lettuce and tomato,for serving
- Zesty Burger Sauce:
- 2 tablespoons BBQ sauce
- 2 tablespoons mayonnaise
- ¼teaspoon ground paprika
- freshly ground black pepper

Directions:
1. Preheat the air fryer to 390°F and pour a little water into the bottom of the air fryer drawer.(This will help prevent the grease that drips into the bottom drawer from burning and smoking.)
2. Combine the bourbon and brown sugar in a small bowl.Place the bacon strips in the air fryer basket and brush with the brown sugar mixture.Air-fry at 390°F for 4 minutes.Flip the bacon over,brush with more brown sugar and air-fry at 390°F for an additional 4 minutes until crispy.
3. While the bacon is cooking,make the burger patties.Combine the ground beef,onion,BBQ sauce,salt and pepper in a large bowl.Mix together thoroughly with your hands and shape the meat into 2 patties.
4. Transfer the burger patties to the air fryer basket and air-fry the burgers at 370°F for 15 to 20 minutes,depending on how you like your burger cooked(15 minutes for rare to medium-rare;20 minutes for well-done).Flip the burgers over halfway through the cooking process.
5. While the burgers are air-frying,make the burger sauce by combining the BBQ sauce,mayonnaise,paprika and freshly ground black pepper in a bowl.
6. When the burgers are cooked to your liking,top each patty with a slice of Colby Jack cheese and air-fry for an additional minute,just to melt the cheese.(You might want to pin the cheese slice to the burger with a toothpick to prevent it from blowing off in your air fryer.)Spread the sauce on the inside of the Kaiser rolls,place the burgers on the rolls,top with the bourbon bacon,lettuce and tomato and enjoy!

Natchitoches Meat Pies

Servings: 8
Cooking Time: 12 Minutes
Ingredients:
- Filling
- ½pound lean ground beef
- ¼cup finely chopped onion
- ¼cup finely chopped green bell pepper
- ⅛teaspoon salt
- ½teaspoon garlic powder
- ½teaspoon red pepper flakes
- 1 tablespoon low sodium Worcestershire sauce

- Crust
- 2 cups self-rising flour
- ¼ cup butter, finely diced
- 1 cup milk
- Egg Wash
- 1 egg
- 1 tablespoon water or milk
- oil for misting or cooking spray

Directions:
1. Mix all filling ingredients well and shape into 4 small patties.
2. Cook patties in air fryer basket at 390°F for 10 to 12 minutes or until well done.
3. Place patties in large bowl and use fork and knife to crumble meat into very small pieces. Set aside.
4. To make the crust, use a pastry blender or fork to cut the butter into the flour until well mixed. Add milk and stir until dough stiffens.
5. Divide dough into 8 equal portions.
6. On a lightly floured surface, roll each portion of dough into a circle. The circle should be thin and about 5 inches in diameter, but don't worry about getting a perfect shape. Uneven circles result in a rustic look that many people prefer.
7. Spoon 2 tablespoons of meat filling onto each dough circle.
8. Brush egg wash all the way around the edge of dough circle, about ½-inch deep.
9. Fold each circle in half and press dough with tines of a dinner fork to seal the edges all the way around.
10. Brush tops of sealed meat pies with egg wash.
11. Cook filled pies in a single layer in air fryer basket at 360°F for 4 minutes. Spray tops with oil or cooking spray, turn pies over, and spray bottoms with oil or cooking spray. Cook for an additional 2 minutes.
12. Repeat previous step to cook remaining pies.

Argentinian Steak Asado Salad

Servings: 2
Cooking Time: 35 Minutes
Ingredients:
- 1 jalapeño pepper, sliced thin
- ¼ cup shredded pepper Jack cheese
- 1 avocado, peeled and pitted
- ¼ cup diced tomatoes
- ½ diced shallot
- 2 tsp chopped cilantro
- 2 tsp lime juice
- ½ lb flank steak
- 1 garlic clove, minced
- 1 tsp ground cumin
- Salt and pepper to taste
- ¼ lime
- 3 cups mesclun mix
- ½ cup pico de gallo

Directions:
1. Mash the avocado in a small bowl. Add tomatoes, shallot, cilantro, lime juice, salt, and pepper. Set aside. Season the steak with garlic, salt, pepper, and cumin.
2. Preheat air fryer to 400°F. Put the steak into the greased frying basket. Bake 8-10 minutes, flipping once until your desired doneness. Remove and let rest. Squeeze the lime over the steak and cut into thin slices. For one serving, plate half of mesclun, 2 tbsp of cheese, and ¼ cup guacamole. Place half of the steak slices on top t, then add ¼ cup pico de gallo and jalapeño if desired.

Tonkatsu

Servings: 3
Cooking Time: 10 Minutes
Ingredients:
- ½ cup All-purpose flour or tapioca flour
- 1 Large egg white(s), well beaten
- ¾ cup Plain panko bread crumbs (gluten-free, if a concern)
- 3 4-ounce center-cut boneless pork loin chops (about ½ inch thick)
- Vegetable oil spray

Directions:
1. Preheat the air fryer to 375°F.
2. Set up and fill three shallow soup plates or small pie plates on your counter: one for the flour, one for the beaten egg white(s), and one for the bread crumbs.
3. Set a chop in the flour and roll it to coat all sides, even the ends. Gently shake off any excess flour and set it in the egg white(s). Gently roll and turn it to coat all sides. Let any excess egg white slip back into the rest, then set the chop in the bread crumbs. Turn it several times, pressing gently to get an even coating on all sides and the ends. Generously coat the breaded chop with vegetable oil spray, then set it aside so you can dredge, coat, and spray the remaining chop(s).
4. Set the chops in the basket with as much air space between them as possible. Air-fry undisturbed for 10 minutes, or until golden brown and crisp.
5. Use kitchen tongs to transfer the chops to a wire rack and cool for a couple of minutes before serving.

Lamb Meatballs With Quick Tomato Sauce

Servings: 4
Cooking Time: 8 Minutes
Ingredients:
- ½ small onion, finely diced
- 1 clove garlic, minced
- 1 pound ground lamb
- 2 tablespoons fresh parsley, finely chopped (plus more for garnish)
- 2 teaspoons fresh oregano, finely chopped
- 2 tablespoons milk
- 1 egg yolk
- salt and freshly ground black pepper
- ½ cup crumbled feta cheese, for garnish
- Tomato Sauce:
- 2 tablespoons butter
- 1 clove garlic, smashed
- pinch crushed red pepper flakes
- ¼ teaspoon ground cinnamon
- 1 (28-ounce) can crushed tomatoes
- salt, to taste

Directions:
1. Combine all ingredients for the meatballs in a large bowl and mix just until everything is combined. Shape the mixture into 1½-inch balls or shape the meat between two spoons to make quenelles (little three-sided footballs).
2. Preheat the air fryer to 400°F.
3. While the air fryer is Preheating, start the quick tomato sauce. Place the butter, garlic and red pepper flakes in a sauté pan and heat over medium heat on the stovetop. Let the garlic sizzle a little, but before the butter starts to brown, add the cinnamon and tomatoes. Bring to a simmer and simmer for 15 minutes. Season to taste with salt (but not too much as the feta that you will be sprinkling on at the end will be salty).

4. Brush the bottom of the air fryer basket with a little oil and transfer the meatballs to the air fryer basket in one layer, air-frying in batches if necessary.
5. Air-fry at 400°F for 8 minutes, giving the basket a shake once during the cooking process to turn the meatballs over.
6. To serve, spoon a pool of the tomato sauce onto plates and add the meatballs in a decorative manner. Sprinkle the feta cheese on top and garnish with more fresh parsley. Serve immediately.

Tasty Filet Mignon

Servings: 2
Cooking Time: 30 Minutes
Ingredients:
- 2 filet mignon steaks
- ¼ tsp garlic powder
- Salt and pepper to taste
- 1 tbsp butter, melted

Directions:
1. Preheat air fryer to 370°F. Sprinkle the steaks with salt, garlic and pepper on both sides. Place them in the greased frying basket and Air Fry for 12 minutes to yield a medium-rare steak, turning twice. Transfer steaks to a cutting board, brush them with butter and let rest 5 minutes before serving.

Balsamic Short Ribs

Servings: 2
Cooking Time: 30 Minutes
Ingredients:
- 1/8 tsp Worcestershire sauce
- ¼ cup olive oil
- ¼ cup balsamic vinegar
- ¼ cup chopped basil leaves
- ¼ cup chopped oregano
- 1 tbsp honey
- ¼ cup chopped fresh sage
- 3 cloves garlic, quartered
- ½ tsp salt
- 1 lb beef short ribs

Directions:
1. Add all ingredients, except for the short ribs, to a plastic resealable bag and shake to combine. Reserve 2 tbsp of balsamic mixture in a small bowl. Place short ribs in the plastic bag and massage into ribs. Seal the bag and let marinate in the fridge for 30 minutes up to overnight.
2. Preheat air fryer at 325°F. Place short ribs in the frying basket and Bake for 16 minutes, turn once and brush with extra sauce. Serve warm.

Balsamic London Broil

Servings: 4
Cooking Time: 25 Minutes
Ingredients:
- 2½ lb top round London broil steak
- ¼ cup coconut aminos
- 1 tbsp balsamic vinegar
- 1 tbsp olive oil
- 1 tbsp mustard
- 2 tsp maple syrup
- 2 garlic cloves, minced
- 1 tsp dried oregano
- Salt and pepper to taste
- ¼ tsp smoked paprika
- 2 tbsp red onions, chopped

Directions:
1. Whisk coconut aminos, mustard, vinegar, olive oil, maple oregano, syrup, oregano garlic, red onions, salt, pepper, and paprika in a small bowl. Put the steak in a shallow container and pour the marinade over the steak. Cover and let sit for 20 minutes.
2. Preheat air fryer to 400°F. Transfer the steak to the frying basket and bake for 5 minutes. Flip the steak and bake for another 4 to 6 minutes. Allow sitting for 5 minutes before slicing. Serve warm and enjoy.

Crunchy Veal Cutlets

Servings: 2
Cooking Time: 5 Minutes
Ingredients:
- ½ cup All-purpose flour or tapioca flour
- 1 Large egg(s), well beaten
- ¾ cup Seasoned Italian-style dried bread crumbs (gluten-free, if a concern)
- 2 tablespoons Yellow cornmeal
- 4 Thinly pounded 2-ounce veal leg cutlets (less than ¼ inch thick)
- Olive oil spray

Directions:
1. Preheat the air fryer to 400°F.
2. Set up and fill three shallow soup plates or small pie plates on your counter: one for the flour; one for the egg(s); and one for the bread crumbs, whisked with the cornmeal until well combined.
3. Dredge a veal cutlet in the flour, coating it on both sides. Gently shake off any excess flour, then gently dip it in the beaten egg(s), coating both sides. Let the excess egg slip back into the rest. Dip the cutlet in the bread-crumb mixture, turning it several times and pressing gently to make an even coating on both sides. Coat it on both sides with olive oil spray, then set it aside and continue dredging and coating more cutlets.
4. When the machine is at temperature, set the cutlets in the basket so that they don't touch each other. Air-fry undisturbed for 5 minutes, or until crisp and brown. (If only some of the veal cutlets will fit in one layer for any selected batch—the sizes of air fryer baskets vary dramatically—work in batches as necessary.)
5. Use kitchen tongs to transfer the cutlets to a wire rack. Cool for only 1 to 2 minutes before serving.

Sirloin Steak Bites With Gravy

Servings: 4
Cooking Time: 20 Minutes
Ingredients:
- 1½ lb sirloin steak, cubed
- 1 tbsp olive oil
- 2 tbsp cornstarch, divided
- 2 tbsp soy sauce
- 2 tbsp Worcestershire sauce
- 2 garlic cloves, minced
- Salt and pepper to taste
- ½ tsp smoked paprika
- ½ cup sliced red onion
- 2 fresh thyme sprigs
- ½ cup sliced mushrooms
- 1 cup beef broth
- 1 tbsp butter

Directions:
1. Preheat air fryer to 400°F. Combine beef, olive oil, 1 tablespoon of cornstarch, garlic, pepper, Worcestershire sauce, soy sauce, thyme, salt, and paprika. Arrange the beef on the greased baking dish, then top with onions and mushrooms. Place the dish in the frying basket and bake for 4 minutes. While the beef is baking, whisk beef broth and the rest of the cornstarch in a small bowl. When the beef is ready, add butter and beef broth to the baking dish. Bake for another 5 minutes. Allow resting for 5 minutes. Serve and enjoy.

Wasabi Pork Medallions

Servings:4
Cooking Time:20 Minutes+Marinate Time
Ingredients:
- 1 lb pork medallions
- 1 cup soy sauce
- 1 tbsp mirin
- ½cup olive oil
- 3 cloves garlic,crushed
- 1 tsp fresh grated ginger
- 1 tsp wasabi paste
- 1 tbsp brown sugar

Directions:
1. Place all ingredients,except for the pork,in a resealable bag and shake to combine.Add the pork medallions to the bag,shake again,and place in the fridge to marinate for 2 hours.Preheat air fryer to 360°F.Remove pork medallions from the marinade and place them in the frying basket in rows.Air Fry for 14-16 minutes or until the medallions are cooked through and juicy.Serve.

Beef Short Ribs

Servings:4
Cooking Time:20 Minutes
Ingredients:
- 2 tablespoons soy sauce
- 1 tablespoon sesame oil
- 2 tablespoons brown sugar
- 1 teaspoon ground ginger
- 2 garlic cloves,crushed
- 1 pound beef short ribs

Directions:
1. In a small bowl,mix together the soy sauce,sesame oil,brown sugar,and ginger.Transfer the mixture to a large resealable plastic bag,and place the garlic cloves and short ribs into the bag.Secure and place in the refrigerator for an hour(or overnight).
2. When you're ready to prepare the dish,preheat the air fryer to 330°F.
3. Liberally spray the air fryer basket with olive oil mist and set the beef short ribs in the basket.
4. Cook for 10 minutes,flip the short ribs,and then cook another 10 minutes.
5. Remove the short ribs from the air fryer basket,loosely cover with aluminum foil,and let them rest.The short ribs will continue to cook after they're removed from the basket.Check the internal temperature after 5 minutes to make sure it reached 145°F if you prefer a well-done meat.If it didn't reach 145°F and you would like it to be cooked longer,you can put it back into the air fryer basket at 330°F for another 3 minutes.
6. Remove from the basket and let it rest,covered with aluminum foil,for 5 minutes.Serve immediately.

Broccoli&Mushroom Beef

Servings:4
Cooking Time:30 Minutes
Ingredients:
- 1 lb sirloin strip steak,cubed
- 1 cup sliced cremini mushrooms
- 2 tbsp potato starch
- ½cup beef broth
- 1 tsp soy sauce
- 2½cups broccoli florets
- 1 onion,chopped
- 1 tbsp grated fresh ginger
- 1 cup cooked quinoa

Directions:
1. Add potato starch,broth,and soy sauce to a bowl and mix,then add in the beef and coat thoroughly.Marinate for 5 minutes.Preheat air fryer to 400°F.Set aside the broth and move the beef to a bowl.Add broccoli,onion,mushrooms,and ginger and transfer the bowl to the air fryer.Bake for 12-15 minutes until the beef is golden brown and the veggies soft.Pour the reserved broth over the beef and cook for 2-3 more minutes until the sauce is bubbling.Serve warm over cooked quinoa.

Better-than-chinese-take-out Sesame Beef

Servings:4
Cooking Time:14 Minutes
Ingredients:
- 1¼pounds Beef flank steak
- 2½tablespoons Regular or low-sodium soy sauce or gluten-free tamari sauce
- 2 tablespoons Toasted sesame oil
- 2½teaspoons Cornstarch
- 1 pound 2 ounces(about 4½cups)Frozen mixed vegetables for stir-fry,thawed,seasoning packet discarded
- 3 tablespoons Unseasoned rice vinegar(see here)
- 3 tablespoons Thai sweet chili sauce
- 2 tablespoons Light brown sugar
- 2 tablespoons White sesame seeds
- 2 teaspoons Water
- Vegetable oil spray
- 1½tablespoons Minced peeled fresh ginger
- 1 tablespoon Minced garlic

Directions:
1. Set the flank steak on a cutting board and run your clean fingers across it to figure out which way the meat's fibers are running.(Usually,they run the long way from end to end,or perhaps slightly at an angle lengthwise along the cut.)Cut the flank steak into three pieces parallel to the meat's grain.Then cut each of these pieces into½-inch-wide strips against the grain.
2. Put the meat strips in a large bowl.For a small batch,add 2 teaspoons of the soy or tamari sauce,2 teaspoons of the sesame oil,and½teaspoon of the cornstarch;for a medium batch,add 1 tablespoon of the soy or tamari sauce,1 tablespoon of the sesame oil,and 1 teaspoon of the cornstarch;and for a large batch,add 1½tablespoons of the soy or tamari sauce,1½tablespoons of the sesame oil,and 1½teaspoons of the cornstarch.Toss well until the meat is thoroughly coated in the marinade.Set aside at room temperature.
3. Preheat the air fryer to 400°F.
4. When the machine is at temperature,place the beef strips in the basket in as close to one layer as possible.The strips will overlap or even cover each other.Air-fry for 10 minutes,tossing and rearranging the strips three times so that the covered parts get exposed,until browned and even a little crisp.Pour the strips into a clean bowl.
5. Spread the vegetables in the basket and air-fry undisturbed for 4 minutes,just until they are heated through and somewhat softened.Pour these into the bowl with the meat strips.Turn off the air fryer.
6. Whisk the rice vinegar,sweet chili sauce,brown sugar,sesame seeds,the remaining soy sauce,and the remaining sesame oil in a small bowl until well combined.For a small batch,whisk the remaining 1 teaspoon cornstarch with the water in a second small bowl to make a smooth slurry;for medium batch,whisk the remaining 1½teaspoons cornstarch with the water in a second small bowl to make a smooth slurry;and for a large batch,whisk the remaining 2 teaspoons cornstarch with the water in a second small bowl to make a smooth slurry.

7. Generously coat the inside of a large wok with vegetable oil spray, then set the wok over high heat for a few minutes. Add the ginger and garlic; stir-fry for 10 seconds or so, just until fragrant. Add the meat and vegetables; stir-fry for 1 minute to heat through.
8. Add the rice vinegar mixture and continue stir-frying until the sauce is bubbling, less than 1 minute. Add the cornstarch slurry and stir-fry until the sauce has thickened, just a few seconds. Remove the wok from the heat and serve hot.

Wasabi-coated Pork Loin Chops

Servings: 3
Cooking Time: 14 Minutes
Ingredients:
- 1½ cups Wasabi peas
- ¼ cup Plain panko bread crumbs
- 1 Large egg white(s)
- 2 tablespoons Water
- 3 5-to 6-ounce boneless center-cut pork loin chops (about ½ inch thick)

Directions:
1. Preheat the air fryer to 375°F.
2. Put the wasabi peas in a food processor. Cover and process until finely ground, about like panko bread crumbs. Add the bread crumbs and pulse a few times to blend.
3. Set up and fill two shallow soup plates or small pie plates on your counter: one for the egg white(s), whisked with the water until uniform; and one for the wasabi pea mixture.
4. Dip a pork chop in the egg white mixture, coating the chop on both sides as well as around the edge. Allow any excess egg white mixture to slip back into the rest, then set the chop in the wasabi pea mixture. Press gently and turn it several times to coat evenly on both sides and around the edge. Set aside, then dip and coat the remaining chop(s).
5. Set the chops in the basket with as much air space between them as possible. Air-fry, turning once at the 6-minute mark, for 12 minutes, or until the chops are crisp and browned and an instant-read meat thermometer inserted into the center of a chop registers 145°F. If the machine is at 360°F, you may need to add 2 minutes to the cooking time.
6. Use kitchen tongs to transfer the chops to a wire rack. Cool for a couple of minutes before serving.

Sriracha Pork Strips With Rice

Servings: 4
Cooking Time: 30 Minutes+Chilling Time
Ingredients:
- ½ cup lemon juice
- 2 tbsp lemon marmalade
- 1 tbsp avocado oil
- 1 tbsp tamari
- 2 tsp sriracha
- 1 tsp yellow mustard
- 1 lb pork shoulder strips
- 4 cups cooked white rice
- ¼ cup chopped cilantro
- 1 tsp black pepper

Directions:
1. Whisk the lemon juice, lemon marmalade, avocado oil, tamari, sriracha, and mustard in a bowl. Reserve half of the marinade. Toss pork strips with half of the marinade and let marinate covered in the fridge for 30 minutes.
2. Preheat air fryer at 350°F. Place pork strips in the frying basket and Air Fry for 17 minutes, tossing twice. Transfer them to a bowl and stir in the remaining marinade. Serve over cooked rice and scatter with cilantro and pepper.

Mini Meatloaves With Pancetta

Servings: 4
Cooking Time: 40 Minutes
Ingredients:
- ¼ cup grated Parmesan
- 1/3 cup quick-cooking oats
- 2 tbsp milk
- 3 tbsp ketchup
- 3 tbsp Dijon mustard
- 1 egg
- 1 tsp dried oregano
- Salt and pepper to taste
- 1 lb lean ground beef
- 4 pancetta slices, uncooked

Directions:
1. Preheat the air fryer to 375°F. Combine the oats, milk, 1 tbsp of ketchup, 1 tbsp of mustard, the egg, oregano, Parmesan cheese, salt, and pepper, and mix. Add the beef and mix with your hands, then form 4 mini loaves. Wrap each mini loaf with pancetta, covering the meat.
2. Combine the remaining ketchup and mustard and set aside. Line the frying basket with foil and poke holes in it, then set the loaves in the basket. Brush with the ketchup/mustard mix. Bake for 17-22 minutes or until cooked and golden. Serve and enjoy!

Homemade Pork Gyoza

Servings: 4
Cooking Time: 50 Minutes
Ingredients:
- 8 wonton wrappers
- 4 oz ground pork, browned
- 1 green apple
- 1 tsp rice vinegar
- 1 tbsp vegetable oil
- ½ tbsp oyster sauce
- 1 tbsp soy sauce
- A pinch of white pepper

Directions:
1. Preheat air fryer to 350°F. Combine the oyster sauce, soy sauce, rice vinegar, and white pepper in a small bowl. Add in the pork and stir thoroughly. Peel and core the apple, and slice into small cubes. Add the apples to the meat mixture, and combine thoroughly. Divide the filling between the wonton wrappers. Wrap the wontons into triangles and seal with a bit of water. Brush the wrappers with vegetable oil. Place them in the greased frying basket. Bake for 25 minutes until crispy golden brown on the outside and juicy and delicious on the inside. Serve.

Greek Pork Chops

Servings: 4
Cooking Time: 30 Minutes
Ingredients:
- 3 tbsp grated Halloumi cheese
- 4 pork chops
- 1 tsp Greek seasoning
- Salt and pepper to taste
- ¼ cup all-purpose flour
- 2 tbsp bread crumbs

Directions:
1. Preheat air fryer to 380°F. Season the pork chops with Greek seasoning, salt and pepper. In a shallow bowl, add flour. In another shallow bowl, combine the crumbs and Halloumi. Dip the chops in the flour, then in the bread crumbs. Place them in the fryer and spray with cooking oil. Bake for 12-14 minutes, flipping once. Serve warm.

Chile Con Carne Galette

Servings: 4
Cooking Time: 30 Minutes
Ingredients:
- 1 can chili beans in chili sauce
- ½ cup canned fire-roasted diced tomatoes, drained
- ½ cup grated Mexican cheese blend
- 2 tsp olive oil
- ½ lb ground beef
- ½ cup dark beer
- ½ onion, diced
- 1 carrot, peeled and diced
- 1 celery stalk, diced
- ½ tsp ground cumin
- ½ tsp chili powder
- ¼ tsp salt
- 1 cup corn chips
- 3 tbsp beef broth
- 2 tsp corn masa

Directions:
1. Warm the olive oil in a skillet over-high heat for 30 seconds. Add in ground beef, onion, carrot, and celery and cook for 5 minutes until the beef is no longer pink. Drain the fat. Mix 3 tbsp beef broth and 2 tsp corn mass until smooth and then toss it in beans, chili sauce, dark beer, tomatoes, cumin, chili powder, and salt. Cook until thickened. Turn the heat off.
2. Preheat air fryer at 350ºF. Spoon beef mixture into a cake pan, then top with corn chips, followed by cheese blend. Place cake pan in the frying basket and Bake for 6 minutes. Let rest for 10 minutes before serving.

Tamari-seasoned Pork Strips

Servings: 4
Cooking Time: 40 Minutes
Ingredients:
- 3 tbsp olive oil
- 2 tbsp tamari
- 2 tsp red chili paste
- 2 tsp yellow mustard
- 2 tsp granulated sugar
- 1 lb pork shoulder strips
- 1 cup white rice, cooked
- 6 scallions, chopped
- ½ tsp garlic powder
- 1 tbsp lemon juice
- 1 tsp lemon zest
- ½ tsp salt

Directions:
1. Add 2 tbsp of olive oil, tamari, chili paste, mustard, and sugar to a bowl and whisk until everything is well mixed. Set aside half of the marinade. Toss pork strips in the remaining marinade and put in the fridge for 30 minutes.
2. Preheat air fryer to 350ºF. Place the pork strips in the frying basket and Air Fry for 16-18 minutes, tossing once. Transfer cooked pork to the bowl along with the remaining marinade and toss to coat. Set aside. In a medium bowl, stir in the cooked rice, garlic, lemon juice, lemon zest, and salt and cover. Spread on a serving plate. Arrange the pork strips over and top with scallions. Serve.

Friendly Bbq Baby Back Ribs

Servings: 4
Cooking Time: 35 Minutes
Ingredients:
- 1 rack baby back ribs, halved
- 1 tsp onion powder
- 1 tsp garlic powder
- 1 tsp brown sugar
- 1 tsp dried oregano
- 1 tsp ancho chili powder
- 1 tsp mustard powder
- Salt and pepper to taste
- ½ cup barbecue sauce

Directions:
1. Mix the onion powder, garlic powder, brown sugar, oregano, salt, mustard, ancho chili and pepper in a small bowl. Rub the seasoning all over the meat of the ribs. Cover the ribs in plastic wrap or foil. Sit for 30 minutes.
2. Preheat air fryer to 360°F. Place all of the ribs in the air fryer. Bake for 15 minutes, then use tongs to flip the ribs. Cook for another 15 minutes. Transfer to a serving dish and drizzle with barbecue sauce. Serve and enjoy!

Tacos Norteños

Servings: 4
Cooking Time: 25 Minutes
Ingredients:
- ½ cup minced purple onions
- 5 radishes, julienned
- 2 tbsp white wine vinegar
- ½ tsp granulated sugar
- Salt and pepper to taste
- ¼ cup olive oil
- ½ tsp ground cumin
- 1 flank steak
- 10 mini flour tortillas
- 1 cup shredded red cabbage
- ½ cup cucumber slices
- ½ cup fresh radish slices

Directions:
1. Combine the radishes, vinegar, sugar, and salt in a bowl. Let sit covered in the fridge until ready to use. Whisk the olive oil, salt, black pepper and cumin in a bowl. Toss in flank steak and let marinate in the fridge for 30 minutes.
2. Preheat air fryer at 325ºF. Place flank steak in the frying basket and Bake for 18-20 minutes, tossing once. Let rest onto a cutting board for 5 minutes before slicing thinly against the grain. Add steak slices to flour tortillas along with red cabbage, chopped purple onions, cucumber slices, radish slices and fresh radish slices. Serve warm.

Paprika Fried Beef

Servings: 4
Cooking Time: 30 Minutes
Ingredients:
- Celery salt to taste
- 4 beef cube steaks
- ½ cup milk
- 1 cup flour
- 2 tsp paprika
- 1 egg
- 1 cup bread crumbs
- 2 tbsp olive oil

Directions:
1. Preheat air fryer to 350ºF. Place the cube steaks in a zipper sealed bag or between two sheets of cling wrap. Gently pound the steaks until they are slightly thinner. Set aside. In a bowl, mix together milk, flour, paprika, celery salt, and egg until just combined. In a separate bowl, mix together the crumbs and olive oil. Take the steaks and dip them into the buttermilk batter, shake off some of the excess, and return to a plate for 5 minutes. Next, dip the steaks in the bread crumbs, patting the crumbs into both sides. Air Fry the steaks until the crust is crispy and brown, 12-16 minutes. Serve warm.

Skirt Steak Fajitas

Servings: 4
Cooking Time: 30 Minutes
Ingredients:
- 2 tablespoons olive oil
- ¼ cup lime juice
- 1 clove garlic, minced
- ½ teaspoon ground cumin
- ½ teaspoon hot sauce
- ½ teaspoon salt
- 2 tablespoons chopped fresh cilantro
- 1 pound skirt steak
- 1 onion, sliced
- 1 teaspoon chili powder
- 1 red pepper, sliced
- 1 green pepper, sliced
- salt and freshly ground black pepper
- 8 flour tortillas
- shredded lettuce, crumbled Queso Fresco (or grated Cheddar cheese), sliced black olives, diced tomatoes, sour cream and guacamole for serving

Directions:
1. Combine the olive oil, lime juice, garlic, cumin, hot sauce, salt and cilantro in a shallow dish. Add the skirt steak and turn it over several times to coat all sides. Pierce the steak with a needle-style meat tenderizer or paring knife. Marinate the steak in the refrigerator for at least 3 hours, or overnight. When you are ready to cook, remove the steak from the refrigerator and let it sit at room temperature for 30 minutes.
2. Preheat the air fryer to 400°F.
3. Toss the onion slices with the chili powder and a little olive oil and transfer them to the air fryer basket. Air-fry at 400°F for 5 minutes. Add the red and green peppers to the air fryer basket with the onions, season with salt and pepper and air-fry for 8 more minutes, until the onions and peppers are soft. Transfer the vegetables to a dish and cover with aluminum foil to keep warm.
4. Place the skirt steak in the air fryer basket and pour the marinade over the top. Air-fry at 400°F for 12 minutes. Flip the steak over and air-fry at 400°F for an additional 5 minutes. (The time needed for your steak will depend on the thickness of the skirt steak. 17 minutes should bring your steak to roughly medium.) Transfer the cooked steak to a cutting board and let the steak rest for a few minutes. If the peppers and onions need to be heated, return them to the air fryer for just 1 to 2 minutes.
5. Thinly slice the steak at an angle, cutting against the grain of the steak. Serve the steak with the onions and peppers, the warm tortillas and the fajita toppings on the side so that everyone can make their own fajita.

Pepperoni Bagel Pizzas

Servings: 4
Cooking Time: 20 Minutes
Ingredients:
- 2 bagels, halved horizontally
- 2 cups shredded mozzarella
- ¼ cup grated Parmesan
- 1 cup passata
- 1/3 cup sliced pepperoni
- 2 scallions, chopped
- 2 tbsp minced fresh chives
- 1 tsp red chili flakes

Directions:
1. Preheat the air fryer to 375°F. Put the bagel halves, cut side up, in the frying basket. Bake for 2-3 minutes until golden. Remove and top them with passata, pepperoni, scallions, and cheeses. Put the bagels topping-side up to the frying basket and cook for 8-12 more minutes or until the bagels are hot and the cheese has melted and is bubbling. Top with the chives and chili flakes and serve.

Cheeseburger Sliders With Pickle Sauce

Servings: 4
Cooking Time: 20 Minutes
Ingredients:
- 4 iceberg lettuce leaves, each halved lengthwise
- 2 red onion slices, rings separated
- ¼ cup shredded Swiss cheese
- 1 lb ground beef
- 1 tbsp Dijon mustard
- Salt and pepper to taste
- ¼ tsp shallot powder
- 2 tbsp mayonnaise
- 2 tsp ketchup
- ½ tsp mustard powder
- ½ tsp dill pickle juice
- ⅛ tsp onion powder
- ⅛ tsp garlic powder
- ⅛ tsp sweet paprika
- 8 tomato slices
- ½ cucumber, thinly sliced

Directions:
1. In a large bowl, use your hands to mix beef, Swiss cheese, mustard, salt, shallot, and black pepper. Do not overmix. Form 8 patties ½-inch thick. Mix together mayonnaise, ketchup, mustard powder, pickle juice, onion and garlic powder, and paprika in a medium bowl. Stir until smooth.
2. Preheat air fryer to 400°F. Place the sliders in the greased frying basket and Air Fry for about 8-10 minutes, flipping once until preferred doneness. Serve on top of lettuce halves with a slice of tomato, a slider, onion, a smear of special sauce, and cucumber.

Fusion Tender Flank Steak

Servings: 4
Cooking Time: 25 Minutes
Ingredients:
- 2 tbsp cilantro, chopped
- 2 tbsp chives, chopped
- ¼ tsp red pepper flakes
- 1 jalapeño pepper, minced
- 1 lime, juiced
- 3 tbsp olive oil
- Salt and pepper to taste
- 2 tbsp sesame oil
- 5 tbsp tamari sauce
- 3 tsp honey
- 1 tbsp grated fresh ginger
- 2 green onions, minced
- 2 garlic cloves, minced
- 1¼ pounds flank steak

Directions:
1. Combine the jalapeño pepper, cilantro, chives, lime juice, olive oil, salt, and pepper in a bowl. Set aside. Mix the sesame oil, tamari sauce, honey, ginger, green onions, garlic, and pepper flakes in another bowl. Stir until the honey is dissolved. Put the steak into the bowl and massage the marinade onto the meat. Marinate for 2 hours in the fridge. Preheat air fryer to 390 F.
2. Remove the steak from the marinade and place it in the greased frying basket. Air Fry for about 6 minutes, flip, and continue cooking for 6-8 more minutes. Allow to rest for a few minutes, slice thinly against the grain and top with the prepared dressing. Serve and enjoy!

Peppered Steak Bites

Servings: 4
Cooking Time: 14 Minutes
Ingredients:
- 1 pound sirloin steak, cut into 1-inch cubes
- ½ teaspoon coarse sea salt
- 1 teaspoon coarse black pepper
- 2 teaspoons Worcestershire sauce
- ½ teaspoon garlic powder
- ¼ teaspoon red pepper flakes
- ¼ cup chopped parsley

Directions:
1. Preheat the air fryer to 390°F.
2. In a large bowl, place the steak cubes and toss with the salt, pepper, Worcestershire sauce, garlic powder, and red pepper flakes.
3. Pour the steak into the air fryer basket and cook for 10 to 14 minutes, depending on how well done you prefer your bites. Starting at the 8-minute mark, toss the steak bites every 2 minutes to check for doneness.
4. When the steak is cooked, remove it from the basket to a serving bowl and top with the chopped parsley. Allow the steak to rest for 5 minutes before serving.

Pork Loin

Servings: 8
Cooking Time: 50 Minutes
Ingredients:
- 1 tablespoon lime juice
- 1 tablespoon orange marmalade
- 1 teaspoon coarse brown mustard
- 1 teaspoon curry powder
- 1 teaspoon dried lemongrass
- 2-pound boneless pork loin roast
- salt and pepper
- cooking spray

Directions:
1. Mix together the lime juice, marmalade, mustard, curry powder, and lemongrass.
2. Rub mixture all over the surface of the pork loin. Season to taste with salt and pepper.
3. Spray air fryer basket with nonstick spray and place pork roast diagonally in basket.
4. Cook at 360°F for approximately 50 minutes, until roast registers 130°F on a meat thermometer.
5. Wrap roast in foil and let rest for 10 minutes before slicing.

Easy-peasy Beef Sliders

Servings: 4
Cooking Time: 25 Minutes
Ingredients:
- 1 lb ground beef
- ¼ tsp cumin
- ¼ tsp mustard power
- 1/3 cup grated yellow onion
- ½ tsp smoked paprika
- Salt and pepper to taste

Directions:
1. Preheat air fryer to 350ºF. Combine the ground beef, cumin, mustard, onion, paprika, salt, and black pepper in a bowl. Form mixture into 8 patties and make a slight indentation in the middle of each. Place beef patties in the greased frying basket and Air Fry for 8-10 minutes, flipping once. Serve right away and enjoy!

Honey Mesquite Pork Chops

Servings: 2
Cooking Time: 10 Minutes
Ingredients:
- 2 tablespoons mesquite seasoning
- ¼ cup honey
- 1 tablespoon olive oil
- 1 tablespoon water
- freshly ground black pepper
- 2 bone-in center cut pork chops (about 1 pound)

Directions:
1. Whisk the mesquite seasoning, honey, olive oil, water and freshly ground black pepper together in a shallow glass dish. Pierce the chops all over and on both sides with a fork or meat tenderizer. Add the pork chops to the marinade and massage the marinade into the chops. Cover and marinate for 30 minutes.
2. Preheat the air fryer to 330°F.
3. Transfer the pork chops to the air fryer basket and pour half of the marinade over the chops, reserving the remaining marinade. Air-fry the pork chops for 6 minutes. Flip the pork chops over and pour the remaining marinade on top. Air-fry for an additional 3 minutes at 330°F. Then, increase the air fryer temperature to 400°F and air-fry the pork chops for an additional minute.
4. Transfer the pork chops to a serving plate, and let them rest for 5 minutes before serving. If you'd like a sauce for these chops, pour the cooked marinade from the bottom of the air fryer over the top.

Calzones South Of The Border

Servings: 8
Cooking Time: 8 Minutes
Ingredients:
- Filling
- ¼ pound ground pork sausage
- ½ teaspoon chile powder
- ¼ teaspoon ground cumin
- ⅛ teaspoon garlic powder
- ⅛ teaspoon onion powder
- ⅛ teaspoon oregano
- ½ cup ricotta cheese
- 1 ounce sharp Cheddar cheese, shredded
- 2 ounces Pepper Jack cheese, shredded
- 1 4-ounce can chopped green chiles, drained
- oil for misting or cooking spray
- salsa, sour cream, or guacamole
- Crust
- 2 cups white wheat flour, plus more for kneading and rolling
- 1 package (¼ ounce) RapidRise yeast
- 1 teaspoon salt
- ½ teaspoon chile powder
- ½ teaspoon ground cumin
- 1 cup warm water (115°F to 125°F)
- 2 teaspoons olive oil

Directions:
1. Crumble sausage into air fryer baking pan and stir in the filling seasonings: chile powder, cumin, garlic powder, onion powder, and oregano. Cook at 390°F for 2 minutes. Stir, breaking apart, and cook for 3 to 4 minutes, until well done. Remove and set aside on paper towels to drain.
2. To make dough, combine flour, yeast, salt, chile powder, and cumin. Stir in warm water and oil until soft dough forms. Turn

out onto lightly floured board and knead for 3 or 4 minutes. Let dough rest for 10 minutes.
3. Place the three cheeses in a medium bowl. Add cooked sausage and chiles and stir until well mixed.
4. Cut dough into 8 pieces.
5. Working with 4 pieces of the dough, press each into a circle about 5 inches in diameter. Top each dough circle with 2 heaping tablespoons of filling. Fold over into a half-moon shape and press edges together. Seal edges firmly to prevent leakage. Spray both sides with oil or cooking spray.
6. Place 4 calzones in air fryer basket and cook at 360°F for 5 minutes. Mist with oil or spray and cook for 3 minutes, until crust is done and nicely browned.
7. While the first batch is cooking, press out the remaining dough, fill, and shape into calzones.
8. Spray both sides with oil or cooking spray and cook for 5 minutes. If needed, mist with oil and continue cooking for 3 minutes longer. This second batch will cook a little faster than the first because your air fryer is already hot.
9. Serve plain or with salsa, sour cream, or guacamole.

Beef And Spinach Braciole

Servings: 4
Cooking Time: 92 Minutes
Ingredients:
- 7-inch oven-safe baking pan or casserole
- ½ onion, finely chopped
- 1 teaspoon olive oil
- ⅓ cup red wine
- 2 cups crushed tomatoes
- 1 teaspoon Italian seasoning
- ½ teaspoon garlic powder
- ¼ teaspoon crushed red pepper flakes
- 2 tablespoons chopped fresh parsley
- 2 top round steaks (about 1½ pounds)
- salt and freshly ground black pepper
- 2 cups fresh spinach, chopped
- 1 clove minced garlic
- ½ cup roasted red peppers, julienned
- ½ cup grated pecorino cheese
- ¼ cup pine nuts, toasted and rough chopped
- 2 tablespoons olive oil

Directions:
1. Preheat the air fryer to 400°F.
2. Toss the onions and olive oil together in a 7-inch metal baking pan or casserole dish. Air-fry at 400°F for 5 minutes, stirring a couple times during the cooking process. Add the red wine, crushed tomatoes, Italian seasoning, garlic powder, red pepper flakes and parsley and stir. Cover the pan tightly with aluminum foil, lower the air fryer temperature to 350°F and continue to air-fry for 15 minutes.
3. While the sauce is simmering, prepare the beef. Using a meat mallet, pound the beef until it is ¼-inch thick. Season both sides of the beef with salt and pepper. Combine the spinach, garlic, red peppers, pecorino cheese, pine nuts and olive oil in a medium bowl. Season with salt and freshly ground black pepper. Spread the mixture evenly over the steaks. Starting at one of the short ends, roll the beef around the filling, tucking in the sides as you roll to ensure the filling is completely enclosed. Secure the beef rolls with toothpicks.
4. Remove the baking pan with the sauce from the air fryer and set it aside. Preheat the air fryer to 400°F.
5. Brush or spray the beef rolls with a little olive oil and air-fry at 400°F for 12 minutes, rotating the beef during the cooking process for even browning. When the beef is browned, submerge the rolls into the sauce in the baking pan, cover the pan with foil and return it to the air fryer. Air-fry at 250°F for 60 minutes.
6. Remove the beef rolls from the sauce. Cut each roll into slices and serve with pasta, ladling some of the sauce overtop.

Basil Cheese & Ham Stromboli

Servings: 6
Cooking Time: 30 Minutes
Ingredients:
- 1 can refrigerated pizza dough
- ½ cup shredded mozzarella
- ½ red bell pepper, sliced
- 2 tsp all-purpose flour
- 6 Havarti cheese slices
- 12 deli ham slices
- ½ tsp dried basil
- 1 tsp garlic powder
- ½ tsp oregano
- Black pepper to taste

Directions:
1. Preheat air fryer to 400°F. Flour a flat work surface and roll out the pizza dough. Use a knife to cut into 6 equal-sized rectangles. On each rectangle, add 1 slice of Havarti, 1 tbsp of mozzarella, 2 slices of ham, and some red pepper slices. Season with basil, garlic, oregano, and black pepper. Fold one side of the dough over the filling to the opposite side. Press the edges with the back of a fork to seal them. Place one batch of stromboli in the fryer and lightly spray with cooking oil. Air Fry for 10 minutes. Serve and enjoy!

Garlic And Oregano Lamb Chops

Servings: 4
Cooking Time: 17 Minutes
Ingredients:
- 1½ tablespoons Olive oil
- 1 tablespoon Minced garlic
- 1 teaspoon Dried oregano
- 1 teaspoon Finely minced orange zest
- ¾ teaspoon Fennel seeds
- ¾ teaspoon Table salt
- ¾ teaspoon Ground black pepper
- 6 4-ounce, 1-inch-thick lamb loin chops

Directions:
1. Mix the olive oil, garlic, oregano, orange zest, fennel seeds, salt, and pepper in a large bowl. Add the chops and toss well to coat. Set aside as the air fryer heats, tossing one more time.
2. Preheat the air fryer to 400°F.
3. Set the chops bone side down in the basket (that is, so they stand up on their bony edge) with as much air space between them as possible. Air-fry undisturbed for 14 minutes for medium-rare, or until an instant-read meat thermometer inserted into the thickest part of a chop (without touching bone) registers 132°F (not USDA-approved). Or air-fry undisturbed for 17 minutes for well done, or until an instant-read meat thermometer registers 145°F (USDA-approved).
4. Use kitchen tongs to transfer the chops to a wire rack. Cool for 5 minutes before serving.

Aromatic Pork Tenderloin

Servings:6
Cooking Time:65 Minutes
Ingredients:
- 1 pork tenderloin
- 2 tbsp olive oil
- 2 garlic cloves,minced
- 1 tsp dried sage
- 1 tsp dried marjoram
- 1 tsp dried thyme
- 1 tsp paprika
- Salt and pepper to taste

Directions:
1. Preheat air fryer to 360°F.Drizzle oil over the tenderloin,then rub garlic,sage,marjoram,thyme,paprika,salt and pepper all over.Place the tenderloin in the greased frying basket and Bake for 45 minutes.Flip the pork and cook for another 15 minutes.Check the temperature for doneness.Let the cooked tenderloin rest for 10 minutes before slicing.Serve and enjoy!

T-bone Steak With Roasted Tomato,Corn And Asparagus Salsa

Servings:2
Cooking Time:15-20 Minutes
Ingredients:
- 1(20-ounce)T-bone steak
- salt and freshly ground black pepper
- Salsa
- 1½cups cherry tomatoes
- ¾cup corn kernels(fresh,or frozen and thawed)
- 1½cups sliced asparagus(1-inch slices)(about½bunch)
- 1 tablespoon+1 teaspoon olive oil,divided
- salt and freshly ground black pepper
- 1½teaspoons red wine vinegar
- 3 tablespoons chopped fresh basil
- 1 tablespoon chopped fresh chives

Directions:
1. Preheat the air fryer to 400°F.
2. Season the steak with salt and pepper and air-fry at 400°F for 10 minutes(medium-rare),12 minutes(medium),or 15 minutes(well-done),flipping the steak once halfway through the cooking time.
3. In the meantime,toss the tomatoes,corn and asparagus in a bowl with a teaspoon or so of olive oil,salt and freshly ground black pepper.
4. When the steak has finished cooking,remove it to a cutting board,tent loosely with foil and let it rest.Transfer the vegetables to the air fryer and air-fry at 400°F for 5 minutes,shaking the basket once or twice during the cooking process.Transfer the cooked vegetables back into the bowl and toss with the red wine vinegar,remaining olive oil and fresh herbs.
5. To serve,slice the steak on the bias and serve with some of the salsa on top.

Fish And Seafood Recipes

Shrimp-jalapeño Poppers In Prosciutto

Servings:4
Cooking Time:30 Minutes
Ingredients:
- 1 lb shelled tail on shrimp,deveined,sliced down the spine
- 2 jalapeños,diced
- 2 tbsp grated cheddar
- 3 tbsp mascarpone cheese
- ¼tsp garlic powder
- 1 tbsp mayonnaise
- ¼tsp ground black pepper
- 20 prosciutto slices
- ¼cup chopped parsley
- 1 lemon

Directions:
1. Preheat air fryer at 400ºF.Combine the mascarpone and cheddar cheeses,jalapeños,garlic,mayonnaise,and black pepper in a bowl.Press cheese mixture into shrimp.Wrap 1 piece of prosciutto around each shrimp to hold in the cheese mixture.Place wrapped shrimp in the frying basket and Air Fry for 8-10 minutes,flipping once.To serve,scatter with parsley and squeeze lemon.

Basil Crab Cakes With Fresh Salad

Servings:2
Cooking Time:25 Minutes
Ingredients:
- 8 oz lump crabmeat
- 2 tbsp mayonnaise
- ½tsp Dijon mustard
- ½tsp lemon juice
- ½tsp lemon zest
- 2 tsp minced yellow onion
- ¼tsp prepared horseradish
- ¼cup flour
- 1 egg white,beaten
- 1 tbsp basil,minced
- 1 tbsp olive oil
- 2 tsp white wine vinegar
- Salt and pepper to taste
- 4 oz arugula
- ½cup blackberries
- ¼cup pine nuts
- 2 lemon wedges

Directions:
1. Preheat air fryer to 400ºF.Combine the crabmeat,mayonnaise,mustard,lemon juice and zest,onion,horseradish,flour,egg white,and basil in a bowl.Form mixture into 4 patties.Place the patties in the lightly greased frying basket and Air Fry for 10 minutes,flipping once.Combine olive oil,vinegar,salt,and pepper in a bowl.Toss in the arugula and share into 2 medium bowls.Add 2 crab cakes to each bowl and scatter with blackberries,pine nuts,and lemon wedges.Serve warm.

Hot Calamari Rings

Servings:4
Cooking Time:25 Minutes
Ingredients:
- ½cup all-purpose flour
- 2 tsp hot chili powder
- 2 eggs
- 1 tbsp milk
- 1 cup bread crumbs
- Salt and pepper to taste
- 1 lb calamari rings
- 1 lime,quartered
- ½cup aioli sauce

Directions:
1. Preheat air fryer at 400ºF.In a shallow bowl,add flour and hot chili powder.In another bowl,mix the eggs and milk.In a third bowl,mix the breadcrumbs,salt and pepper.Dip calamari rings in flour mix first,then in eggs mix and shake off excess.Then,roll ring through breadcrumb mixture.Place calamari rings in the greased frying basket and Air Fry for 4 minutes,tossing once.Squeeze lime quarters over calamari.Serve with aioli sauce.

Old Bay Lobster Tails

Servings:2
Cooking Time:20 Minutes
Ingredients:
- ¼cup green onions,sliced
- 2 uncooked lobster tails
- 1 tbsp butter,melted
- ½tsp Old Bay Seasoning
- 1 tbsp chopped parsley
- 1 tsp dried sage
- 1 tsp dried thyme
- 1 garlic clove,chopped
- 1 tbsp basil paste
- 2 lemon wedges

Directions:
1. Preheat air fryer at 400ºF.Using kitchen shears,cut down the middle of each lobster tail on the softer side.Carefully run your finger between lobster meat and shell to loosen the meat.Place lobster tails,cut side-up,in the frying basket and Air Fry for 4 minutes.Brush the tail meat with butter and season with old bay seasoning,sage,thyme,garlic,green onions,basil paste and cook for another 4 minutes.Scatter with parsley and serve with lemon wedges.Enjoy!

Speedy Shrimp Paella

Servings:4
Cooking Time:20 Minutes
Ingredients:
- 2 cups cooked rice
- 1 red bell pepper,chopped
- ¼cup vegetable broth
- ½tsp turmeric
- ½tsp dried thyme
- 1 cup cooked small shrimp
- ½cup baby peas
- 1 tomato,diced

Directions:
1. Preheat air fryer to 340°F.Gently combine rice,red bell pepper,broth,turmeric,and thyme in a baking pan.Bake in the air fryer until the rice is hot,about 9 minutes.Remove the pan from the air fryer and gently stir in shrimp,peas,and tomato.Return to the air fryer and cook until bubbling and all ingredients are hot,5-8 minutes.Serve and enjoy!

Autenthic Greek Fish Pitas

Servings: 4
Cooking Time: 25 Minutes
Ingredients:
- 1 lb pollock, cut into 1-inch pieces
- ¼ cup olive oil
- 1 tsp salt
- ½ tsp dried oregano
- ½ tsp dried thyme
- ½ tsp garlic powder
- ¼ tsp chili powder
- 4 pitas
- 1 cup grated lettuce
- 4 Kalamata olives, chopped
- 2 tomatoes, diced
- 1 cup Greek yogurt

Directions:
1. Preheat air fryer to 380°F. Coat the pollock with olive oil, salt, oregano, thyme, garlic powder, and chili powder in a bowl. Put the pollock into the frying basket and Air Fry for 15 minutes. Serve inside pitas with lettuce, tomato, olives and Greek yogurt. Enjoy!

Tuna Nuggets In Hoisin Sauce

Servings: 4
Cooking Time: 7 Minutes
Ingredients:
- ½ cup hoisin sauce
- 2 tablespoons rice wine vinegar
- 2 teaspoons sesame oil
- 1 teaspoon garlic powder
- 2 teaspoons dried lemongrass
- ¼ teaspoon red pepper flakes
- ½ small onion, quartered and thinly sliced
- 8 ounces fresh tuna, cut into 1-inch cubes
- cooking spray
- 3 cups cooked jasmine rice

Directions:
1. Mix the hoisin sauce, vinegar, sesame oil, and seasonings together.
2. Stir in the onions and tuna nuggets.
3. Spray air fryer baking pan with nonstick spray and pour in tuna mixture.
4. Cook at 390°F for 3 minutes. Stir gently.
5. Cook 2 minutes and stir again, checking for doneness. Tuna should be barely cooked through, just beginning to flake and still very moist. If necessary, continue cooking and stirring in 1-minute intervals until done.
6. Serve warm over hot jasmine rice.

Cheese & Crab Stuffed Mushrooms

Servings: 2
Cooking Time: 30 Minutes
Ingredients:
- 6 oz lump crabmeat, shells discarded
- 6 oz mascarpone cheese, softened
- 2 jalapeño peppers, minced
- ¼ cup diced red onions
- 2 tsp grated Parmesan cheese
- 2 portobello mushroom caps
- 2 tbsp butter, divided
- ½ tsp prepared horseradish
- ¼ tsp Worcestershire sauce
- ¼ tsp smoked paprika
- Salt and pepper to taste
- ¼ cup bread crumbs

Directions:
1. Melt 1 tbsp of butter in a skillet over heat for 30 seconds. Add in onion and cook for 3 minutes until tender. Stir in mascarpone cheese, Parmesan cheese, horseradish, jalapeño peppers, Worcestershire sauce, paprika, salt and pepper and cook for 2 minutes until smooth. Fold in crabmeat. Spoon mixture into mushroom caps. Set aside.
2. Preheat air fryer at 350°F. Microwave the remaining butter until melted. Stir in breadcrumbs. Scatter over stuffed mushrooms. Place mushrooms in the greased frying basket and Bake for 8 minutes. Serve immediately.

Masala Fish'n'Chips

Servings: 4
Cooking Time: 30 Minutes
Ingredients:
- 2 russet potatoes, cut into strips
- 4 pollock fillets
- Salt and pepper to taste
- ½ tsp garam masala
- 1 egg white
- ¾ cup bread crumbs
- 2 tbsp olive oil

Directions:
1. Preheat air fryer to 400°F. Sprinkle the pollock fillets with salt, pepper, and garam masala. In a shallow bowl, beat egg whites until foamy. In a separate bowl, stir together bread crumbs and 1 tablespoon olive oil until completely combined. Dip the fillets into the egg white, then coat with the bread crumbs. In a bowl, toss the potato strips with 1 tbsp olive oil. Place them in the frying basket and Air Fry for 10 minutes. Slide-out the basket, shake the chips and place a metal holder over them. Arrange the fish fillets on the metal holder and cook for 10-12 minutes, flipping once. Serve warm.

Sweet Potato - wrapped Shrimp

Servings: 3
Cooking Time: 6 Minutes
Ingredients:
- 24 Long spiralized sweet potato strands
- Olive oil spray
- ¼ teaspoon Garlic powder
- ¼ teaspoon Table salt
- Up to a ⅛ teaspoon Cayenne
- 12 Large shrimp (20–25 per pound), peeled and deveined

Directions:
1. Preheat the air fryer to 400°F.
2. Lay the spiralized sweet potato strands on a large swath of paper towels and straighten out the strands to long ropes. Coat them with olive oil spray, then sprinkle them with the garlic powder, salt, and cayenne.
3. Pick up 2 strands and wrap them around the center of a shrimp, with the ends tucked under what now becomes the bottom side of the shrimp. Continue wrapping the remainder of the shrimp.
4. Set the shrimp bottom side down in the basket with as much air space between them as possible. Air-fry undisturbed for 6 minutes, or until the sweet potato strands are crisp and the shrimp are pink and firm.
5. Use kitchen tongs to transfer the shrimp to a wire rack. Cool for only a minute or two before serving.

Lime Halibut Parcels

Servings: 4
Cooking Time: 45 Minutes
Ingredients:
- 1 lime, sliced
- 4 halibut fillets
- 1 tsp dried thyme
- Salt and pepper to taste
- 1 shredded carrot
- 1 red bell pepper, sliced
- ½ cup sliced celery
- 2 tbsp butter

Directions:
1. Preheat the air fryer to 400°F. Tear off four 14-inch lengths of parchment paper and fold each piece in half crosswise. Put the lime slices in the center of half of each piece of paper, then top with halibut. Sprinkle each filet with thyme, salt, and pepper, then top each with ¼ of the carrots, bell pepper, and celery. Add a dab of butter. Fold the parchment paper in half and crimp the edges all around to enclose the halibut and vegetables. Put one parchment bundle in the basket, add a raised rack, and add another bundle. Bake for 12-14 minutes or until the bundle puff up. The fish should flake with a fork; put the bundles in the oven to keep warm. Repeat for the second batch of parchment bundles. Hot steam will be released when the bundles are opened.

Popcorn Crawfish

Servings: 4
Cooking Time: 18 Minutes
Ingredients:
- ½ cup flour, plus 2 tablespoons
- ½ teaspoon garlic powder
- 1½ teaspoons Old Bay Seasoning
- ½ teaspoon onion powder
- ½ cup beer, plus 2 tablespoons
- 12-ounce package frozen crawfish tail meat, thawed and drained
- oil for misting or cooking spray
- Coating
- 1½ cups panko crumbs
- 1 teaspoon Old Bay Seasoning
- ½ teaspoon ground black pepper

Directions:
1. In a large bowl, mix together the flour, garlic powder, Old Bay Seasoning, and onion powder. Stir in beer to blend.
2. Add crawfish meat to batter and stir to coat.
3. Combine the coating ingredients in food processor and pulse to finely crush the crumbs. Transfer crumbs to shallow dish.
4. Preheat air fryer to 390°F.
5. Pour the crawfish and batter into a colander to drain. Stir with a spoon to drain excess batter.
6. Working with a handful of crawfish at a time, roll in crumbs and place on a cookie sheet. It's okay if some of the smaller pieces of crawfish meat stick together.
7. Spray breaded crawfish with oil or cooking spray and place all at once into air fryer basket.
8. Cook at 390°F for 5 minutes. Shake basket or stir and mist again with olive oil or spray. Cook 5 more minutes, shake basket again, and mist lightly again. Continue cooking 5 more minutes, until browned and crispy.

Maple Balsamic Glazed Salmon

Servings: 4
Cooking Time: 10 Minutes
Ingredients:
- 4 (6-ounce) fillets of salmon
- salt and freshly ground black pepper
- vegetable oil
- ¼ cup pure maple syrup
- 3 tablespoons balsamic vinegar
- 1 teaspoon Dijon mustard

Directions:
1. Preheat the air fryer to 400°F.
2. Season the salmon well with salt and freshly ground black pepper. Spray or brush the bottom of the air fryer basket with vegetable oil and place the salmon fillets inside. Air-fry the salmon for 5 minutes.
3. While the salmon is air-frying, combine the maple syrup, balsamic vinegar and Dijon mustard in a small saucepan over medium heat and stir to blend well. Let the mixture simmer while the fish is cooking. It should start to thicken slightly, but keep your eye on it so it doesn't burn.
4. Brush the glaze on the salmon fillets and air-fry for an additional 5 minutes. The salmon should feel firm to the touch when finished and the glaze should be nicely browned on top. Brush a little more glaze on top before removing and serving with rice and vegetables, or a nice green salad.

Mediterranean Salmon Cakes

Servings: 4
Cooking Time: 30 Minutes
Ingredients:
- ¼ cup heavy cream
- 5 tbsp mayonnaise
- 2 cloves garlic, minced
- ¼ tsp caper juice
- 2 tsp lemon juice
- 1 tbsp capers
- 1 can salmon
- 2 tsp lemon zest
- 1 egg
- ¼ minced red bell peppers
- ½ cup flour
- ⅛ tsp salt
- 2 tbsp sliced green olives

Directions:
1. Combine heavy cream, 2 tbsp of mayonnaise, garlic, caper juices, capers, and lemon juice in a bowl. Place the resulting caper sauce in the fridge until ready to use.
2. Preheat air fryer to 400°F. Combine canned salmon, lemon zest, egg, remaining mayo, bell peppers, flour, and salt in a bowl. Form into 8 patties. Place the patties in the greased frying basket and Air Fry for 10 minutes, turning once. Let rest for 5 minutes before drizzling with lemon sauce. Garnish with green olives to serve.

Coconut Shrimp With Plum Sauce

Servings: 2
Cooking Time: 30 Minutes
Ingredients:
- ½ lb raw shrimp, peeled
- 2 eggs
- ½ cup breadcrumbs
- 1 tsp red chili powder
- 2 tbsp dried coconut flakes
- Salt and pepper to taste
- ½ cup plum sauce

Directions:

1. Preheat air fryer to 350°F.Whisk the eggs with salt and pepper in a bowl.Dip in the shrimp,fully submerging.Combine the bread crumbs,coconut flakes,chili powder,salt,and pepper in another bowl until evenly blended.Coat the shrimp in the crumb mixture and place them in the foil-lined frying basket.Air Fry for 14-16 minutes.Halfway through the cooking time,shake the basket.Serve with plum sauce for dipping and enjoy!

Mojito Fish Tacos

Servings:4
Cooking Time:30 Minutes
Ingredients:
- 1½cups chopped red cabbage
- 1 lb cod fillets
- 2 tsp olive oil
- 3 tbsp lemon juice
- 1 large carrot,grated
- 1 tbsp white rum
- ½cup salsa
- 1/3 cup Greek yogurt
- 4 soft tortillas

Directions:
1. Preheat air fryer to 390°F.Rub the fish with olive oil,then a splash with a tablespoon of lemon juice.Place in the fryer and Air Fry for 9-12 minutes.The fish should flake when done.Mix the remaining lemon juice,red cabbage,carrots,salsa,rum,and yogurt in a bowl.Take the fish out of the fryer and tear into large pieces.Serve with tortillas and cabbage mixture.Enjoy!

Salty German-style Shrimp Pancakes

Servings:4
Cooking Time:15 Minutes
Ingredients:
- 1 tbsp butter
- 3 eggs,beaten
- ½cup flour
- ½cup milk
- ⅛tsp salt
- 1 cup salsa
- 1 cup cooked shrimp,minced
- 2 tbsp cilantro,chopped

Directions:
1. Preheat air fryer to 390°F.Mix the eggs,flour,milk,and salt in a bowl until frothy.Pour the batter into a greased baking pan and place in the air fryer.Bake for 15 minutes or until the pancake is puffed and golden.Flip the pancake onto a plate.Mix salsa,shrimp,and cilantro.Top the pancake and serve.

Perfect Soft-shelled Crabs

Servings:2
Cooking Time:12 Minutes
Ingredients:
- ½cup All-purpose flour
- 1 tablespoon Old Bay seasoning
- 1 Large egg(s),well beaten
- 1 cup(about 3 ounces)Ground oyster crackers
- 2 2½-ounce cleaned soft-shelled crab(s),about 4 inches across
- Vegetable oil spray

Directions:
1. Preheat the air fryer to 375°F(or 380°F or 390°F,if one of these is the closest setting).
2. Set up and fill three shallow soup plates or small pie plates on your counter:one for the flour,whisked with the Old Bay until well combined;one for the beaten egg(s);and one for the cracker crumbs.
3. Set a soft-shelled crab in the flour mixture and turn to coat evenly and well on all sides,even inside the legs.Dip the crab into the egg(s)and coat well,turning at least once,again getting some of the egg between the legs.Let any excess egg slip back into the rest,then set the crab in the cracker crumbs.Turn several times,pressing very gently to get the crab evenly coated with crumbs,even between the legs.Generously coat the crab on all sides with vegetable oil spray.Set it aside if you're making more than one and coat these in the same way.
4. Set the crab(s)in the basket with as much air space between them as possible.They may overlap slightly,particularly at the ends of their legs,depending on the basket's size.Air-fry undisturbed for 12 minutes,or until very crisp and golden brown.If the machine is at 390°F,the crabs may be done in only 10 minutes.
5. Use kitchen tongs to gently transfer the crab(s)to a wire rack.Cool for a couple of minutes before serving.

Crispy Smelts

Servings:3
Cooking Time:20 Minutes
Ingredients:
- 1 pound Cleaned smelts
- 3 tablespoons Tapioca flour
- Vegetable oil spray
- To taste Coarse sea salt or kosher salt

Directions:
1. Preheat the air fryer to 400°F.
2. Toss the smelts and tapioca flour in a large bowl until the little fish are evenly coated.
3. Lay the smelts out on a large cutting board.Lightly coat both sides of each fish with vegetable oil spray.
4. When the machine is at temperature,set the smelts close together in the basket,with a few even overlapping on top.Air-fry undisturbed for 20 minutes,until lightly browned and crisp.
5. Remove the basket from the machine and turn out the fish onto a wire rack.The smelts will most likely come out as one large block,or maybe in a couple of large pieces.Cool for a minute or two,then sprinkle the smelts with salt and break the block(s)into much smaller sections or individual fish to serve.

Curried Sweet-and-spicy Scallops

Servings:3
Cooking Time:5 Minutes
Ingredients:
- 6 tablespoons Thai sweet chili sauce
- 2 cups(from about 5 cups cereal)Crushed Rice Krispies or other rice-puff cereal
- 2 teaspoons Yellow curry powder,purchased or homemade(see here)
- 1 pound Sea scallops
- Vegetable oil spray

Directions:
1. Preheat the air fryer to 400°F.
2. Set up and fill two shallow soup plates or small pie plates on your counter:one for the chili sauce and one for crumbs,mixed with the curry powder.
3. Dip a scallop into the chili sauce,coating it on all sides.Set it in the cereal mixture and turn several times to coat evenly.Gently shake off any excess and set the scallop on a cutting board.Continue dipping and coating the remaining scallops.Coat them all on all sides with the vegetable oil spray.

4. Set the scallops in the basket with as much air space between them as possible. Air-fry undisturbed for 5 minutes, or until lightly browned and crunchy.
5. Remove the basket. Set aside for 2 minutes to let the coating set up. Then gently pour the contents of the basket onto a platter and serve at once.

Black Olive & Shrimp Salad

Servings: 4
Cooking Time: 15 Minutes
Ingredients:
- 1 lb cleaned shrimp, deveined
- ½ cup olive oil
- 4 garlic cloves, minced
- 1 tbsp balsamic vinegar
- ¼ tsp cayenne pepper
- ¼ tsp dried basil
- ¼ tsp salt
- ¼ tsp onion powder
- 1 tomato, diced
- ¼ cup black olives

Directions:
1. Preheat air fryer to 380°F. Place the olive oil, garlic, balsamic, cayenne, basil, onion powder and salt in a bowl and stir to combine. Divide the tomatoes and black olives between 4 small ramekins. Top with shrimp and pour a quarter of the oil mixture over the shrimp. Bake for 6-8 minutes until the shrimp are cooked through. Serve.

Sweet & Spicy Swordfish Kebabs

Servings: 4
Cooking Time: 30 Minutes
Ingredients:
- ½ cup canned pineapple chunks, drained, juice reserved
- 1 lb swordfish steaks, cubed
- ½ cup large red grapes
- 1 tbsp honey
- 2 tsp grated fresh ginger
- 1 tsp olive oil
- Pinch cayenne pepper

Directions:
1. Preheat air fryer to 370°F. Poke 8 bamboo skewers through the swordfish, pineapple, and grapes. Mix the honey, 1 tbsp of pineapple juice, ginger, olive oil, and cayenne in a bowl, then use a brush to rub the mix on the kebabs. Allow the marinate to sit on the kebab for 10 minutes. Grill the kebabs for 8-12 minutes until the fish is cooked through and the fruit is soft and glazed. Brush the kebabs again with the mix, then toss the rest of the marinade. Serve warm and enjoy!

Oyster Shrimp With Fried Rice

Servings: 4
Cooking Time: 40 Minutes
Ingredients:
- 1 lb peeled shrimp, deveined
- 1 shallot, chopped
- 2 garlic cloves, minced
- 1 tbsp olive oil
- 1 tbsp butter
- 2 eggs, beaten
- 2 cups cooked rice
- 1 cup baby peas
- 2 tbsp fish sauce
- 1 tbsp oyster sauce

Directions:
1. Preheat the air fryer to 370°F. Combine the shrimp, shallot, garlic, and olive oil in a cake pan. Put the cake pan in the air fryer and Bake the shrimp for 5-7 minutes, stirring once until shrimp are no pinker. Remove into a bowl, and set aside. Put the butter in the hot cake pan to melt. Add the eggs and return to the fryer. Bake for 4-6 minutes, stirring once until the eggs are set. Remove the eggs from the pan and set aside.
2. Add the rice, peas, oyster sauce, and fish sauce to the pan and return it to the fryer. Bake for 12-15 minutes, stirring once halfway through. Pour in the shrimp and eggs and stir. Cook for 2-3 more minutes until everything is hot.

Catfish Nuggets

Servings: 4
Cooking Time: 7 Minutes Per Batch
Ingredients:
- 2 medium catfish fillets, cut in chunks (approximately 1 x 2 inch)
- salt and pepper
- 2 eggs
- 2 tablespoons skim milk
- ½ cup cornstarch
- 1 cup panko breadcrumbs, crushed
- oil for misting or cooking spray

Directions:
1. Season catfish chunks with salt and pepper to your liking.
2. Beat together eggs and milk in a small bowl.
3. Place cornstarch in a second small bowl.
4. Place breadcrumbs in a third small bowl.
5. Dip catfish chunks in cornstarch, dip in egg wash, shake off excess, then roll in breadcrumbs.
6. Spray all sides of catfish chunks with oil or cooking spray.
7. Place chunks in air fryer basket in a single layer, leaving space between for air circulation.
8. Cook at 390°F for 4 minutes, turn, and cook an additional 3 minutes, until fish flakes easily and outside is crispy brown.
9. Repeat steps 7 and 8 to cook remaining catfish nuggets.

Mojo Sea Bass

Servings: 2
Cooking Time: 15 Minutes
Ingredients:
- 1 tbsp butter, melted
- ¼ tsp chili powder
- 2 cloves garlic, minced
- 1 tbsp lemon juice
- ¼ tsp salt
- 2 sea bass fillets
- 2 tsp chopped cilantro

Directions:
1. Preheat air fryer to 370ºF. Whisk the butter, chili powder, garlic, lemon juice, and salt in a bowl. Rub mixture over the tops of each fillet. Place the fillets in the frying basket and Air Fry for 7 minutes. Let rest for 5 minutes. Divide between 2 plates and garnish with cilantro to serve.

Almond-crusted Fish

Servings: 4
Cooking Time: 10 Minutes
Ingredients:
- 4 4-ounce fish fillets
- ¾ cup breadcrumbs
- ¼ cup sliced almonds, crushed
- 2 tablespoons lemon juice
- ⅛ teaspoon cayenne
- salt and pepper

- ¾ cup flour
- 1 egg, beaten with 1 tablespoon water
- oil for misting or cooking spray

Directions:
1. Split fish fillets lengthwise down the center to create 8 pieces.
2. Mix breadcrumbs and almonds together and set aside.
3. Mix the lemon juice and cayenne together. Brush on all sides of fish.
4. Season fish to taste with salt and pepper.
5. Place the flour on a sheet of wax paper.
6. Roll fillets in flour, dip in egg wash, and roll in the crumb mixture.
7. Mist both sides of fish with oil or cooking spray.
8. Spray air fryer basket and lay fillets inside.
9. Cook at 390°F for 5 minutes, turn fish over, and cook for an additional 5 minutes or until fish is done and flakes easily.

Lemon-dill Salmon Burgers

Servings: 4
Cooking Time: 8 Minutes
Ingredients:
- 2 (6-ounce) fillets of salmon, finely chopped by hand or in a food processor
- 1 cup fine breadcrumbs
- 1 teaspoon freshly grated lemon zest
- 2 tablespoons chopped fresh dill weed
- 1 teaspoon salt
- freshly ground black pepper
- 2 eggs, lightly beaten
- 4 brioche or hamburger buns
- lettuce, tomato, red onion, avocado, mayonnaise or mustard, to serve

Directions:
1. Preheat the air fryer to 400°F.
2. Combine all the ingredients in a bowl. Mix together well and divide into four balls. Flatten the balls into patties, making an indentation in the center of each patty with your thumb (this will help the burger stay flat as it cooks) and flattening the sides of the burgers so that they fit nicely into the air fryer basket.
3. Transfer the burgers to the air fryer basket and air-fry for 4 minutes. Flip the burgers over and air-fry for another 3 to 4 minutes, until nicely browned and firm to the touch.
4. Serve on soft brioche buns with your choice of topping–lettuce, tomato, red onion, avocado, mayonnaise or mustard.

Dilly Red Snapper

Servings: 4
Cooking Time: 40 Minutes
Ingredients:
- Salt and pepper to taste
- ½ tsp ground cumin
- ¼ tsp cayenne
- ¼ teaspoon paprika
- 1 whole red snapper
- 2 tbsp butter
- 2 garlic cloves, minced
- ¼ cup dill
- 4 lemon wedges

Directions:
1. Preheat air fryer to 360°F. Combine salt, pepper, cumin, paprika and cayenne in a bowl. Brush the fish with butter, then rub with the seasoning mix. Stuff the minced garlic and dill inside the cavity of the fish. Put the snapper into the basket of the air fryer and Roast for 20 minutes. Flip the snapper over and Roast for 15 more minutes. Serve with lemon wedges and enjoy!

Fish Piccata With Crispy Potatoes

Servings: 4
Cooking Time: 30 Minutes
Ingredients:
- 4 cod fillets
- 1 tbsp butter
- 2 tsp capers
- 1 garlic clove, minced
- 2 tbsp lemon juice
- ½ lb asparagus, trimmed
- 2 large potatoes, cubed
- 1 tbsp olive oil
- Salt and pepper to taste
- ¼ tsp garlic powder
- 1 tsp dried rosemary
- 1 tsp dried parsley
- 1 tsp chopped dill

Directions:
1. Preheat air fryer to 380°F. Place each fillet on a large piece of foil. Top each fillet with butter, capers, dill, garlic, and lemon juice. Fold the foil over the fish and seal the edges to make a pouch. Mix asparagus, parsley, potatoes, olive oil, salt, rosemary, garlic powder, and pepper in a large bowl. Place asparagus in the frying basket. Roast for 4 minutes, then shake the basket. Top vegetable with foil packets and Roast for another 8 minutes. Turn off air fryer and let it stand for 5 minutes. Serve warm and enjoy.

Southeast Asian-style Tuna Steaks

Servings: 4
Cooking Time: 20 Minutes
Ingredients:
- 1 stalk lemongrass, bent in half
- 4 tuna steaks
- 2 tbsp soy sauce
- 2 tsp sesame oil
- 2 tsp rice wine vinegar
- 1 tsp grated fresh ginger
- ⅛ tsp pepper
- 3 tbsp lemon juice
- 2 tbsp chopped cilantro
- 1 sliced red chili

Directions:
1. Preheat air fryer to 390°F. Place the tuna steak on a shallow plate. Mix together soy sauce, sesame oil, rice wine vinegar, and ginger in a small bowl. Pour over the tuna, rubbing the marinade gently into both sides of the fish. Marinate for about 10 minutes. Then sprinkle with pepper. Place the lemongrass in the frying basket and top with tuna steaks. Add the remaining lemon juice and 1 tablespoon of water in the pan below the basket. Bake until the tuna is cooked through, 8-10 minutes. Discard the lemongrass before topping with cilantro and red chili. Serve and enjoy!

Easy Asian-style Tuna

Servings: 4
Cooking Time: 25 Minutes
Ingredients:
- 1 jalapeño pepper, minced
- ½ tsp Chinese five-spice
- 4 tuna steaks
- ½ tsp toasted sesame oil
- 2 garlic cloves, grated

- 1 tbsp grated fresh ginger
- Black pepper to taste
- 2 tbsp lemon juice

Directions:
1. Preheat air fryer to 380°F. Pour sesame oil over the tuna steaks and let them sit while you make the marinade. Combine the jalapeño, garlic, ginger, five-spice powder, black pepper, and lemon juice in a bowl, then brush the mix on the fish. Let it sit for 10 minutes. Air Fry the tuna in the fryer for 6-11 minutes until it is cooked through and flakes easily when pressed with a fork. Serve warm.

Horseradish Tuna Croquettes

Servings: 4
Cooking Time: 40 Minutes
Ingredients:
- 1 can tuna in water, drained
- 1/3 cup mayonnaise
- 1 tbsp minced celery
- 1 green onion, sliced
- 2 tsp dried dill
- 1 tsp lime juice
- 1 cup bread crumbs
- 1 egg
- 1 tsp prepared horseradish

Directions:
1. Preheat air fryer to 370°F. Add the tuna, mayonnaise, celery, green onion, dill, lime juice, ¼ cup bread crumbs, egg, and horseradish in a bowl and mix to combine. Mold the mixture into 12 rectangular mound shapes. Roll each croquette in a shallow dish with 3/4 cup of bread crumbs. Place croquettes in the lightly greased frying basket and Air Fry for 12 minutes on all sides. Serve.

Tex-mex Fish Tacos

Servings: 3
Cooking Time: 7 Minutes
Ingredients:
- ¾ teaspoon Chile powder
- ¼ teaspoon Ground cumin
- ¼ teaspoon Dried oregano
- 3 5-ounce skinless mahi-mahi fillets
- Vegetable oil spray
- 3 Corn or flour tortillas
- 6 tablespoons Diced tomatoes
- 3 tablespoons Regular, low-fat, or fat-free sour cream

Directions:
1. Preheat the air fryer to 400°F.
2. Stir the chile powder, cumin, and oregano in a small bowl until well combined.
3. Coat each piece of fish all over (even the sides and ends) with vegetable oil spray. Sprinkle the spice mixture evenly over all sides of the fillets. Lightly spray them again.
4. When the machine is at temperature, set the fillets in the basket with as much air space between them as possible. Air-fry undisturbed for 7 minutes, until lightly browned and firm but not hard.
5. Use a nonstick-safe spatula to transfer the fillets to a wire rack. Microwave the tortillas on high for a few seconds, until supple. Put a fillet in each tortilla and top each with 2 tablespoons diced tomatoes and 1 tablespoon sour cream.

Piña Colada Shrimp

Servings: 4
Cooking Time: 25 Minutes
Ingredients:
- 1 lb large shrimp, deveined and shelled
- 1 can crushed pineapple
- ½ cup sour cream
- ¼ cup pineapple preserves
- 2 egg whites
- 1 tbsp dark rum
- 2/3 cup cornstarch
- 2/3 cup sweetened coconut
- 1 cup panko bread crumbs

Directions:
1. Preheat air fryer to 400°F. Drain the crushed pineapple and reserve the juice. Next, transfer the pineapple to a small bowl and mix with sour cream and preserves. Set aside. In a shallow bowl, beat egg whites with 1 tbsp of the reserved pineapple juice and rum. On a separate plate, add the cornstarch. On another plate, stir together coconut and bread crumbs. Coat the shrimp with the cornstarch. Then, dip the shrimp into the egg white mixture. Shake off drips and then coat with the coconut mixture. Place the shrimp in the greased frying basket. Air Fry until crispy and golden, 7 minutes. Serve warm.

King Prawns Al Ajillo

Servings: 4
Cooking Time: 15 Minutes
Ingredients:
- 1¼ lb peeled king prawns, deveined
- ½ cup grated Parmesan
- 1 tbsp olive oil
- 1 tbsp lemon juice
- ½ tsp garlic powder
- 2 garlic cloves, minced

Directions:
1. Preheat the air fryer to 350°F. In a large bowl, add the prawns and sprinkle with olive oil, lemon juice, and garlic powder. Toss in the minced garlic and Parmesan, then toss to coat. Put the prawns in the frying basket and Air Fry for 10-15 minutes or until the prawns cook through. Shake the basket once while cooking. Serve immediately.

Holiday Shrimp Scampi

Servings: 4
Cooking Time: 25 Minutes
Ingredients:
- 1½ lb peeled shrimp, deveined
- ¼ tsp lemon pepper seasoning
- 6 garlic cloves, minced
- 1 tsp salt
- ½ tsp grated lemon zest
- 3 tbsp fresh lemon juice
- 3 tbsp sunflower oil
- 3 tbsp butter
- 2 tsp fresh thyme leaves
- 1 lemon, cut into wedges

Directions:
1. Preheat the air fryer to 400°F. Combine the shrimp and garlic in a cake pan, then sprinkle with salt and lemon pepper seasoning. Toss to coat, then add the lemon zest, lemon juice, oil, and butter. Place the cake pan in the frying basket and Bake for 10-13 minutes, stirring once until no longer pink. Sprinkle with thyme leaves. Serve hot with lemon wedges on the side.

Catalan-style Crab Samfaina

Servings:4
Cooking Time:30 Minutes
Ingredients:
- 1 peeled eggplant,cubed
- 1 zucchini,cubed
- 1 onion,chopped
- 1 red bell pepper,chopped
- 2 large tomatoes,chopped
- 1 tbsp olive oil
- ½tsp dried thyme
- ½tsp dried basil
- Salt and pepper to taste
- 1½cups cooked crab meat

Directions:
1. Preheat air fryer to 400°F.In a pan,mix together all ingredients,except the crabmeat.Place the pan in the air fryer and Bake for 9 minutes.Remove the bowl and stir in the crabmeat.Return to the air fryer and roast for another 2-5 minutes until the vegetables are tender and ratatouille bubbling.Serve hot.

British Fish&Chips

Servings:4
Cooking Time:40 Minutes
Ingredients:
- 2 peeled russet potatoes,thinly sliced
- 1 egg white
- 1 tbsp lemon juice
- 1/3 cup ground almonds
- 2 bread slices,crumbled
- ½tsp dried basil
- 4 haddock fillets

Directions:
1. Preheat air fryer to 390°F.Lay the potato slices in the frying basket and Air Fry for 11-15 minutes.Turn the fries a couple of times while cooking.While the fries are cooking,whisk the egg white and lemon juice together in a bowl.On a plate,combine the almonds,breadcrumbs,and basil.First,one at a time,dip the fillets into the egg mix and then coat in the almond/breadcrumb mix.Lay the fillets on a wire rack until the fries are done.Preheat the oven to 350°F.After the fries are done,move them to a pan and place in the oven to keep warm.Put the fish in the frying basket and Air Fry for 10-14 minutes or until cooked through,golden,and crispy.Serve with the fries.

Old Bay Fish`n`Chips

Servings:4
Cooking Time:40 Minutes
Ingredients:
- 2 russet potatoes,peeled
- 2 tbsp olive oil
- 4 tilapia filets
- ¼cup flour
- Salt and pepper to taste
- 1 tsp Old Bay seasoning
- 1 lemon,zested
- 1 egg,beaten
- 1 cup panko bread crumbs
- 3 tbsp tartar sauce

Directions:
1. Preheat the air fryer to 400°F.Slice the potatoes into ½-inch-thick chips and drizzle with olive oil.Sprinkle with salt.Add the fries to the frying basket and Air Fry for 12-16 minutes,shaking once.Remove the potatoes to a plate.Cover loosely with foil to keep warm.Sprinkle the fish with salt and season with black pepper,lemon zest,and Old Bay seasoning,then lay on a plate.Put the egg in a shallow bowl and spread the panko on a separate plate.Dip the fish in the flour,then the egg,then the panko.Press to coat completely.Add half the fish to the frying basket and spray with cooking oil.Set a raised rack on the frying basket,top with the other half of the fish,and spray with cooking oil.Air Fry for 8-10 minutes until the fish flakes.Serve the fish and chips with tartar sauce.

Chinese Fish Noodle Bowls

Servings:4
Cooking Time:40 Minutes
Ingredients:
- 1 can crushed pineapple,drained
- 1 shallot,minced
- 2 tbsp chopped cilantro
- 2½tsp lime juice
- 1 tbsp honey
- Salt and pepper to taste
- 1½cups grated red cabbage
- ¼chopped green beans
- 2 grated baby carrots
- ½tsp granulated sugar
- 2 tbsp mayonnaise
- 1 clove garlic,minced
- 8 oz cooked rice noodles
- 2 tsp sesame oil
- 1 tsp sesame seeds
- 4 cod fillets
- 1 tsp Chinese five-spice

Directions:
1. Preheat air fryer at 350ºF.Combine the pineapple,shallot,1 tbsp of cilantro,honey,2 tsp of lime juice,salt,and black pepper in a bowl.Let chill the salsa covered in the fridge until ready to use.Mix the cabbage,green beans,carrots,sugar,remaining lime juice,mayonnaise,garlic,salt,and pepper in a bowl.Let chill covered in the fridge until ready to use.In a bowl,toss cooked noodles and sesame oil,stirring occasionally to avoid sticking.
2. Sprinkle cod fillets with salt and five-spice.Place them in the greased frying basket and Air Fry for 10 minutes until the fish is opaque and flakes easily with a fork.Divide noodles into 4 bowls,top each with salsa,slaw,and fish.Serve right away sprinkled with another tbsp of cilantro and sesame seeds.

Five Spice Red Snapper With Green Onions And Orange Salsa

Servings:2
Cooking Time:8 Minutes
Ingredients:
- 2 oranges,peeled,segmented and chopped
- 1 tablespoon minced shallot
- 1 to 3 teaspoons minced red Jalapeño or Serrano pepper
- 1 tablespoon chopped fresh cilantro
- lime juice,to taste
- salt,to taste
- 2(5-to 6-ounce)red snapper fillets
- ½teaspoon Chinese five spice powder
- salt and freshly ground black pepper
- vegetable or olive oil,in a spray bottle
- 4 green onions,cut into 2-inch lengths

Directions:
1. Start by making the salsa.Cut the peel off the oranges,slicing around the oranges to expose the flesh.Segment

the oranges by cutting in between the membranes of the orange.Chop the segments roughly and combine in a bowl with the shallot,Jalapeño or Serrano pepper,cilantro,lime juice and salt.Set the salsa aside.
2. Preheat the air fryer to 400°F.
3. Season the fish fillets with the five-spice powder,salt and freshly ground black pepper.Spray both sides of the fish fillets with oil.Toss the green onions with a little oil.
4. Transfer the fish to the air fryer basket and scatter the green onions around the fish.Air-fry at 400°F for 8 minutes.
5. Remove the fish from the air fryer,along with the fried green onions.Serve with white rice and a spoonful of the salsa on top.

Fish Sticks With Tartar Sauce

Servings:2
Cooking Time:6 Minutes
Ingredients:
- 12 ounces cod or flounder
- ½cup flour
- ½teaspoon paprika
- 1 teaspoon salt
- lots of freshly ground black pepper
- 2 eggs,lightly beaten
- 1½cups panko breadcrumbs
- 1 teaspoon salt
- vegetable oil
- Tartar Sauce:
- ¼cup mayonnaise
- 2 teaspoons lemon juice
- 2 tablespoons finely chopped sweet pickles
- salt and freshly ground black pepper

Directions:
1. Cut the fish into¾-inch wide sticks or strips.Set up a dredging station.Combine the flour,paprika,salt and pepper in a shallow dish.Beat the eggs lightly in a second shallow dish.Finally,mix the breadcrumbs and salt in a third shallow dish.Coat the fish sticks by dipping the fish into the flour,then the egg and finally the breadcrumbs,coating on all sides in each step and pressing the crumbs firmly onto the fish.Place the finished sticks on a plate or baking sheet while you finish all the sticks.
2. Preheat the air fryer to 400°F.
3. Spray the fish sticks with the oil and spray or brush the bottom of the air fryer basket.Place the fish into the basket and air-fry at 400°F for 4 minutes,turn the fish sticks over,and air-fry for another 2 minutes.
4. While the fish is cooking,mix the tartar sauce ingredients together.
5. Serve the fish sticks warm with the tartar sauce and some French fries on the side.

Catalan Sardines With Romesco Sauce

Servings:2
Cooking Time:15 Minutes
Ingredients:
- 2 cans skinless,boneless sardines in oil,drained
- ½cup warmed romesco sauce
- ½cup bread crumbs

Directions:
1. Preheat air fryer to 350ºF.In a shallow dish,add bread crumbs.Roll in sardines to coat.Place sardines in the greased frying basket and Air Fry for 6 minutes,turning once.Serve with romesco sauce.

Salmon Croquettes

Servings:4
Cooking Time:8 Minutes
Ingredients:
- 1 tablespoon oil
- ½cup breadcrumbs
- 1 14.75-ounce can salmon,drained and all skin and fat removed
- 1 egg,beaten
- ⅓cup coarsely crushed saltine crackers(about 8 crackers)
- ½teaspoon Old Bay Seasoning
- ½teaspoon onion powder
- ½teaspoon Worcestershire sauce

Directions:
1. Preheat air fryer to 390°F.
2. In a shallow dish,mix oil and breadcrumbs until crumbly.
3. In a large bowl,combine the salmon,egg,cracker crumbs,Old Bay,onion powder,and Worcestershire.Mix well and shape into 8 small patties about½-inch thick.
4. Gently dip each patty into breadcrumb mixture and turn to coat well on all sides.
5. Cook at 390°F for 8minutes or until outside is crispy and browned.

Fish Nuggets With Broccoli Dip

Servings:4
Cooking Time:40 Minutes
Ingredients:
- 1 lb cod fillets,cut into chunks
- 1½cups broccoli florets
- ¼cup grated Parmesan
- 3 garlic cloves,peeled
- 3 tbsp sour cream
- 2 tbsp lemon juice
- 2 tbsp olive oil
- 2 egg whites
- 1 cup panko bread crumbs
- 1 tsp dried dill
- Salt and pepper to taste

Directions:
1. Preheat the air fryer to 400°F.Put the broccoli and garlic in the greased frying basket and Air Fry for 5-7 minutes or until tender.Remove to a blender and add sour cream,lemon juice,olive oil,and½tsp of salt and process until smooth.Set the sauce aside.Beat the egg whites until frothy in a shallow bowl.On a plate,combine the panko,Parmesan,dill,pepper,and the remaining½tsp of salt.Dip the cod fillets in the egg whites,then the breadcrumbs,pressing to coat.Put half the cubes in the frying basket and spray with cooking oil.Air Fry for 6-8 minutes or until the fish is cooked through.Serve the fish with the sauce and enjoy!

Fish Tacos With Jalapeño-lime Sauce

Servings:4
Cooking Time:7 Minutes
Ingredients:
- Fish Tacos
- 1 pound fish fillets
- ¼teaspoon cumin
- ¼teaspoon coriander
- ⅛teaspoon ground red pepper
- 1 tablespoon lime zest
- ¼teaspoon smoked paprika

- 1 teaspoon oil
- cooking spray
- 6–8 corn or flour tortillas(6-inch size)
- Jalapeño-Lime Sauce
- ½cup sour cream
- 1 tablespoon lime juice
- ¼teaspoon grated lime zest
- ½teaspoon minced jalapeño(flesh only)
- ¼teaspoon cumin
- Napa Cabbage Garnish
- 1 cup shredded Napa cabbage
- ¼cup slivered red or green bell pepper
- ¼cup slivered onion

Directions:
1. Slice the fish fillets into strips approximately½-inch thick.
2. Put the strips into a sealable plastic bag along with the cumin,coriander,red pepper,lime zest,smoked paprika,and oil.Massage seasonings into the fish until evenly distributed.
3. Spray air fryer basket with nonstick cooking spray and place seasoned fish inside.
4. Cook at 390°F for approximately 5minutes.Shake basket to distribute fish.Cook an additional 2 minutes,until fish flakes easily.
5. While the fish is cooking,prepare the Jalapeño-Lime Sauce by mixing the sour cream,lime juice,lime zest,jalapeño,and cumin together to make a smooth sauce.Set aside.
6. Mix the cabbage,bell pepper,and onion together and set aside.
7. To warm refrigerated tortillas,wrap in damp paper towels and microwave for 30 to 60 seconds.
8. To serve,spoon some of fish into a warm tortilla.Add one or two tablespoons Napa Cabbage Garnish and drizzle with Jalapeño-Lime Sauce.

Sinaloa Fish Fajitas

Servings:4
Cooking Time:30 Minutes
Ingredients:
- 1 lemon,thinly sliced
- 16 oz red snapper filets
- 1 tbsp olive oil
- 1 tbsp cayenne pepper
- ½tsp salt
- 2 cups shredded coleslaw
- 1 carrot,shredded
- 2 tbsp orange juice
- ½cup salsa
- 4 flour tortillas
- ½cup sour cream
- 2 avocados,sliced

Directions:
1. Preheat the air fryer to 350°F.Lay the lemon slices at the bottom of the basket.Drizzle the fillets with olive oil and sprinkle with cayenne pepper and salt.Lay the fillets on top of the lemons and Bake for 6-9 minutes or until the fish easily flakes.While the fish cooks,toss the coleslaw,carrot,orange juice,and salsa in a bowl.When the fish is done,remove it and cover.Toss the lemons.Air Fry the tortillas for 2-3 minutes to warm up.Add the fish to the tortillas and top with a cabbage mix,sour cream,and avocados.Serve and enjoy!

Crab Cakes On A Budget

Servings:4
Cooking Time:12 Minutes
Ingredients:
- 8 ounces imitation crabmeat
- 4 ounces leftover cooked fish(such as cod,pollock,or haddock)
- 2 tablespoons minced green onion
- 2 tablespoons minced celery
- ¾cup crushed saltine cracker crumbs
- 2 tablespoons light mayonnaise
- 1 teaspoon prepared yellow mustard
- 1 tablespoon Worcestershire sauce,plus 2 teaspoons
- 2 teaspoons dried parsley flakes
- ½teaspoon dried dill weed,crushed
- ½teaspoon garlic powder
- ½teaspoon Old Bay Seasoning
- ½cup panko breadcrumbs
- oil for misting or cooking spray

Directions:
1. Use knives or a food processor to finely shred crabmeat and fish.
2. In a large bowl,combine all ingredients except panko and oil.Stir well.
3. Shape into 8 small,fat patties.
4. Carefully roll patties in panko crumbs to coat.Spray both sides with oil or cooking spray.
5. Place patties in air fryer basket and cook at 390°F for 12 minutes or until golden brown and crispy.

Herb-crusted Sole

Servings:4
Cooking Time:20 Minutes
Ingredients:
- ½lemon,juiced and zested
- 4 sole fillets
- ½tsp dried thyme
- ½tsp dried marjoram
- ½tsp dried parsley
- Black pepper to taste
- 1 bread slice,crumbled
- 2 tsp olive oil

Directions:
1. Preheat air fryer to 320°F.In a bowl,combine the lemon zest,thyme,marjoram,parsley,pepper,breadcrumbs,and olive oil and stir.Arrange the sole fillets on a lined baking pan,skin-side down.Pour the lemon juice over the fillets,then press them firmly into the breadcrumb mixture to coat.Air Fry for 8-11 minutes,until the breadcrumbs are crisp and golden brown.Serve warm.

Coconut-shrimp Po' Boys

Servings:4
Cooking Time:5 Minutes
Ingredients:
- ½cup cornstarch
- 2 eggs
- 2 tablespoons milk
- ¾cup shredded coconut
- ½cup panko breadcrumbs
- 1 pound(31–35 count)shrimp,peeled and deveined
- Old Bay Seasoning
- oil for misting or cooking spray
- 2 large hoagie rolls
- honey mustard or light mayonnaise
- 1½cups shredded lettuce
- 1 large tomato,thinly sliced

Directions:
1. Place cornstarch in a shallow dish or plate.
2. In another shallow dish,beat together eggs and milk.
3. In a third dish mix the coconut and panko crumbs.

4. Sprinkle shrimp with Old Bay Seasoning to taste.
5. Dip shrimp in cornstarch to coat lightly,dip in egg mixture,shake off excess,and roll in coconut mixture to coat well.
6. Spray both sides of coated shrimp with oil or cooking spray.
7. Cook half the shrimp in a single layer at 390°F for 5minutes.
8. Repeat to cook remaining shrimp.
9. To Assemble
10. Split each hoagie lengthwise,leaving one long edge intact.
11. Place in air fryer basket and cook at 390°F for 1 to 2minutes or until heated through.
12. Remove buns,break apart,and place on 4 plates,cut side up.
13. Spread with honey mustard and/or mayonnaise.
14. Top with shredded lettuce,tomato slices,and coconut shrimp.

Restaurant-style Breaded Shrimp

Servings:2
Cooking Time:35 Minutes
Ingredients:
- ½lb fresh shrimp,peeled
- 2 eggs,beaten
- ½cup breadcrumbs
- ½onion,finely chopped
- ½tsp ground ginger
- ½tsp garlic powder
- ½tsp turmeric
- ½tsp red chili powder
- Salt and pepper to taste
- ½tsp amchur powder

Directions:
1. Preheat air fryer to 350°F.Place the beaten eggs in a bowl and dip in the shrimp.Blend the bread crumbs with all the dry ingredients in another bowl.Add in the shrimp and toss to coat.Place the coated shrimp in the greased frying basket.Air Fry for 12-14 minutes until the breaded crust of the shrimp is golden brown.Toss the basket two or three times during the cooking time.Serve.

Sea Bass With Fruit Salsa

Servings:4
Cooking Time:30 Minutes
Ingredients:
- 3 halved nectarines,pitted
- 4 sea bass fillets
- 2 tsp olive oil
- 3 plums,halved and pitted
- 1 cup red grapes
- 1 tbsp lemon juice
- 1 tbsp honey
- ½tsp dried thyme

Directions:
1. Preheat air fryer to 390°F.Lay the sea bass fillets in the frying basket,then spritz olive oil over the top.Air Fry for 4 minutes.Take the basket out of the fryer and add the nectarines and plums.Pour the grapes over,spritz with lemon juice and honey,then add a pinch of thyme.Put the basket back into the fryer and Bake for 5-9 minutes.The fish should flake when finished,and the fruits should be soft.Serve hot.

Flounder Fillets

Servings:4
Cooking Time:8 Minutes
Ingredients:
- 1 egg white
- 1 tablespoon water
- 1 cup panko breadcrumbs
- 2 tablespoons extra-light virgin olive oil
- 4 4-ounce flounder fillets
- salt and pepper
- oil for misting or cooking spray

Directions:
1. Preheat air fryer to 390°F.
2. Beat together egg white and water in shallow dish.
3. In another shallow dish,mix panko crumbs and oil until well combined and crumbly(best done by hand).
4. Season flounder fillets with salt and pepper to taste.Dip each fillet into egg mixture and then roll in panko crumbs,pressing in crumbs so that fish is nicely coated.
5. Spray air fryer basket with nonstick cooking spray and add fillets.Cook at 390°F for 3minutes.
6. Spray fish fillets but do not turn.Cook 5 minutes longer or until golden brown and crispy.Using a spatula,carefully remove fish from basket and serve.

Rich Salmon Burgers With Broccoli Slaw

Servings:4
Cooking Time:25 Minutes
Ingredients:
- 1 lb salmon fillets
- 1 egg
- ¼cup dill,chopped
- 1 cup bread crumbs
- Salt to taste
- ½tsp cayenne pepper
- 1 lime,zested
- 1 tsp fish sauce
- 4 buns
- 3 cups chopped broccoli
- ½cup shredded carrots
- ¼cup sunflower seeds
- 2 garlic cloves,minced
- 1 cup Greek yogurt

Directions:
1. Preheat air fryer to 360°F.Blitz the salmon fillets in your food processor until they are finely chopped.Remove to a large bowl and add egg,dill,bread crumbs,salt,and cayenne.Stir to combine.Form the mixture into 4 patties.Put them into the frying basket and Bake for 10 minutes,flipping once.Combine broccoli,carrots,sunflower seeds,garlic,salt,lime,fish sauce,and Greek yogurt in a bowl.Serve the salmon burgers onto buns with broccoli slaw.Enjoy!

Easy-peasy Shrimp

Servings:2
Cooking Time:15 Minutes
Ingredients:
- 1 lb tail-on shrimp,deveined
- 2 tbsp butter,melted
- 1 tbsp lemon juice
- 1 tbsp dill,chopped

Directions:
1. Preheat air fryer to 350ºF.Combine shrimp and butter in a bowl.Place shrimp in the greased frying basket and Air Fry for 6 minutes,flipping once.Squeeze lemon juice over and top with dill.Serve hot.

Salmon Puttanesca En Papillotte With Zucchini

Servings: 2
Cooking Time: 17 Minutes
Ingredients:
- 1 small zucchini, sliced into ¼-inch thick half moons
- 1 teaspoon olive oil
- salt and freshly ground black pepper
- 2 (5-ounce) salmon fillets
- 1 beefsteak tomato, chopped (about 1 cup)
- 1 tablespoon capers, rinsed
- 10 black olives, pitted and sliced
- 2 tablespoons dry vermouth or white wine 2 tablespoons butter
- ¼ cup chopped fresh basil, chopped

Directions:
1. Preheat the air fryer to 400°F.
2. Toss the zucchini with the olive oil, salt and freshly ground black pepper. Transfer the zucchini into the air fryer basket and air-fry for 5 minutes, shaking the basket once or twice during the cooking process.
3. Cut out 2 large rectangles of parchment paper–about 13-inches by 15-inches each. Divide the air-fried zucchini between the two pieces of parchment paper, placing the vegetables in the center of each rectangle.
4. Place a fillet of salmon on each pile of zucchini. Season the fish very well with salt and pepper. Toss the tomato, capers, olives and vermouth (or white wine) together in a bowl. Divide the tomato mixture between the two fish packages, placing it on top of the fish fillets and pouring any juice out of the bowl onto the fish. Top each fillet with a tablespoon of butter.
5. Fold up each parchment square. Bring two edges together and fold them over a few times, leaving some space above the fish. Twist the open sides together and upwards so they can serve as handles for the packet, but don't let them extend beyond the top of the air fryer basket.
6. Place the two packages into the air fryer and air-fry at 400°F for 12 minutes. The packages should be puffed up and slightly browned when fully cooked. Once cooked, let the fish sit in the parchment for 2 minutes.
7. Serve the fish in the parchment paper, or if desired, remove the parchment paper before serving. Garnish with a little fresh basil.

Caribbean Jerk Cod Fillets

Servings: 2
Cooking Time: 20 Minutes
Ingredients:
- ¼ cup chopped cooked shrimp
- ¼ cup diced mango
- 1 tomato, diced
- 2 tbsp diced red onion
- 1 tbsp chopped parsley
- ¼ tsp ginger powder
- 2 tsp lime juice
- Salt and pepper to taste
- 2 cod fillets
- 2 tsp Jerk seasoning

Directions:
1. In a bowl, combine the shrimp, mango, tomato, red onion, parsley, ginger powder, lime juice, salt, and black pepper. Let chill the salsa in the fridge until ready to use.
2. Preheat air fryer to 350ºF. Sprinkle cod fillets with Jerk seasoning. Place them in the greased frying basket and Air Fry for 10 minutes or until the cod is opaque and flakes easily with a fork. Divide between 2 medium plates. Serve topped with the Caribbean salsa.

Blackened Red Snapper

Servings: 4
Cooking Time: 8 Minutes
Ingredients:
- 1½ teaspoons black pepper
- ¼ teaspoon thyme
- ¼ teaspoon garlic powder
- ⅛ teaspoon cayenne pepper
- 1 teaspoon olive oil
- 4 4-ounce red snapper fillet portions, skin on
- 4 thin slices lemon
- cooking spray

Directions:
1. Mix the spices and oil together to make a paste. Rub into both sides of the fish.
2. Spray air fryer basket with nonstick cooking spray and lay snapper steaks in basket, skin-side down.
3. Place a lemon slice on each piece of fish.
4. Cook at 390°F for 8 minutes. The fish will not flake when done, but it should be white through the center.

Yummy Salmon Burgers With Salsa Rosa

Servings: 4
Cooking Time: 35 Minutes + Chilling Time
Ingredients:
- ¼ cup minced red onion
- ¼ cup slivered onions
- ½ cup mayonnaise
- 2 tsp ketchup
- 1 tsp brandy
- 2 tsp orange juice
- 1 lb salmon fillets
- 5 tbsp panko bread crumbs
- 1 garlic clove, minced
- 1 large egg, lightly beaten
- 1 tbsp Dijon mustard
- 1 tsp fresh lemon juice
- 1 tbsp chopped parsley
- Salt to taste
- 4 buns
- 8 Boston lettuce leaves

Directions:
1. Mix the mayonnaise, ketchup, brandy, and orange juice in a bowl until blended. Set aside the resulting salsa rosa until ready to serve. Cut a 4-oz section of salmon and place in a food processor. Pulse until it turns into a paste. Chop the remaining salmon into cubes and transfer to a bowl along with the salmon paste. Add the panko, minced onion, garlic, egg, mustard, lemon juice, parsley, and salt. Toss to combine. Divide into 5 patties about ¾-inch thick. Refrigerate for 30 minutes.
2. Preheat air fryer to 400°F. Place the patties in the greased frying basket. Air Fry for 12-14 minutes, flipping once until golden. Serve each patty on a bun, 2 lettuce leaves, 2 tbsp of salsa rosa, and slivered onions. Enjoy!

Salmon

Servings: 4
Cooking Time: 8 Minutes
Ingredients:
- Marinade
- 3 tablespoons low-sodium soy sauce
- 3 tablespoons rice vinegar
- 3 tablespoons ketchup
- 3 tablespoons olive oil
- 3 tablespoons brown sugar
- 1 teaspoon garlic powder
- ½ teaspoon ground ginger
- 4 salmon fillets (½-inch thick, 3 to 4 ounces each)
- cooking spray

Directions:
1. Mix all marinade ingredients until well blended.
2. Place salmon in sealable plastic bag or shallow container with lid. Pour marinade over fish and turn to coat well. Refrigerate for 30 minutes.
3. Drain marinade, and spray air fryer basket with cooking spray.
4. Place salmon in basket, skin-side down.
5. Cook at 360°F for 10 minutes, watching closely to avoid overcooking. Salmon is done when just beginning to flake and still very moist.

Family Fish Nuggets With Tartar Sauce

Servings: 4
Cooking Time: 30 Minutes
Ingredients:
- ½ cup mayonnaise
- 1 tbsp yellow mustard
- ½ cup diced dill pickles
- Salt and pepper to taste
- 1 egg, beaten
- ¼ cup cornstarch
- ¼ cup flour
- 1 lb cod, cut into sticks

Directions:
1. In a bowl, whisk the mayonnaise, mustard, pickles, salt, and pepper. Set aside the resulting tarter sauce.
2. Preheat air fryer to 350ºF. Add the beaten egg to a bowl. In another bowl, combine cornstarch, flour, salt, and pepper. Dip fish nuggets in the egg and roll them in the flour mixture. Place fish nuggets in the lightly greased frying basket and Air Fry for 10 minutes, flipping once. Serve with the sauce on the side.

Shrimp Patties

Servings: 4
Cooking Time: 10 Minutes
Ingredients:
- ½ pound shelled and deveined raw shrimp
- ¼ cup chopped red bell pepper
- ¼ cup chopped green onion
- ¼ cup chopped celery
- 2 cups cooked sushi rice
- ½ teaspoon garlic powder
- ½ teaspoon Old Bay Seasoning
- ½ teaspoon salt
- 2 teaspoons Worcestershire sauce
- ½ cup plain breadcrumbs
- oil for misting or cooking spray

Directions:
1. Finely chop the shrimp. You can do this in a food processor, but it takes only a few pulses. Be careful not to overprocess into mush.
2. Place shrimp in a large bowl and add all other ingredients except the breadcrumbs and oil. Stir until well combined.
3. Preheat air fryer to 390°F.
4. Shape shrimp mixture into 8 patties, no more than ½-inch thick. Roll patties in breadcrumbs and mist with oil or cooking spray.
5. Place 4 shrimp patties in air fryer basket and cook at 390°F for 10 minutes, until shrimp cooks through and outside is crispy.
6. Repeat step 5 to cook remaining shrimp patties.

Fish Goujons With Tartar Sauce

Servings: 4
Cooking Time: 20 Minutes
Ingredients:
- ¼ cup flour
- Salt and pepper to taste
- ¼ tsp smoked paprika
- ¼ tsp dried oregano
- 1 tsp dried thyme
- 1 egg
- 4 haddock fillets
- 1 lemon, thinly sliced
- ½ cup tartar sauce

Directions:
1. Preheat air fryer to 400°F. Combine flour, salt, pepper, paprika, thyme, and oregano in a wide bowl. Whisk egg and 1 teaspoon water in another wide bowl. Slice each fillet into 4 strips. Dip the strips in the egg mixture. Then roll them in the flour mixture and coat completely. Arrange the fish strips on the greased frying basket. Air Fry for 4 minutes. Flip the fish and Air Fry for another 4 to 5 minutes until crisp. Serve warm with lemon slices and tartar sauce on the side and enjoy.

Easy Scallops With Lemon Butter

Servings: 3
Cooking Time: 4 Minutes
Ingredients:
- 1 tablespoon Olive oil
- 2 teaspoons Minced garlic
- 1 teaspoon Finely grated lemon zest
- ½ teaspoon Red pepper flakes
- ¼ teaspoon Table salt
- 1 pound Sea scallops
- 3 tablespoons Butter, melted
- 1½ tablespoons Lemon juice

Directions:
1. Preheat the air fryer to 400°F.
2. Gently stir the olive oil, garlic, lemon zest, red pepper flakes, and salt in a bowl. Add the scallops and stir very gently until they are evenly and well coated.
3. When the machine is at temperature, arrange the scallops in a single layer in the basket. Some may touch. Air-fry undisturbed for 4 minutes, or until the scallops are opaque and firm.
4. While the scallops cook, stir the melted butter and lemon juice in a serving bowl. When the scallops are ready, pour them from the basket into this bowl. Toss well before serving.

Old Bay Crab Cake Burgers

Servings:4
Cooking Time:30 Minutes
Ingredients:
- ½cup panko bread crumbs
- 1 egg,beaten
- 1 tbsp hummus
- 1 tsp Dijon mustard
- ¼cup minced parsley
- 2 spring onions,chopped
- ½tsp red chili powder
- 1 tbsp lemon juice
- ½tsp Old Bay seasoning
- ⅛tsp sweet paprika
- Salt and pepper to taste
- 10 oz lump crabmeat
- ¼cup mayonnaise
- 2 tbsp minced dill pickle
- 1 tsp fresh lemon juice
- ¾tsp Cajun seasoning
- 4 Boston lettuce leaves
- 4 buns,split

Directions:
1. Mix the crumbs,egg,hummus,mustard,parsley,lemon juice,red chili,spring onions,Old Bay seasoning,paprika,salt,and pepper in a large bowl.Fold in crabmeat until just coated without overmixing.Divide into 4 equal parts,about ½cup each,and shape into patties,about ¾-inch thick.Preheat air fryer to 400°F.
2. Place the cakes in the greased frying basket and Air Fry for 10 minutes,flipping them once until the edges are golden.Meanwhile,mix mayonnaise,lemon juice and Cajun seasoning in a small bowl until well blended.Set aside.When you are ready to serve,start with the bottom of the bun.Add a lettuce leaf,then a crab cake.Top with a heaping tbsp of Cajun mayo,minced pickles,and top with the bun and enjoy.

Saucy Shrimp

Servings:4
Cooking Time:30 Minutes
Ingredients:
- 1 lb peeled shrimp,deveined
- ½cup grated coconut
- ¼cup bread crumbs
- ¼cup flour
- ¼tsp smoked paprika
- Salt and pepper to taste
- 1 egg
- 2 tbsp maple syrup
- ½tsp rice vinegar
- 1 tbsp hot sauce
- ⅛tsp red pepper flakes
- ¼cup orange juice
- 1 tsp cornstarch
- ½cup banana ketchup
- 1 lemon,sliced

Directions:
1. Preheat air fryer to 350°F.Combine coconut,bread crumbs,flour,paprika,black pepper,and salt in a bowl.In a separate bowl,whisk egg and 1 teaspoon water.Dip one shrimp into the egg bowl and shake off excess drips.Dip the shrimp in the bread crumb mixture and coat it completely.Continue the process for all of the shrimp.Arrange the shrimp on the greased frying basket.Air Fry for 5 minutes,then use tongs to flip the shrimp.Cook for another 2-3 minutes.
2. To make the sauce,add maple syrup,banana ketchup,hot sauce,vinegar,and red pepper flakes in a small saucepan over medium heat.Make a slurry in a small bowl with orange juice and cornstarch.Stir in slurry and continue stirring.Bring the sauce to a boil and cook for 5 minutes.When the sauce begins to thicken,remove from heat and allow to sit for 5 minutes.Serve shrimp warm along with sauce and lemon slices on the side.

Shrimp,Chorizo And Fingerling Potatoes

Servings:4
Cooking Time:16 Minutes
Ingredients:
- ½red onion,chopped into 1-inch chunks
- 8 fingerling potatoes,sliced into 1-inch slices or halved lengthwise
- 1 teaspoon olive oil
- salt and freshly ground black pepper
- 8 ounces raw chorizo sausage,sliced into 1-inch chunks
- 16 raw large shrimp,peeled,deveined and tails removed
- 1 lime
- ¼cup chopped fresh cilantro
- chopped orange zest(optional)

Directions:
1. Preheat the air fryer to 380°F.
2. Combine the red onion and potato chunks in a bowl and toss with the olive oil,salt and freshly ground black pepper.
3. Transfer the vegetables to the air fryer basket and air-fry for 6 minutes,shaking the basket a few times during the cooking process.
4. Add the chorizo chunks and continue to air-fry for another 5 minutes.
5. Add the shrimp,season with salt and continue to air-fry,shaking the basket every once in a while,for another 5 minutes.
6. Transfer the tossed shrimp,chorizo and potato to a bowl and squeeze some lime juice over the top to taste.Toss in the fresh cilantro,orange zest and a drizzle of olive oil,and season again to taste.
7. Serve with a fresh green salad.

Nutty Shrimp With Amaretto Glaze

Servings:10
Cooking Time:10 Minutes
Ingredients:
- 1 cup flour
- ½teaspoon baking powder
- 1 teaspoon salt
- 2 eggs,beaten
- ½cup milk
- 2 tablespoons olive or vegetable oil
- 2 cups sliced almonds
- 2 pounds large shrimp(about 32 to 40 shrimp),peeled and deveined,tails left on
- 2 cups amaretto liqueur

Directions:
1. Combine the flour,baking powder and salt in a large bowl.Add the eggs,milk and oil and stir until it forms a smooth batter.Coarsely crush the sliced almonds into a second shallow dish with your hands.
2. Dry the shrimp well with paper towels.Dip the shrimp into the batter and shake off any excess batter,leaving just enough to lightly coat the shrimp.Transfer the shrimp to the dish with the almonds and coat completely.Place the coated shrimp on a plate

or baking sheet and when all the shrimp have been coated,freeze the shrimp for an 1 hour,or as long as a week before air-frying.
3. Preheat the air fryer to 400°F.
4. Transfer 8 frozen shrimp at a time to the air fryer basket.Air-fry for 6 minutes.Turn the shrimp over and air-fry for an additional 4 minutes.Repeat with the remaining shrimp.
5. While the shrimp are cooking,bring the Amaretto to a boil in a small saucepan on the stovetop.Lower the heat and simmer until it has reduced and thickened into a glaze–about 10 minutes.
6. Remove the shrimp from the air fryer and brush both sides with the warm amaretto glaze.Serve warm.

Shrimp Al Pesto

Servings:4
Cooking Time:10 Minutes
Ingredients:
- 1 lb peeled shrimp,deveined
- ¼cup pesto sauce
- 1 lime,sliced
- 2 cups cooked farro

Directions:
1. Preheat air fryer to 360°F.Coat the shrimp with the pesto sauce in a bowl.Put the shrimp in a single layer in the frying basket.Put the lime slices over the shrimp and Roast for 5 minutes.Remove lime and discard.Serve the shrimp over a bed of farro pilaf.Enjoy!

Fish Cakes

Servings:4
Cooking Time:10 Minutes
Ingredients:
- ¾cup mashed potatoes(about 1 large russet potato)
- 12 ounces cod or other white fish
- salt and pepper
- oil for misting or cooking spray
- 1 large egg
- ¼cup potato starch
- ½cup panko breadcrumbs
- 1 tablespoon fresh chopped chives
- 2 tablespoons minced onion

Directions:
1. Peel potatoes,cut into cubes,and cook on stovetop till soft.
2. Salt and pepper raw fish to taste.Mist with oil or cooking spray,and cook in air fryer at 360°F for 6 to 8minutes,until fish flakes easily.If fish is crowded,rearrange halfway through cooking to ensure all pieces cook evenly.
3. Transfer fish to a plate and break apart to cool.
4. Beat egg in a shallow dish.
5. Place potato starch in another shallow dish,and panko crumbs in a third dish.
6. When potatoes are done,drain in colander and rinse with cold water.
7. In a large bowl,mash the potatoes and stir in the chives and onion.Add salt and pepper to taste,then stir in the fish.
8. If needed,stir in a tablespoon of the beaten egg to help bind the mixture.
9. Shape into 8 small,fat patties.Dust lightly with potato starch,dip in egg,and roll in panko crumbs.Spray both sides with oil or cooking spray.
10. Cook at 360°F for 10 minutes,until golden brown and crispy.

Butternut Squash - wrapped Halibut Fillets

Servings:3
Cooking Time:11 Minutes
Ingredients:
- 15 Long spiralized peeled and seeded butternut squash strands
- 3 5-to 6-ounce skinless halibut fillets
- 3 tablespoons Butter,melted
- ¾teaspoon Mild paprika
- ¾teaspoon Table salt
- ¾teaspoon Ground black pepper

Directions:
1. Preheat the air fryer to 375°F.
2. Hold 5 long butternut squash strands together and wrap them around a fillet.Set it aside and wrap any remaining fillet(s).
3. Mix the melted butter,paprika,salt,and pepper in a small bowl.Brush this mixture over the squash-wrapped fillets on all sides.
4. When the machine is at temperature,set the fillets in the basket with as much air space between them as possible.Air-fry undisturbed for 10 minutes,or until the squash strands have browned but not burned.If the machine is at 360°F,you may need to add 1 minute to the cooking time.In any event,watch the fish carefully after the 8-minute mark.
5. Use a nonstick-safe spatula to gently transfer the fillets to a serving platter or plates.Cool for only a minute or so before serving.

Quick Tuna Tacos

Servings:4
Cooking Time:20 Minutes
Ingredients:
- 2 cups torn romaine lettuce
- 1 lb fresh tuna steak,cubed
- 1 tbsp grated fresh ginger
- 2 garlic cloves,minced
- ½tsp toasted sesame oil
- 4 tortillas
- ¼cup mild salsa
- 1 red bell pepper,sliced

Directions:
1. Preheat air fryer to 390°F.Combine the tuna,ginger,garlic,and sesame oil in a bowl and allow to marinate for 10 minutes.Lay the marinated tuna in the fryer and Grill for 4-7 minutes.Serve right away with tortillas,mild salsa,lettuce,and bell pepper for delicious tacos.

Lemon&Herb Crusted Salmon

Servings:4
Cooking Time:20 Minutes
Ingredients:
- 1/3 cup crushed potato chips
- 4 skinless salmon fillets
- 3 tbsp honey mustard
- ½tsp lemon zest
- ½tsp dried thyme
- ½tsp dried basil
- ¼cup panko bread crumbs
- 2 tbsp olive oil

Directions:
1. Preheat air fryer to 320°F.Place the salmon on a work surface.Mix together mustard,lemon zest,thyme,and basil in a small bowl.Spread on top of the salmon evenly.In a separate small bowl,mix together bread crumbs and potato chips before drizzling with olive oil.Place the salmon in the frying basket.Bake until the salmon is cooked through and the topping is crispy and brown,about 10 minutes.Serve hot and enjoy!

Korean-style Fried Calamari

Servings: 4
Cooking Time: 25 Minutes
Ingredients:
- 2 tbsp tomato paste
- 1 tbsp gochujang
- 1 tbsp lime juice
- 1 tsp lime zest
- 1 tsp smoked paprika
- ½ tsp salt
- 1 cup bread crumbs
- 1/3 lb calamari rings

Directions:
1. Preheat air fryer to 400ºF. Whisk tomato paste, gochujang, lime juice and zest, paprika, and salt in a bowl. In another bowl, add in the bread crumbs. Dredge calamari rings in the tomato mixture, shake off excess, then roll through the crumbs. Place calamari rings in the greased frying basket and Air Fry for 4-5 minutes, flipping once. Serve.

Horseradish-crusted Salmon Fillets

Servings: 3
Cooking Time: 8 Minutes
Ingredients:
- ½ cup Fresh bread crumbs (see the headnote)
- 4 tablespoons (¼ cup/½ stick) Butter, melted and cooled
- ¼ cup Jarred prepared white horseradish
- Vegetable oil spray
- 4 6-ounce skin-on salmon fillets (for more information, see here)

Directions:
1. Preheat the air fryer to 400°F.
2. Mix the bread crumbs, butter, and horseradish in a bowl until well combined.
3. Take the basket out of the machine. Generously spray the skin side of each fillet. Pick them up one by one with a nonstick-safe spatula and set them in the basket skin side down with as much air space between them as possible. Divide the bread-crumb mixture between the fillets, coating the top of each fillet with an even layer. Generously coat the bread-crumb mixture with vegetable oil spray.
4. Return the basket to the machine and air-fry undisturbed for 8 minutes, or until the topping has lightly browned and the fish is firm but not hard.
5. Use a nonstick-safe spatula to transfer the salmon fillets to serving plates. Cool for 5 minutes before serving. Because of the butter in the topping, it will stay very hot for quite a while. Take care, especially if you're serving these fillets to children.

Poultry Recipes

Crispy Cordon Bleu

Servings: 4
Cooking Time: 25 Minutes
Ingredients:
- 4 deli ham slices, halved lengthwise
- 2 tbsp grated Parmesan
- 4 chicken breast halves
- Salt and pepper to taste
- 8 Swiss cheese slices
- 1 egg
- 2 egg whites
- ¾ cup bread crumbs
- 1 tsp garlic powder
- 1 tsp onion powder
- 1 tsp mustard powder

Directions:
1. Preheat air fryer to 400°F. Season the chicken cutlets with salt and pepper. On one cutlet, put a half slice of ham and cheese on the top. Roll the chicken tightly, then set aside. Beat the eggs and egg whites in a shallow bowl. Put the crumbs, Parmesan, garlic, onion, and mustard powder, in a second bowl. Dip the cutlet in the egg bowl and then in the crumb mix. Press so that they stick to the chicken. Put the rolls of chicken seam side down in the greased frying basket and Air Fry for 12-14 minutes, flipping once until golden and cooked through. Serve.

Smoky Chicken Fajita Bowl

Servings: 4
Cooking Time: 35 Minutes + Chilling Time
Ingredients:
- 1 jalapeño, sliced and seeded
- ½ cup queso fresco crumbles
- 1 tbsp olive oil
- 2 tsp flour
- ¼ tsp chili powder
- ¼ tsp fajita seasoning
- ¼ tsp smoked paprika
- ¼ tsp ground cumin
- ½ tsp granular honey
- ⅛ tsp onion powder
- ⅛ tsp garlic powder
- 1 lb chicken breast strips
- 4 tomatoes, diced
- ½ diced red onion
- 4 tbsp sour cream
- 1 avocado, diced

Directions:
1. Combine the olive oil, flour, all the spices, and chicken strips in a bowl. Let chill in the fridge for 30 minutes.
2. Preheat air fryer to 400ºF. Place the chicken strips in the frying basket and Air Fry for 8 minutes, shaking once. Divide between 4 medium bowls. Add tomatoes, jalapeño, onion, queso fresco, sour cream, and avocado to the bowls. Serve right away.

Asian-style Orange Chicken

Servings: 4
Cooking Time: 25 Minutes
Ingredients:
- 1 lb chicken breasts, cubed
- Salt and pepper to taste
- 6 tbsp cornstarch
- 1 cup orange juice
- ¼ cup orange marmalade
- ¼ cup ketchup
- ½ tsp ground ginger
- 2 tbsp soy sauce
- 1 1/3 cups edamame beans

Directions:
1. Preheat the air fryer to 375°F. Sprinkle the cubes with salt and pepper. Coat with 4 tbsp of cornstarch and set aside on a wire rack. Mix the orange juice, marmalade, ketchup, ginger, soy sauce, and the remaining cornstarch in a cake pan, then stir in the beans. Set the pan in the frying basket and Bake for 5-8 minutes, stirring once during cooking until the sauce is thick and bubbling. Remove from the fryer and set aside. Put the chicken in the frying basket and fry for 10-12 minutes, shaking the basket once. Stir the chicken into the sauce and beans in the pan. Return to the fryer and reheat for 2 minutes.

Super-simple Herby Turkey

Servings: 4
Cooking Time: 35 Minutes
Ingredients:
- 2 turkey tenderloins
- 2 tbsp olive oil
- Salt and pepper to taste
- 2 tbsp minced rosemary
- 1 tbsp minced thyme
- 1 tbsp minced sage

Directions:
1. Preheat the air fryer to 350°F. Brush the tenderloins with olive oil and sprinkle with salt and pepper. Mix rosemary, thyme, and sage, then rub the seasoning onto the meat. Put the tenderloins in the frying basket and Bake for 22-27 minutes, flipping once until cooked through. Lay the turkey on a serving plate, cover with foil, and let stand for 5 minutes. Slice before serving.

Asian Meatball Tacos

Servings: 4
Cooking Time: 10 Minutes
Ingredients:
- 1 pound lean ground turkey
- 3 tablespoons soy sauce
- 1 tablespoon brown sugar
- ½ teaspoon onion powder
- ½ teaspoon garlic powder
- 1 tablespoon sesame seeds
- 1 English cucumber
- 4 radishes
- 2 tablespoons white wine vinegar
- 1 lime, juiced and divided
- 1 tablespoon avocado oil
- Salt, to taste
- ½ cup Greek yogurt
- 1 to 3 teaspoons Sriracha, based on desired spiciness
- 1 cup shredded cabbage
- ¼ cup chopped cilantro
- Eight 6-inch flour tortillas

Directions:
1. Preheat the air fryer to 360°F.
2. In a large bowl, mix the ground turkey, soy sauce, brown sugar, onion powder, garlic powder, and sesame seeds. Form the meat into 1-inch meatballs and place in the air fryer

basket.Cook for 5 minutes,shake the basket,and cook another 5 minutes.Using a food thermometer,make sure the internal temperature of the meatballs is 165°F.
3. Meanwhile,dice the cucumber and radishes and place in a medium bowl.Add the white wine vinegar,1 teaspoon of the lime juice,and the avocado oil,and stir to coat.Season with salt to desired taste.
4. In a large bowl,mix the Greek yogurt,Sriracha,and the remaining lime juice,and stir.Add in the cabbage and cilantro;toss well to create a slaw.
5. In a heavy skillet,heat the tortillas over medium heat for 1 to 2 minutes on each side,or until warmed.
6. To serve,place a tortilla on a plate,top with 5 meatballs,then with cucumber and radish salad,and finish with 2 tablespoons of cabbage slaw.

Buttered Turkey Breasts

Servings:6
Cooking Time:65 Minutes
Ingredients:
- ½cup butter,melted
- 6 garlic cloves,minced
- 1 tsp dried oregano
- ½tsp dried thyme
- ½tsp dried rosemary
- Salt and pepper to taste
- 4 lb bone-in turkey breast
- 1 tbsp chopped cilantro

Directions:
1. Preheat air fryer to 350°F.Combine butter,garlic,oregano,salt,and pepper in a small bowl.Place the turkey breast on a plate and coat the entire turkey with the butter mixture.Put the turkey breast-side down in the frying basket and scatter with thyme and rosemary.Bake for 20 minutes.Flip the turkey so that the breast side is up,then bake for another 20-30 minutes until it has an internal temperature of 165°F.Allow to rest for 10 minutes before carving.Serve sprinkled with cilantro.

Simple Salsa Chicken Thighs

Servings:2
Cooking Time:35 Minutes
Ingredients:
- 1 lb boneless,skinless chicken thighs
- 1 cup mild chunky salsa
- ½tsp taco seasoning
- 2 lime wedges for serving

Directions:
1. Preheat air fryer to 350ºF.Add chicken thighs into a baking pan and pour salsa and taco seasoning over.Place the pan in the frying basket and Air Fry for 30 minutes until golden brown.Serve with lime wedges.

Indian-inspired Chicken Skewers

Servings:4
Cooking Time:40 Minutes+Chilling Time
Ingredients:
- 1 lb boneless,skinless chicken thighs,cubed
- 1 red onion,diced
- 1 tbsp grated ginger
- 2 tbsp lime juice
- 1 cup canned coconut milk
- 2 tbsp tomato paste
- 2 tbsp olive oil
- 1 tbsp ground cumin
- 1 tbsp ground coriander
- 1 tsp cayenne pepper
- 1 tsp ground turmeric
- ½tsp red chili powder
- ¼tsp curry powder
- 2 tsp salt
- 2 tbsp chopped cilantro

Directions:
1. Toss red onion,ginger,lime juice,coconut milk,tomato paste,olive oil,cumin,coriander,cayenne pepper,turmeric,chili powder,curry powder,salt,and chicken until fully coated.Let chill in the fridge for 2 hours.
2. Preheat air fryer to 350ºF.Thread chicken onto 8 skewers and place them on a kebab rack.Place rack in the frying basket and Air Fry for 12 minutes.Discard marinade.Garnish with cilantro to serve.

Popcorn Chicken Tenders With Vegetables

Servings:4
Cooking Time:30 Minutes
Ingredients:
- 2 tbsp cooked popcorn,ground
- Salt and pepper to taste
- 1 lb chicken tenders
- ½cup bread crumbs
- ½tsp dried thyme
- 1 tbsp olive oil
- 2 carrots,sliced
- 12 baby potatoes

Directions:
1. Preheat air fryer to 380°F.Season the chicken tenders with salt and pepper.In a shallow bowl,mix the crumbs,popcorn,thyme,and olive oil until combined.Coat the chicken with mixture.Press firmly,so the crumbs adhere.Arrange the carrots and baby potatoes in the greased frying basket and top them with the chicken tenders.Bake for 9-10 minutes.Shake the basket and continue cooking for another 9-10 minutes,until the vegetables are tender.Serve and enjoy!

Satay Chicken Skewers

Servings:4
Cooking Time:35 Minutes
Ingredients:
- 2 chicken breasts,cut into strips
- 1½tbsp Thai red curry paste
- ¼cup peanut butter
- 1 tbsp maple syrup
- 1 tbsp tamari
- 1 tbsp lime juice
- 2 tsp chopped onions
- ¼tsp minced ginger
- 1 clove garlic,minced
- 1 cup coconut milk
- 1 tsp fish sauce
- 1 tbsp chopped cilantro

Directions:
1. Mix the peanut butter,maple syrup,tamari,lime juice,¼tsp of sriracha,onions,ginger,garlic,and 2 tbsp of water in a bowl.Reserve 1 tbsp of the sauce.Set aside.Combine the reserved peanut sauce,fish sauce,coconut milk,Thai red curry paste,cilantro and chicken strips in a bowl and let marinate in the fridge for 15 minutes.
2. Preheat air fryer at 350ºF.Thread chicken strips onto skewers and place them on a kebab rack.Place rack in the frying basket and Air Fry for 12 minutes.Serve with previously prepared peanut sauce on the side.

Maple Bacon Wrapped Chicken Breasts

Servings: 2
Cooking Time: 18 Minutes
Ingredients:
- 2 (6-ounce) boneless, skinless chicken breasts
- 2 tablespoons maple syrup, divided
- freshly ground black pepper
- 6 slices thick-sliced bacon
- fresh celery or parsley leaves
- Ranch Dressing:
- ¼ cup mayonnaise
- ¼ cup buttermilk
- ¼ cup Greek yogurt
- 1 tablespoon chopped fresh chives
- 1 tablespoon chopped fresh parsley
- 1 tablespoon chopped fresh dill
- 1 tablespoon lemon juice
- salt and freshly ground black pepper

Directions:
1. Brush the chicken breasts with half the maple syrup and season with freshly ground black pepper. Wrap three slices of bacon around each chicken breast, securing the ends with toothpicks.
2. Preheat the air fryer to 380°F.
3. Air-fry the chicken for 6 minutes. Then turn the chicken breasts over, pour more maple syrup on top and air-fry for another 6 minutes. Turn the chicken breasts one more time, brush the remaining maple syrup all over and continue to air-fry for a final 6 minutes.
4. While the chicken is cooking, prepare the dressing by combining all the dressing ingredients together in a bowl.
5. When the chicken has finished cooking, remove the toothpicks and serve each breast with a little dressing drizzled over each one. Scatter lots of fresh celery or parsley leaves on top.

Turkey & Rice Frittata

Servings: 4
Cooking Time: 30 Minutes
Ingredients:
- 6 large eggs
- ½ tsp dried thyme
- ½ cup rice, cooked
- ½ cup pulled turkey, cooked
- ½ cup fresh baby spinach
- 1 red bell pepper, chopped
- 2 tsp Parmesan cheese, grated

Directions:
1. Preheat air fryer to 320°F. Put the rice, turkey, spinach, and red bell pepper in a greased pan. Whisk the eggs, and thyme, then pour over the rice mix. Top with Parmesan cheese and Bake for 15 minutes, until the frittata is puffy and golden. Serve hot and enjoy!

Mushroom & Turkey Bread Pizza

Servings: 4
Cooking Time: 35 Minutes
Ingredients:
- 10 cooked turkey sausages, sliced
- 1 cup shredded mozzarella cheese
- 1 cup shredded Cheddar cheese
- 1 French loaf bread
- 2 tbsp butter, softened
- 1 tsp garlic powder
- 1 1/3 cups marinara sauce
- 1 tsp Italian seasoning
- 2 scallions, chopped
- 1 cup mushrooms, sliced

Directions:
1. Preheat the air fryer to 370°F. Cut the bread in half crosswise, then split each half horizontally. Combine butter and garlic powder, then spread on the cut sides of the bread. Bake the halves in the fryer for 3-5 minutes or until the leaves start to brown. Set the toasted bread on a work surface and spread marinara sauce over the top. Sprinkle the Italian seasoning, then top with sausages, scallions, mushrooms, and cheeses. Set the pizzas in the air fryer and Bake for 8-12 minutes or until the cheese is melted and starting to brown. Serve hot.

Chicken Pinchos Morunos

Servings: 4
Cooking Time: 35 Minutes
Ingredients:
- 1 yellow summer squash, sliced
- 3 chicken breasts
- ¼ cup plain yogurt
- 2 tbsp olive oil
- 1 tsp sweet pimentón
- 1 tsp dried thyme
- ½ tsp sea salt
- ½ tsp garlic powder
- ½ tsp ground cumin
- 2 red bell peppers
- 3 scallions
- 16 large green olives

Directions:
1. Preheat the air fryer to 400°F. Combine yogurt, olive oil, pimentón, thyme, cumin, salt, and garlic in a bowl and add the chicken. Stir to coat. Cut the bell peppers and scallions into 1-inch pieces. Remove the chicken from the marinade; set aside the rest of the marinade. Thread the chicken, peppers, scallions, squash, and olives onto the soaked skewers. Brush the kebabs with marinade. Discard any remaining marinade. Lay the kebabs in the frying basket. Add a raised rack and put the rest of the kebabs on it. Bake for 18-23 minutes, flipping once around minute 10. Serve hot.

Italian Roasted Chicken Thighs

Servings: 6
Cooking Time: 14 Minutes
Ingredients:
- 6 boneless chicken thighs
- ½ teaspoon dried oregano
- ½ teaspoon garlic powder
- ½ teaspoon sea salt
- ½ teaspoon black pepper
- ¼ teaspoon crushed red pepper flakes

Directions:
1. Pat the chicken thighs with paper towel.
2. In a small bowl, mix the oregano, garlic powder, salt, pepper, and crushed red pepper flakes. Rub the spice mixture onto the chicken thighs.
3. Preheat the air fryer to 400°F.
4. Place the chicken thighs in the air fryer basket and spray with cooking spray. Cook for 10 minutes, turn over, and cook another 4 minutes. When cooking completes, the internal temperature should read 165°F.

Sunday Chicken Skewers

Servings: 4
Cooking Time: 25 Minutes
Ingredients:
- 1 green bell pepper, cut into chunks
- 1 red bell pepper, cut into chunks
- 4 chicken breasts, cubed
- 1 tbsp chicken seasoning
- Salt and pepper to taste
- 16 cherry tomatoes
- 8 pearl onions, peeled

Directions:
1. Preheat air fryer to 360°F. Season the cubes with chicken seasoning, salt, and pepper. Thread metal skewers with chicken, bell pepper chunks, cherry tomatoes, and pearl onions. Put the kabobs in the greased frying basket. Bake for 14-16 minutes, flipping once until cooked through. Let cool slightly. Serve.

Buttery Chicken Legs

Servings: 4
Cooking Time: 50 Minutes
Ingredients:
- 1 tsp baking powder
- 1 tsp dried mustard
- 1 tsp smoked paprika
- 1 tsp garlic powder
- 1 tsp dried thyme
- Salt and pepper to taste
- 1½ lb chicken legs
- 3 tbsp butter, melted

Directions:
1. Preheat air fryer to 370°F. Combine all ingredients, except for butter, in a bowl until coated. Place the chicken legs in the greased frying basket. Air Fry for 18 minutes, flipping once and brushing with melted butter on both sides. Let chill onto a serving plate for 5 minutes before serving.

Cornflake Chicken Nuggets

Servings: 4
Cooking Time: 25 Minutes
Ingredients:
- 1 egg white
- 1 tbsp lemon juice
- ½ tsp dried basil
- ½ tsp ground paprika
- 1 lb chicken breast fingers
- ½ cup ground cornflakes
- 2 slices bread, crumbled

Directions:
1. Preheat air fryer to 400°F. Whisk the egg white, lemon juice, basil, and paprika, then add the chicken and stir. Combine the cornflakes and breadcrumbs on a plate, then put the chicken fingers in the mix to coat. Put the nuggets in the frying basket and Air Fry for 10-13 minutes, turning halfway through, until golden, crisp and cooked through. Serve hot!

Crispy Chicken Parmesan

Servings: 4
Cooking Time: 12 Minutes
Ingredients:
- 4 skinless, boneless chicken breasts, pounded thin to ¼-inch thickness
- 1 teaspoon salt, divided
- ½ teaspoon black pepper, divided
- 1 cup flour
- 2 eggs
- 1 cup panko breadcrumbs
- ½ teaspoon dried oregano
- ½ cup grated Parmesan cheese

Directions:
1. Pat the chicken breasts with a paper towel. Season the chicken with ½ teaspoon of the salt and ¼ teaspoon of the pepper.
2. In a medium bowl, place the flour.
3. In a second bowl, whisk the eggs.
4. In a third bowl, place the breadcrumbs, oregano, cheese, and the remaining ½ teaspoon of salt and ¼ teaspoon of pepper.
5. Dredge the chicken in the flour and shake off the excess. Dip the chicken into the eggs and then into the breadcrumbs. Set the chicken on a plate and repeat with the remaining chicken pieces.
6. Preheat the air fryer to 360°F.
7. Place the chicken in the air fryer basket and spray liberally with cooking spray. Cook for 8 minutes, turn the chicken breasts over, and cook another 4 minutes. When golden brown, check for an internal temperature of 165°F.

Katsu Chicken Thighs

Servings: 4
Cooking Time: 35 Minutes
Ingredients:
- 1½ lb boneless, skinless chicken thighs
- 3 tbsp tamari sauce
- 3 tbsp lemon juice
- ½ tsp ground ginger
- Black pepper to taste
- 6 tbsp cornstarch
- 1 cup chicken stock
- 2 tbsp hoisin sauce
- 2 tbsp light brown sugar
- 2 tbsp sesame seeds

Directions:
1. Preheat the air fryer to 400°F. After cubing the chicken thighs, put them in a cake pan. Add a tbsp of tamari sauce, a tbsp of lemon juice, ginger, and black pepper. Mix and let marinate for 10 minutes. Remove the chicken and coat it in 4 tbsp of cornstarch; set aside. Add the rest of the marinade to the pan and add the stock, hoisin sauce, brown sugar, and the remaining tamari sauce, lemon juice, and cornstarch. Mix well. Put the pan in the frying basket and Air Fry for 5-8 minutes or until bubbling and thick, stirring once. Remove and set aside. Put the chicken in the frying basket and Fry for 15-18 minutes, shaking the basket once. Remove the chicken to the sauce in the pan and return to the fryer to reheat for 2 minutes. Sprinkle with the sesame seeds and serve.

Cajun Fried Chicken

Servings: 3
Cooking Time: 35 Minutes
Ingredients:
- 1 cup Cajun seasoning
- ½ tsp mango powder
- 6 chicken legs, bone-in

Directions:
1. Preheat air fryer to 360°F. Place half of the Cajun seasoning and 3/4 cup of water in a bowl and mix well to dissolve any lumps. Add the remaining Cajun seasoning and mango powder to a shallow bowl and stir to combine. Dip the chicken in the batter, then coat it in the mango seasoning. Lightly spritz the chicken with cooking spray. Place the chicken in the air fryer and Air Fry for 14-16 minutes, turning once until the chicken is cooked and the coating is brown. Serve and enjoy!

Mustardy Chicken Bites

Servings:4
Cooking Time:20 Minutes+Chilling Time
Ingredients:
- 2 tbsp horseradish mustard
- 1 tbsp mayonnaise
- 1 tbsp olive oil
- 2 chicken breasts,cubes
- 1 tbsp parsley

Directions:
1. Combine all ingredients,excluding parsley,in a bowl.Let marinate covered in the fridge for 30 minutes.Preheat air fryer at 350ºF.Place chicken cubes in the greased frying basket and Air Fry for 9 minutes,tossing once.Serve immediately sprinkled with parsley.

Lemon Sage Roast Chicken

Servings:4
Cooking Time:60 Minutes
Ingredients:
- 1(4-pound)chicken
- 1 bunch sage,divided
- 1 lemon,zest and juice
- salt and freshly ground black pepper

Directions:
1. Preheat the air fryer to 350°F and pour a little water into the bottom of the air fryer drawer.(This will help prevent the grease that drips into the bottom drawer from burning and smoking.)
2. Run your fingers between the skin and flesh of the chicken breasts and thighs.Push a couple of sage leaves up underneath the skin of the chicken on each breast and each thigh.
3. Push some of the lemon zest up under the skin of the chicken next to the sage.Sprinkle some of the zest inside the chicken cavity,and reserve any leftover zest.Squeeze the lemon juice all over the chicken and in the cavity as well.
4. Season the chicken,inside and out,with the salt and freshly ground black pepper.Set a few sage leaves aside for the final garnish.Crumple up the remaining sage leaves and push them into the cavity of the chicken,along with one of the squeezed lemon halves.
5. Place the chicken breast side up into the air fryer basket and air-fry for 20 minutes at 350°F.Flip the chicken over so that it is breast side down and continue to air-fry for another 20 minutes.Return the chicken to breast side up and finish air-frying for 20 more minutes.The internal temperature of the chicken should register 165°F in the thickest part of the thigh when fully cooked.Remove the chicken from the air fryer and let it rest on a cutting board for at least 5 minutes.
6. Cut the rested chicken into pieces,sprinkle with the reserved lemon zest and garnish with the reserved sage leaves.

Gluten-free Nutty Chicken Fingers

Servings:4
Cooking Time:10 Minutes
Ingredients:
- ½cup gluten-free flour
- ½teaspoon garlic powder
- ¼teaspoon onion powder
- ¼teaspoon black pepper
- ¼teaspoon salt
- 1 cup walnuts,pulsed into coarse flour
- ½cup gluten-free breadcrumbs
- 2 large eggs
- 1 pound boneless,skinless chicken tenders

Directions:
1. Preheat the air fryer to 400°F.
2. In a medium bowl,mix the flour,garlic,onion,pepper,and salt.Set aside.
3. In a separate bowl,mix the walnut flour and breadcrumbs.
4. In a third bowl,whisk the eggs.
5. Liberally spray the air fryer basket with olive oil spray.
6. Pat the chicken tenders dry with a paper towel.Dredge the tenders one at a time in the flour,then dip them in the egg,and toss them in the breadcrumb coating.Repeat until all tenders are coated.
7. Set each tender in the air fryer,leaving room on each side of the tender to allow for flipping.
8. When the basket is full,cook 5 minutes,flip,and cook another 5 minutes.Check the internal temperature after cooking completes;it should read 165°F.If it does not,cook another 2 to 4 minutes.
9. Remove the tenders and let cool 5 minutes before serving.Repeat until all the tenders are cooked.

Teriyaki Chicken Legs

Servings:2
Cooking Time:20 Minutes
Ingredients:
- 4 tablespoons teriyaki sauce
- 1 tablespoon orange juice
- 1 teaspoon smoked paprika
- 4 chicken legs
- cooking spray

Directions:
1. Mix together the teriyaki sauce,orange juice,and smoked paprika.Brush on all sides of chicken legs.
2. Spray air fryer basket with nonstick cooking spray and place chicken in basket.
3. Cook at 360°F for 6minutes.Turn and baste with sauce.Cook for 6 moreminutes,turn and baste.Cook for 8 minutes more,until juices run clear when chicken is pierced with a fork.

Boss Chicken Cobb Salad

Servings:2
Cooking Time:30 Minutes
Ingredients:
- 4 oz cooked bacon,crumbled
- ¼cup diced peeled red onion
- ½cup crumbled blue cheese
- 1 egg
- 1 tbsp honey
- 1 tbsp Dijon mustard
- ½tsp apple cider vinegar
- 2 chicken breasts,cubed
- 3/4 cup bread crumbs
- Salt and pepper to taste
- 3 cups torn iceberg lettuce
- 2 cups baby spinach
- ½cup ranch dressing
- ½avocado,diced
- 1 beefsteak tomato,diced
- 1 hard-boiled egg,diced
- 2 tbsp parsley

Directions:
1. Preheat air fryer at 350ºF.Mix the egg,honey,mustard,and vinegar in a bowl.Toss in chicken cubes to coat.Shake off excess marinade of chicken.In another bowl,combine breadcrumbs,salt,and pepper.Dredge chicken cubes in the mixture.Place chicken cubes in the greased frying basket.Air Fry for 8-10 minutes,tossing once.In a salad bowl,combine lettuce,baby spinach,and ranch dressing and toss to coat.Add in the cooked chicken and the remaining ingredients.Serve immediately.

Vip's Club Sandwiches

Servings: 4
Cooking Time: 50 Minutes
Ingredients:
- 1 cup buttermilk
- 1 egg
- 1 cup bread crumbs
- 1 tsp garlic powder
- Salt and pepper to taste
- 4 chicken cutlets
- 3 tbsp butter, melted
- 4 hamburger buns
- 4 tbsp mayonnaise
- 4 tsp yellow mustard
- 8 dill pickle chips
- 4 pieces iceberg lettuce
- ½ sliced avocado
- 4 slices cooked bacon
- 8 vine-ripe tomato slices
- 1 tsp chia seeds

Directions:
1. Preheat air fryer at 400°F. Beat the buttermilk and egg in a bowl. In another bowl, combine breadcrumbs, garlic powder, salt, and black pepper. Dip chicken cutlets in the egg mixture, then dredge them in the breadcrumbs mixture. Brush chicken cutlets lightly with melted butter on both sides, place them in the greased frying basket, and Air Fry for 18-20 minutes. Spread the mayonnaise on the top buns and mustard on the bottom buns. Add chicken onto bottom buns and top with pickles, lettuce, chia seeds, avocado, bacon, and tomato. Cover with the top buns. Serve and enjoy!

Masala Chicken With Charred Vegetables

Servings: 4
Cooking Time: 35 Minutes
Ingredients:
- 8 boneless, skinless chicken thighs
- ¼ cup yogurt
- 3 garlic cloves, minced
- 1 tbsp lime juice
- 1 tsp ginger-garlic paste
- 1 tsp garam masala
- ¼ tsp ground turmeric
- ¼ tsp red pepper flakes
- 1¼ tsp salt
- 7 oz shishito peppers
- 2 vine tomatoes, quartered
- 1 tbsp chopped cilantro
- 1 lime, cut into wedges

Directions:
1. Mix yogurt, garlic, lime juice, ginger paste, garam masala, turmeric, flakes, and salt in a bowl. Place the thighs in a zipper bag and pour in the marinade. Massage the chicken to coat and refrigerate for 2 hours.
2. Preheat air fryer to 400°F. Remove the chicken from the bag and discard the marinade. Put the chicken in the greased frying basket and Arr Fry for 13-15 minutes, flipping once until browned and thoroughly cooked. Set chicken aside and cover with foil. Lightly spray shishitos and tomatoes with cooking oil. Place in the frying basket and Bake for 8 minutes, shaking the basket once until soft and slightly charred. Sprinkle with salt. Top the chicken and veggies with cilantro and lemon wedges.

Spinach And Feta Stuffed Chicken Breasts

Servings: 4
Cooking Time: 27 Minutes
Ingredients:
- 1(10-ounce) package frozen spinach, thawed and drained well
- 1 cup feta cheese, crumbled
- ½ teaspoon freshly ground black pepper
- 4 boneless chicken breasts
- salt and freshly ground black pepper
- 1 tablespoon olive oil

Directions:
1. Prepare the filling. Squeeze out as much liquid as possible from the thawed spinach. Rough chop the spinach and transfer it to a mixing bowl with the feta cheese and the freshly ground black pepper.
2. Prepare the chicken breast. Place the chicken breast on a cutting board and press down on the chicken breast with one hand to keep it stabilized. Make an incision about 1-inch long in the fattest side of the breast. Move the knife up and down inside the chicken breast, without poking through either the top or the bottom, or the other side of the breast. The inside pocket should be about 3-inches long, but the opening should only be about 1-inch wide. If this is too difficult, you can make the incision longer, but you will have to be more careful when cooking the chicken breast since this will expose more of the stuffing.
3. Once you have prepared the chicken breasts, use your fingers to stuff the filling into each pocket, spreading the mixture down as far as you can.
4. Preheat the air fryer to 380°F.
5. Lightly brush or spray the air fryer basket and the chicken breasts with olive oil. Transfer two of the stuffed chicken breasts to the air fryer. Air-fry for 12 minutes, turning the chicken breasts over halfway through the cooking time. Remove the chicken to a resting plate and air-fry the second two breasts for 12 minutes. Return the first batch of chicken to the air fryer with the second batch and air-fry for 3 more minutes. When the chicken is cooked, an instant read thermometer should register 165°F in the thickest part of the chicken, as well as in the stuffing.
6. Remove the chicken breasts and let them rest on a cutting board for 2 to 3 minutes. Slice the chicken on the bias and serve with the slices fanned out.

Teriyaki Chicken Drumsticks

Servings: 2
Cooking Time: 17 Minutes
Ingredients:
- 2 tablespoons soy sauce*
- ¼ cup dry sherry
- 1 tablespoon brown sugar
- 2 tablespoons water
- 1 tablespoon rice wine vinegar
- 1 clove garlic, crushed
- 1-inch fresh ginger, peeled and sliced
- pinch crushed red pepper flakes
- 4 to 6 bone-in, skin-on chicken drumsticks
- 1 tablespoon cornstarch
- fresh cilantro leaves

Directions:
1. Make the marinade by combining the soy sauce, dry sherry, brown sugar, water, rice vinegar, garlic, ginger and crushed red pepper flakes. Pour the marinade over the chicken legs, cover and let the chicken marinate for 1 to 4 hours in the refrigerator.

2. Preheat the air fryer to 380°F.
3. Transfer the chicken from the marinade to the air fryer basket,transferring any extra marinade to a small saucepan.Air-fry at 380°F for 8 minutes.Flip the chicken over and continue to air-fry for another 6 minutes,watching to make sure it doesn't brown too much.
4. While the chicken is cooking,bring the reserved marinade to a simmer on the stovetop.Dissolve the cornstarch in 2 tablespoons of water and stir this into the saucepan.Bring to a boil to thicken the sauce.Remove the garlic clove and slices of ginger from the sauce and set aside.
5. When the time is up on the air fryer,brush the thickened sauce on the chicken and air-fry for 3 more minutes.Remove the chicken from the air fryer and brush with the remaining sauce.
6. Serve over rice and sprinkle the cilantro leaves on top.

Sweet-and-sour Chicken

Servings:6
Cooking Time:10 Minutes
Ingredients:
- 1 cup pineapple juice
- 1 cup plus 3 tablespoons cornstarch,divided
- ¼cup sugar
- ¼cup ketchup
- ¼cup apple cider vinegar
- 2 tablespoons soy sauce or tamari
- 1 teaspoon garlic powder,divided
- ¼cup flour
- 1 tablespoon sesame seeds
- ½teaspoon salt
- ¼teaspoon ground black pepper
- 2 large eggs
- 2 pounds chicken breasts,cut into 1-inch cubes
- 1 red bell pepper,cut into 1-inch pieces
- 1 carrot,sliced into¼-inch-thick rounds

Directions:
1. In a medium saucepan,whisk together the pineapple juice,3 tablespoons of the cornstarch,the sugar,the ketchup,the apple cider vinegar,the soy sauce or tamari,and½teaspoon of the garlic powder.Cook over medium-low heat,whisking occasionally as the sauce thickens,about 6 minutes.Stir and set aside while preparing the chicken.
2. Preheat the air fryer to 370°F.
3. In a medium bowl,place the remaining 1 cup of cornstarch,the flour,the sesame seeds,the salt,the remaining½teaspoon of garlic powder,and the pepper.
4. In a second medium bowl,whisk the eggs.
5. Working in batches,place the cubed chicken in the cornstarch mixture to lightly coat;then dip it into the egg mixture,and return it to the cornstarch mixture.Shake off the excess and place the coated chicken in the air fryer basket.Spray with cooking spray and cook for 5 minutes,shake the basket,and spray with more cooking spray.Cook an additional 3 to 5 minutes,or until completely cooked and golden brown.
6. On the last batch of chicken,add the bell pepper and carrot to the basket and cook with the chicken.
7. Place the cooked chicken and vegetables into a serving bowl and toss with the sweet-and-sour sauce to serve.

Daadi Chicken Salad

Servings:2
Cooking Time:30 Minutes
Ingredients:
- ½cup chopped golden raisins
- 1 Granny Smith apple,grated
- 2 chicken breasts
- Salt and pepper to taste
- ¾cup mayonnaise
- 1 tbsp lime juice
- 1 tsp curry powder
- ½sliced avocado
- 1 scallion,minced
- 2 tbsp chopped pecans
- 1 tsp poppy seeds

Directions:
1. Preheat air fryer at 350ºF.Sprinkle chicken breasts with salt and pepper,place them in the greased frying basket,and Air Fry for 8-10 minutes,tossing once.Let rest for 5 minutes before cutting.In a salad bowl,combine chopped chicken,mayonnaise,lime juice,curry powder,raisins,apple,avocado,scallion,and pecans.Let sit covered in the fridge until ready to eat.Before serve sprinkled with the poppy seeds.

Sage&Paprika Turkey Cutlets

Servings:4
Cooking Time:15 Minutes
Ingredients:
- ½cup bread crumbs
- ¼tsp paprika
- Salt and pepper to taste
- ⅛tsp dried sage
- ⅛tsp garlic powder
- ¼tsp ground cumin
- 1 egg
- 4 turkey breast cutlets
- 2 tbsp chopped chervil

Directions:
1. Preheat air fryer to 380°F.Combine the bread crumbs,paprika,salt,black pepper,sage,cumin,and garlic powder in a bowl and mix well.Beat the egg in another bowl until frothy.Dip the turkey cutlets into the egg mixture,then coat them in the bread crumb mixture.Put the breaded turkey cutlets in the frying basket.Bake for 4 minutes.Turn the cutlets over,then Bake for 4 more minutes.Decorate with chervil and serve.

Southern-fried Chicken Livers

Servings:4
Cooking Time:12 Minutes
Ingredients:
- 2 eggs
- 2 tablespoons water
- ¾cup flour
- 1½cups panko breadcrumbs
- ½cup plain breadcrumbs
- 1 teaspoon salt
- ½teaspoon black pepper
- 20 ounces chicken livers,salted to taste
- oil for misting or cooking spray

Directions:
1. Beat together eggs and water in a shallow dish.Place the flour in a separate shallow dish.
2. In the bowl of a food processor,combine the panko,plain breadcrumbs,salt,and pepper.Process until well mixed and panko crumbs are finely crushed.Place crumbs in a third shallow dish.
3. Dip livers in flour,then egg wash,and then roll in panko mixture to coat well with crumbs.

4. Spray both sides of livers with oil or cooking spray.Cooking in two batches,place livers in air fryer basket in single layer.
5. Cook at 390°F for 7minutes.Spray livers,turn over,and spray again.Cook for 5 more minutes,until done inside and coating is golden brown.
6. Repeat to cook remaining livers.

Pecan Turkey Cutlets

Servings:4
Cooking Time:12 Minutes
Ingredients:
- ¾cup panko breadcrumbs
- ¼teaspoon salt
- ¼teaspoon pepper
- ¼teaspoon dry mustard
- ¼teaspoon poultry seasoning
- ½cup pecans
- ¼cup cornstarch
- 1 egg,beaten
- 1 pound turkey cutlets,½-inch thick
- salt and pepper
- oil for misting or cooking spray

Directions:
1. Place the panko crumbs,¼teaspoon salt,¼teaspoon pepper,mustard,and poultry seasoning in food processor.Process until crumbs are finely crushed.Add pecans and process in short pulses just until nuts are finely chopped.Go easy so you don't overdo it!
2. Preheat air fryer to 360°F.
3. Place cornstarch in one shallow dish and beaten egg in another.Transfer coating mixture from food processor into a third shallow dish.
4. Sprinkle turkey cutlets with salt and pepper to taste.
5. Dip cutlets in cornstarch and shake off excess.Then dip in beaten egg and roll in crumbs,pressing to coat well.Spray both sides with oil or cooking spray.
6. Place 2 cutlets in air fryer basket in a single layer and cook for 12 minutes or until juices run clear.
7. Repeat step 6 to cook remaining cutlets.

Chicken Skewers

Servings:4
Cooking Time:55 Minutes
Ingredients:
- 1 lb boneless skinless chicken thighs,cut into pieces
- 1 sweet onion,cut into 1-inch pieces
- 1 zucchini,cut into 1-inch pieces
- 1 red bell pepper,cut into 1-inch pieces
- ¼cup olive oil
- 1 tsp garlic powder
- 1 tsp shallot powder
- 1 tsp ground cumin
- ½tsp dried oregano
- ½tsp dried thyme
- ¼cup lemon juice
- 1 tbsp apple cider vinegar
- 12 grape tomatoes

Directions:
1. Combine the olive oil,garlic powder,shallot powder,cumin,oregano,thyme,lemon juice,and vinegar in a bowl;mix well.Alternate skewering the chicken,bell pepper,onion,zucchini,and tomatoes.Once all of the skewers are prepared,place them in a greased baking dish and pour the olive oil marinade over the top.Turn to coat.Cover with plastic wrap and refrigerate.

2. Preheat air fryer to 380°F.Remove the skewers from the marinade and arrange them in a single layer on the frying basket.Bake for 25 minutes,rotating once.Let the skewers sit for 5 minutes.Serve and enjoy!

Rich Turkey Burgers

Servings:4
Cooking Time:30 Minutes
Ingredients:
- 2 tbsp finely grated Emmental
- 1/3 cup minced onions
- ¼cup grated carrots
- 2 garlic cloves,minced
- 2 tsp olive oil
- 1 tsp dried marjoram
- 1 egg
- 1 lb ground turkey

Directions:
1. Preheat air fryer to 400°F.Mix the onions,carrots,garlic,olive oil,marjoram,Emmental,and egg in a bowl,then add the ground turkey.Use your hands to mix the ingredients together.Form the mixture into 4 patties.Set them in the air fryer and Air Fry for 18-20 minutes,flipping once until cooked through and golden.Serve.

Fancy Chicken Piccata

Servings:4
Cooking Time:30 Minutes
Ingredients:
- 1 lb chicken breasts,cut into cutlets
- Salt and pepper to taste
- 2 egg whites
- 2/3 cup bread crumbs
- 1 tsp Italian seasoning
- 1 tbsp whipped butter
- ½cup chicken broth
- ½onion powder
- ¼cup fino sherry
- Juice of 1 lemon
- 1 tbsp capers,drained
- 1 lemon,sliced
- 2 tbsp chopped parsley

Directions:
1. Preheat air fryer to 370°F.Place the cutlets between two sheets of parchment paper.Pound to a¼-inch thickness and season with salt and pepper.Beat egg whites with 1 tsp of water in a bowl.Put the bread crumbs,Parmesan cheese,onion powder,and Italian seasoning in a second bowl.Dip the cutlet in the egg bowl,and then in the crumb mix.Put the cutlets in the greased frying basket.Air Fry for 6 minutes,flipping once until crispy and golden.
2. Melt butter in a skillet.Stir in broth,sherry,lemon juice,lemon halves,and black pepper.Bring to a boil over high heat until the sauce is reduced by half,4 minutes.Remove from heat.Pick out the lemon rinds and discard them.Stir in capers.Plate a cutlet,spoon some sauce over and garnish with lemon sleeves and parsley to serve.

Garlic Chicken

Servings:4
Cooking Time:30 Minutes
Ingredients:
- 4 bone-in skinless chicken thighs
- 1 tbsp olive oil
- 1 tbsp lemon juice
- 3 tbsp cornstarch

- 1 tsp dried sage
- Black pepper to taste
- 20 garlic cloves, unpeeled

Directions:
1. Preheat air fryer to 370°F. Brush the chicken with olive oil and lemon juice, then drizzle cornstarch, sage, and pepper. Put the chicken in the frying basket and scatter the garlic cloves on top. Roast for 25 minutes or until the garlic is soft, and the chicken is cooked through. Serve.

Parmesan Crusted Chicken Cordon Bleu

Servings: 2
Cooking Time: 14 Minutes

Ingredients:
- 2 (6-ounce) boneless, skinless chicken breasts
- salt and freshly ground black pepper
- 1 tablespoon Dijon mustard
- 4 slices Swiss cheese
- 4 slices deli-sliced ham
- ¼ cup all-purpose flour*
- 1 egg, beaten
- ¾ cup panko breadcrumbs*
- ⅓ cup grated Parmesan cheese
- olive oil, in a spray bottle

Directions:
1. Butterfly the chicken breasts. Place the chicken breast on a cutting board and press down on the breast with the palm of your hand. Slice into the long side of the chicken breast, parallel to the cutting board, but not all the way through to the other side. Open the chicken breast like a "book". Place a piece of plastic wrap over the chicken breast and gently pound it with a meat mallet to make it evenly thick.
2. Season the chicken with salt and pepper. Spread the Dijon mustard on the inside of each chicken breast. Layer one slice of cheese on top of the mustard, then top with the 2 slices of ham and the other slice of cheese.
3. Starting with the long edge of the chicken breast, roll the chicken up to the other side. Secure it shut with 1 or 2 toothpicks.
4. Preheat the air fryer to 350°F.
5. Set up a dredging station with three shallow dishes. Place the flour in the first dish. Place the beaten egg in the second shallow dish. Combine the panko breadcrumbs and Parmesan cheese together in the third shallow dish. Dip the stuffed and rolled chicken breasts in the flour, then the beaten egg and then roll in the breadcrumb-cheese mixture to cover on all sides. Press the crumbs onto the chicken breasts with your hands to make sure they are well adhered. Spray the chicken breasts with olive oil and transfer to the air fryer basket.
6. Air-fry at 350°F for 14 minutes, flipping the breasts over halfway through the cooking time. Let the chicken rest for a few minutes before removing the toothpicks, slicing and serving.

Chicken & Rice Sautée

Servings: 4
Cooking Time: 25 Minutes

Ingredients:
- 1 can pineapple chunks, drained, ¼ cup juice reserved
- 1 cup cooked long-grain rice
- 1 lb chicken breasts, cubed
- 1 red onion, chopped
- 1 tbsp peanut oil
- 1 peeled peach, cubed
- 1 tbsp cornstarch
- ½ tsp ground ginger
- ¼ tsp chicken seasoning

Directions:
1. Preheat air fryer to 400°F. Combine the chicken, red onion, pineapple, and peanut oil in a metal bowl, then put the bowl in the fryer. Air Fry for 9 minutes, remove and stir. Toss the peach in and put the bowl back into the fryer for 3 minutes. Slide out and stir again. Mix the reserved pineapple juice, corn starch, ginger, and chicken seasoning in a bowl, then pour over the chicken mixture and stir well. Put the bowl back into the fryer and cook for 3 more minutes or until the chicken is cooked through and the sauce is thick. Serve over cooked rice.

Chicken Nuggets

Servings: 20
Cooking Time: 14 Minutes Per Batch

Ingredients:
- 1 pound boneless, skinless chicken thighs, cut into 1-inch chunks
- ¾ teaspoon salt
- ½ teaspoon black pepper
- ½ teaspoon garlic powder
- ½ teaspoon onion powder
- ½ cup flour
- 2 eggs, beaten
- ½ cup panko breadcrumbs
- 3 tablespoons plain breadcrumbs
- oil for misting or cooking spray

Directions:
1. In the bowl of a food processor, combine chicken, ½ teaspoon salt, pepper, garlic powder, and onion powder. Process in short pulses until chicken is very finely chopped and well blended.
2. Place flour in one shallow dish and beaten eggs in another. In a third dish or plastic bag, mix together the panko crumbs, plain breadcrumbs, and ¼ teaspoon salt.
3. Shape chicken mixture into small nuggets. Dip nuggets in flour, then eggs, then panko crumb mixture.
4. Spray nuggets on both sides with oil or cooking spray and place in air fryer basket in a single layer, close but not overlapping.
5. Cook at 360°F for 10 minutes. Spray with oil and cook 4 minutes, until chicken is done and coating is golden brown.
6. Repeat step 5 to cook remaining nuggets.

Cajun Chicken Kebabs

Servings: 4
Cooking Time: 30 Minutes

Ingredients:
- 3 tbsp lemon juice
- 2 tsp olive oil
- 2 tbsp chopped parsley
- ½ tsp dried oregano
- ½ Cajun seasoning
- 1 lb chicken breasts, cubed
- 1 cup cherry tomatoes
- 1 zucchini, cubed

Directions:
1. Preheat air fryer to 400°F. Combine the lemon juice, olive oil, parsley, oregano, and Cajun seasoning in a bowl. Toss in the chicken and stir, making sure all pieces are coated. Allow to marinate for 10 minutes. Take 8 bamboo skewers and poke the chicken, tomatoes, and zucchini, alternating the pieces. Use a brush to put more marinade on them, then lay them in the air fryer. Air Fry the kebabs for 15 minutes, turning once, or until the chicken is cooked through, with no pink showing. Get rid of the leftover marinade. Serve and enjoy!

Ranch Chicken Tortillas

Servings: 4
Cooking Time: 35 Minutes
Ingredients:
- 2 chicken breasts
- 1 tbsp Ranch seasoning
- 1 tbsp taco seasoning
- 1 cup flour
- 1 egg
- ½ cup bread crumbs
- 4 flour tortillas
- 1½ cups shredded lettuce
- 3 tbsp ranch dressing
- 2 tbsp cilantro, chopped

Directions:
1. Preheat air fryer to 370°F. Slice the chicken breasts into cutlets by cutting in half horizontally on a cutting board. Rub with ranch and taco seasonings. In one shallow bowl, add flour. In another shallow bowl, beat the egg. In the third shallow bowl, add bread crumbs.
2. Lightly spray the air fryer basket with cooking oil. First, dip the cutlet in the flour, dredge in egg, and then finish by coating with bread crumbs. Place the cutlets in the fryer and Bake for 6-8 minutes. Flip them and cook further for 4 minutes until crisp. Allow the chicken to cook for a few minutes, then cut into strips. Divide into 4 equal portions along with shredded lettuce, ranch dressing, cilantro and tortillas. Serve and enjoy!

Poblano Bake

Servings: 4
Cooking Time: 11 Minutes Per Batch
Ingredients:
- 2 large poblano peppers (approx. 5½ inches long excluding stem)
- ¾ pound ground turkey, raw
- ¾ cup cooked brown rice
- 1 teaspoon chile powder
- ½ teaspoon ground cumin
- ½ teaspoon garlic powder
- 4 ounces sharp Cheddar cheese, grated
- 1 8-ounce jar salsa, warmed

Directions:
1. Slice each pepper in half lengthwise so that you have four wide, flat pepper halves.
2. Remove seeds and membrane and discard. Rinse inside and out.
3. In a large bowl, combine turkey, rice, chile powder, cumin, and garlic powder. Mix well.
4. Divide turkey filling into 4 portions and stuff one into each of the 4 pepper halves. Press lightly to pack down.
5. Place 2 pepper halves in air fryer basket and cook at 390°F for 10 minutes or until turkey is well done.
6. Top each pepper half with ¼ of the grated cheese. Cook 1 more minute or just until cheese melts.
7. Repeat steps 5 and 6 to cook remaining pepper halves.
8. To serve, place each pepper half on a plate and top with ¼ cup warm salsa.

Chicken Rochambeau

Servings: 4
Cooking Time: 20 Minutes
Ingredients:
- 1 tablespoon butter
- 4 chicken tenders, cut in half crosswise
- salt and pepper
- ¼ cup flour
- oil for misting
- 4 slices ham, ¼-to-⅜-inches thick and large enough to cover an English muffin
- 2 English muffins, split
- Sauce
- 2 tablespoons butter
- ½ cup chopped green onions
- ½ cup chopped mushrooms
- 2 tablespoons flour
- 1 cup chicken broth
- ¼ teaspoon garlic powder
- 1½ teaspoons Worcestershire sauce

Directions:
1. Place 1 tablespoon of butter in air fryer baking pan and cook at 390°F for 2 minutes to melt.
2. Sprinkle chicken tenders with salt and pepper to taste, then roll in the ¼ cup of flour.
3. Place chicken in baking pan, turning pieces to coat with melted butter.
4. Cook at 390°F for 5 minutes. Turn chicken pieces over, and spray tops lightly with olive oil. Cook 5 minutes longer or until juices run clear. The chicken will not brown.
5. While chicken is cooking, make the sauce: In a medium saucepan, melt the 2 tablespoons of butter.
6. Add onions and mushrooms and sauté until tender, about 3 minutes.
7. Stir in the flour. Gradually add broth, stirring constantly until you have a smooth gravy.
8. Add garlic powder and Worcestershire sauce and simmer on low heat until sauce thickens, about 5 minutes.
9. When chicken is cooked, remove baking pan from air fryer and set aside.
10. Place ham slices directly into air fryer basket and cook at 390°F for 5 minutes or until hot and beginning to sizzle a little. Remove and set aside on top of the chicken for now.
11. Place the English muffin halves in air fryer basket and cook at 390°F for 1 minute.
12. Open air fryer and place a ham slice on top of each English muffin half. Stack 2 pieces of chicken on top of each ham slice. Cook at 390°F for 1 to 2 minutes to heat through.
13. Place each English muffin stack on a serving plate and top with plenty of sauce.

Saucy Chicken Thighs

Servings: 4
Cooking Time: 35 Minutes
Ingredients:
- 8 boneless, skinless chicken thighs
- 1 tbsp Italian seasoning
- Salt and pepper to taste
- 2 garlic cloves, minced
- ½ tsp apple cider vinegar
- ½ cup honey
- ¼ cup Dijon mustard

Directions:
1. Preheat air fryer to 400°F. Season the chicken with Italian seasoning, salt, and black pepper. Place in the greased frying basket and Bake for 15 minutes, flipping once halfway through cooking.
2. While the chicken is cooking, add garlic, honey, vinegar, and Dijon mustard in a saucepan and stir-fry over medium heat for 4 minutes or until the sauce has thickened and warmed through. Transfer the thighs to a serving dish and drizzle with honey-mustard sauce. Serve and enjoy!

Farmer's Fried Chicken

Servings:4
Cooking Time:55 Minutes
Ingredients:
- 3 lb whole chicken,cut into breasts,drumsticks,and thighs
- 2 cups flour
- 4 tsp salt
- 4 tsp dried basil
- 4 tsp dried thyme
- 2 tsp dried shallot powder
- 2 tsp smoked paprika
- 1 tsp mustard powder
- 1 tsp celery salt
- 1 cup kefir
- ¼ cup honey

Directions:
1. Preheat the air fryer to 370°F.Combine the flour,salt,basil,thyme,shallot,paprika,mustard powder,and celery salt in a bowl.Pour into a glass jar.Mix the kefir and honey in a large bowl and add the chicken,stir to coat.Marinate for 15 minutes at room temperature.Remove the chicken from the kefir mixture;discard the rest.Put 2/3 cup of the flour mix onto a plate and dip the chicken.Shake gently and put on a wire rack for 10 minutes.Line the frying basket with round parchment paper with holes punched in it.Place the chicken in a single layer and spray with cooking oil.Air Fry for 18-25 minutes,flipping once around minute 10.Serve hot.

Windsor's Chicken Salad

Servings:4
Cooking Time:30 Minutes
Ingredients:
- ½ cup halved seedless red grapes
- 2 chicken breasts,cubed
- Salt and pepper to taste
- ¾ cup mayonnaise
- 1 tbsp lemon juice
- 2 tbsp chopped parsley
- ½ cup chopped celery
- 1 shallot,diced

Directions:
1. Preheat air fryer to 350°F.Sprinkle chicken with salt and pepper.Place the chicken cubes in the frying basket and Air Fry for 9 minutes,flipping once.In a salad bowl,combine the cooked chicken,mayonnaise,lemon juice,parsley,grapes,celery,and shallot and let chill covered in the fridge for 1 hour up to overnight.

Maewoon Chicken Legs

Servings:4
Cooking Time:30 Minutes+Chilling Time
Ingredients:
- 4 scallions,sliced,whites and greens separated
- ¼ cup tamari
- 2 tbsp sesame oil
- 1 tsp sesame seeds
- ¼ cup honey
- 2 tbsp gochujang
- 2 tbsp ketchup
- 4 cloves garlic,minced
- ½ tsp ground ginger
- Salt and pepper to taste
- 1 tbsp parsley
- 1½ lb chicken legs

Directions:
1. Whisk all ingredients,except chicken and scallion greens,in a bowl.Reserve ¼ cup of marinade.Toss chicken legs in the remaining marinade and chill for 30 minutes.
2. Preheat air fryer at 400ºF.Place chicken legs in the greased frying basket and Air Fry for 10 minutes.Turn chicken.Cook for 8 more minutes.Let sit in a serving dish for 5 minutes.Coat the cooked chicken with the reserved marinade and scatter with scallion greens,sesame seeds and parsley to serve.

German Chicken Frikadellen

Servings:6
Cooking Time:20 Minutes
Ingredients:
- 1 lb ground chicken
- 1 egg
- 3/4 cup bread crumbs
- ¼ cup diced onions
- 1 grated carrot
- 1 tsp yellow mustard
- Salt and pepper to taste
- ¼ cup chopped parsley

Directions:
1. Preheat air fryer at 350ºF.In a bowl,combine the ground chicken,egg,crumbs,onions,carrot,parsley,salt,and pepper.Mix well with your hands.Form mixture into meatballs.Place them in the frying basket and Air Fry for 8-10 minutes,tossing once until golden.Serve right away.

Paprika Chicken Drumettes

Servings:2
Cooking Time:30 Minutes
Ingredients:
- 1 lb chicken drumettes
- 1 cup buttermilk
- 3/4 cup bread crumbs
- ½ tsp smoked paprika
- 1 tsp chicken seasoning
- ½ tsp garlic powder
- Salt and pepper to taste
- 3 tsp of lemon juice

Directions:
1. Mix drumettes and buttermilk in a bowl and let sit covered in the fridge overnight.Preheat air fryer at 350ºF.In a shallow bowl,combine the remaining ingredients.Shake excess buttermilk off drumettes and dip them in the breadcrumb mixture.Place breaded drumettes in the greased frying basket and Air Fry for 12 minutes.Increase air fryer temperature to 400ºF,toss chicken,and cook for 8 minutes.Let rest for 5 minutes before serving.

Fiesta Chicken Plate

Servings:4
Cooking Time:15 Minutes
Ingredients:
- 1 pound boneless,skinless chicken breasts(2 large breasts)
- 2 tablespoons lime juice
- 1 teaspoon cumin
- ½ teaspoon salt
- ½ cup grated Pepper Jack cheese
- 1 16-ounce can refried beans
- ½ cup salsa
- 2 cups shredded lettuce
- 1 medium tomato,chopped
- 2 avocados,peeled and sliced
- 1 small onion,sliced into thin rings
- sour cream

- tortilla chips(optional)

Directions:
1. Split each chicken breast in half lengthwise.
2. Mix lime juice,cumin,and salt together and brush on all surfaces of chicken breasts.
3. Place in air fryer basket and cook at 390°F for 15 minutes,until well done.
4. Divide the cheese evenly over chicken breasts and cook for an additional minute to melt cheese.
5. While chicken is cooking,heat refried beans on stovetop or in microwave.
6. When ready to serve,divide beans among 4 plates.Place chicken breasts on top of beans and spoon salsa over.Arrange the lettuce,tomatoes,and avocados artfully on each plate and scatter with the onion rings.
7. Pass sour cream at the table and serve with tortilla chips if desired.

Jerk Chicken Drumsticks

Servings:2
Cooking Time:20 Minutes
Ingredients:
- 1 or 2 cloves garlic
- 1 inch of fresh ginger
- 2 serrano peppers,(with seeds if you like it spicy,seeds removed for less heat)
- 1 teaspoon ground allspice
- 1 teaspoon ground nutmeg
- 1 teaspoon chili powder
- ½teaspoon dried thyme
- ½teaspoon ground cinnamon
- ½teaspoon paprika
- 1 tablespoon brown sugar
- 1 teaspoon soy sauce
- 2 tablespoons vegetable oil
- 6 skinless chicken drumsticks

Directions:
1. Combine all the ingredients except the chicken in a small chopper or blender and blend to a paste.Make slashes into the meat of the chicken drumsticks and rub the spice blend all over the chicken(a pair of plastic gloves makes this really easy).Transfer the rubbed chicken to a non-reactive covered container and let the chicken marinate for at least 30 minutes or overnight in the refrigerator.
2. Preheat the air fryer to 400°F.
3. Transfer the drumsticks to the air fryer basket.Air-fry for 10 minutes.Turn the drumsticks over and air-fry for another 10 minutes.Serve warm with some rice and vegetables or a green salad.

The Ultimate Chicken Bulgogi

Servings:4
Cooking Time:30 Minutes
Ingredients:
- 1½lb boneless,skinless chicken thighs,cubed
- 1 cucumber,thinly sliced
- ¼cup apple cider vinegar
- 4 garlic cloves,minced
- ¼tsp ground ginger
- ⅛tsp red pepper flakes
- 2 tsp honey
- ⅛tsp salt
- 2 tbsp tamari
- 2 tsp sesame oil
- 2 tsp granular honey
- 2 tbsp lemon juice
- ½tsp lemon zest
- 3 scallions,chopped
- 2 cups cooked white rice
- 2 tsp roasted sesame seeds

Directions:
1. In a bowl,toss the cucumber,vinegar,half of the garlic,half of the ginger,pepper flakes,honey,and salt and store in the fridge covered.Combine the tamari,sesame oil,granular honey,lemon juice,remaining garlic,remaining ginger,and chicken in a large bowl.Toss to coat and marinate in the fridge for 10 minutes.
2. Preheat air fryer to 350ºF.Place chicken in the frying basket,do not discard excess marinade.Air Fry for 11 minutes,shaking once and pouring excess marinade over.Place the chicken bulgogi over the cooked rice and scatter with scallion greens,pickled cucumbers,and sesame seeds.Serve and enjoy!

Irresistible Cheesy Chicken Sticks

Servings:2
Cooking Time:30 Minutes
Ingredients:
- 6 mozzarella sticks
- 1 cup flour
- 2 eggs,beaten
- 1 lb ground chicken
- 1½cups breadcrumbs
- ¼tsp crushed chilis
- ¼tsp cayenne pepper
- ½tsp garlic powder
- ¼tsp shallot powder
- ½tsp oregano

Directions:
1. Preheat air fryer to 390°F.Combine crushed chilis,cayenne pepper,garlic powder,shallot powder,and oregano in a bowl.Add the ground chicken and mix well with your hands until evenly combined.In another mixing bowl,beat the eggs until fluffy and until the yolks and whites are fully combined,and set aside.
2. Pour the beaten eggs,flour,and bread crumbs into 3 separate bowls.Roll the mozzarella sticks in the flour,then dip them in the beaten eggs.With hands,wrap the stick in a thin layer of the chicken mixture.Finally,coat the sticks in the crumbs.Place the sticks in the greased frying basket fryer and Air Fry for 18-20 minutes,turning once until crispy.Serve hot.

Turkey Scotch Eggs

Servings:4
Cooking Time:30 Minutes
Ingredients:
- 1½lb ground turkey
- 1 tbsp ground cumin
- 1 tsp ground coriander
- 2 garlic cloves,minced
- 3 raw eggs
- 1½cups bread crumbs
- 6 hard-cooked eggs,peeled
- ½cup flour

Directions:
1. Preheat air fryer to 370°F.Place the ground turkey,cumin,coriander,garlic,one egg,and½cup of bread crumbs in a large bowl and mix until well incorporated.
2. Divide into 6 equal portions,then flatten each into long ovals.Set aside.In a shallow bowl,beat the remaining raw eggs.In another shallow bowl,add flour.Do the same with

another plate for bread crumbs.Roll each cooked egg in flour,then wrap with one oval of chicken sausage until completely covered.
3. Roll again in flour,then coat in the beaten egg before rolling in bread crumbs.Arrange the eggs in the greased frying basket.Air Fry for 12-14 minutes,flipping once until the sausage is cooked and the eggs are brown.Serve.

Peanut Butter-barbeque Chicken

Servings:4
Cooking Time:20 Minutes
Ingredients:
- 1 pound boneless,skinless chicken thighs
- salt and pepper
- 1 large orange
- ½ cup barbeque sauce
- 2 tablespoons smooth peanut butter
- 2 tablespoons chopped peanuts for garnish(optional)
- cooking spray

Directions:
1. Season chicken with salt and pepper to taste.Place in a shallow dish or plastic bag.
2. Grate orange peel,squeeze orange and reserve 1 tablespoon of juice for the sauce.
3. Pour remaining juice over chicken and marinate for 30minutes.
4. Mix together the reserved 1 tablespoon of orange juice,barbeque sauce,peanut butter,and 1 teaspoon grated orange peel.
5. Place ¼ cup of sauce mixture in a small bowl for basting.Set remaining sauce aside to serve with cooked chicken.
6. Preheat air fryer to 360°F.Spray basket with nonstick cooking spray.
7. Remove chicken from marinade,letting excess drip off.Place in air fryer basket and cook for 5minutes.Turn chicken over and cook 5minutes longer.
8. Brush both sides of chicken lightly with sauce.
9. Cook chicken 5minutes,then turn thighs one more time,again brushing both sides lightly with sauce.Cook for 5 moreminutes or until chicken is done and juices run clear.
10. Serve chicken with remaining sauce on the side and garnish with chopped peanuts if you like.

Chicken Parmesan

Servings:4
Cooking Time:11 Minutes
Ingredients:
- 4 chicken tenders
- Italian seasoning
-
- salt
- ¼ cup cornstarch
- ½ cup Italian salad dressing
- ¼ cup panko breadcrumbs
- ¼ cup grated Parmesan cheese,plus more for serving
- oil for misting or cooking spray
- 8 ounces spaghetti,cooked
- 1 24-ounce jar marinara sauce

Directions:
1. Pound chicken tenders with meat mallet or rolling pin until about ¼-inch thick.
2. Sprinkle both sides with Italian seasoning and salt to taste.
3. Place cornstarch and salad dressing in 2 separate shallow dishes.
4. In a third shallow dish,mix together the panko crumbs and Parmesan cheese.
5. Dip flattened chicken in cornstarch,then salad dressing.Dip in the panko mixture,pressing into the chicken so the coating sticks well.
6. Spray both sides with oil or cooking spray.Place in air fryer basket in single layer.
7. Cook at 390°F for 5minutes.Spray with oil again,turning chicken to coat both sides.See tip about turning.
8. Cook for an additional 6 minutes or until chicken juices run clear and outside is browned.
9. While chicken is cooking,heat marinara sauce and stir into cooked spaghetti.
10. To serve,divide spaghetti with sauce among 4 dinner plates,and top each with a fried chicken tender.Pass additional Parmesan at the table for those who want extra cheese.

Apricot Glazed Chicken Thighs

Servings:2
Cooking Time:22 Minutes
Ingredients:
- 4 bone-in chicken thighs(about 2 pounds)
- olive oil
- 1 teaspoon salt
- ¼ teaspoon freshly ground black pepper
- ½ teaspoon onion powder
- ¾ cup apricot preserves 1½ tablespoons Dijon mustard
- ½ teaspoon dried thyme
- 1 teaspoon soy sauce
- fresh thyme leaves,for garnish

Directions:
1. Preheat the air fryer to 380°F.
2. Brush or spray both the air fryer basket and the chicken with the olive oil.Combine the salt,pepper and onion powder and season both sides of the chicken with the spice mixture.
3. Place the seasoned chicken thighs,skin side down in the air fryer basket.Air-fry for 10 minutes.
4. While chicken is cooking,make the glaze by combining the apricot preserves,Dijon mustard,thyme and soy sauce in a small bowl.
5. When the time is up on the air fryer,spoon half of the apricot glaze over the chicken thighs and air-fry for 2 minutes.Then flip the chicken thighs over so that the skin side is facing up and air-fry for an additional 8 minutes.Finally,spoon and spread the rest of the glaze evenly over the chicken thighs and air-fry for a final 2 minutes.Transfer the chicken to a serving platter and sprinkle the fresh thyme leaves on top.

Vegetarians Recipes

Authentic Mexican Esquites

Servings:4
Cooking Time:25 Minutes
Ingredients:
- 4 ears of corn,husk and silk removed
- 1 tbsp ground coriander
- 1 tbsp smoked paprika
- 1 tsp sea salt
- 1 tsp garlic powder
- 1 tsp onion powder
- 1 tsp dried lime peel
- 1 tsp cayenne pepper
- 3 tbsp mayonnaise
- 3 tbsp grated Cotija cheese
- 1 tbsp butter,melted
- 1 tsp epazote seasoning

Directions:
1. Preheat the air fryer to 400°F.Combine the coriander,paprika,salt,garlic powder,onion powder,lime peel,epazote and cayenne pepper in a small bowl and mix well.Pour into a small glass jar.Put the corn in the greased frying basket and Bake for 6-8 minutes or until the corn is crispy but tender.Make sure to rearrange the ears halfway through cooking.
2. While the corn is frying,combine the mayonnaise,cheese,and melted butter in a small bowl.Spread the mixture over the cooked corn,return to the fryer,and Bake for 3-5 minutes more or until the corn has brown spots.Remove from the fryer and sprinkle each cob with about½tsp of the spice mix.

Curried Potato,Cauliflower And Pea Turnovers

Servings:4
Cooking Time:40 Minutes
Ingredients:
- Dough:
- 2 cups all-purpose flour
- ½teaspoon baking powder
- 1 teaspoon salt
- freshly ground black pepper
- ¼teaspoon dried thyme
- ¼cup canola oil
- ½to⅔cup water
- Turnover Filling:
- 1 tablespoon canola or vegetable oil
- 1 onion,finely chopped
- 1 clove garlic,minced
- 1 tablespoon grated fresh ginger
- ½teaspoon cumin seeds
- ½teaspoon fennel seeds
- 1 teaspoon curry powder
- 2 russet potatoes,diced
- 2 cups cauliflower florets
- ½cup frozen peas
- 2 tablespoons chopped fresh cilantro
- salt and freshly ground black pepper
- 2 tablespoons butter,melted
- mango chutney,for serving

Directions:
1. Start by making the dough.Combine the flour,baking powder,salt,pepper and dried thyme in a mixing bowl or the bowl of a stand mixer.Drizzle in the canola oil and pinch it together with your fingers to turn the flour into a crumby mixture.Stir in the water(enough to bring the dough together).Knead the dough for 5 minutes or so until it is smooth.Add a little more water or flour as needed.Let the dough rest while you make the turnover filling.
2. Preheat a large skillet on the stovetop over medium-high heat.Add the oil and sautéthe onion until it starts to become tender–about 4 minutes.Add the garlic and ginger and continue to cook for another minute.Add the dried spices and toss everything to coat.Add the potatoes and cauliflower to the skillet and pour in 1½cups of water.Simmer everything together for 20 to 25 minutes,or until the potatoes are soft and most of the water has evaporated.If the water has evaporated and the vegetables still need more time,just add a little water and continue to simmer until everything is tender.Stir well,crushing the potatoes and cauliflower a little as you do so.Stir in the peas and cilantro,season to taste with salt and freshly ground black pepper and set aside to cool.
3. Divide the dough into 4 balls.Roll the dough balls out into¼-inch thick circles.Divide the cooled potato filling between the dough circles,placing a mound of the filling on one side of each piece of dough,leaving an empty border around the edge of the dough.Brush the edges of the dough with a little water and fold one edge of circle over the filling to meet the other edge of the circle,creating a half moon.Pinch the edges together with your fingers and then press the edge with the tines of a fork to decorate and seal.
4. Preheat the air fryer to 380°F.
5. Spray or brush the air fryer basket with oil.Brush the turnovers with the melted butter and place 2 turnovers into the air fryer basket.Air-fry for 15 minutes.Flip the turnovers over and air-fry for another 5 minutes.Repeat with the remaining 2 turnovers.
6. These will be very hot when they come out of the air fryer.Let them cool for at least 20 minutes before serving warm with mango chutney.

Vegetable Couscous

Servings:4
Cooking Time:10 Minutes
Ingredients:
- 4 ounces white mushrooms,sliced
- ½medium green bell pepper,julienned
- 1 cup cubed zucchini
- ¼small onion,slivered
- 1 stalk celery,thinly sliced
- ¼teaspoon ground coriander
- ¼teaspoon ground cumin
- salt and pepper
- 1 tablespoon olive oil
- Couscous
- ¾cup uncooked couscous
- 1 cup vegetable broth or water
- ½teaspoon salt(omit if using salted broth)

Directions:
1. Combine all vegetables in large bowl.Sprinkle with coriander,cumin,and salt and pepper to taste.Stir well,add olive oil,and stir again to coat vegetables evenly.
2. Place vegetables in air fryer basket and cook at 390°F for 5minutes.Stir and cook for 5 more minutes,until tender.
3. While vegetables are cooking,prepare the couscous:Place broth or water and salt in large saucepan.Heat to boiling,stir in couscous,cover,and remove from heat.
4. Let couscous sit for 5minutes,stir in cooked vegetables,and serve hot.

Veggie Fried Rice

Servings: 4
Cooking Time: 25 Minutes
Ingredients:
- 1 cup cooked brown rice
- ⅓ cup chopped onion
- ½ cup chopped carrots
- ½ cup chopped bell peppers
- ½ cup chopped broccoli florets
- 3 tablespoons low-sodium soy sauce
- 1 tablespoon sesame oil
- 1 teaspoon ground ginger
- 1 teaspoon ground garlic powder
- ½ teaspoon black pepper
- ⅛ teaspoon salt
- 2 large eggs

Directions:
1. Preheat the air fryer to 370°F.
2. In a large bowl, mix together the brown rice, onions, carrots, bell pepper, and broccoli.
3. In a small bowl, whisk together the soy sauce, sesame oil, ginger, garlic powder, pepper, salt, and eggs.
4. Pour the egg mixture into the rice and vegetable mixture and mix together.
5. Liberally spray a 7-inch springform pan (or compatible air fryer dish) with olive oil. Add the rice mixture to the pan and cover with aluminum foil.
6. Place a metal trivet into the air fryer basket and set the pan on top. Cook for 15 minutes. Carefully remove the pan from basket, discard the foil, and mix the rice. Return the rice to the air fryer basket, turning down the temperature to 350°F and cooking another 10 minutes.
7. Remove and let cool 5 minutes. Serve warm.

Effortless Mac 'n' Cheese

Servings: 4
Cooking Time: 15 Minutes
Ingredients:
- 1 cup heavy cream
- 1 cup milk
- ½ cup mozzarella cheese
- 2 tsp grated Parmesan cheese
- 16 oz cooked elbow macaroni

Directions:
1. Preheat air fryer to 400°F. Whisk the heavy cream, milk, mozzarella cheese, and Parmesan cheese until smooth in a bowl. Stir in the macaroni and pour into a baking dish. Cover with foil and Bake in the air fryer for 6 minutes. Remove foil and Bake until cooked through and bubbly, 3-5 minutes. Serve warm.

Zucchini Tamale Pie

Servings: 4
Cooking Time: 45 Minutes
Ingredients:
- 1 cup canned diced tomatoes with juice
- 1 zucchini, diced
- 3 tbsp safflower oil
- 1 cup cooked pinto beans
- 3 garlic cloves, minced
- 1 tbsp corn masa flour
- 1 tsp dried oregano
- ½ tsp ground cumin
- 1 tsp onion powder
- Salt to taste
- ½ tsp red chili flakes
- ½ cup ground cornmeal
- 1 tsp nutritional yeast
- 2 tbsp chopped cilantro
- ½ tsp lime zest

Directions:
1. Warm 2 tbsp of the oil in a skillet over medium heat and sauté the zucchini for 3 minutes or until they begin to brown. Add the beans, tomatoes, garlic, flour, oregano, cumin, onion powder, salt, and chili flakes. Cook over medium heat, stirring often, about 5 minutes until the mix is thick and no liquid remains. Remove from heat. Spray a baking pan with oil and pour the mix inside. Smooth out the top and set aside.
2. In a pot over high heat, add the cornmeal, 1½ cups of water, and salt. Whisk constantly as the mix begins to boil. Once it boils, reduce the heat to low. Add the yeast and oil and continue to cook, stirring often, for 10 minutes or until the mix is thick and hard to stir. Remove. Preheat air fryer to 325°F. Add the cilantro and lime zest into the cornmeal mix and thoroughly combine. Using a rubber spatula, spread it evenly over the filling in the baking pan to form a crust topping. Put in the frying basket and Bake for 20 minutes or until the top is golden. Let it cool for 5 to 10 minutes, then cut and serve.

Pine Nut Eggplant Dip

Servings: 4
Cooking Time: 35 Minutes
Ingredients:
- 2½ tsp olive oil
- 1 eggplant, halved lengthwise
- 1/2 cup Parmesan cheese
- 2 tsp pine nuts
- 1 tbsp chopped walnuts
- ¼ cup tahini
- 1 tbsp lemon juice
- 2 cloves garlic, minced
- 1/8 tsp ground cumin
- 1 tsp smoked paprika
- Salt and pepper to taste
- 1 tbsp chopped parsley

Directions:
1. Preheat air fryer at 375°F. Rub olive oil over eggplant and pierce the eggplant flesh 3 times with a fork. Place eggplant, flat side down, in the frying basket and Bake for 25 minutes. Let cool onto a cutting board for 5 minutes until cool enough to handle. Scoop out eggplant flesh. Add pine nuts and walnuts to the basket and Air Fry for 2 minutes, shaking every 30 seconds to ensure they don´t burn. Set aside in a bowl.
2. In a food processor, blend eggplant flesh, tahini, lemon juice, garlic, smoked paprika, cumin, salt, and pepper until smooth. Transfer to a bowl. Scatter with the roasted pine nuts, Parmesan cheese, and parsley. Drizzle the dip with the remaining olive oil. Serve and enjoy!

Cheesy Eggplant Rounds

Servings: 4
Cooking Time: 35 Minutes
Ingredients:
- 1 eggplant, peeled
- 2 eggs
- ½ cup all-purpose flour
- ¾ cup bread crumbs
- 2 tbsp grated Swiss cheese
- Salt and pepper to taste
- ¾ cup tomato passata
- ½ cup shredded Parmesan

- ½ cup shredded mozzarella

Directions:
1. Preheat air fryer to 400°F. Slice the eggplant into ½-inch rounds. Set aside. Set out three small bowls. In the first bowl, add flour. In the second bowl, beat the eggs. In the third bowl, mix the crumbs, 2 tbsp of grated Swiss cheese, salt, and pepper. Dip each eggplant in the flour, then dredge in egg, then coat with bread crumb mixture. Arrange the eggplant rounds on the greased frying basket and spray with cooking oil. Bake for 7 minutes. Top each eggplant round with 1 tsp passata and ½ tbsp each of shredded Parmesan and mozzarella. Cook until the cheese melts, 2-3 minutes. Serve warm and enjoy!

Sushi-style Deviled Eggs

Servings: 4
Cooking Time: 20 Minutes
Ingredients:
- ¼ cup crabmeat, shells discarded
- 4 eggs
- 2 tbsp mayonnaise
- ½ tsp soy sauce
- ¼ avocado, diced
- ¼ tsp wasabi powder
- 2 tbsp diced cucumber
- 1 sheet nori, sliced
- 8 jarred pickled ginger slices
- 1 tsp toasted sesame seeds
- 2 spring onions, sliced

Directions:
1. Preheat air fryer to 260°F. Place the eggs in muffin cups to avoid bumping around and cracking during the cooking process. Add silicone cups to the frying basket and Air Fry for 15 minutes. Remove and plunge the eggs immediately into an ice bath to cool, about 5 minutes. Carefully peel and slice them in half lengthwise. Spoon yolks into a separate medium bowl and arrange white halves on a large plate. Mash the yolks with a fork. Stir in mayonnaise, soy sauce, avocado, and wasabi powder until smooth. Mix in cucumber and spoon into white halves. Scatter eggs with crabmeat, nori, pickled ginger, spring onions and sesame seeds to serve.

Hellenic Zucchini Bites

Servings: 4
Cooking Time: 20 Minutes
Ingredients:
- 8 pitted Kalamata olives, halved
- 2 tsp olive oil
- 1 zucchini, sliced
- ½ tsp salt
- ½ tsp Greek oregano
- ½ cup marinara sauce
- ½ cup feta cheese crumbles
- 2 tbsp chopped dill

Directions:
1. Preheat air fryer to 350°F. Brush olive oil over both sides of the zucchini circles. Lay out slices on a large plate and sprinkle with salt. Then, top with marinara sauce, feta crumbles, Greek oregano and olives. Place the topped circles in the frying basket and Air Fry for 5 minutes. Garnish with chopped dill to serve.

Berbere Eggplant Dip

Servings: 4
Cooking Time: 35 Minutes
Ingredients:
- 1 eggplant, halved lengthwise
- 3 tsp olive oil
- 2 tsp pine nuts
- ¼ cup tahini
- 1 tbsp lemon juice
- 2 cloves garlic, minced
- ¼ tsp berbere seasoning
- ⅛ tsp ground cumin
- Salt and pepper to taste
- 1 tbsp chopped parsley

Directions:
1. Preheat air fryer to 370°F. Brush the eggplant with some olive oil. With a fork, pierce the eggplant flesh a few times. Place them, flat sides-down, in the frying basket. Air Fry for 25 minutes. Transfer the eggplant to a cutting board and let cool for 3 minutes until easy to handle. Place pine nuts in the frying basket and Air Fry for 2 minutes, shaking every 30 seconds. Set aside in a bowl.
2. Scoop out the eggplant flesh and add to a food processor. Add in tahini, lemon juice, garlic, berbere seasoning, cumin, salt, and black pepper and pulse until smooth. Transfer to a serving bowl. Scatter with toasted pine nuts, parsley, and the remaining olive oil. Serve immediately.

Vegan Buddha Bowls (2)

Servings: 4
Cooking Time: 20 Minutes
Ingredients:
- 1 carrot, peeled and julienned
- ½ onion, sliced into half-moons
- ¼ cup apple cider vinegar
- ½ tsp ground ginger
- ⅛ tsp cayenne pepper
- 1 parsnip, diced
- 1 tsp avocado oil
- 4 oz extra-firm tofu, cubed
- ½ tsp five-spice powder
- ½ tsp chili powder
- 2 tsp fresh lime zest
- 1 cup fresh arugula
- ½ cup cooked quinoa
- 2 tbsp canned kidney beans
- 2 tbsp canned sweetcorn
- 1 avocado, diced
- 2 tbsp pine nuts

Directions:
1. Preheat air fryer to 350°F. Combine carrot, vinegar, ginger, and cayenne in a bowl. In another bowl, combine onion, parsnip, and avocado oil. In a third bowl, mix the tofu, five-spice powder, and chili powder.
2. Place the onion mixture in the greased basket. Air Fry for 6 minutes. Stir in tofu mixture and cook for 8 more minutes. Mix in lime zest. Divide arugula, cooked quinoa, kidney beans, sweetcorn, drained carrots, avocado, pine nuts, and tofu mixture between 2 bowls. Serve.

Harissa Veggie Fries

Servings: 4
Cooking Time: 55 Minutes
Ingredients:
- 1 pound red potatoes, cut into rounds
- 1 onion, diced
- 1 green bell pepper, diced
- 1 red bell pepper, diced
- 2 tbsp olive oil
- Salt and pepper to taste
- ¾ tsp garlic powder
- ¾ tsp harissa seasoning

Directions:

1. Combine all ingredients in a large bowl and mix until potatoes are well coated and seasoned.Preheat air fryer to 350°F.Pour all of the contents in the bowl into the frying basket.Bake for 35 minutes,shaking every 10 minutes,until golden brown and soft.Serve hot.

Thyme Lentil Patties

Servings:2
Cooking Time:35 Minutes
Ingredients:
- ½cup grated American cheese
- 1 cup cooked lentils
- ¼tsp dried thyme
- 2 eggs,beaten
- Salt and pepper to taste
- 1 cup bread crumbs

Directions:
1. Preheat air fryer to 350°F.Put the eggs,lentils,and cheese in a bowl and mix to combine.Stir in half the bread crumbs,thyme,salt,and pepper.Form the mixture into 2 patties and coat them in the remaining bread crumbs.Transfer to the greased frying basket.Air Fry for 14-16 minutes until brown,flipping once.Serve.

Bell Pepper & Lentil Tacos

Servings:2
Cooking Time:40 Minutes
Ingredients:
- 2 corn tortilla shells
- ½cup cooked lentils
- ½white onion,sliced
- ½red pepper,sliced
- ½green pepper,sliced
- ½yellow pepper,sliced
- ½cup shredded mozzarella
- ½tsp Tabasco sauce

Directions:
1. Preheat air fryer to 320°F.Sprinkle half of the mozzarella cheese over one of the tortillas,then top with lentils,Tabasco sauce,onion,and peppers.Scatter the remaining mozzarella cheese,cover with the other tortilla and place in the frying basket.Bake for 6 minutes,flipping halfway through cooking.Serve and enjoy!

Garlicky Brussel Sprouts With Saffron Aioli

Servings:4
Cooking Time:20 Minutes
Ingredients:
- 1 lb Brussels sprouts,halved
- 1 tsp garlic powder
- Salt and pepper to taste
- ½cup mayonnaise
- ½tbsp olive oil
- 1 tbsp Dijon mustard
- 1 tsp minced garlic
- Salt and pepper to taste
- ½tsp liquid saffron

Directions:
1. Preheat air fryer to 380°F.Combine the Brussels sprouts,garlic powder,salt and pepper in a large bowl.Place in the fryer and spray with cooking oil.Bake for 12-14 minutes,shaking once,until just brown.
2. Meanwhile,in a small bowl,mix mayonnaise,olive oil,mustard,garlic,saffron,salt and pepper.When the Brussels sprouts are slightly cool,serve with aioli.Enjoy!

Vegetable Hand Pies

Servings:8
Cooking Time:10 Minutes Per Batch
Ingredients:
- ¾cup vegetable broth
- 8 ounces potatoes
- ¾cup frozen chopped broccoli,thawed
- ¼cup chopped mushrooms
- 1 tablespoon cornstarch
- 1 tablespoon milk
- 1 can organic flaky biscuits(8 large biscuits)
- oil for misting or cooking spray

Directions:
1. Place broth in medium saucepan over low heat.
2. While broth is heating,grate raw potato into a bowl of water to prevent browning.You will need¾cup grated potato.
3. Roughly chop the broccoli.
4. Drain potatoes and put them in the broth along with the broccoli and mushrooms.Cook on low for 5 minutes.
5. Dissolve cornstarch in milk,then stir the mixture into the broth.Cook about a minute,until mixture thickens a little.Remove from heat and cool slightly.
6. Separate each biscuit into 2 rounds.Divide vegetable mixture evenly over half the biscuit rounds,mounding filling in the center of each.
7. Top the four rounds with filling,then the other four rounds and crimp the edges together with a fork.
8. Spray both sides with oil or cooking spray and place 4 pies in a single layer in the air fryer basket.
9. Cook at 330°F for approximately 10 minutes.
10. Repeat with the remaining biscuits.The second batch may cook more quickly because the fryer will be hot.

Vegetarian Paella

Servings:3
Cooking Time:50 Minutes
Ingredients:
- ½cup chopped artichoke hearts
- ½sliced red bell peppers
- 4 mushrooms,thinly sliced
- ½cup canned diced tomatoes
- ½cup canned chickpeas
- 3 tbsp hot sauce
- 2 tbsp lemon juice
- 1 tbsp allspice
- 1 cup rice

Directions:
1. Preheat air fryer to 400°F.Combine the artichokes,peppers,mushrooms,tomatoes and their juices,chickpeas,hot sauce,lemon juice,and allspice in a baking pan.Roast for 10 minutes.Pour in rice and 2 cups of boiling water,cover with aluminum foil,and Roast for 22 minutes.Discard the foil and Roast for 3 minutes until the top is crisp.Let cool slightly before stirring.Serve.

Sweet Corn Bread

Servings:6
Cooking Time:35 Minutes
Ingredients:
- 2 eggs,beaten
- ½cup cornmeal
- ½cup pastry flour
- 1/3 cup sugar
- 1 tsp lemon zest
- ½tbsp baking powder
- ¼tsp salt

- ¼ tsp baking soda
- ½ tbsp lemon juice
- ½ cup milk
- ¼ cup sunflower oil

Directions:
1. Preheat air fryer to 350°F. Add the cornmeal, flour, sugar, lemon zest, baking powder, salt, and baking soda in a bowl. Stir with a whisk until combined. Add the eggs, lemon juice, milk, and oil to another bowl and stir well. Add the wet mixture to the dry mixture and stir gently until combined. Spray a baking pan with oil. Pour the batter in and Bake in the fryer for 25 minutes or until golden and a knife inserted in the center comes out clean. Cut into wedges and serve.

Lentil Burritos With Cilantro Chutney

Servings: 4
Cooking Time: 30 Minutes
Ingredients:
- 1 cup cilantro chutney
- 1 lb cooked potatoes, mashed
- 2 tsp sunflower oil
- 3 garlic cloves, minced
- 1½ tbsp fresh lime juice
- 1½ tsp cumin powder
- 1 tsp onion powder
- 1 tsp coriander powder
- Salt to taste
- ½ tsp turmeric
- ¼ tsp cayenne powder
- 4 large flour tortillas
- 1 cup cooked lentils
- ½ cup shredded cabbage
- ¼ cup minced red onions

Directions:
1. Preheat air fryer to 390°F. Place the mashed potatoes, sunflower oil, garlic, lime, cumin, onion powder, coriander, salt, turmeric, and cayenne in a large bowl. Stir well until combined. Lay the tortillas out flat on the counter. In the middle of each, distribute the potato filling. Add some of the lentils, cabbage, and red onions on top of the potatoes. Close the wraps by folding the bottom of the tortillas up and over the filling, then folding the sides in, then roll the bottom up to form a burrito. Place the wraps in the greased frying basket, seam side down. Air Fry for 6-8 minutes, flipping once until golden and crispy. Serve topped with cilantro chutney.

Tropical Salsa

Servings: 4
Cooking Time: 15 Minutes
Ingredients:
- 1 cup pineapple cubes
- ½ apple, cubed
- Salt to taste
- ¼ tsp olive oil
- 2 tomatoes, diced
- 1 avocado, diced
- 3-4 strawberries, diced
- ¼ cup diced red onion
- 1 tbsp chopped cilantro
- 1 tbsp chopped parsley
- 2 cloves garlic, minced
- ½ tsp granulated sugar
- ½ lime, juiced

Directions:
1. Preheat air fryer at 400°F. Combine pineapple cubes, apples, olive oil, and salt in a bowl. Place pineapple in the greased frying basket, and Air Fry for 8 minutes, shaking once. Transfer it to a bowl. Toss in tomatoes, avocado, strawberries, onion, cilantro, parsley, garlic, sugar, lime juice, and salt. Let chill in the fridge before using.

Bite-sized Blooming Onions

Servings: 4
Cooking Time: 35 Minutes + Cooling Time
Ingredients:
- 1 lb cipollini onions
- 1 cup flour
- 1 tsp salt
- ½ tsp paprika
- 1 tsp cayenne pepper
- 2 eggs
- 2 tbsp milk

Directions:
1. Preheat the air fryer to 375°F. Carefully peel the onions and cut a ½ inch off the stem ends and trim the root ends. Place them root-side down on the cutting surface and cut the onions into quarters. Be careful not to cut al the way to the bottom. Cut each quarter into 2 sections and pull the wedges apart without breaking them.
2. In a shallow bowl, add the flour, salt, paprika, and cayenne, and in a separate shallow bowl, beat the eggs with the milk. Dip the onions in the flour, then dip in the egg mix, coating evenly, and then in the flour mix again. Shake off excess flour. Put the onions in the frying basket, cut-side up, and spray with cooking oil. Air Fry for 10-15 minutes until the onions are crispy on the outside, tender on the inside. Let cool for 10 minutes, then serve.

Pizza Portobello Mushrooms

Servings: 2
Cooking Time: 18 Minutes
Ingredients:
- 2 portobello mushroom caps, gills removed (see Figure 13-1)
- 1 teaspoon extra-virgin olive oil
- ¼ cup diced onion
- 1 teaspoon minced garlic
- 1 medium zucchini, shredded
- 1 teaspoon dried oregano
- ½ teaspoon black pepper
- ¼ teaspoon salt
- ⅓ cup marinara sauce
- ¼ cup shredded part-skim mozzarella cheese
- ¼ teaspoon red pepper flakes
- 2 tablespoons Parmesan cheese
- 2 tablespoons chopped basil

Directions:
1. Preheat the air fryer to 370°F.
2. Lightly spray the mushrooms with an olive oil mist and place into the air fryer to cook for 10 minutes, cap side up.
3. Add the olive oil to a pan and sauté the onion and garlic together for about 2 to 4 minutes. Stir in the zucchini, oregano, pepper, and salt, and continue to cook. When the zucchini has cooked down (usually about 4 to 6 minutes), add in the marinara sauce. Remove from the heat and stir in the mozzarella cheese.
4. Remove the mushrooms from the air fryer basket when cooking completes. Reset the temperature to 350°F.
5. Using a spoon, carefully stuff the mushrooms with the zucchini marinara mixture.
6. Return the stuffed mushrooms to the air fryer basket and cook for 5 to 8 minutes, or until the cheese is lightly

browned.You should be able to easily insert a fork into the mushrooms when they're cooked.
7. Remove the mushrooms and sprinkle the red pepper flakes,Parmesan cheese,and fresh basil over the top.
8. Serve warm.

Cheese&Bean Burgers

Servings:2
Cooking Time:35 Minutes
Ingredients:
- 1 cup cooked black beans
- ½cup shredded cheddar
- 1 egg,beaten
- Salt and pepper to taste
- 1 cup bread crumbs
- ½cup grated carrots

Directions:
1. Preheat air fryer to 350°F.Mash the beans with a fork in a bowl.Mix in the cheese,salt,and pepper until evenly combined.Stir in half of the bread crumbs and egg.Shape the mixture into 2 patties.Coat each patty with the remaining bread crumbs and spray with cooking oil.Air Fry for 14-16 minutes,turning once.When ready,removeto a plate.Top with grated carrots and serve.

Stuffed Portobellos

Servings:4
Cooking Time:45 Minutes
Ingredients:
- 1 cup cherry tomatoes
- 2¼tsp olive oil
- 3 tbsp grated mozzarella
- 1 cup chopped baby spinach
- 1 garlic clove,minced
- ¼tsp dried oregano
- ¼tsp dried thyme
- Salt and pepper to taste
- ¼cup bread crumbs
- 4 portobello mushrooms,stemmed and gills removed
- 1 tbsp chopped parsley

Directions:
1. Preheat air fryer to 360°F.Combine tomatoes,¼teaspoon olive oil,and salt in a small bowl.Arrange in a single layer in the parchment-lined frying basket and Air Fry for 10 minutes.Stir and flatten the tomatoes with the back of a spoon,then Air Fry for another 6-8 minutes.Transfer the tomatoes to a medium bowl and combine with spinach,garlic,oregano,thyme,pepper,bread crumbs,and the rest of the olive oil.
2. Place the mushrooms on a work surface with the gills facing up.Spoon tomato mixture and mozzarella cheese equally into the mushroom caps and transfer the mushrooms to the frying basket.Air Fry for 8-10 minutes until the mushrooms have softened and the tops are golden.Garnish with chopped parsley and serve.

Stuffed Zucchini Boats

Servings:2
Cooking Time:20 Minutes
Ingredients:
- olive oil
- ½cup onion,finely chopped
- 1 clove garlic,finely minced
- ½teaspoon dried oregano
- ¼teaspoon dried thyme
- ¾cup couscous
- 1½cups chicken stock,divided
- 1 tomato,seeds removed and finely chopped
- ½cup coarsely chopped Kalamata olives
- ½cup grated Romano cheese
- ¼cup pine nuts,toasted
- 1 tablespoon chopped fresh parsley
- 1 teaspoon salt
- freshly ground black pepper
- 1 egg,beaten
- 1 cup grated mozzarella cheese,divided
- 2 thick zucchini

Directions:
1. Preheat a sautépan on the stovetop over medium-high heat.Add the olive oil and sautéthe onion until it just starts to soften–about 4 minutes.Stir in the garlic,dried oregano and thyme.Add the couscous and sautéfor just a minute.Add 1¼cups of the chicken stock and simmer over low heat for 3 to 5 minutes,until liquid has been absorbed and the couscous is soft.Remove the pan from heat and set it aside to cool slightly.
2. Fluff the couscous and add the tomato,Kalamata olives,Romano cheese,pine nuts,parsley,salt and pepper.Mix well.Add the remaining chicken stock,the egg and½cup of the mozzarella cheese.Stir to ensure everything is combined.
3. Cut each zucchini in half lengthwise.Then,trim each half of the zucchini into four 5-inch lengths.(Save the trimmed ends of the zucchini for another use.)Use a spoon to scoop out the center of the zucchini,leaving some flesh around the sides.Brush both sides of the zucchini with olive oil and season the cut side with salt and pepper.
4. Preheat the air fryer to 380°F.
5. Divide the couscous filling between the four zucchini boats.Use your hands to press the filling together and fill the inside of the zucchini.The filling should be mounded into the boats and rounded on top.
6. Transfer the zucchini boats to the air fryer basket and drizzle the stuffed zucchini boats with olive oil.Air-fry for 19 minutes.Then,sprinkle the remaining mozzarella cheese on top of the zucchini,pressing it down onto the filling lightly to prevent it from blowing around in the air fryer.Air-fry for one more minute to melt the cheese.Transfer the finished zucchini boats to a serving platter and garnish with the chopped parsley.

Easy Zucchini Lasagna Roll-ups

Servings:2
Cooking Time:40 Minutes
Ingredients:
- 2 medium zucchini
- 2 tbsp lemon juice
- 1½cups ricotta cheese
- 1 tbsp allspice
- 2 cups marinara sauce
- 1/3 cup mozzarella cheese

Directions:
1. Preheat air fryer to 400°F.Cut the ends of each zucchini,then slice into 1/4-inch thick pieces and drizzle with lemon juice.Roast for 5 minutes until slightly tender.Let cool slightly.Combine ricotta cheese and allspice in a bowl;set aside.Spread 2 tbsp of marinara sauce on the bottom of a baking pan.Spoon 1-2 tbsp of the ricotta mixture onto each slice,roll up each slice and place them spiral-side up in the pan.Scatter with the remaining ricotta mixture and drizzle with marinara sauce.Top with mozzarella cheese and Bake at 360ºF for 20 minutes until the cheese is bubbly and golden brown.Serve warm.

Vegetarian Eggplant "pizzas"

Servings: 4
Cooking Time: 25 Minutes
Ingredients:
- ½ cup diced baby bella mushrooms
- 3 tbsp olive oil
- ¼ cup diced onions
- ½ cup pizza sauce
- 1 eggplant, sliced
- 1 tsp salt
- 1 cup shredded mozzarella
- ¼ cup chopped oregano

Directions:
1. Warm 2 tsp of olive oil in a skillet over medium heat. Add in onion and mushrooms and stir-fry for 4 minutes until tender. Stir in pizza sauce. Turn the heat off.
2. Preheat air fryer to 375°F. Brush the eggplant slices with the remaining olive oil on both sides. Lay out slices on a large plate and season with salt. Then, top with the sauce mixture and shredded mozzarella. Place the eggplant pizzas in the frying basket and Air Fry for 5 minutes. Garnish with oregano to serve.

Caprese-style Sandwiches

Servings: 2
Cooking Time: 20 Minutes
Ingredients:
- 2 tbsp balsamic vinegar
- 4 sandwich bread slices
- 2 oz mozzarella shreds
- 3 tbsp pesto sauce
- 2 tomatoes, sliced
- 8 basil leaves
- 8 baby spinach leaves
- 2 tbsp olive oil

Directions:
1. Preheat air fryer at 350°F. Drizzle balsamic vinegar on the bottom of bread slices and smear with pesto sauce. Then, layer mozzarella cheese, tomatoes, baby spinach leaves and basil leaves on top. Add top bread slices. Rub the outside top and bottom of each sandwich with olive oil. Place them in the frying basket and Bake for 5 minutes, flipping once. Serve right away.

Ricotta Veggie Potpie

Servings: 4
Cooking Time: 30 Minutes
Ingredients:
- 1¼ cup flour
- ¾ cup ricotta cheese
- 1 tbsp olive oil
- 1 potato, peeled and diced
- ¼ cup diced mushrooms
- ¼ cup diced carrots
- ¼ cup diced celery
- ¼ cup diced yellow onion
- 1 garlic clove, minced
- 1 tbsp unsalted butter
- 1 cup milk
- ½ tsp ground black pepper
- 1 tsp dried thyme
- 2 tbsp dill, chopped

Directions:
1. Preheat air fryer to 350°F. Combine 1 cup flour and ricotta cheese in a medium bowl and stir until the dough comes together. Heat oil over medium heat in a small skillet. Stir in potato, mushroom, carrots, dill, thyme, celery, onion, and garlic. Cook for 4-5 minutes, often stirring, until the onions are soft and translucent.
2. Add butter and melt, then stir in the rest of the flour. Slowly pour in the milk and keep stirring. Simmer for 5 minutes until the sauce has thickened, then stir in pepper and thyme. Spoon the vegetable mixture into four 6-ounce ramekins. Cut the dough into 4 equal sections and work it into rounds that fit over the size of the ramekins. Top the ramekins with the dough, then place the ramekins in the frying basket. Bake for 10 minutes until the crust is golden. Serve hot and enjoy.

Mexican Twice Air-fried Sweet Potatoes

Servings: 2
Cooking Time: 42 Minutes
Ingredients:
- 2 large sweet potatoes
- olive oil
- salt and freshly ground black pepper
- ⅓ cup diced red onion
- ⅓ cup diced red bell pepper
- ½ cup canned black beans, drained and rinsed
- ½ cup corn kernels, fresh or frozen
- ½ teaspoon chili powder
- 1½ cups grated pepper jack cheese, divided
- Jalapeño peppers, sliced

Directions:
1. Preheat the air fryer to 400°F.
2. Rub the outside of the sweet potatoes with olive oil and season with salt and freshly ground black pepper. Transfer the potatoes into the air fryer basket and air-fry at 400°F for 30 minutes, rotating the potatoes a few times during the cooking process.
3. While the potatoes are air-frying, start the potato filling. Preheat a large sautépan over medium heat on the stovetop. Add the onion and pepper and sautéfor a few minutes, until the vegetables start to soften. Add the black beans, corn, and chili powder and sautéfor another 3 minutes. Set the mixture aside.
4. Remove the sweet potatoes from the air fryer and let them rest for 5 minutes. Slice off one inch of the flattest side of both potatoes. Scrape the potato flesh out of the potatoes, leaving half an inch of potato flesh around the edge of the potato. Place all the potato flesh into a large bowl and mash it with a fork. Add the black bean mixture and 1 cup of the pepper jack cheese to the mashed sweet potatoes. Season with salt and freshly ground black pepper and mix well. Stuff the hollowed out potato shells with the black bean and sweet potato mixture, mounding the filling high in the potatoes.
5. Transfer the stuffed potatoes back into the air fryer basket and air-fry at 370°F for 10 minutes. Sprinkle the remaining cheese on top of each stuffed potato, lower the heat to 340°F and air-fry for an additional 2 minutes to melt the cheese. Top with a couple slices of Jalapeño pepper and serve warm with a green salad.

Easy Cheese & Spinach Lasagna

Servings: 6
Cooking Time: 50 Minutes
Ingredients:
- 1 zucchini, cut into strips
- 1 tbsp butter
- 4 garlic cloves, minced
- ½ yellow onion, diced
- 1 tsp dried oregano
- ¼ tsp red pepper flakes
- 1 can diced tomatoes
- 4 oz ricotta

- 3 tbsp grated mozzarella
- ½ cup grated cheddar
- 3 tsp grated Parmesan cheese
- ⅛ cup chopped basil
- 2 tbsp chopped parsley
- Salt and pepper to taste
- ¼ tsp ground nutmeg

Directions:
1. Preheat air fryer to 375°F. Melt butter in a medium skillet over medium heat. Stir in half of the garlic and onion and cook for 2 minutes. Stir in oregano and red pepper flakes and cook for 1 minute. Reduce the heat to medium-low and pour in crushed tomatoes and their juices. Cover the skillet and simmer for 5 minutes.
2. Mix ricotta, mozzarella, cheddar cheese, rest of the garlic, basil, black pepper, and nutmeg in a large bowl. Arrange a layer of zucchini strips in the baking dish. Scoop 1/3 of the cheese mixture and spread evenly over the zucchini. Spread 1/3 of the tomato sauce over the cheese. Repeat the steps two more times, then top the lasagna with Parmesan cheese. Bake in the frying basket for 25 minutes until the mixture is bubbling and the mozzarella is melted. Allow sitting for 10 minutes before cutting. Serve warm sprinkled with parsley and enjoy!

Spicy Vegetable And Tofu Shake Fry

Servings: 4
Cooking Time: 17 Minutes
Ingredients:
- 4 teaspoons canola oil, divided
- 2 tablespoons rice wine vinegar
- 1 tablespoon sriracha chili sauce
- ¼ cup soy sauce*
- ½ teaspoon toasted sesame oil
- 1 teaspoon minced garlic
- 1 tablespoon minced fresh ginger
- 8 ounces extra firm tofu
- ½ cup vegetable stock or water
- 1 tablespoon honey
- 1 tablespoon cornstarch
- ½ red onion, chopped
- 1 red or yellow bell pepper, chopped
- 1 cup green beans, cut into 2-inch lengths
- 4 ounces mushrooms, sliced
- 2 scallions, sliced
- 2 tablespoons fresh cilantro leaves
- 2 teaspoons toasted sesame seeds

Directions:
1. Combine 1 tablespoon of the oil, vinegar, sriracha sauce, soy sauce, sesame oil, garlic and ginger in a small bowl. Cut the tofu into bite-sized cubes and toss the tofu in with the marinade while you prepare the other vegetables. When you are ready to start cooking, remove the tofu from the marinade and set it aside. Add the water, honey and cornstarch to the marinade and bring to a simmer on the stovetop, just until the sauce thickens. Set the sauce aside.
2. Preheat the air fryer to 400°F.
3. Toss the onion, pepper, green beans and mushrooms in a bowl with a little canola oil and season with salt. Air-fry at 400°F for 11 minutes, shaking the basket and tossing the vegetables every few minutes. When the vegetables are cooked to your preferred doneness, remove them from the air fryer and set aside.
4. Add the tofu to the air fryer basket and air-fry at 400°F for 6 minutes, shaking the basket a few times during the cooking process. Add the vegetables back to the basket and air-fry for another minute. Transfer the vegetables and tofu to a large bowl, add the scallions and cilantro leaves and toss with the sauce. Serve over rice with sesame seeds sprinkled on top.

Tomato & Squash Stuffed Mushrooms

Servings: 2
Cooking Time: 15 Minutes
Ingredients:
- 12 whole white button mushrooms
- 3 tsp olive oil
- 2 tbsp diced zucchini
- 1 tsp soy sauce
- ¼ tsp salt
- 2 tbsp tomato paste
- 1 tbsp chopped parsley

Directions:
1. Preheat air fryer to 350ºF. Remove the stems from the mushrooms. Chop the stems finely and set in a bowl. Brush 1 tsp of olive oil around the top ridge of mushroom caps. To the bowl of the stem, add all ingredients, except for parsley, and mix. Divide and press mixture into tops of mushroom caps. Place the mushrooms in the frying basket and Air Fry for 5 minutes. Top with parsley. Serve.

Falafels

Servings: 12
Cooking Time: 10 Minutes
Ingredients:
- 1 pouch falafel mix
- 2–3 tablespoons plain breadcrumbs
- oil for misting or cooking spray

Directions:
1. Prepare falafel mix according to package directions.
2. Preheat air fryer to 390°F.
3. Place breadcrumbs in shallow dish or on wax paper.
4. Shape falafel mixture into 12 balls and flatten slightly. Roll in breadcrumbs to coat all sides and mist with oil or cooking spray.
5. Place falafels in air fryer basket in single layer and cook for 5 minutes. Shake basket, and continue cooking for 5 minutes, until they brown and are crispy.

Crunchy Rice Paper Samosas

Servings: 2
Cooking Time: 20 Minutes
Ingredients:
- 1 boiled potato, mashed
- ¼ cup green peas
- 1 tsp garam masala powder
- ½ tsp ginger garlic paste
- ½ tsp cayenne pepper
- ½ tsp turmeric powder
- Salt and pepper to taste
- 3 rice paper wrappers

Directions:
1. Preheat air fryer to 350°F. Place the mashed potatoes in a bowl. Add the peas, garam masala powder, ginger garlic paste, cayenne pepper, turmeric powder, salt, and pepper and stir until ingredients are evenly blended.
2. Lay the rice paper wrappers out on a lightly floured surface. Divide the potato mixture between the wrappers and fold the top edges over to seal. Transfer the samosas to the greased frying basket and Air Fry for 12 minutes, flipping once until the samosas are crispy and flaky. Remove and leave to cool for 5 minutes. Serve and enjoy!

Roasted Vegetable, Brown Rice And Black Bean Burrito

Servings: 2
Cooking Time: 20 Minutes
Ingredients:
- ½ zucchini, sliced ¼-inch thick
- ½ red onion, sliced
- 1 yellow bell pepper, sliced
- 2 teaspoons olive oil
- salt and freshly ground black pepper
- 2 burrito size flour tortillas
- 1 cup grated pepper jack cheese
- ½ cup cooked brown rice
- ½ cup canned black beans, drained and rinsed
- ¼ teaspoon ground cumin
- 1 tablespoon chopped fresh cilantro
- fresh salsa, guacamole and sour cream, for serving

Directions:
1. Preheat the air fryer to 400°F.
2. Toss the vegetables in a bowl with the olive oil, salt and freshly ground black pepper. Air-fry at 400°F for 12 to 15 minutes, shaking the basket a few times during the cooking process. The vegetables are done when they are cooked to your liking.
3. In the meantime, start building the burritos. Lay the tortillas out on the counter. Sprinkle half of the cheese in the center of the tortillas. Combine the rice, beans, cumin and cilantro in a bowl, season to taste with salt and freshly ground black pepper and then divide the mixture between the two tortillas. When the vegetables have finished cooking, transfer them to the two tortillas, placing the vegetables on top of the rice and beans. Sprinkle the remaining cheese on top and then roll the burritos up, tucking in the sides of the tortillas as you roll. Brush or spray the outside of the burritos with olive oil and transfer them to the air fryer.
4. Air-fry at 360°F for 8 minutes, turning them over when there are about 2 minutes left. The burritos will have slightly brown spots, but will still be pliable.
5. Serve with some fresh salsa, guacamole and sour cream.

Spinach And Cheese Calzone

Servings: 2
Cooking Time: 10 Minutes
Ingredients:
- ⅔ cup frozen chopped spinach, thawed
- 1 cup grated mozzarella cheese
- 1 cup ricotta cheese
- ½ teaspoon Italian seasoning
- ½ teaspoon salt
- freshly ground black pepper
- 1 store-bought or homemade pizza dough*(about 12 to 16 ounces)
- 2 tablespoons olive oil
- pizza or marinara sauce(optional)

Directions:
1. Drain and squeeze all the water out of the thawed spinach and set it aside. Mix the mozzarella cheese, ricotta cheese, Italian seasoning, salt and freshly ground black pepper together in a bowl. Stir in the chopped spinach.
2. Divide the dough in half. With floured hands or on a floured surface, stretch or roll one half of the dough into a 10-inch circle. Spread half of the cheese and spinach mixture on half of the dough, leaving about one inch of dough empty around the edge.
3. Fold the other half of the dough over the cheese mixture, almost to the edge of the bottom dough to form a half moon. Fold the bottom edge of dough up over the top edge and crimp the dough around the edges in order to make the crust and seal the calzone. Brush the dough with olive oil. Repeat with the second half of dough to make the second calzone.
4. Preheat the air fryer to 360°F.
5. Brush or spray the air fryer basket with olive oil. Air-fry the calzones one at a time for 10 minutes, flipping the calzone over half way through. Serve with warm pizza or marinara sauce if desired.

Zucchini Tacos

Servings: 3
Cooking Time: 20 Minutes
Ingredients:
- 1 small zucchini, sliced
- 1 yellow onion, sliced
- ¼ tsp garlic powder
- Salt and pepper to taste
- 1 can refried beans
- 6 corn tortillas, warm
- 1 cup guacamole
- 1 tbsp cilantro, chopped

Directions:
1. Preheat air fryer to 390°F. Place the zucchini and onion in the greased frying basket. Spray with more oil and sprinkle with garlic, salt, and pepper to taste. Roast for 6 minutes. Remove, shake, or stir, then cook for another 6 minutes, until the veggies are golden and tender.
2. In a pan, heat the refried beans over low heat. Stir often. When warm enough, remove from heat and set aside. Place a corn tortilla on a plate and fill it with beans, roasted vegetables, and guacamole. Top with cilantro to serve.

Roasted Vegetable Pita Pizza

Servings: 4
Cooking Time: 20 Minutes
Ingredients:
- 1 medium red bell pepper, seeded and cut into quarters
- 1 teaspoon extra-virgin olive oil
- ⅛ teaspoon black pepper
- ⅛ teaspoon salt
- Two 6-inch whole-grain pita breads
- 6 tablespoons pesto sauce
- ¼ small red onion, thinly sliced
- ½ cup shredded part-skim mozzarella cheese

Directions:
1. Preheat the air fryer to 400°F.
2. In a small bowl, toss the bell peppers with the olive oil, pepper, and salt.
3. Place the bell peppers in the air fryer and cook for 15 minutes, shaking every 5 minutes to prevent burning.
4. Remove the peppers and set aside. Turn the air fryer temperature down to 350°F.
5. Lay the pita bread on a flat surface. Cover each with half the pesto sauce; then top with even portions of the red bell peppers and onions. Sprinkle cheese over the top. Spray the air fryer basket with olive oil mist.
6. Carefully lift the pita bread into the air fryer basket with a spatula.
7. Cook for 5 to 8 minutes, or until the outer edges begin to brown and the cheese is melted.
8. Serve warm with desired sides.

Roasted Vegetable Thai Green Curry

Servings: 4
Cooking Time: 16 Minutes
Ingredients:
- 1(13-ounce)can coconut milk
- 3 tablespoons green curry paste
- 1 tablespoon soy sauce*
- 1 tablespoon rice wine vinegar
- 1 teaspoon sugar
- 1 teaspoon minced fresh ginger
- ½ onion, chopped
- 3 carrots, sliced
- 1 red bell pepper, chopped
- olive oil
- 10 stalks of asparagus, cut into 2-inch pieces
- 3 cups broccoli florets
- basmati rice for serving
- fresh cilantro
- crushed red pepper flakes(optional)

Directions:
1. Combine the coconut milk, green curry paste, soy sauce, rice wine vinegar, sugar and ginger in a medium saucepan and bring to a boil on the stovetop. Reduce the heat and simmer for 20 minutes while you cook the vegetables. Set aside.
2. Preheat the air fryer to 400°F.
3. Toss the onion, carrots, and red pepper together with a little olive oil and transfer the vegetables to the air fryer basket. Air-fry at 400°F for 10 minutes, shaking the basket a few times during the cooking process. Add the asparagus and broccoli florets and air-fry for an additional 6 minutes, again shaking the basket for even cooking.
4. When the vegetables are cooked to your liking, toss them with the green curry sauce and serve in bowls over basmati rice. Garnish with fresh chopped cilantro and crushed red pepper flakes.

Vietnamese Gingered Tofu

Servings: 4
Cooking Time: 25 Minutes
Ingredients:
- 1 package extra-firm tofu, cubed
- 4 tsp shoyu
- 1 tsp onion powder
- ½ tsp garlic powder
- ½ tsp ginger powder
- ½ tsp turmeric powder
- Black pepper to taste
- 2 tbsp nutritional yeast
- 1 tsp dried rosemary
- 1 tsp dried dill
- 2 tsp cornstarch
- 2 tsp sunflower oil

Directions:
1. Sprinkle the tofu with shoyu and toss to coat. Add the onion, garlic, ginger, turmeric, and pepper. Gently toss to coat. Add the yeast, rosemary, dill, and cornstarch. Toss to coat. Dribble with the oil and toss again.
2. Preheat air fryer to 390°F. Spray the fryer basket with oil, put the tofu in the basket and Bake for 7 minutes. Remove, shake gently, and cook for another 7 minutes or until the tofu is crispy and golden. Serve warm.

Balsamic Caprese Hasselback

Servings: 4
Cooking Time: 15 Minutes
Ingredients:
- 4 tomatoes
- 12 fresh basil leaves
- 1 ball fresh mozzarella
- Salt and pepper to taste
- 1 tbsp olive oil
- 2 tsp balsamic vinegar
- 1 tbsp basil, torn

Directions:
1. Preheat air fryer to 325°F. Remove the bottoms from the tomatoes to create a flat surface. Make 4 even slices on each tomato, 3/4 of the way down. Slice the mozzarella and the cut into 12 pieces. Stuff 1 basil leaf and a piece of mozzarella into each slice. Sprinkle with salt and pepper. Place the stuffed tomatoes in the frying basket and Air Fry for 3 minutes. Transfer to a large serving plate. Drizzle with olive oil and balsamic vinegar and scatter the basil over. Serve and enjoy!

General Tso's Cauliflower

Servings: 4
Cooking Time: 15 Minutes
Ingredients:
- 1 head cauliflower cut into florets
- ¾ cup all-purpose flour, divided*
- 3 eggs, lightly beaten
- 1 cup panko breadcrumbs*
- canola or peanut oil, in a spray bottle
- 2 tablespoons oyster sauce
- ¼ cup soy sauce
- 2 teaspoons chili paste
- 2 tablespoons rice wine vinegar
- 2 tablespoons sugar
- ¼ cup water
- white or brown rice for serving
- steamed broccoli

Directions:
1. Set up dredging station using three bowls. Place the cauliflower in a large bowl and sprinkle ¼ cup of the flour over the top. Place the eggs in a second bowl and combine the panko breadcrumbs and remaining ½ cup flour in a third bowl. Toss the cauliflower in the flour to coat all the florets thoroughly. Dip the cauliflower florets in the eggs and finally toss them in the breadcrumbs to coat on all sides. Place the coated cauliflower florets on a baking sheet and spray generously with canola or peanut oil.
2. Preheat the air fryer to 400°F.
3. Air-fry the cauliflower at 400°F for 15 minutes, flipping the florets over for the last 3 minutes of the cooking process and spraying again with oil.
4. While the cauliflower is air-frying, make the General Tso Sauce. Combine the oyster sauce, soy sauce, chili paste, rice wine vinegar, sugar and water in a saucepan and bring the mixture to a boil on the stove top. Lower the heat and let it simmer for 10 minutes, stirring occasionally.
5. When the timer is up on the air fryer, transfer the cauliflower to a large bowl, pour the sauce over it all and toss to coat. Serve with white or brown rice and some steamed broccoli.

Thai Peanut Veggie Burgers

Servings:6
Cooking Time:14 Minutes
Ingredients:
- One 15.5-ounce can cannellini beans
- 1 teaspoon minced garlic
- ¼cup chopped onion
- 1 Thai chili pepper,sliced
- 2 tablespoons natural peanut butter
- ½teaspoon black pepper
- ½teaspoon salt
- ⅓cup all-purpose flour(optional)
- ½cup cooked quinoa
- 1 large carrot,grated
- 1 cup shredded red cabbage
- ¼cup peanut dressing
- ¼cup chopped cilantro
- 6 Hawaiian rolls
- 6 butterleaf lettuce leaves

Directions:
1. Preheat the air fryer to 350°F.
2. To a blender or food processor fitted with a metal blade,add the beans,garlic,onion,chili pepper,peanut butter,pepper,and salt.Pulse for 5 to 10 seconds.Do not over process.The mixture should be coarse,not smooth.
3. Remove from the blender or food processor and spoon into a large bowl.Mix in the cooked quinoa and carrots.At this point,the mixture should begin to hold together to form small patties.If the dough appears to be too sticky(meaning you likely processed a little too long),add the flour to hold the patties together.
4. Using a large spoon,form 8 equal patties out of the batter.
5. Liberally spray a metal trivet with olive oil spray and set in the air fryer basket.Place the patties into the basket,leaving enough space to be able to turn them with a spatula.
6. Cook for 7 minutes,flip,and cook another 7 minutes.
7. Remove from the heat and repeat with additional patties.
8. To serve,place the red cabbage in a bowl and toss with peanut dressing and cilantro.Place the veggie burger on a bun,and top with a slice of lettuce and cabbage slaw.

Quinoa&Black Bean Stuffed Peppers

Servings:4
Cooking Time:30 Minutes
Ingredients:
- ½cup vegetable broth
- ½cup quinoa
- 1 can black beans
- ½cup diced red onion
- 1 garlic clove,minced
- ½tsp salt
- ½tsp ground cumin
- ¼tsp paprika
- ¼tsp ancho chili powder
- 4 bell peppers,any color
- ½cup grated cheddar
- ¼cup chopped cilantro
- ½cup red enchilada sauce

Directions:
1. Add vegetable broth and quinoa to a small saucepan over medium heat.Bring to a boil,then cover and let it simmer for 5 minutes.Turn off the heat.
2. Preheat air fryer to 350°F.Transfer quinoa to a medium bowl and stir in black beans,onion,red enchilada sauce,ancho chili powder,garlic,salt,cumin,and paprika.Cut the top¼-inch off the bell peppers.Remove seeds and membranes.Scoop quinoa filling into each pepper and top with cheddar cheese.Transfer peppers to the frying basket and bake for 10 minutes until peppers are soft and filling is heated through.Garnish with cilantro.Serve warm along with salsa.Enjoy!

Vegetarian Shepherd's Pie

Servings:4
Cooking Time:40 Minutes
Ingredients:
- 1 russet potato,peeled and diced
- 1 tbsp olive oil
- 2 tbsp balsamic vinegar
- ¼cup cheddar shreds
- 2 tbsp milk
- Salt and pepper to taste
- 2 tsp avocado oil
- 1 cup beefless grounds
- ½onion,diced
- 3 cloves garlic
- 1 carrot,diced
- ¼diced green bell peppers
- 1 celery stalk,diced
- 2/3 cup tomato sauce
- 1 tsp chopped rosemary
- 1 tbsp sesame seeds
- 1 tsp thyme leaves
- 1 lemon

Directions:
1. Add salted water to a pot over high heat and bring it to a boil.Add in diced potatoes and cook for 5 minutes until fork tender.Drain and transfer it to a bowl.Add in the olive oil cheddar shreds,milk,salt,and pepper and mash it until smooth.Set the potato topping aside.
2. Preheat air fryer at 350ºF.Place avocado oil,beefless grounds,garlic,onion,carrot,bell pepper,and celery in a skillet over medium heat and cook for 4 minutes until the veggies are tender.Stir in the remaining ingredients and turn the heat off.Spoon the filling into a greased cake pan.Top with the potato topping.
3. Using tines of a fork,create shallow lines along the top of mashed potatoes.Place cake pan in the frying basket and Bake for 12 minutes.Let rest for 10 minutes before serving sprinkled with sesame seeds and squeezed lemon.

Quinoa Burgers With Feta Cheese And Dill

Servings:6
Cooking Time:10 Minutes
Ingredients:
- 1 cup quinoa(red,white or multi-colored)
- 1½cups water
- 1 teaspoon salt
- freshly ground black pepper
- 1½cups rolled oats
- 3 eggs,lightly beaten
- ¼cup minced white onion
- ½cup crumbled feta cheese
- ¼cup chopped fresh dill
- salt and freshly ground black pepper
- vegetable or canola oil,in a spray bottle
- whole-wheat hamburger buns(or gluten-free hamburger buns*)
- arugula
- tomato,sliced
- red onion,sliced
- mayonnaise

Directions:
1. Make the quinoa: Rinse the quinoa in cold water in a saucepan, swirling it with your hand until any dry husks rise to the surface. Drain the quinoa as well as you can and then put the saucepan on the stovetop to dry and toast the quinoa. Turn the heat to medium-high and shake the pan regularly until you see the quinoa moving easily and can hear the seeds moving in the pan, indicating that they are dry. Add the water, salt and pepper. Bring the liquid to a boil and then reduce the heat to low or medium-low. You should see just a few bubbles, not a boil. Cover with a lid, leaving it askew and simmer for 20 minutes. Turn the heat off and fluff the quinoa with a fork. If there's any liquid left in the bottom of the pot, place it back on the burner for another 3 minutes or so. Spread the cooked quinoa out on a sheet pan to cool.
2. Combine the room temperature quinoa in a large bowl with the oats, eggs, onion, cheese and dill. Season with salt and pepper and mix well (remember that feta cheese is salty). Shape the mixture into 6 patties with flat sides (so they fit more easily into the air fryer). Add a little water or a few more rolled oats if necessary to get the mixture to be the right consistency to make patties.
3. Preheat the air-fryer to 400°F.
4. Spray both sides of the patties generously with oil and transfer them to the air fryer basket in one layer (you will probably have to cook these burgers in batches, depending on the size of your air fryer). Air-fry each batch at 400°F for 10 minutes, flipping the burgers over halfway through the cooking time.
5. Build your burger on the whole-wheat hamburger buns with arugula, tomato, red onion and mayonnaise.

Chicano Rice Bowls

Servings: 4
Cooking Time: 10 Minutes
Ingredients:
- 1 cup sour cream
- 2 tbsp milk
- 1 tsp ground cumin
- 1 tsp chili powder
- 1/8 tsp cayenne pepper
- 1 tbsp tomato paste
- 1 white onion, chopped
- 1 clove garlic, minced
- ½ tsp ground turmeric
- ½ tsp salt
- 1 cup canned black beans
- 1 cup canned corn kernels
- 1 tsp olive oil
- 4 cups cooked brown rice
- 3 tomatoes, diced
- 1 avocado, diced

Directions:
1. Whisk the sour cream, milk, cumin, ground turmeric, chili powder, cayenne pepper, and salt in a bowl. Let chill covered in the fridge until ready to use.
2. Preheat air fryer at 350°F. Combine beans, white onion, tomato paste, garlic, corn, and olive oil in a bowl. Transfer it into the frying basket and Air Fry for 5 minutes. Divide cooked rice into 4 serving bowls. Top each with bean mixture, tomatoes, and avocado and drizzle with sour cream mixture over. Serve immediately.

Cheddar-bean Flautas

Servings: 4
Cooking Time: 15 Minutes
Ingredients:
- 8 corn tortillas
- 1 can refried beans
- 1 cup shredded cheddar
- 1 cup guacamole

Directions:
1. Preheat air fryer to 390°F. Wet the tortillas with water. Spray the frying basket with oil and stack the tortillas inside. Air Fry for 1 minute. Remove to a flat surface, laying them out individually. Scoop an equal amount of beans in a line down the center of each tortilla. Top with cheddar cheese. Roll the tortilla sides over the filling and put seam-side down in the greased frying basket. Air Fry for 7 minutes or until the tortillas are golden and crispy. Serve immediately topped with guacamole.

Pineapple & Veggie Souvlaki

Servings: 4
Cooking Time: 35 Minutes
Ingredients:
- 1 can pineapple rings in pineapple juice
- 1 red bell pepper, stemmed and seeded
- 1/3 cup butter
- 2 tbsp apple cider vinegar
- 2 tbsp hot sauce
- 1 tbsp allspice
- 1 tsp ground nutmeg
- 16 oz feta cheese
- 1 red onion, peeled
- 8 mushrooms, quartered

Directions:
1. Preheat air fryer to 400°F. Whisk the butter, pineapple juice, apple vinegar, hot sauce, allspice, and nutmeg until smooth. Set aside. Slice feta cheese into 16 cubes, then the bell pepper into 16 chunks, and finally red onion into 8 wedges, separating each wedge into 2 pieces.
2. Cut pineapple ring into quarters. Place veggie cubes and feta into the butter bowl and toss to coat. Thread the veggies, tofu, and pineapple onto 8 skewers, alternating 16 pieces on each skewer. Grill for 15 minutes until golden brown and cooked. Serve warm.

Smoked Paprika Sweet Potato Fries

Servings: 4
Cooking Time: 35 Minutes
Ingredients:
- 2 sweet potatoes, peeled
- 1½ tbsp cornstarch
- 1 tbsp canola oil
- 1 tbsp olive oil
- 1 tsp smoked paprika
- 1 tsp garlic powder
- Salt and pepper to taste
- 1 cup cocktail sauce

Directions:
1. Cut the potatoes lengthwise to form French fries. Put in a resealable plastic bag and add cornstarch. Seal and shake to coat the fries. Combine the canola oil, olive oil, paprika, garlic powder, salt, and pepper fries in a large bowl. Add the sweet potato fries and mix to combine.
2. Preheat air fryer to 380°F. Place fries in the greased basket and fry for 20-25 minutes, shaking the basket once until crisp. Drizzle with Cocktail sauce to serve.

Honey Pear Chips

Servings: 4
Cooking Time: 30 Minutes
Ingredients:
- 2 firm pears, thinly sliced
- 1 tbsp lemon juice
- ½ tsp ground cinnamon
- 1 tsp honey

Directions:
1. Preheat air fryer to 380°F. Arrange the pear slices on the parchment-lined cooking basket. Drizzle with lemon juice and honey and sprinkle with cinnamon. Air Fry for 6-8 minutes, shaking the basket once, until golden. Leave to cool. Serve immediately or save for later in an airtight container. Good for 2 days.

Cheesy Enchilada Stuffed Baked Potatoes

Servings: 4
Cooking Time: 37 Minutes
Ingredients:
- 2 medium russet potatoes, washed
- One 15-ounce can mild red enchilada sauce
- One 15-ounce can low-sodium black beans, rinsed and drained
- 1 teaspoon taco seasoning
- ½ cup shredded cheddar cheese
- 1 medium avocado, halved
- ½ teaspoon garlic powder
- ¼ teaspoon black pepper
- ¼ teaspoon salt
- 2 teaspoons fresh lime juice
- 2 tablespoon chopped red onion
- ¼ cup chopped cilantro

Directions:
1. Preheat the air fryer to 390°F.
2. Puncture the outer surface of the potatoes with a fork.
3. Set the potatoes inside the air fryer basket and cook for 20 minutes, rotate, and cook another 10 minutes.
4. In a large bowl, mix the enchilada sauce, black beans, and taco seasoning.
5. When the potatoes have finished cooking, carefully remove them from the air fryer basket and let cool for 5 minutes.
6. Using a pair of tongs to hold the potato if it's still too hot to touch, slice the potato in half lengthwise. Use a spoon to scoop out the potato flesh and add it into the bowl with the enchilada sauce. Mash the potatoes with the enchilada sauce mixture, creating a uniform stuffing.
7. Place the potato skins into an air-fryer-safe pan and stuff the halves with the enchilada stuffing. Sprinkle the cheese over the top of each potato.
8. Set the air fryer temperature to 350°F, return the pan to the air fryer basket, and cook for another 5 to 7 minutes to heat the potatoes and melt the cheese.
9. While the potatoes are cooking, take the avocado and scoop out the flesh into a small bowl. Mash it with the back of a fork; then mix in the garlic powder, pepper, salt, lime juice, and onion. Set aside.
10. When the potatoes have finished cooking, remove the pan from the air fryer and place the potato halves on a plate. Top with avocado mash and fresh cilantro. Serve immediately.

Spicy Bean Patties

Servings: 4
Cooking Time: 20 Minutes
Ingredients:
- 1 cup canned black beans
- 1 bread slice, torn
- 2 tbsp spicy brown mustard
- 1 tbsp chili powder
- 1 egg white
- 2 tbsp grated carrots
- ¼ diced green bell pepper
- 1-2 jalapeño peppers, diced
- ¼ tsp ground cumin
- ¼ tsp smoked paprika
- 2 tbsp cream cheese
- 1 tbsp olive oil

Directions:
1. Preheat air fryer at 350ºF. Using a fork, mash beans until smooth. Stir in the remaining ingredients, except olive oil. Form mixture into 4 patties. Place bean patties in the greased frying basket and Air Fry for 6 minutes, turning once, and brush with olive oil. Serve immediately.

Asparagus, Mushroom And Cheese Soufflés

Servings: 3
Cooking Time: 21 Minutes
Ingredients:
- butter
- grated Parmesan cheese
- 3 button mushrooms, thinly sliced
- 8 spears asparagus, sliced ½-inch long
- 1 teaspoon olive oil
- 1 tablespoon butter
- 4½ teaspoons flour
- pinch paprika
- pinch ground nutmeg
- salt and freshly ground black pepper
- ½ cup milk
- ½ cup grated Gruyère cheese or other Swiss cheese (about 2 ounces)
- 2 eggs, separated

Directions:
1. Butter three 6-ounce ramekins and dust with grated Parmesan cheese. (Butter the ramekins and then coat the butter with Parmesan by shaking it around in the ramekin and dumping out any excess.)
2. Preheat the air fryer to 400°F.
3. Toss the mushrooms and asparagus in a bowl with the olive oil. Transfer the vegetables to the air fryer and air-fry for 7 minutes, shaking the basket once or twice to redistribute the Ingredients while they cook.
4. While the vegetables are cooking, make the soufflé base. Melt the butter in a saucepan on the stovetop over medium heat. Add the flour, stir and cook for a minute or two. Add the paprika, nutmeg, salt and pepper. Whisk in the milk and bring the mixture to a simmer to thicken. Remove the pan from the heat and add the cheese, stirring to melt. Let the mixture cool for just a few minutes and then whisk the egg yolks in, one at a time. Stir in the cooked mushrooms and asparagus. Let this soufflé base cool.

Ninja Foodi 2-Basket Air Fryer

5. In a separate bowl, whisk the egg whites to soft peak stage(the point at which the whites can almost stand up on the end of your whisk). Fold the whipped egg whites into the soufflé base, adding a little at a time.
6. Preheat the air fryer to 330°F.
7. Transfer the batter carefully to the buttered ramekins, leaving about½-inch at the top. Place the ramekins into the air fryer basket and air-fry for 14 minutes. The soufflés should have risen nicely and be brown on top. Serve immediately.

Quinoa Green Pizza

Servings: 2
Cooking Time: 25 Minutes
Ingredients:
- ¾ cup quinoa flour
- ½ tsp dried basil
- ½ tsp dried oregano
- 1 tbsp apple cider vinegar
- 1/3 cup ricotta cheese
- 2/3 cup chopped broccoli
- ½ tsp garlic powder

Directions:
1. Preheat air fryer to 350°F. Whisk quinoa flour, basil, oregano, apple cider vinegar, and ½ cup of water until smooth. Set aside. Cut 2 pieces of parchment paper. Place the quinoa mixture on one paper, top with another piece, and flatten to create a crust. Discard the top piece of paper. Bake for 5 minutes, turn and discard the other piece of paper. Spread the ricotta cheese over the crust, scatter with broccoli, and sprinkle with garlic. Grill at 400ºF for 5 minutes until golden brown. Serve warm.

Powerful Jackfruit Fritters

Servings: 4
Cooking Time: 30 Minutes
Ingredients:
- 1 can jackfruit, chopped
- 1 egg, beaten
- 1 tbsp Dijon mustard
- 1 tbsp mayonnaise
- 1 tbsp prepared horseradish
- 2 tbsp grated yellow onion
- 2 tbsp chopped parsley
- 2 tbsp chopped nori
- 2 tbsp flour
- 1 tbsp Cajun seasoning
- ¼ tsp garlic powder
- ¼ tsp salt
- 2 lemon wedges

Directions:
1. In a bowl, combine jackfruit, egg, mustard, mayonnaise, horseradish, onion, parsley, nori, flour, Cajun seasoning, garlic, and salt. Let chill in the fridge for 15 minutes. Preheat air fryer to 350°F. Divide the mixture into 12 balls. Place them in the frying basket and Air Fry for 10 minutes. Serve with lemon wedges.

Corn And Pepper Jack Chile Rellenos With Roasted Tomato Sauce

Servings: 3
Cooking Time: 30 Minutes
Ingredients:
- 3 Poblano peppers
- 1 cup all-purpose flour*
- salt and freshly ground black pepper
- 2 eggs, lightly beaten
- 1 cup plain breadcrumbs*
- olive oil, in a spray bottle
- Sauce
- 2 cups cherry tomatoes
- 1 Jalapeño pepper, halved and seeded
- 1 clove garlic
- ¼ red onion, broken into large pieces
- 1 tablespoon olive oil
- salt, to taste
- 2 tablespoons chopped fresh cilantro
- Filling
- olive oil
- ¼ red onion, finely chopped
- 1 teaspoon minced garlic
- 1 cup corn kernels, fresh or frozen
- 2 cups grated pepper jack cheese

Directions:
1. Start by roasting the peppers. Preheat the air fryer to 400°F. Place the peppers into the air fryer basket and air-fry at 400°F for 10 minutes, turning them over halfway through the cooking time. Remove the peppers from the basket and cover loosely with foil.
2. While the peppers are cooling, make the roasted tomato sauce. Place all sauce Ingredients except for the cilantro into the air fryer basket and air-fry at 400°F for 10 minutes, shaking the basket once or twice. When the sauce Ingredients have finished air-frying, transfer everything to a blender or food processor and blend or process to a smooth sauce, adding a little warm water to get the desired consistency. Season to taste with salt, add the cilantro and set aside.
3. While the sauce Ingredients are cooking in the air fryer, make the filling. Heat a skillet on the stovetop over medium heat. Add the olive oil and sauté the red onion and garlic for 4 to 5 minutes. Transfer the onion and garlic to a bowl, stir in the corn and cheese, and set aside.
4. Set up a dredging station with three shallow dishes. Place the flour, seasoned with salt and pepper, in the first shallow dish. Place the eggs in the second dish, and fill the third shallow dish with the breadcrumbs. When the peppers have cooled, carefully slice into one side of the pepper to create an opening. Pull the seeds out of the peppers and peel away the skins, trying not to tear the pepper. Fill each pepper with some of the corn and cheese filling and close the pepper up again by folding one side of the opening over the other. Carefully roll each pepper in the seasoned flour, then into the egg and finally into the breadcrumbs to coat on all sides, trying not to let the pepper fall open. Spray the peppers on all sides with a little olive oil.
5. Air-fry two peppers at a time at 350°F for 6 minutes. Turn the peppers over and air-fry for another 4 minutes. Serve the peppers warm on a bed of the roasted tomato sauce.

Rice & Bean Burritos

Servings: 4
Cooking Time: 20 Minutes

Ingredients:
- 1 bell pepper, sliced
- ½ red onion, thinly sliced
- 2 garlic cloves, peeled
- 1 tbsp olive oil
- 1 cup cooked brown rice
- 1 can pinto beans
- ½ tsp salt
- ¼ tsp chili powder
- ¼ tsp ground cumin
- ¼ tsp smoked paprika
- 1 tbsp lime juice
- 4 tortillas
- 2 tsp grated Parmesan cheese
- 1 avocado, diced
- 4 tbsp salsa
- 2 tbsp chopped cilantro

Directions:
1. Preheat air fryer to 400°F. Combine bell pepper, onion, garlic, and olive oil. Place in the frying basket and Roast for 5 minutes. Shake and roast for another 5 minutes.
2. Remove the garlic from the basket and mince finely. Add to a large bowl along with brown rice, pinto beans, salt, chili powder, cumin, paprika, and lime juice. Divide the roasted vegetable mixture between the tortillas. Top with rice mixture, Parmesan, avocado, cilantro, and salsa. Fold in the sides, then roll the tortillas over the filling. Serve.

Sandwiches And Burgers Recipes

Philly Cheesesteak Sandwiches

Servings:3
Cooking Time:9 Minutes
Ingredients:
- ¾pound Shaved beef
- 1 tablespoon Worcestershire sauce(gluten-free,if a concern)
- ¼teaspoon Garlic powder
- ¼teaspoon Mild paprika
- 6 tablespoons(1½ounces)Frozen bell pepper strips(do not thaw)
- 2 slices,broken into rings Very thin yellow or white medium onion slice(s)
- 6 ounces(6 to 8 slices)Provolone cheese slices
- 3 Long soft rolls such as hero,hoagie,or Italian sub rolls,or hot dog buns(gluten-free,if a concern),split open lengthwise

Directions:
1. Preheat the air fryer to 400°F.
2. When the machine is at temperature,spread the shaved beef in the basket,leaving a½-inch perimeter around the meat for good air flow.Sprinkle the meat with the Worcestershire sauce,paprika,and garlic powder.Spread the peppers and onions on top of the meat.
3. Air-fry undisturbed for 6 minutes,or until cooked through.Set the cheese on top of the meat.Continue air-frying undisturbed for 3 minutes,or until the cheese has melted.
4. Use kitchen tongs to divide the meat and cheese layers in the basket between the rolls or buns.Serve hot.

Inside Out Cheeseburgers

Servings:2
Cooking Time:20 Minutes
Ingredients:
- ¾pound lean ground beef
- 3 tablespoons minced onion
- 4 teaspoons ketchup
- 2 teaspoons yellow mustard
- salt and freshly ground black pepper
- 4 slices of Cheddar cheese,broken into smaller pieces
- 8 hamburger dill pickle chips

Directions:
1. Combine the ground beef,minced onion,ketchup,mustard,salt and pepper in a large bowl.Mix well to thoroughly combine the ingredients.Divide the meat into four equal portions.
2. To make the stuffed burgers,flatten each portion of meat into a thin patty.Place 4 pickle chips and half of the cheese onto the center of two of the patties,leaving a rim around the edge of the patty exposed.Place the remaining two patties on top of the first and press the meat together firmly,sealing the edges tightly.With the burgers on a flat surface,press the sides of the burger with the palm of your hand to create a straight edge.This will help keep the stuffing inside the burger while it cooks.
3. Preheat the air fryer to 370°F.
4. Place the burgers inside the air fryer basket and air-fry for 20 minutes,flipping the burgers over halfway through the cooking time.
5. Serve the cheeseburgers on buns with lettuce and tomato.

Asian Glazed Meatballs

Servings:4
Cooking Time:10 Minutes
Ingredients:
- 1 large shallot,finely chopped
- 2 cloves garlic,minced
- 1 tablespoon grated fresh ginger
- 2 teaspoons fresh thyme,finely chopped
- 1½cups brown mushrooms,very finely chopped(a food processor works well here)
- 2 tablespoons soy sauce
- freshly ground black pepper
- 1 pound ground beef
- ½pound ground pork
- 3 egg yolks
- 1 cup Thai sweet chili sauce(spring roll sauce)
- ¼cup toasted sesame seeds
- 2 scallions,sliced

Directions:
1. Combine the shallot,garlic,ginger,thyme,mushrooms,soy sauce,freshly ground black pepper,ground beef and pork,and egg yolks in a bowl and mix the ingredients together.Gently shape the mixture into 24 balls,about the size of a golf ball.
2. Preheat the air fryer to 380°F.
3. Working in batches,air-fry the meatballs for 8 minutes,turning the meatballs over halfway through the cooking time.Drizzle some of the Thai sweet chili sauce on top of each meatball and return the basket to the air fryer,air-frying for another 2 minutes.Reserve the remaining Thai sweet chili sauce for serving.
4. As soon as the meatballs are done,sprinkle with toasted sesame seeds and transfer them to a serving platter.Scatter the scallions around and serve warm.

Thanksgiving Turkey Sandwiches

Servings:3
Cooking Time:10 Minutes
Ingredients:
- 1½cups Herb-seasoned stuffing mix(not cornbread-style;gluten-free,if a concern)
- 1 Large egg white(s)
- 2 tablespoons Water
- 3 5-to 6-ounce turkey breast cutlets
- Vegetable oil spray
- 4½tablespoons Purchased cranberry sauce,preferably whole berry
- ⅛teaspoon Ground cinnamon
- ⅛teaspoon Ground dried ginger
- 4½tablespoons Regular,low-fat,or fat-free mayonnaise(gluten-free,if a concern)
- 6 tablespoons Shredded Brussels sprouts
- 3 Kaiser rolls(gluten-free,if a concern),split open

Directions:
1. Preheat the air fryer to 375°F.
2. Put the stuffing mix in a heavy zip-closed bag,seal it,lay it flat on your counter,and roll a rolling pin over the bag to crush the stuffing mix to the consistency of rough sand.(Or you can pulse the stuffing mix to the desired consistency in a food processor.)
3. Set up and fill two shallow soup plates or small pie plates on your counter:one for the egg white(s),whisked with the water until foamy;and one for the ground stuffing mix.
4. Dip a cutlet in the egg white mixture,coating both sides and letting any excess egg white slip back into the rest.Set the cutlet in the ground stuffing mix and coat it evenly on both sides,pressing gently to coat well on both sides.Lightly coat the

cutlet on both sides with vegetable oil spray,set it aside,and continue dipping and coating the remaining cutlets in the same way.
5. Set the cutlets in the basket and air-fry undisturbed for 10 minutes,or until crisp and brown.Use kitchen tongs to transfer the cutlets to a wire rack to cool for a few minutes.
6. Meanwhile,stir the cranberry sauce with the cinnamon and ginger in a small bowl.Mix the shredded Brussels sprouts and mayonnaise in a second bowl until the vegetable is evenly coated.
7. Build the sandwiches by spreading about 1½ tablespoons of the cranberry mixture on the cut side of the bottom half of each roll.Set a cutlet on top,then spread about 3 tablespoons of the Brussels sprouts mixture evenly over the cutlet.Set the other half of the roll on top and serve warm.

Chicken Spiedies

Servings:3
Cooking Time:12 Minutes
Ingredients:
- 1¼ pounds Boneless skinless chicken thighs,trimmed of any fat blobs and cut into 2-inch pieces
- 3 tablespoons Red wine vinegar
- 2 tablespoons Olive oil
- 2 tablespoons Minced fresh mint leaves
- 2 tablespoons Minced fresh parsley leaves
- 2 teaspoons Minced fresh dill fronds
- ¾ teaspoon Fennel seeds
- ¾ teaspoon Table salt
- Up to a ¼ teaspoon Red pepper flakes
- 3 Long soft rolls,such as hero,hoagie,or Italian sub rolls(gluten-free,if a concern),split open lengthwise
- 4½ tablespoons Regular or low-fat mayonnaise(not fat-free;gluten-free,if a concern)
- 1½ tablespoons Distilled white vinegar
- 1½ teaspoons Ground black pepper

Directions:
1. Mix the chicken,vinegar,oil,mint,parsley,dill,fennel seeds,salt,and red pepper flakes in a zip-closed plastic bag.Seal,gently massage the marinade ingredients into the meat,and refrigerate for at least 2 hours or up to 6 hours.(Longer than that and the meat can turn rubbery.)
2. Set the plastic bag out on the counter(to make the contents a little less frigid).Preheat the air fryer to 400°F.
3. When the machine is at temperature,use kitchen tongs to set the chicken thighs in the basket(discard any remaining marinade)and air-fry undisturbed for 6 minutes.Turn the thighs over and continue air-frying undisturbed for 6 minutes more,until well browned,cooked through,and even a little crunchy.
4. Dump the contents of the basket onto a wire rack and cool for 2 or 3 minutes.Divide the chicken evenly between the rolls.Whisk the mayonnaise,vinegar,and black pepper in a small bowl until smooth.Drizzle this sauce over the chicken pieces in the rolls.

Best-ever Roast Beef Sandwiches

Servings:6
Cooking Time:30-50 Minutes
Ingredients:
- 2½ teaspoons Olive oil
- 1½ teaspoons Dried oregano
- 1½ teaspoons Dried thyme
- 1½ teaspoons Onion powder
- 1½ teaspoons Table salt
- 1½ teaspoons Ground black pepper
- 3 pounds Beef eye of round
- 6 Round soft rolls,such as Kaiser rolls or hamburger buns(gluten-free,if a concern),split open lengthwise
- ¾ cup Regular,low-fat,or fat-free mayonnaise(gluten-free,if a concern)
- 6 Romaine lettuce leaves,rinsed
- 6 Round tomato slices(¼ inch thick)

Directions:
1. Preheat the air fryer to 350°F.
2. Mix the oil,oregano,thyme,onion powder,salt,and pepper in a small bowl.Spread this mixture all over the eye of round.
3. When the machine is at temperature,set the beef in the basket and air-fry for 30 to 50 minutes(the range depends on the size of the cut),turning the meat twice,until an instant-read meat thermometer inserted into the thickest piece of the meat registers 130°F for rare,140°F for medium,or 150°F for well-done.
4. Use kitchen tongs to transfer the beef to a cutting board.Cool for 10 minutes.If serving now,carve into ⅛-inch-thick slices.Spread each roll with 2 tablespoons mayonnaise and divide the beef slices between the rolls.Top with a lettuce leaf and a tomato slice and serve.Or set the beef in a container,cover,and refrigerate for up to 3 days to make cold roast beef sandwiches anytime.

Perfect Burgers

Servings:3
Cooking Time:13 Minutes
Ingredients:
- 1 pound 2 ounces 90% lean ground beef
- 1½ tablespoons Worcestershire sauce(gluten-free,if a concern)
- ½ teaspoon Ground black pepper
- 3 Hamburger buns(gluten-free if a concern),split open

Directions:
1. Preheat the air fryer to 375°F.
2. Gently mix the ground beef,Worcestershire sauce,and pepper in a bowl until well combined but preserving as much of the meat's fibers as possible.Divide this mixture into two 5-inch patties for the small batch,three 5-inch patties for the medium,or four 5-inch patties for the large.Make a thumbprint indentation in the center of each patty,about halfway through the meat.
3. Set the patties in the basket in one layer with some space between them.Air-fry undisturbed for 10 minutes,or until an instant-read meat thermometer inserted into the center of a burger registers 160°F(a medium-well burger).You may need to add 2 minutes cooking time if the air fryer is at 360°F.
4. Use a nonstick-safe spatula,and perhaps a flatware fork for balance,to transfer the burgers to a cutting board.Set the buns cut side down in the basket in one layer(working in batches as necessary)and air-fry undisturbed for 1 minute,to toast a bit and warm up.Serve the burgers in the warm buns.

Chicken Club Sandwiches

Servings:3
Cooking Time:15 Minutes
Ingredients:
- 3 5-to 6-ounce boneless skinless chicken breasts
- 6 Thick-cut bacon strips(gluten-free,if a concern)
- 3 Long soft rolls,such as hero,hoagie,or Italian sub rolls(gluten-free,if a concern)
- 3 tablespoons Regular,low-fat,or fat-free mayonnaise(gluten-free,if a concern)
- 3 Lettuce leaves,preferably romaine or iceberg
- 6 ¼-inch-thick tomato slices

Directions:
1. Preheat the air fryer to 375°F.
2. Wrap each chicken breast with 2 strips of bacon, spiraling the bacon around the meat, slightly overlapping the strips on each revolution. Start the second strip of bacon farther down the breast but on a line with the start of the first strip so they both end at a lined-up point on the chicken breast.
3. When the machine is at temperature, set the wrapped breasts bacon-seam side down in the basket with space between them. Air-fry undisturbed for 12 minutes, until the bacon is browned, crisp, and cooked through and an instant-read meat thermometer inserted into the center of a breast registers 165°F. You may need to add 2 minutes in the air fryer if the temperature is at 360°F.
4. Use kitchen tongs to transfer the breasts to a wire rack. Split the rolls open lengthwise and set them cut side down in the basket. Air-fry for 1 minute, or until warmed through.
5. Use kitchen tongs to transfer the rolls to a cutting board. Spread 1 tablespoon mayonnaise on the cut side of one half of each roll. Top with a chicken breast, lettuce leaf, and tomato slice. Serve warm.

Crunchy Falafel Balls

Servings: 8
Cooking Time: 16 Minutes
Ingredients:
- 2½ cups Drained and rinsed canned chickpeas
- ¼ cup Olive oil
- 3 tablespoons All-purpose flour
- 1½ teaspoons Dried oregano
- 1½ teaspoons Dried sage leaves
- 1½ teaspoons Dried thyme
- ¾ teaspoon Table salt
- Olive oil spray

Directions:
1. Preheat the air fryer to 400°F.
2. Place the chickpeas, olive oil, flour, oregano, sage, thyme, and salt in a food processor. Cover and process into a paste, stopping the machine at least once to scrape down the inside of the canister.
3. Scrape down and remove the blade. Using clean, wet hands, form 2 tablespoons of the paste into a ball, then continue making 9 more balls for a small batch, 15 more for a medium one, and 19 more for a large batch. Generously coat the balls in olive oil spray.
4. Set the balls in the basket in one layer with a little space between them and air-fry undisturbed for 16 minutes, or until well browned and crisp.
5. Dump the contents of the basket onto a wire rack. Cool for 5 minutes before serving.

Chicken Saltimbocca Sandwiches

Servings: 3
Cooking Time: 11 Minutes
Ingredients:
- 3 5-to 6-ounce boneless skinless chicken breasts
- 6 Thin prosciutto slices
- 6 Provolone cheese slices
- 3 Long soft rolls, such as hero, hoagie, or Italian sub rolls (gluten-free, if a concern), split open lengthwise
- 3 tablespoons Pesto, purchased or homemade (see the headnote)

Directions:
1. Preheat the air fryer to 400°F.
2. Wrap each chicken breast with 2 prosciutto slices, spiraling the prosciutto around the breast and overlapping the slices a bit to cover the breast. The prosciutto will stick to the chicken more readily than bacon does.
3. When the machine is at temperature, set the wrapped chicken breasts in the basket and air-fry undisturbed for 10 minutes, or until the prosciutto is frizzled and the chicken is cooked through.
4. Overlap 2 cheese slices on each breast. Air-fry undisturbed for 1 minute, or until melted. Take the basket out of the machine.
5. Smear the insides of the rolls with the pesto, then use kitchen tongs to put a wrapped and cheesy chicken breast in each roll.

Eggplant Parmesan Subs

Servings: 2
Cooking Time: 13 Minutes
Ingredients:
- 4 Peeled eggplant slices (about ½ inch thick and 3 inches in diameter)
- Olive oil spray
- 2 tablespoons plus 2 teaspoons Jarred pizza sauce, any variety except creamy
- ¼ cup (about ⅔ ounce) Finely grated Parmesan cheese
- 2 Small, long soft rolls, such as hero, hoagie, or Italian sub rolls (gluten-free, if a concern), split open lengthwise

Directions:
1. Preheat the air fryer to 350°F.
2. When the machine is at temperature, coat both sides of the eggplant slices with olive oil spray. Set them in the basket in one layer and air-fry undisturbed for 10 minutes, until lightly browned and softened.
3. Increase the machine's temperature to 375°F (or 370°F, if that's the closest setting—unless the machine is already at 360°F, in which case leave it alone). Top each eggplant slice with 2 teaspoons pizza sauce, then 1 tablespoon cheese. Air-fry undisturbed for 2 minutes, or until the cheese has melted.
4. Use a nonstick-safe spatula, and perhaps a flatware fork for balance, to transfer the eggplant slices cheese side up to a cutting board. Set the roll(s) cut side down in the basket in one layer (working in batches as necessary) and air-fry undisturbed for 1 minute, to toast the rolls a bit and warm them up. Set 2 eggplant slices in each warm roll.

Chili Cheese Dogs

Servings: 3
Cooking Time: 12 Minutes
Ingredients:
- ¾ pound Lean ground beef
- 1½ tablespoons Chile powder
- 1 cup plus 2 tablespoons Jarred sofrito
- 3 Hot dogs (gluten-free, if a concern)
- 3 Hot dog buns (gluten-free, if a concern), split open lengthwise
- 3 tablespoons Finely chopped scallion
- 9 tablespoons (a little more than 2 ounces) Shredded Cheddar cheese

Directions:
1. Crumble the ground beef into a medium or large saucepan set over medium heat. Brown well, stirring often to break up the clumps. Add the chile powder and cook for 30 seconds, stirring the whole time. Stir in the sofrito and bring to a simmer. Reduce the heat to low and simmer, stirring occasionally, for 5 minutes. Keep warm.
2. Preheat the air fryer to 400°F.
3. When the machine is at temperature, put the hot dogs in the basket and air-fry undisturbed for 10 minutes, or until the hot dogs are bubbling and blistered, even a little crisp.

Ninja Foodi 2-Basket Air Fryer | 109

4. Use kitchen tongs to put the hot dogs in the buns. Top each with a ½ cup of the ground beef mixture, 1 tablespoon of the minced scallion, and 3 tablespoons of the cheese. (The scallion should go under the cheese so it superheats and wilts a bit.) Set the filled hot dog buns in the basket and air-fry undisturbed for 2 minutes, or until the cheese has melted.
5. Remove the basket from the machine. Cool the chili cheese dogs in the basket for 5 minutes before serving.

Thai-style Pork Sliders

Servings: 4
Cooking Time: 15 Minutes
Ingredients:
- 11 ounces Ground pork
- 2½ tablespoons Very thinly sliced scallions, white and green parts
- 4 teaspoons Minced peeled fresh ginger
- 2½ teaspoons Fish sauce(gluten-free, if a concern)
- 2 teaspoons Thai curry paste(see the headnote; gluten-free, if a concern)
- 2 teaspoons Light brown sugar
- ¾ teaspoon Ground black pepper
- 4 Slider buns(gluten-free, if a concern)

Directions:
1. Preheat the air fryer to 375°F.
2. Gently mix the pork, scallions, ginger, fish sauce, curry paste, brown sugar, and black pepper in a bowl until well combined. With clean, wet hands, form about ⅓ cup of the pork mixture into a slider about 2½ inches in diameter. Repeat until you use up all the meat—3 sliders for the small batch, 4 for the medium, and 6 for the large. (Keep wetting your hands to help the patties adhere.)
3. When the machine is at temperature, set the sliders in the basket in one layer. Air-fry undisturbed for 14 minutes, or until the sliders are golden brown and caramelized at their edges and an instant-read meat thermometer inserted into the center of a slider registers 160°F.
4. Use a nonstick-safe spatula, and perhaps a flatware fork for balance, to transfer the sliders to a cutting board. Set the buns cut side down in the basket in one layer(working in batches as necessary)and air-fry undisturbed for 1 minute, to toast a bit and warm up. Serve the sliders warm in the buns.

Dijon Thyme Burgers

Servings: 3
Cooking Time: 18 Minutes
Ingredients:
- 1 pound lean ground beef
- ⅓ cup panko breadcrumbs
- ¼ cup finely chopped onion
- 3 tablespoons Dijon mustard
- 1 tablespoon chopped fresh thyme
- 4 teaspoons Worcestershire sauce
- 1 teaspoon salt
- freshly ground black pepper
- Topping(optional):
- 2 tablespoons Dijon mustard
- 1 tablespoon dark brown sugar
- 1 teaspoon Worcestershire sauce
- 4 ounces sliced Swiss cheese, optional

Directions:
1. Combine all the burger ingredients together in a large bowl and mix well. Divide the meat into 4 equal portions and then form the burgers, being careful not to over-handle the meat. One good way to do this is to throw the meat back and forth from one hand to another, packing the meat each time you catch it. Flatten the balls into patties, making an indentation in the center of each patty with your thumb(this will help it stay flat as it cooks)and flattening the sides of the burgers so that they will fit nicely into the air fryer basket.
2. Preheat the air fryer to 370°F.
3. If you don't have room for all four burgers, air-fry two or three burgers at a time for 8 minutes. Flip the burgers over and air-fry for another 6 minutes.
4. While the burgers are cooking combine the Dijon mustard, dark brown sugar, and Worcestershire sauce in a small bowl and mix well. This optional topping to the burgers really adds a boost of flavor at the end. Spread the Dijon topping evenly on each burger. If you cooked the burgers in batches, return the first batch to the cooker at this time–it's ok to place the fourth burger on top of the others in the center of the basket. Air-fry the burgers for another 3 minutes.
5. Finally, if desired, top each burger with a slice of Swiss cheese. Lower the air fryer temperature to 330°F and air-fry for another minute to melt the cheese. Serve the burgers on toasted brioche buns, dressed the way you like them.

White Bean Veggie Burgers

Servings: 3
Cooking Time: 13 Minutes
Ingredients:
- 1⅓ cups Drained and rinsed canned white beans
- 3 tablespoons Rolled oats(not quick-cooking or steel-cut; gluten-free, if a concern)
- 3 tablespoons Chopped walnuts
- 2 teaspoons Olive oil
- 2 teaspoons Lemon juice
- 1½ teaspoons Dijon mustard(gluten-free, if a concern)
- ¾ teaspoon Dried sage leaves
- ¼ teaspoon Table salt
- Olive oil spray
- 3 Whole-wheat buns or gluten-free whole-grain buns(if a concern), split open

Directions:
1. Preheat the air fryer to 400°F.
2. Place the beans, oats, walnuts, oil, lemon juice, mustard, sage, and salt in a food processor. Cover and process to make a coarse paste that will hold its shape, about like wet sugar-cookie dough, stopping the machine to scrape down the inside of the canister at least once.
3. Scrape down and remove the blade. With clean and wet hands, form the bean paste into two 4-inch patties for the small batch, three 4-inch patties for the medium, or four 4-inch patties for the large batch. Generously coat the patties on both sides with olive oil spray.
4. Set them in the basket with some space between them and air-fry undisturbed for 12 minutes, or until lightly brown and crisp at the edges. The tops of the burgers will feel firm to the touch.
5. Use a nonstick-safe spatula, and perhaps a flatware fork for balance, to transfer the burgers to a cutting board. Set the buns cut side down in the basket in one layer(working in batches as necessary)and air-fry undisturbed for 1 minute, to toast a bit and warm up. Serve the burgers warm in the buns.

Inside-out Cheeseburgers

Servings: 3
Cooking Time: 9-11 Minutes
Ingredients:
- 1 pound 2 ounces 90% lean ground beef
- ¾ teaspoon Dried oregano
- ¾ teaspoon Table salt
- ¾ teaspoon Ground black pepper
- ¼ teaspoon Garlic powder

- 6 tablespoons(about 1½ounces)Shredded Cheddar,Swiss,or other semi-firm cheese,or a purchased blend of shredded cheeses
- 3 Hamburger buns(gluten-free,if a concern),split open

Directions:
1. Preheat the air fryer to 375°F.
2. Gently mix the ground beef,oregano,salt,pepper,and garlic powder in a bowl until well combined without turning the mixture to mush.Form it into two 6-inch patties for the small batch,three for the medium,or four for the large.
3. Place 2 tablespoons of the shredded cheese in the center of each patty.With clean hands,fold the sides of the patty up to cover the cheese,then pick it up and roll it gently into a ball to seal the cheese inside.Gently press it back into a 5-inch burger without letting any cheese squish out.Continue filling and preparing more burgers,as needed.
4. Place the burgers in the basket in one layer and air-fry undisturbed for 8 minutes for medium or 10 minutes for well-done.(An instant-read meat thermometer won't work for these burgers because it will hit the mostly melted cheese inside and offer a hotter temperature than the surrounding meat.)
5. Use a nonstick-safe spatula,and perhaps a flatware fork for balance,to transfer the burgers to a cutting board.Set the buns cut side down in the basket in one layer(working in batches as necessary)and air-fry undisturbed for 1 minute,to toast a bit and warm up.Cool the burgers a few minutes more,then serve them warm in the buns.

Black Bean Veggie Burgers

Servings:3
Cooking Time:10 Minutes
Ingredients:
- 1 cup Drained and rinsed canned black beans
- ⅓cup Pecan pieces
- ⅓cup Rolled oats(not quick-cooking or steel-cut;gluten-free,if a concern)
- 2 tablespoons(or 1 small egg)Pasteurized egg substitute,such as Egg Beaters(gluten-free,if a concern)
- 2 teaspoons Red ketchup-like chili sauce,such as Heinz
- ¼teaspoon Ground cumin
- ¼teaspoon Dried oregano
- ¼teaspoon Table salt
- ¼teaspoon Ground black pepper
- Olive oil
- Olive oil spray

Directions:
1. Preheat the air fryer to 400°F.
2. Put the beans,pecans,oats,egg substitute or egg,chili sauce,cumin,oregano,salt,and pepper in a food processor.Cover and process to a coarse paste that will hold its shape like sugar-cookie dough,adding olive oil in 1-teaspoon increments to get the mixture to blend smoothly.The amount of olive oil is actually dependent on the internal moisture content of the beans and the oats.Figure on about 1 tablespoon(three 1-teaspoon additions)for the smaller batch,with proportional increases for the other batches.A little too much olive oil can't hurt,but a dry paste will fall apart as it cooks and a far-too-wet paste will stick to the basket.
3. Scrape down and remove the blade.Using clean,wet hands,form the paste into two 4-inch patties for the small batch,three 4-inch patties for the medium,or four 4-inch patties for the large batch,setting them one by one on a cutting board.Generously coat both sides of the patties with olive oil spray.
4. Set them in the basket in one layer.Air-fry undisturbed for 10 minutes,or until lightly browned and crisp at the edges.
5. Use a nonstick-safe spatula,and perhaps a flatware fork for balance,to transfer the burgers to a wire rack.Cool for 5 minutes before serving.

Mexican Cheeseburgers

Servings:4
Cooking Time:22 Minutes
Ingredients:
- 1¼pounds ground beef
- ¼cup finely chopped onion
- ½cup crushed yellow corn tortilla chips
- 1(1.25-ounce)packet taco seasoning
- ¼cup canned diced green chilies
- 1 egg,lightly beaten
- 4 ounces pepper jack cheese,grated
- 4(12-inch)flour tortillas
- shredded lettuce,sour cream,guacamole,salsa(for topping)

Directions:
1. Combine the ground beef,minced onion,crushed tortilla chips,taco seasoning,green chilies,and egg in a large bowl.Mix thoroughly until combined–your hands are good tools for this.Divide the meat into four equal portions and shape each portion into an oval-shaped burger.
2. Preheat the air fryer to 370°F.
3. Air-fry the burgers for 18 minutes,turning them over halfway through the cooking time.Divide the cheese between the burgers,lower fryer to 340°F and air-fry for an additional 4 minutes to melt the cheese.(This will give you a burger that is medium-well.If you prefer your cheeseburger medium-rare,shorten the cooking time to about 15 minutes and then add the cheese and proceed with the recipe.)
4. While the burgers are cooking,warm the tortillas wrapped in aluminum foil in a 350°F oven,or in a skillet with a little oil over medium-high heat for a couple of minutes.Keep the tortillas warm until the burgers are ready.
5. To assemble the burgers,spread sour cream over three quarters of the tortillas and top each with some shredded lettuce and salsa.Place the Mexican cheeseburgers on the lettuce and top with guacamole.Fold the tortillas around the burger,starting with the bottom and then folding the sides in over the top.(A little sour cream can help hold the seam of the tortilla together.)Serve immediately.

Chicken Gyros

Servings:4
Cooking Time:14 Minutes
Ingredients:
- 4 4-to 5-ounce boneless skinless chicken thighs,trimmed of any fat blobs
- 2 tablespoons Lemon juice
- 2 tablespoons Red wine vinegar
- 2 tablespoons Olive oil
- 2 teaspoons Dried oregano
- 2 teaspoons Minced garlic
- 1 teaspoon Table salt
- 1 teaspoon Ground black pepper
- 4 Pita pockets(gluten-free,if a concern)
- ½cup Chopped tomatoes
- ½cup Bottled regular,low-fat,or fat-free ranch dressing(gluten-free,if a concern)

Directions:
1. Mix the thighs,lemon juice,vinegar,oil,oregano,garlic,salt,and pepper in a zip-closed bag.Seal,gently massage the marinade into the meat through the plastic,and refrigerate for at least 2 hours or up to 6 hours.(Longer than that and the meat can turn rubbery.)

2. Set the plastic bag out on the counter(to make the contents a little less frigid).Preheat the air fryer to 375°F.
3. When the machine is at temperature,use kitchen tongs to place the thighs in the basket in one layer.Discard the marinade.Air-fry the chicken thighs undisturbed for 12 minutes,or until browned and an instant-read meat thermometer inserted into the thickest part of one thigh registers 165°F.You may need to air-fry the chicken 2 minutes longer if the machine's temperature is 360°F.
4. Use kitchen tongs to transfer the thighs to a cutting board.Cool for 5 minutes,then set one thigh in each of the pita pockets.Top each with 2 tablespoons chopped tomatoes and 2 tablespoons dressing.Serve warm.

Chicken Apple Brie Melt

Servings:3
Cooking Time:13 Minutes
Ingredients:
- 3 5-to 6-ounce boneless skinless chicken breasts
- Vegetable oil spray
- 1½teaspoons Dried herbes de Provence
- 3 ounces Brie,rind removed,thinly sliced
- 6 Thin cored apple slices
- 3 French rolls(gluten-free,if a concern)
- 2 tablespoons Dijon mustard(gluten-free,if a concern)

Directions:
1. Preheat the air fryer to 375°F.
2. Lightly coat all sides of the chicken breasts with vegetable oil spray.Sprinkle the breasts evenly with the herbes de Provence.
3. When the machine is at temperature,set the breasts in the basket and air-fry undisturbed for 10 minutes.
4. Top the chicken breasts with the apple slices,then the cheese.Air-fry undisturbed for 2 minutes,or until the cheese is melty and bubbling.
5. Use a nonstick-safe spatula and kitchen tongs,for balance,to transfer the breasts to a cutting board.Set the rolls in the basket and air-fry for 1 minute to warm through.(Putting them in the machine without splitting them keeps the insides very soft while the outside gets a little crunchy.)
6. Transfer the rolls to the cutting board.Split them open lengthwise,then spread 1 teaspoon mustard on each cut side.Set a prepared chicken breast on the bottom of a roll and close with its top,repeating as necessary to make additional sandwiches.Serve warm.

Desserts And Sweets

Gingerbread

Servings: 6
Cooking Time: 20 Minutes
Ingredients:
- cooking spray
- 1 cup flour
- 2 tablespoons sugar
- ¾ teaspoon ground ginger
- ¼ teaspoon cinnamon
- 1 teaspoon baking powder
- ½ teaspoon baking soda
- ⅛ teaspoon salt
- 1 egg
- ¼ cup molasses
- ½ cup buttermilk
- 2 tablespoons oil
- 1 teaspoon pure vanilla extract

Directions:
1. Preheat air fryer to 330°F.
2. Spray 6 x 6-inch baking dish lightly with cooking spray.
3. In a medium bowl, mix together all the dry ingredients.
4. In a separate bowl, beat the egg. Add molasses, buttermilk, oil, and vanilla and stir until well mixed.
5. Pour liquid mixture into dry ingredients and stir until well blended.
6. Pour batter into baking dish and cook at 330°F for 20 minutes or until toothpick inserted in center of loaf comes out clean.

Strawberry Pastry Rolls

Servings: 4
Cooking Time: 6 Minutes
Ingredients:
- 3 ounces low-fat cream cheese
- 2 tablespoons plain yogurt
- 2 teaspoons sugar
- ¼ teaspoon pure vanilla extract
- 8 ounces fresh strawberries
- 8 sheets phyllo dough
- butter-flavored cooking spray
- ¼–½ cup dark chocolate chips (optional)

Directions:
1. In a medium bowl, combine the cream cheese, yogurt, sugar, and vanilla. Beat with hand mixer at high speed until smooth, about 1 minute.
2. Wash strawberries and destem. Chop enough of them to measure ½ cup. Stir into cheese mixture.
3. Preheat air fryer to 330°F.
4. Phyllo dough dries out quickly, so cover your stack of phyllo sheets with waxed paper and then place a damp dish towel on top of that. Remove only one sheet at a time as you work.
5. To create one pastry roll, lay out a single sheet of phyllo. Spray lightly with butter-flavored spray, top with a second sheet of phyllo, and spray the second sheet lightly.
6. Place a quarter of the filling (about 3 tablespoons) about ½ inch from the edge of one short side. Fold the end of the phyllo over the filling and keep rolling a turn or two. Fold in both the left and right sides so that the edges meet in the middle of your roll. Then roll up completely. Spray outside of pastry roll with butter spray.
7. When you have 4 rolls, place them in the air fryer basket, seam side down, leaving some space in between each. Cook at 330°F for 6 minutes, until they turn a delicate golden brown.
8. Repeat step 7 for remaining rolls.
9. Allow pastries to cool to room temperature.
10. When ready to serve, slice the remaining strawberries. If desired, melt the chocolate chips in microwave or double boiler. Place 1 pastry on each dessert plate, and top with sliced strawberries. Drizzle melted chocolate over strawberries and onto plate.

Wild Blueberry Sweet Empanadas

Servings: 12
Cooking Time: 8 Minutes
Ingredients:
- 2 cups frozen wild blueberries
- 5 tablespoons chia seeds
- ¼ cup honey
- 1 tablespoon lemon or lime juice
- ¼ cup water
- 1½ cups all-purpose flour
- 1 cup whole-wheat flour
- ½ teaspoon salt
- 1 tablespoon sugar
- ½ cup cold unsalted butter
- 1 egg
- ½ cup plus 2 tablespoons milk, divided
- 1 cup powdered sugar
- 1 teaspoon vanilla extract

Directions:
1. To make the wild blueberry chia jam, place the blueberries, chia seeds, honey, lemon or lime juice, and water into a blender and pulse for 2 minutes. Pour the chia jam into a glass jar or bowl and cover. Store in the refrigerator at least 4 to 8 hours or until the jam is thickened.
2. In a food processor, place the all-purpose flour, whole-wheat flour, salt, sugar, and butter and process for 2 minutes, scraping down the sides of the food processor every 30 seconds. Add in the egg and blend for 30 seconds. Using the pulse button, add in ½ cup of the milk 1 tablespoon at a time or until the dough is moist enough to handle and be rolled into a ball. Let the dough rest at room temperature for 30 minutes.
3. On a floured surface, cut the dough in half; then form a ball and cut each ball into 6 equal pieces, totaling 12 equal pieces. Work with one piece at a time, and cover the remaining dough with a towel. Roll out the dough into a 6-inch round, much like a tortilla, with ¼ inch thickness. Place 4 tablespoons of filling in the center of round, fold over to form a half-circle. Using a fork, crimp the edges together and pierce the top with a fork for air holes. Repeat with the remaining dough and filling.
4. Preheat the air fryer to 350°F.
5. Working in batches, place 3 to 4 empanadas in the air fryer basket and spray with cooking spray. Cook for 8 minutes. Repeat in batches, as needed. Allow the sweet empanadas to cool for 15 minutes. Meanwhile, in a small bowl, whisk together the powdered sugar, the remaining 2 tablespoons of milk, and the vanilla extract. Then drizzle the glaze over the surface and serve.

Ninja Foodi 2-Basket Air Fryer

Mango Cobbler With Raspberries

Servings: 4
Cooking Time: 30 Minutes
Ingredients:
- 1½ cups chopped mango
- 1 cup raspberries
- 1 tbsp brown sugar
- 2 tsp cornstarch
- 1 tsp lemon juice
- 2 tbsp sunflower oil
- 1 tbsp maple syrup
- 1 tsp vanilla
- ½ cup rolled oats
- 1/3 cup flour
- 3 tbsp coconut sugar
- 1 tsp cinnamon
- ¼ tsp nutmeg
- ⅛ tsp salt

Directions:
1. Place the mango, raspberries, brown sugar, cornstarch, and lemon juice in a baking pan. Stir with a rubber spatula until combined. Set aside.
2. In a separate bowl, add the oil, maple syrup, and vanilla and stir well. Toss in the oats, flour, coconut sugar, cinnamon, nutmeg, and salt. Stir until combined. Sprinkle evenly over the mango-raspberry filling. Preheat air fryer to 320°F. Bake for 20 minutes or until the topping is crispy and golden. Enjoy warm.

Strawberry Donuts

Servings: 4
Cooking Time: 55 Minutes
Ingredients:
- ¾ cup Greek yogurt
- 2 tbsp maple syrup
- 1 tbsp vanilla extract
- 2 tsp active dry yeast
- 1½ cups all-purpose flour
- 3 tbsp milk
- ½ cup strawberry jam

Directions:
1. Preheat air fryer to 350°F. Whisk the Greek yogurt, maple syrup, vanilla extract, and yeast until well combined. Then toss in flour until you get a sticky dough. Let rest covered for 10 minutes. Flour a parchment paper on a flat surface, lay the dough, sprinkle with some flour, and flatten to ½-inch thick with a rolling pin.
2. Using a 3-inch cookie cutter, cut the donuts. Repeat the process until no dough is left. Place the donuts in the basket and let rise for 15-20 minutes. Spread some milk on top of each donut and Air Fry for 4 minutes. Turn the donuts, spread more milk, and Air Fry for 4 more minutes until golden brown. Let cool for 15 minutes. Using a knife, cut the donuts 3/4 lengthwise, brush 1 tbsp of strawberry jam on each and close them. Serve.

Puff Pastry Apples

Servings: 4
Cooking Time: 10 Minutes
Ingredients:
- 3 Rome or Gala apples, peeled
- 2 tablespoons sugar
- 1 teaspoon all-purpose flour
- 1 teaspoon ground cinnamon
- ⅛ teaspoon ground ginger
- pinch ground nutmeg
- 1 sheet puff pastry
- 1 tablespoon butter, cut into 4 pieces
- 1 egg, beaten
- vegetable oil
- vanilla ice cream (optional)
- caramel sauce (optional)

Directions:
1. Remove the core from the apple by cutting the four sides off the apple around the core. Slice the pieces of apple into thin half-moons, about ¼-inch thick. Combine the sugar, flour, cinnamon, ginger, and nutmeg in a large bowl. Add the apples to the bowl and gently toss until the apples are evenly coated with the spice mixture. Set aside.
2. Cut the puff pastry sheet into a 12-inch by 12-inch square. Then quarter the sheet into four 6-inch squares. Save any remaining pastry for decorating the apples at the end.
3. Divide the spiced apples between the four puff pastry squares, stacking the apples in the center of each square and placing them flat on top of each other in a circle. Top the apples with a piece of the butter.
4. Brush the four edges of the pastry with the egg wash. Bring the four corners of the pastry together, wrapping them around the apple slices and pinching them together at the top in the style of a "beggars purse" appetizer. Fold the ends of the pastry corners down onto the apple making them look like leaves. Brush the entire apple with the egg wash.
5. Using the leftover dough, make leaves to decorate the apples. Cut out 8 leaf shapes, about 1½-inches long, "drawing" the leaf veins on the pastry leaves with a paring knife. Place 2 leaves on the top of each apple, tucking the ends of the leaves under the pastry in the center of the apples. Brush the top of the leaves with additional egg wash. Sprinkle the entire apple with some granulated sugar.
6. Preheat the air fryer to 350°F.
7. Spray or brush the inside of the air fryer basket with oil. Place the apples in the basket and air-fry for 6 minutes. Carefully turn the apples over–it's easiest to remove one apple, then flip the others over and finally return the last apple to the air fryer. Air-fry for an additional 4 minutes.
8. Serve the puff pastry apples warm with vanilla ice cream and drizzle with some caramel sauce.

Baked Stuffed Pears

Servings: 4
Cooking Time: 15 Minutes + Cooling Time
Ingredients:
- 4 cored pears, halved
- ½ cup chopped cashews
- ½ cup dried cranberries
- ¼ cup agave nectar
- ½ stick butter, softened
- ½ tsp ground cinnamon
- ½ cup apple juice

Directions:
1. Preheat the air fryer to 350°F. Combine the cashews, cranberries, agave nectar, butter, and cinnamon and mix well. Stuff this mixture into the pears, heaping it up on top. Set the pears in a baking pan and pour the apple juice into the bottom of the pan. Put the pan in the fryer and Bake for 10-12 minutes or until the pears are tender. Let cool before serving.

Peach Cobbler

Servings: 4
Cooking Time: 12 Minutes
Ingredients:
- 16 ounces frozen peaches, thawed, with juice (do not drain)
- 6 tablespoons sugar
- 1 tablespoon cornstarch
- 1 tablespoon water
- Crust
- ½ cup flour
- ¼ teaspoon salt
- 3 tablespoons butter
- 1½ tablespoons cold water
- ¼ teaspoon sugar

Directions:
1. Place peaches, including juice, and sugar in air fryer baking pan. Stir to mix well.
2. In a small cup, dissolve cornstarch in the water. Stir into peaches.
3. In a medium bowl, combine the flour and salt. Cut in butter using knives or a pastry blender. Stir in the cold water to make a stiff dough.
4. On a floured board or wax paper, pat dough into a square or circle slightly smaller than your air fryer baking pan. Cut diagonally into 4 pieces.
5. Place dough pieces on top of peaches, leaving a tiny bit of space between the edges. Sprinkle very lightly with sugar, no more than about ¼ teaspoon.
6. Cook at 360°F for 12 minutes, until fruit bubbles and crust browns.

Apple-carrot Cupcakes

Servings: 6
Cooking Time: 25 Minutes
Ingredients:
- 1 cup grated carrot
- 1/3 cup chopped apple
- ¼ cup raisins
- 2 tbsp maple syrup
- 1/3 cup milk
- 1 cup oat flour
- 1 tsp ground cinnamon
- ½ tsp ground ginger
- 1 tsp baking powder
- ½ tsp baking soda
- 1/3 cup chopped walnuts

Directions:
1. Preheat air fryer to 350°F. Combine carrot, apple, raisins, maple syrup, and milk in a bowl. Stir in oat flour, cinnamon, ginger, baking powder, and baking soda until combined. Divide the batter between 6 cupcake molds. Top with chopped walnuts each and press down a little. Bake for 15 minutes until golden brown and a toothpick comes out clean. Let cool completely before serving.

S'mores Pockets

Servings: 6
Cooking Time: 5 Minutes
Ingredients:
- 12 sheets phyllo dough, thawed
- 1½ cups butter, melted
- ¾ cup graham cracker crumbs
- 1 (7-ounce) Giant Hershey's® milk chocolate bar
- 12 marshmallows, cut in half

Directions:
1. Place one sheet of the phyllo on a large cutting board. Keep the rest of the phyllo sheets covered with a slightly damp, clean kitchen towel. Brush the phyllo sheet generously with some melted butter. Place a second phyllo sheet on top of the first and brush it with more butter. Repeat with one more phyllo sheet until you have a stack of 3 phyllo sheets with butter brushed between the layers. Cover the phyllo sheets with one quarter of the graham cracker crumbs leaving a 1-inch border on one of the short ends of the rectangle. Cut the phyllo sheets lengthwise into 3 strips.
2. Take 2 of the strips and crisscross them to form a cross with the empty borders at the top and to the left. Place 2 of the chocolate rectangles in the center of the cross. Place 4 of the marshmallow halves on top of the chocolate. Now fold the pocket together by folding the bottom phyllo strip up over the chocolate and marshmallows. Then fold the right side over, then the top strip down and finally the left side over. Brush all the edges generously with melted butter to seal shut. Repeat with the next three sheets of phyllo, until all the sheets have been used. You will be able to make 2 pockets with every second batch because you will have an extra graham cracker crumb strip from the previous set of sheets.
3. Preheat the air fryer to 350°F.
4. Transfer 3 pockets at a time to the air fryer basket. Air-fry at 350°F for 4 to 5 minutes, until the phyllo dough is light brown in color. Flip the pockets over halfway through the cooking process. Repeat with the remaining 3 pockets.
5. Serve warm.

Raspberry Empanada

Servings: 6
Cooking Time: 35 Minutes
Ingredients:
- 1 can raspberry pie filling
- 1 puff pastry dough
- 1 egg white, beaten

Directions:
1. Preheat air fryer to 370°F. Unroll the two sheets of dough and cut into 4 squares each, or 8 squares total. Scoop ½ to 1 tbsp of the raspberry pie filling in the center of each square. Brush the edges with egg white. Fold diagonally to form a triangle and close the turnover. Press the edges with the back of a fork to seal. Arrange the turnovers in a single layer in the greased basket. Spray the empanadas with cooking oil and Bake for 8 minutes. Let them sit in the air fryer for 3-4 minutes to cool before removing. Repeat for the other batch. Serve and enjoy!

Fast Brownies

Servings: 4
Cooking Time: 25 Minutes
Ingredients:
- ½ cup flour
- 2 tbsp cocoa
- 1/3 cup granulated sugar
- ¼ tsp baking soda
- 3 tbsp butter, melted
- 1 egg
- ¼ tsp salt
- ½ cup chocolate chips
- ¼ cup chopped hazelnuts
- 1 tbsp powdered sugar
- 1 tsp vanilla extract

Directions:
1. Preheat air fryer at 350°F. Combine all ingredients, except chocolate chips, hazelnuts, and powdered sugar, in a bowl. Fold in chocolate chips and pecans. Press mixture into a greased cake pan. Place cake pan in the frying basket and Bake for 12 minutes. Let cool for 10 minutes before slicing into 9 brownies. Scatter with powdered sugar and serve.

Coconut-custard Pie

Servings: 4
Cooking Time: 20 Minutes
Ingredients:
- 1 cup milk
- ¼ cup plus 2 tablespoons sugar
- ¼ cup biscuit baking mix
- 1 teaspoon vanilla
- 2 eggs
- 2 tablespoons melted butter
- cooking spray
- ½ cup shredded, sweetened coconut

Directions:
1. Place all ingredients except coconut in a medium bowl.
2. Using a hand mixer, beat on high speed for 3 minutes.
3. Let sit for 5 minutes.
4. Preheat air fryer to 330°F.
5. Spray a 6-inch round or 6 x 6-inch square baking pan with cooking spray and place pan in air fryer basket.
6. Pour filling into pan and sprinkle coconut over top.
7. Cook pie at 330°F for 20 minutes or until center sets.

Cherry Cheesecake Rolls

Servings: 6
Cooking Time: 30 Minutes
Ingredients:
- 1 can crescent rolls
- 4 oz cream cheese
- 1 tbsp cherry preserves
- 1/3 cup sliced fresh cherries

Directions:
1. Roll out the dough into a large rectangle on a flat work surface. Cut the dough into 12 rectangles by cutting 3 cuts across and 2 cuts down. In a microwave-safe bowl, soften cream cheese for 15 seconds. Stir together with cherry preserves. Mound 2 tsp of the cherries-cheese mix on each piece of dough. Carefully spread the mixture but not on the edges. Top with 2 tsp of cherries each. Roll each triangle to make a cylinder.
2. Preheat air fryer to 350°F. Place the first batch of the rolls in the greased air fryer. Spray the rolls with cooking oil and Bake for 8 minutes. Let cool in the air fryer for 2-3 minutes before removing. Serve.

Ricotta Stuffed Apples

Servings: 4
Cooking Time: 25 Minutes
Ingredients:
- ½ cup cheddar cheese
- ¼ cup raisins
- 2 apples
- ½ tsp ground cinnamon

Directions:
1. Preheat air fryer to 350°F. Combine cheddar cheese and raisins in a bowl and set aside. Chop apples lengthwise and discard the core and stem. Sprinkle each half with cinnamon and stuff each half with 1/4 of the cheddar mixture. Bake for 7 minutes, turn, and Bake for 13 minutes more until the apples are soft. Serve immediately.

Sea-salted Caramel Cookie Cups

Servings: 12
Cooking Time: 12 Minutes
Ingredients:
- ⅓ cup butter
- ¼ cup brown sugar
- 1 teaspoon vanilla extract
- 1 large egg
- 1 cup all-purpose flour
- ½ cup old-fashioned oats
- ½ teaspoon baking soda
- ¼ teaspoon salt
- ⅓ cup sea-salted caramel chips

Directions:
1. Preheat the air fryer to 300°F.
2. In a large bowl, cream the butter with the brown sugar and vanilla. Whisk in the egg and set aside.
3. In a separate bowl, mix the flour, oats, baking soda, and salt. Then gently mix the dry ingredients into the wet. Fold in the caramel chips.
4. Divide the batter into 12 silicon muffin liners. Place the cookie cups into the air fryer basket and cook for 12 minutes or until a toothpick inserted in the center comes out clean.
5. Remove and let cool 5 minutes before serving.

Oreo-coated Peanut Butter Cups

Servings: 8
Cooking Time: 4 Minutes
Ingredients:
- 8 Standard ¾-ounce peanut butter cups, frozen
- ⅓ cup All-purpose flour
- 2 Large egg white(s), beaten until foamy
- 16 Oreos or other creme-filled chocolate sandwich cookies, ground to crumbs in a food processor
- Vegetable oil spray

Directions:
1. Set up and fill three shallow soup plates or small pie plates on your counter: one for the flour, one for the beaten egg white(s), and one for the cookie crumbs.
2. Dip a frozen peanut butter cup in the flour, turning it to coat all sides. Shake off any excess, then set it in the beaten egg white(s). Turn it to coat all sides, then let any excess egg white slip back into the rest. Set the candy bar in the cookie crumbs. Turn to coat on all parts, even the sides. Dip the peanut butter cup back in the egg white(s) as before, then into the cookie crumbs as before, making sure you have a solid, even coating all around the cup. Set aside while you dip and coat the remaining cups.
3. When all the peanut butter cups are dipped and coated, lightly coat them on all sides with the vegetable oil spray. Set them on a plate and freeze while the air fryer heats.
4. Preheat the air fryer to 400°F.
5. Set the dipped cups wider side up in the basket with as much air space between them as possible. Air-fry undisturbed for 4 minutes, or until they feel soft but the coating is set.
6. Turn off the machine and remove the basket from it. Set aside the basket with the fried cups for 10 minutes. Use a nonstick-safe spatula to transfer the fried cups to a wire rack. Cool for at least another 5 minutes before serving.

Black And Blue Clafoutis

Servings: 2
Cooking Time: 15 minutes
Ingredients:
- 6-inch pie pan
- 3 large eggs
- ½ cup sugar
- 1 teaspoon vanilla extract
- 2 tablespoons butter, melted 1 cup milk
- ½ cup all-purpose flour*
- 1 cup blackberries

- 1 cup blueberries
- 2 tablespoons confectioners' sugar

Directions:
1. Preheat the air fryer to 320°F.
2. Combine the eggs and sugar in a bowl and whisk vigorously until smooth, lighter in color and well combined. Add the vanilla extract, butter and milk and whisk together well. Add the flour and whisk just until no lumps or streaks of white remain.
3. Scatter half the blueberries and blackberries in a greased (6-inch) pie pan or cake pan. Pour half of the batter (about 1¼ cups) on top of the berries and transfer the tart pan to the air fryer basket. You can use an aluminum foil sling to help with this by taking a long piece of aluminum foil, folding it in half lengthwise twice until it is roughly 26-inches by 3-inches. Place this under the pie dish and hold the ends of the foil to move the pie dish in and out of the air fryer basket. Tuck the ends of the foil beside the pie dish while it cooks in the air fryer.
4. Air-fry at 320°F for 15 minutes or until the clafoutis has puffed up and is still a little jiggly in the center. Remove the clafoutis from the air fryer, invert it onto a plate and let it cool while you bake the second batch. Serve the clafoutis warm, dusted with confectioners' sugar on top.

Nutty Cookies

Servings: 6
Cooking Time: 25 Minutes
Ingredients:
- ¼ cup pistachios
- ¼ cup evaporated cane sugar
- ¼ cup raw almonds
- ½ cup almond flour
- 1 tsp pure vanilla extract
- 1 egg white

Directions:
1. Preheat air fryer to 375°F. Add ¼ cup of pistachios and almonds into a food processor. Pulse until they resemble crumbles. Roughly chop the rest of the pistachios with a sharp knife. Combine all ingredients in a large bowl until completely incorporated. Form 6 equally-sized balls and transfer to the parchment-lined frying basket. Allow for 1 inch between each portion. Bake for 7 minutes. Cool on a wire rack for 5 minutes. Serve and enjoy.

Mixed Berry Pie

Servings: 4
Cooking Time: 25 Minutes
Ingredients:
- 2/3 cup blackberries, cut into thirds
- ¼ cup sugar
- 2 tbsp cornstarch
- ¼ tsp vanilla extract
- ¼ tsp peppermint extract
- ½ tsp lemon zest
- 1 cup sliced strawberries
- 1 cup raspberries
- 1 refrigerated piecrust
- 1 large egg

Directions:
1. Mix the sugar, cornstarch, vanilla, peppermint extract, and lemon zest in a bowl. Toss in all berries gently until combined. Pour into a greased dish. On a clean workspace, lay out the dough and cut into a 7-inch diameter round. Cover the baking dish with the round and crimp the edges. With a knife, cut 4 slits in the top to vent.
2. Beat 1 egg and 1 tbsp of water to make an egg wash. Brush the egg wash over the crust. Preheat air fryer to 350°F. Put the baking dish into the frying basket. Bake for 15 minutes or until the crust is golden and the berries are bubbling through the vents. Remove from the air fryer and let cool for 15 minutes. Serve warm.

Spiced Fruit Skewers

Servings: 4
Cooking Time: 15 Minutes
Ingredients:
- 2 peeled peaches, thickly sliced
- 3 plums, halved and pitted
- 3 peeled kiwi, quartered
- 1 tbsp honey
- ½ tsp ground cinnamon
- ¼ tsp ground allspice
- ¼ tsp cayenne pepper

Directions:
1. Preheat air fryer to 400°F. Combine the honey, cinnamon, allspice, and cayenne and set aside. Alternate fruits on 8 bamboo skewers, then brush the fruit with the honey mix. Lay the skewers in the air fryer and Air Fry for 3-5 minutes. Allow to chill for 5 minutes before serving.

Banana-almond Delights

Servings: 4
Cooking Time: 30 Minutes
Ingredients:
- 1 ripe banana, mashed
- 1 tbsp almond liqueur
- ½ tsp ground cinnamon
- 2 tbsp coconut sugar
- 1 cup almond flour
- ¼ tsp baking soda
- 8 raw almonds

Directions:
1. Preheat air fryer to 300°F. Add the banana to a bowl and stir in almond liqueur, cinnamon, and coconut sugar until well combined. Toss in almond flour and baking soda until smooth. Make 8 balls out of the mixture. Place the balls onto the parchment-lined frying basket, flatten each into ½-inch thick, and press 1 almond into the center. Bake for 12 minutes, turn and Bake for 6 more minutes. Let cool slightly before serving.

Cinnamon Canned Biscuit Donuts

Servings: 4
Cooking Time: 25 Minutes
Ingredients:
- 1 can jumbo biscuits
- 1 cup cinnamon sugar

Directions:
1. Preheat air fryer to 360°F. Divide biscuit dough into 8 biscuits and place on a flat work surface. Cut a small circle in the center of the biscuit with a small cookie cutter. Place a batch of 4 donuts in the air fryer. Spray with oil and Bake for 8 minutes, flipping once. Drizzle the cinnamon sugar over the donuts and serve.

Cheese Blintzes

Servings: 6
Cooking Time: 10 Minutes
Ingredients:
- 1½ 7½-ounce package(s) farmer cheese
- 3 tablespoons Regular or low-fat cream cheese (not fat-free)
- 3 tablespoons Granulated white sugar
- ¼ teaspoon Vanilla extract
- 6 Egg roll wrappers

- 3 tablespoons Butter, melted and cooled

Directions:
1. Preheat the air fryer to 375°F.
2. Use a flatware fork to mash the farmer cheese, cream cheese, sugar, and vanilla in a small bowl until smooth.
3. Set one egg roll wrapper on a clean, dry work surface. Place ¼ cup of the filling at the edge closest to you, leaving a ½-inch gap before the edge of the wrapper. Dip your clean finger in water and wet the edges of the wrapper. Fold the perpendicular sides over the filling, then roll the wrapper closed with the filling inside. Set it aside seam side down and continue filling the remainder of the wrappers.
4. Brush the wrappers on all sides with the melted butter. Be generous. Set them seam side down in the basket with as much space between them as possible. Air-fry undisturbed for 10 minutes, or until lightly browned.
5. Use a nonstick-safe spatula to transfer the blintzes to a wire rack. Cool for at least 5 minutes or up to 20 minutes before serving.

Tortilla Fried Pies

Servings: 12
Cooking Time: 5 Minutes
Ingredients:
- 12 small flour tortillas (4-inch diameter)
- ½ cup fig preserves
- ¼ cup sliced almonds
- 2 tablespoons shredded, unsweetened coconut
- oil for misting or cooking spray

Directions:
1. Wrap refrigerated tortillas in damp paper towels and heat in microwave 30 seconds to warm.
2. Working with one tortilla at a time, place 2 teaspoons fig preserves, 1 teaspoon sliced almonds, and ½ teaspoon coconut in the center of each.
3. Moisten outer edges of tortilla all around.
4. Fold one side of tortilla over filling to make a half-moon shape and press down lightly on center. Using the tines of a fork, press down firmly on edges of tortilla to seal in filling.
5. Mist both sides with oil or cooking spray.
6. Place hand pies in air fryer basket close but not overlapping. It's fine to lean some against the sides and corners of the basket. You may need to cook in 2 batches.
7. Cook at 390°F for 5 minutes or until lightly browned. Serve hot.
8. Refrigerate any leftover pies in a closed container. To serve later, toss them back in the air fryer basket and cook for 2 or 3 minutes to reheat.

Fruity Oatmeal Crisp

Servings: 6
Cooking Time: 25 Minutes
Ingredients:
- 2 peeled nectarines, chopped
- 1 peeled apple, chopped
- 1/3 cup raisins
- 2 tbsp honey
- 1/3 cup brown sugar
- ¼ cup flour
- ½ cup oatmeal
- 3 tbsp softened butter

Directions:
1. Preheat air fryer to 380°F. Mix together nectarines, apple, raisins, and honey in a baking pan. Set aside. Mix brown sugar, flour, oatmeal and butter in a medium bowl until crumbly. Top the fruit in a greased pan with the crumble. Bake until bubbly and the topping is golden, 10-12 minutes. Serve warm and top with vanilla ice cream if desired.

Nutty Banana Bread

Servings: 6
Cooking Time: 30 Minutes
Ingredients:
- 2 bananas
- 2 tbsp ground flaxseed
- ¼ cup milk
- 1 tbsp apple cider vinegar
- 1 tbsp vanilla extract
- ½ tsp ground cinnamon
- 2 tbsp honey
- ½ cup oat flour
- ½ tsp baking soda
- 3 tbsp butter

Directions:
1. Preheat air fryer to 320°F. Using a fork, mash the bananas until chunky. Mix in flaxseed, milk, apple vinegar, vanilla extract, cinnamon, and honey. Finally, toss in oat flour and baking soda until smooth but still chunky. Divide the batter between 6 cupcake molds. Top with one and a half teaspoons of butter each and swirl it a little. Bake for 18 minutes until golden brown and puffy. Let cool completely before serving.

Home-style Pumpkin Pie Pudding

Servings: 4
Cooking Time: 30 Minutes
Ingredients:
- 1 cup canned pumpkin purée
- ¼ cup sugar
- 3 tbsp all-purpose flour
- 1 tbsp butter, melted
- 1 egg
- 1 orange, zested
- 2 tbsp milk
- 1 tsp vanilla extract
- 4 vanilla wafers, crumbled

Directions:
1. Preheat air fryer to 350°F. Beat the pumpkin puree, sugar, flour, butter, egg, orange zest, milk, and vanilla until well-mixed. Spritz a baking pan with the cooking spray, then pour the pumpkin mix in. Place it in the air fryer and Bake for 11-17 minutes or until golden brown. Take the pudding out of the fryer and let it chill. Serve with vanilla wager crumbs.

British Bread Pudding

Servings: 4
Cooking Time: 30 Minutes
Ingredients:
- 4 bread slices
- 1 cup milk
- ¼ cup sugar
- 2 eggs, beaten
- 1 tbsp vanilla extract
- ½ tsp ground cinnamon

Directions:
1. Preheat air fryer to 320°F. Slice bread into bite-size pieces. Set aside in a small cake pan. Mix the milk, sugar, eggs, vanilla extract, and cinnamon in a bowl until well combined. Pour over the bread and toss to coat. Bake for 20 minutes until crispy and all liquid is absorbed. Slice into 4 pieces. Serve and enjoy!

Carrot-oat Cake Muffins

Servings: 4
Cooking Time: 20 Minutes
Ingredients:
- 3 tbsp butter, softened
- ¼ cup brown sugar
- 1 tbsp maple syrup
- 1 egg white
- ½ tsp vanilla extract
- 1/3 cup finely grated carrots
- ½ cup oatmeal
- 1/3 cup flour
- ½ tsp baking soda
- ¼ cup raisins

Directions:
1. Preheat air fryer to 350°F. Mix the butter, brown sugar, and maple syrup until smooth, then toss in the egg white, vanilla, and carrots. Whisk well and add the oatmeal, flour, baking soda, and raisins. Divide the mixture between muffin cups. Bake in the fryer for 8-10 minutes.

Fried Cannoli Wontons

Servings: 10
Cooking Time: 8 Minutes
Ingredients:
- 8 ounces Neufchâtel cream cheese
- ¼ cup powdered sugar
- 1 teaspoon vanilla extract
- ¼ teaspoon salt
- ¼ cup mini chocolate chips
- 2 tablespoons chopped pecans (optional)
- 20 wonton wrappers
- ¼ cup filtered water

Directions:
1. Preheat the air fryer to 370°F.
2. In a large bowl, use a hand mixer to combine the cream cheese with the powdered sugar, vanilla, and salt. Fold in the chocolate chips and pecans. Set aside.
3. Lay the wonton wrappers out on a flat, smooth surface and place a bowl with the filtered water next to them.
4. Use a teaspoon to evenly divide the cream cheese mixture among the 20 wonton wrappers, placing the batter in the center of the wontons.
5. Wet the tip of your index finger, and gently moisten the outer edges of the wrapper. Then fold each wrapper until it creates a secure pocket.
6. Liberally spray the air fryer basket with olive oil mist.
7. Place the wontons into the basket, and cook for 5 to 8 minutes. When the outer edges begin to brown, remove the wontons from the air fryer basket. Repeat cooking with remaining wontons.
8. Serve warm.

Fall Pumpkin Cake

Servings: 6
Cooking Time: 50 Minutes
Ingredients:
- 1/3 cup pecan pieces
- 5 gingersnap cookies
- 1/3 cup light brown sugar
- 6 tbsp butter, melted
- 3 eggs
- ½ tsp vanilla extract
- 1 cup pumpkin purée
- 2 tbsp sour cream
- ½ cup flour
- ¼ cup tapioca flour
- ½ tsp cornstarch
- ½ cup granulated sugar
- ½ tsp baking soda
- 1 tsp baking powder
- 1 tsp pumpkin pie spice
- 6 oz mascarpone cheese
- 1 1/3 cups powdered sugar
- 1 tsp cinnamon
- 2 tbsp butter, softened
- 1 tbsp milk
- 1 tbsp flaked almonds

Directions:
1. Blitz the pecans, gingersnap cookies, brown sugar, and 3 tbsp of melted butter in a food processor until combined. Press mixture into the bottom of a lightly greased cake pan. Preheat air fryer at 350ºF. In a bowl, whisk the eggs, remaining melted butter, ½ tsp of vanilla extract, pumpkin purée, and sour cream. In another bowl, combine the flour, tapioca flour, cornstarch, granulated sugar, baking soda, baking powder, and pumpkin pie spice. Add wet ingredients to dry ingredients and combine. Do not overmix. Pour the batter into a cake pan and cover it with aluminum foil. Place cake pan in the frying basket and Bake for 30 minutes. Remove the foil and cook for another 5 minutes. Let cool onto a cooling rack for 10 minutes. Then, turn cake onto a large serving platter. In a small bowl, whisk the mascarpone cheese, powdered sugar, remaining vanilla extract, cinnamon, softened butter, and milk. Spread over cooled cake and cut into slices. Serve sprinkled with almonds and enjoy!

Pumpkin Brownies

Servings: 4
Cooking Time: 30 Minutes
Ingredients:
- ¼ cup canned pumpkin
- ½ cup maple syrup
- 2 eggs, beaten
- 1 tbsp vanilla extract
- ¼ cup tapioca flour
- ¼ cup flour
- ½ tsp baking powder

Directions:
1. Preheat air fryer to 320°F. Mix the pumpkin, maple syrup, eggs, and vanilla extract in a bowl. Toss in tapioca flour, flour, and baking powder until smooth. Pour the batter into a small round cake pan and Bake for 20 minutes until a toothpick comes out clean. Let cool completely before slicing into 4 brownies. Serve and enjoy!

Chewy Coconut Cake

Servings: 6
Cooking Time: 18-22 Minutes
Ingredients:
- ¾ cup plus 2½ tablespoons All-purpose flour
- ¾ teaspoon Baking powder
- ⅛ teaspoon Table salt
- 7½ tablespoons (1 stick minus ½ tablespoon) Butter, at room temperature
- 1/3 cup plus 1 tablespoon Granulated white sugar
- 5 tablespoons Packed light brown sugar
- 5 tablespoons Pasteurized egg substitute, such as Egg Beaters
- 2 teaspoons Vanilla extract
- ½ cup Unsweetened shredded coconut (see here)
- Baking spray

Directions:

1. Preheat the air fryer to 325°F(or 330°F,if that's the closest setting).
2. Mix the flour,baking powder,and salt in a small bowl until well combined.
3. Using an electric hand mixer at medium speed,beat the butter,granulated white sugar,and brown sugar in a medium bowl until creamy and smooth,about 3 minutes,occasionally scraping down the inside of the bowl.Beat in the egg substitute or egg and vanilla until smooth.
4. Scrape down and remove the beaters.Fold in the flour mixture with a rubber spatula just until all the flour is moistened.Fold in the coconut until the mixture is a uniform color.
5. Use the baking spray to generously coat the inside of a 6-inch round cake pan for a small batch,a 7-inch round cake pan for a medium batch,or an 8-inch round cake pan for a large batch.Scrape and spread the batter into the pan,smoothing the batter out to an even layer.
6. Set the pan in the basket and air-fry for 18 minutes for a 6-inch layer,20 minutes for a 7-inch layer,or 22 minutes for an 8-inch layer,or until the cake is well browned and set even if there's a little soft give right at the center.Start checking it at the 16-minute mark to know where you are.
7. Use hot pads or silicone baking mitts to transfer the cake pan to a wire rack.Cool for at least 1 hour or up to 4 hours.Use a nonstick-safe knife to slice the cake into wedges right in the pan,lifting them out one by one.

Mixed Berry Hand Pies

Servings:4
Cooking Time:15 Minutes
Ingredients:
- ¾cup sugar
- ½teaspoon ground cinnamon
- 1 tablespoon cornstarch
- 1 cup blueberries
- 1 cup blackberries
- 1 cup raspberries,divided
- 1 teaspoon water
- 1 package refrigerated pie dough(or your own homemade pie dough)
- 1 egg,beaten

Directions:
1. Combine the sugar,cinnamon,and cornstarch in a small saucepan.Add the blueberries,blackberries,and½cup of the raspberries.Toss the berries gently to coat them evenly.Add the teaspoon of water to the saucepan and turn the stovetop on to medium-high heat,stirring occasionally.Once the berries break down,release their juice and start to simmer(about 5 minutes),simmer for another couple of minutes and then transfer the mixture to a bowl,stir in the remaining½cup of raspberries and let it cool.
2. Preheat the air fryer to 370°F.
3. Cut the pie dough into four 5-inch circles and four 6-inch circles.
4. Spread the 6-inch circles on a flat surface.Divide the berry filling between all four circles.Brush the perimeter of the dough circles with a little water.Place the 5-inch circles on top of the filling and press the perimeter of the dough circles together to seal.Roll the edges of the bottom circle up over the top circle to make a crust around the filling.Press a fork around the crust to make decorative indentations and to seal the crust shut.Brush the pies with egg wash and sprinkle a little sugar on top.Poke a small hole in the center of each pie with a paring knife to vent the dough.
5. Air-fry two pies at a time.Brush or spray the air fryer basket with oil and place the pies into the basket.Air-fry for 9 minutes.Turn the pies over and air-fry for another 6 minutes.Serve warm or at room temperature.

Honeyed Tortilla Fritters

Servings:8
Cooking Time:10 Minutes
Ingredients:
- 2 tbsp granulated sugar
- ½tsp ground cinnamon
- 1 tsp vanilla powder
- Salt to taste
- 8 flour tortillas,quartered
- 2 tbsp butter,melted
- 4 tsp honey
- 1 tbsp almond flakes

Directions:
1. Preheat air fryer at 400ºF.Combine the sugar,cinnamon,vanilla powder,and salt in a bowl.Set aside.Brush tortilla quarters with melted butter and sprinkle with sugar mixture.Place tortilla quarters in the frying basket and Air Fry for 4 minutes,turning once.Let cool on a large plate for 5 minutes until hardened.Drizzle with honey and scatter with almond flakes to serve.

Baked Apple

Servings:6
Cooking Time:20 Minutes
Ingredients:
- 3 small Honey Crisp or other baking apples
- 3 tablespoons maple syrup
- 3 tablespoons chopped pecans
- 1 tablespoon firm butter,cut into 6 pieces

Directions:
1. Put½cup water in the drawer of the air fryer.
2. Wash apples well and dry them.
3. Split apples in half.Remove core and a little of the flesh to make a cavity for the pecans.
4. Place apple halves in air fryer basket,cut side up.
5. Spoon 1½teaspoons pecans into each cavity.
6. Spoon½tablespoon maple syrup over pecans in each apple.
7. Top each apple with½teaspoon butter.
8. Cook at 360°F for 20 minutes,until apples are tender.

Banana Bread Cake

Servings:6
Cooking Time:18-22 Minutes
Ingredients:
- ¾cup plus 2 tablespoons All-purpose flour
- ½teaspoon Baking powder
- ¼teaspoon Baking soda
- ¼teaspoon Table salt
- 4 tablespoons(¼cup/½stick)Butter,at room temperature
- ½cup Granulated white sugar
- 2 Small ripe bananas,peeled
- 5 tablespoons Pasteurized egg substitute,such as Egg Beaters
- ¼cup Buttermilk
- ¾teaspoon Vanilla extract
- Baking spray(see here)

Directions:
1. Preheat the air fryer to 325°F(or 330°F,if that's the closest setting).
2. Mix the flour,baking powder,baking soda,and salt in a small bowl until well combined.
3. Using an electric hand mixer at medium speed,beat the butter and sugar in a medium bowl until creamy and smooth,about 3 minutes,occasionally scraping down the inside of the bowl.
4. Beat in the bananas until smooth.Then beat in egg substitute or egg,buttermilk,and vanilla until uniform.(The

batter may look curdled at this stage.The flour mixture will smooth it out.)Add the flour mixture and beat at low speed until smooth and creamy.
5. Use the baking spray to generously coat the inside of a 6-inch round cake pan for a small batch,a 7-inch round cake pan for a medium batch,or an 8-inch round cake pan for a large batch.Scrape and spread the batter into the pan,smoothing the batter out to an even layer.
6. Set the pan in the basket and air-fry for 18 minutes for a 6-inch layer,20 minutes for a 7-inch layer,or 22 minutes for an 8-inch layer,or until the cake is well browned and set even if there's a little soft give right at the center.Start checking it at the 16-minute mark to know where you are.
7. Use hot pads or silicone baking mitts to transfer the cake pan to a wire rack.To unmold,set a cutting board over the baking pan and invert both the board and the pan.Lift the still-warm pan off the cake layer.Set the wire rack on top of that layer and invert all of it with the cutting board so that the cake layer is now right side up on the wire rack.Remove the cutting board and continue cooling the cake for at least 10 minutes or to room temperature,about 40 minutes,before slicing into wedges.

Roasted Pears

Servings:4
Cooking Time:10 Minutes
Ingredients:
- 2 Ripe pears,preferably Anjou,stemmed,peeled,halved lengthwise,and cored
- 2 tablespoons Butter,melted
- 2 teaspoons Granulated white sugar
- Grated nutmeg
- ¼cup Honey
- ½cup(about 1½ounces)Shaved Parmesan cheese

Directions:
1. Preheat the air fryer to 400°F.
2. Brush each pear half with about 1½teaspoons of the melted butter,then sprinkle their cut sides with½teaspoon sugar.Grate a pinch of nutmeg over each pear.
3. When the machine is at temperature,set the pear halves cut side up in the basket with as much air space between them as possible.Air-fry undisturbed for 10 minutes,or until hot and softened.
4. Use a nonstick-safe spatula,and perhaps a flatware tablespoon for balance,to transfer the pear halves to a serving platter or plates.Cool for a minute or two,then drizzle each pear half with 1 tablespoon of the honey.Lay about 2 tablespoons of shaved Parmesan over each half just before serving.

Dark Chokolate Cookies

Servings:4
Cooking Time:50 Minutes
Ingredients:
- 1/3 cup brown sugar
- 2 tbsp butter,softened
- 1 egg yolk
- 2/3 cup flour
- 5 tbsp peanut butter
- ¼tsp baking soda
- 1 tsp dark rum
- ½cup dark chocolate chips

Directions:
1. Preheat air fryer to 310°F.Beat butter and brown sugar in a bowl until fluffy.Stir in the egg yolk.Add flour,3 tbsp of peanut butter,baking soda,and rum until well mixed.Spread the batter into a parchment-lined baking pan.Bake in the air fryer until the cooking is lightly brown and just set,7-10 minutes.Remove from the fryer and let cool for 10 minutes.
2. After,remove the cookie from the pan and the parchment paper and cool on the wire rack.When cooled,combine the chips with the remaining peanut butter in a heatproof cup.Place in the air fryer and Bake until melted,2 minutes.Remove and stir.Spread on the cooled cookies and serve.

Apple&Blueberry Crumble

Servings:4
Cooking Time:20 Minutes
Ingredients:
- 5 apples,peeled and diced
- ½lemon,zested and juiced
- ½cup blueberries
- 1 cup brown sugar
- 1 tsp cinnamon
- ½cup butter
- ½cup flour

Directions:
1. Preheat air fryer to 340°F.Place the apple chunks,blueberries,lemon juice and zest,half of the butter,half of the brown sugar,and cinnamon in a greased baking dish.Combine thoroughly until all is well mixed.Combine the flour with the remaining butter and brown sugar in a separate bowl.Stir until it forms a crumbly consistency.Spread the mixture over the fruit.Bake in the air fryer for 10-15 minutes until golden and bubbling.Serve and enjoy!

Cheesecake Wontons

Servings:16
Cooking Time:6 Minutes
Ingredients:
- ¼cup Regular or low-fat cream cheese(not fat-free)
- 2 tablespoons Granulated white sugar
- 1½tablespoons Egg yolk
- ¼teaspoon Vanilla extract
- ⅛teaspoon Table salt
- 1½tablespoons All-purpose flour
- 16 Wonton wrappers(vegetarian,if a concern)
- Vegetable oil spray

Directions:
1. Preheat the air fryer to 400°F.
2. Using a flatware fork,mash the cream cheese,sugar,egg yolk,and vanilla in a small bowl until smooth.Add the salt and flour and continue mashing until evenly combined.
3. Set a wonton wrapper on a clean,dry work surface so that one corner faces you(so that it looks like a diamond on your work surface).Set 1 teaspoon of the cream cheese mixture in the middle of the wrapper but just above a horizontal line that would divide the wrapper in half.Dip your clean finger in water and run it along the edges of the wrapper.Fold the corner closest to you up and over the filling,lining it up with the corner farthest from you,thereby making a stuffed triangle.Press gently to seal.Wet the two triangle tips nearest you,then fold them up and together over the filling.Gently press together to seal and fuse.Set aside and continue making more stuffed wontons,11 more for the small batch,15 more for the medium batch,or 23 more for the large one.
4. Lightly coat the stuffed wrappers on all sides with vegetable oil spray.Set them with the fused corners up in the basket with as much air space between them as possible.Air-fry undisturbed for 6 minutes,or until golden brown and crisp.
5. Gently dump the contents of the basket onto a wire rack.Cool for at least 5 minutes before serving.

Cheese & Honey Stuffed Figs

Servings: 4
Cooking Time: 15 Minutes
Ingredients:
- 8 figs, stem off
- 2 oz cottage cheese
- ¼tsp ground cinnamon
- ¼tsp orange zest
- ¼tsp vanilla extract
- 2 tbsp honey
- 1 tbsp olive oil

Directions:
1. Preheat air fryer to 360°F. Cut an "X" in the top of each fig 1/3 way through, leaving intact the base. Mix together the cottage cheese, cinnamon, orange zest, vanilla extract and 1 tbsp of honey in a bowl. Spoon the cheese mixture into the cavity of each fig. Put the figs in a single layer in the frying basket. Drizzle the olive oil over the top of the figs and Roast for 10 minutes. Drizzle with the remaining honey. Serve and enjoy!

Giant Buttery Oatmeal Cookie

Servings: 4
Cooking Time: 16 Minutes
Ingredients:
- 1 cup Rolled oats (not quick-cooking or steel-cut oats)
- ½cup All-purpose flour
- ½teaspoon Baking soda
- ½teaspoon Ground cinnamon
- ½teaspoon Table salt
- 3½tablespoons Butter, at room temperature
- ⅓cup Packed dark brown sugar
- 1½tablespoons Granulated white sugar
- 3 tablespoons (or 1 medium egg, well beaten) Pasteurized egg substitute, such as Egg Beaters
- ¾teaspoon Vanilla extract
- ⅓cup Chopped pecans
- Baking spray

Directions:
1. Preheat the air fryer to 350°F.
2. Stir the oats, flour, baking soda, cinnamon, and salt in a bowl until well combined.
3. Using an electric hand mixer at medium speed, beat the butter, brown sugar, and granulated white sugar until creamy and thick, about 3 minutes, scraping down the inside of the bowl occasionally. Beat in the egg substitute or egg (as applicable) and vanilla until uniform.
4. Scrape down and remove the beaters. Fold in the flour mixture and pecans with a rubber spatula just until all the flour is moistened and the nuts are even throughout the dough.
5. For a small air fryer, coat the inside of a 6-inch round cake pan with baking spray. For a medium air fryer, coat the inside of a 7-inch round cake pan with baking spray. And for a large air fryer, coat the inside of an 8-inch round cake pan with baking spray. Scrape and gently press the dough into the prepared pan, spreading it into an even layer to the perimeter.
6. Set the pan in the basket and air-fry undisturbed for 16 minutes, or until puffed and browned.
7. Transfer the pan to a wire rack and cool for 10 minutes. Loosen the cookie from the perimeter with a spatula, then invert the pan onto a cutting board and let the cookie come free. Remove the pan and reinvert the cookie onto the wire rack. Cool for 5 minutes more before slicing into wedges to serve.

Carrot Cake With Cream Cheese Icing

Servings: 6
Cooking Time: 55 Minutes
Ingredients:
- 1¼cups all-purpose flour
- 1 teaspoon baking powder
- ½teaspoon baking soda
- 1 teaspoon ground cinnamon
- ¼teaspoon ground nutmeg
- ¼teaspoon salt
- 2 cups grated carrot (about 3 to 4 medium carrots or 2 large)
- ¾cup granulated sugar
- ¼cup brown sugar
- 2 eggs
- ¾cup canola or vegetable oil
- For the icing:
- 8 ounces cream cheese, softened at room, Temperature: 8 tablespoons butter (4 ounces or 1 stick), softened at room, Temperature: 1 cup powdered sugar
- 1 teaspoon pure vanilla extract

Directions:
1. Grease a 7-inch cake pan.
2. Combine the flour, baking powder, baking soda, cinnamon, nutmeg and salt in a bowl. Add the grated carrots and toss well. In a separate bowl, beat the sugars and eggs together until light and frothy. Drizzle in the oil, beating constantly. Fold the egg mixture into the dry ingredients until everything is just combined and you no longer see any traces of flour. Pour the batter into the cake pan and wrap the pan completely in greased aluminum foil.
3. Preheat the air fryer to 350°F.
4. Lower the cake pan into the air fryer basket using a sling made of aluminum foil (fold a piece of aluminum foil into a strip about 2-inches wide by 24-inches long). Fold the ends of the aluminum foil into the air fryer, letting them rest on top of the cake. Air-fry for 40 minutes. Remove the aluminum foil cover and air-fry for an additional 15 minutes or until a skewer inserted into the center of the cake comes out clean and the top is nicely browned.
5. While the cake is cooking, beat the cream cheese, butter, powdered sugar and vanilla extract together using a hand mixer, stand mixer or food processor (or a lot of elbow grease!).
6. Remove the cake pan from the air fryer and let the cake cool in the cake pan for 10 minutes or so. Then remove the cake from the pan and let it continue to cool completely. Frost the cake with the cream cheese icing and serve.

Vanilla-strawberry Muffins

Servings: 4
Cooking Time: 25 Minutes
Ingredients:
- ¼cup diced strawberries
- 2 tbsp powdered sugar
- 1 cup flour
- ½tsp baking soda
- 1/3 cup granulated sugar
- ¼tsp salt
- 1 tsp vanilla extract
- 1 egg
- 1 tbsp butter, melted
- ½cup diced strawberries
- 2 tbsp chopped walnuts
- 6 tbsp butter, softened

- 1½ cups powdered sugar
- 1/8 tsp peppermint extract

Directions:
1. Preheat air fryer at 375°F. Combine flour, baking soda, granulated sugar, and salt in a bowl. In another bowl, combine the vanilla, egg, walnuts and melted butter. Pour wet ingredients into dry ingredients and toss to combine. Fold in half of the strawberries and spoon mixture into 8 greased silicone cupcake liners.
2. Place cupcakes in the frying basket and Bake for 6-8 minutes. Let cool onto a cooling rack for 10 minutes. Blend the remaining strawberries in a food processor until smooth. Slowly add powdered sugar to softened butter while beating in a bowl. Stir in peppermint extract and puréed strawberries until blended. Spread over cooled cupcakes. Serve sprinkled with powdered sugar

Orange-chocolate Cake

Servings: 6
Cooking Time: 35 Minutes
Ingredients:
- ¾ cup flour
- ½ cup sugar
- 7 tbsp cocoa powder
- ½ tsp baking soda
- ½ cup milk
- 2½ tbsp sunflower oil
- ½ tbsp orange juice
- 2 tsp vanilla
- 2 tsp orange zest
- 3 tbsp butter, softened
- 1¼ cups powdered sugar

Directions:
1. Use a whisk to combine the flour, sugar, 2 tbsp of cocoa powder, baking soda, and a pinch of salt in a bowl. Once combined, add milk, sunflower oil, orange juice, and orange zest. Stir until combined. Preheat the air fryer to 350°F. Pour the batter into a greased cake pan and Bake for 25 minutes or until a knife inserted in the center comes out clean.
2. Use an electric beater to beat the butter and powdered sugar together in a bowl. Add the remaining cocoa powder and vanilla and whip until fluffy. Scrape the sides occasionally. Refrigerate until ready to use. Allow the cake to cool completely, then run a knife around the edges of the baking pan. Turn it upside-down on a plate so it can be frosted on the sides and top. When the frosting is no longer cold, use a butter knife or small spatula to frost the sides and top. Cut into slices and enjoy!

Honey-roasted Mixed Nuts

Servings: 8
Cooking Time: 15 Minutes
Ingredients:
- ½ cup raw, shelled pistachios
- ½ cup raw almonds
- 1 cup raw walnuts
- 2 tablespoons filtered water
- 2 tablespoons honey
- 1 tablespoon vegetable oil
- 2 tablespoons sugar
- ½ teaspoon salt

Directions:
1. Preheat the air fryer to 300°F.
2. Lightly spray an air-fryer-safe pan with olive oil; then place the pistachios, almonds, and walnuts inside the pan and place the pan inside the air fryer basket.
3. Cook for 15 minutes, shaking the basket every 5 minutes to rotate the nuts.
4. While the nuts are roasting, boil the water in a small pan and stir in the honey and oil. Continue to stir while cooking until the water begins to evaporate and a thick sauce is formed. Note: The sauce should stick to the back of a wooden spoon when mixed. Turn off the heat.
5. Remove the nuts from the air fryer (cooking should have just completed) and spoon the nuts into the stovetop pan. Use a spatula to coat the nuts with the honey syrup.
6. Line a baking sheet with parchment paper and spoon the nuts onto the sheet. Lightly sprinkle the sugar and salt over the nuts and let cool in the refrigerator for at least 2 hours.
7. When the honey and sugar have hardened, store the nuts in an airtight container in the refrigerator.

Giant Vegan Chocolate Chip Cookie

Servings: 4
Cooking Time: 16 Minutes
Ingredients:
- ⅔ cup All-purpose flour
- 5 tablespoons Rolled oats (not quick-cooking or steel-cut oats)
- ¼ teaspoon Baking soda
- ¼ teaspoon Table salt
- 5 tablespoons Granulated white sugar
- ¼ cup Vegetable oil
- 2½ tablespoons Tahini (see here)
- 2½ tablespoons Maple syrup
- 2 teaspoons Vanilla extract
- ⅔ cup Vegan semisweet or bittersweet chocolate chips
- Baking spray

Directions:
1. Preheat the air fryer to 325°F (or 330°F, if that's the closest setting).
2. Whisk the flour, oats, baking soda, and salt in a bowl until well combined.
3. Using an electric hand mixer at medium speed, beat the sugar, oil, tahini, maple syrup, and vanilla until rich and creamy, about 3 minutes, scraping down the inside of the bowl occasionally.
4. Scrape down and remove the beaters. Fold in the flour mixture and chocolate chips with a rubber spatula just until all the flour is moistened and the chocolate chips are even throughout the dough.
5. For a small air fryer, coat the inside of a 6-inch round cake pan with baking spray. For a medium air fryer, coat the inside of a 7-inch round cake pan with baking spray. And for a large air fryer, coat the inside of an 8-inch round cake pan with baking spray. Scrape and gently press the dough into the prepared pan, spreading it into an even layer to the perimeter.
6. Set the pan in the basket and air-fry undisturbed for 16 minutes, or until puffed, browned, and firm to the touch.
7. Transfer the pan to a wire rack and cool for 10 minutes. Loosen the cookie from the perimeter with a spatula, then invert the pan onto a cutting board and let the cookie come free. Remove the pan and reinvert the cookie onto the wire rack. Cool for 5 minutes more before slicing into wedges to serve.

Fluffy Orange Cake

Servings: 6
Cooking Time: 30 Minutes

Ingredients:
- 1/3 cup cornmeal
- 1¼ cups flour
- ¾ cup white sugar
- 1 tsp baking soda
- ¼ cup safflower oil
- 1¼ cups orange juice
- 1 tsp orange zest
- ¼ cup powdered sugar

Directions:
1. Preheat air fryer to 340°F. Mix cornmeal, flour, sugar, baking soda, safflower oil, 1 cup of orange juice, and orange zest in a medium bowl. Mix until combined.
2. Pour the batter into a greased baking pan and set into the air fryer. Bake until a toothpick in the center of the cake comes out clean. Remove the cake and place it on a cooling rack. Use the toothpick to make 20 holes in the cake. Meanwhile, combine the rest of the juice with the powdered sugar in a small bowl. Drizzle the glaze over the hot cake and allow it to absorb. Leave to cool completely, then cut into pieces. Serve and enjoy!

RECIPE INDEX

A

Almond And Sun-dried Tomato Crusted Pork Chops 53
Almond Green Beans 40
Almond-crusted Fish 67
Almond-crusted Zucchini Fries 36
Antipasto-stuffed Cherry Tomatoes 13
Apple&Blueberry Crumble 121
Apple&Turkey Breakfast Sausages 28
Apple-carrot Cupcakes 115
Apricot Glazed Chicken Thighs 91
Argentinian Steak Asado Salad 54
Aromatic Mushroom Omelet 28
Aromatic Pork Tenderloin 62
Asian Glazed Meatballs 107
Asian Meatball Tacos 79
Asian-style Orange Chicken 79
Asparagus 41
Asparagus,Mushroom And Cheese Soufflés 104
Autenthic Greek Fish Pitas 64
Authentic Mexican Esquites 92
Avocado Fries 12

B

Baba Ghanouj 22
Baby Back Ribs 53
Bacon Puff Pastry Pinwheels 25
Bacon-wrapped Asparagus 40
Bagel Chips 17
Bagels With Avocado&Tomatoes 29
Baked Apple 120
Baked Stuffed Pears 114
Balsamic Beef&Veggie Skewers 47
Balsamic Caprese Hasselback 101
Balsamic London Broil 55
Balsamic Short Ribs 55
Banana Bread Cake 120
Banana Bread 30
Banana-almond Delights 117
Barbecue-style London Broil 52
Basil Cheese&Ham Stromboli 61
Basil Crab Cakes With Fresh Salad 63
Bbq Back Ribs 48
Bbq Chips 12
Beef And Spinach Braciole 61
Beef Brazilian Empanadas 49
Beef Meatballs With Herbs 49
Beef Short Ribs 56
Beer Battered Onion Rings 19
Beer-battered Onion Rings 12
Bell Pepper&Lentil Tacos 95
Berbere Eggplant Dip 94
Best-ever Roast Beef Sandwiches 108
Better-than-chinese-take-out Sesame Beef 56
Bite-sized Blooming Onions 96
Black And Blue Clafoutis 116
Black Bean Veggie Burgers 111
Black Olive&Shrimp Salad 67
Blackened Red Snapper 74

Blooming Onion 15
Blueberry Applesauce Oat Cake 26
Blueberry Pannenkoek(dutch Pancake) 29
Boneless Ribeyes 51
Boss Chicken Cobb Salad 83
Bourbon Bacon Burgers 53
Breakfast Burrito With Sausage 32
Breakfast Chimichangas 29
Breakfast Sausage Bites 32
British Bread Pudding 118
British Fish&Chips 70
Broccoli&Mushroom Beef 56
Buffalo Wings 14
Buttered Turkey Breasts 80
Butternut Squash–wrapped Halibut Fillets 77
Buttery Chicken Legs 82
Buttery Stuffed Tomatoes 39

C

Cajun Chicken Kebabs 87
Cajun Fried Chicken 82
Calzones South Of The Border 60
Caprese-style Sandwiches 98
Caribbean Jerk Cod Fillets 74
Carrot Cake With Cream Cheese Icing 122
Carrot-oat Cake Muffins 119
Catalan Sardines With Romesco Sauce 71
Catalan-style Crab Samfaina 70
Catfish Nuggets 67
Cauliflower 39
Charred Radicchio Salad 42
Cheddar&Sausage Tater Tots 29
Cheddar-bean Flautas 103
Cheese Arancini 20
Cheese Blintzes 117
Cheese&Bacon Pasta Bake 44
Cheese&Bean Burgers 97
Cheese&Crab Stuffed Mushrooms 64
Cheese&Honey Stuffed Figs 122
Cheeseburger Sliders With Pickle Sauce 59
Cheesecake Wontons 121
Cheesy Breaded Eggplants 36
Cheesy Eggplant Rounds 93
Cheesy Enchilada Stuffed Baked Potatoes 104
Cheesy Green Wonton Triangles 19
Cherry Cheesecake Rolls 116
Cherry-apple Oatmeal Cups 26
Chewy Coconut Cake 119
Chicano Rice Bowls 103
Chicken Apple Brie Melt 112
Chicken Club Sandwiches 108
Chicken Fried Steak 51
Chicken Gyros 111
Chicken Nuggets 87
Chicken Parmesan 91
Chicken Pinchos Morunos 81
Chicken Rochambeau 88
Chicken Saltimbocca Sandwiches 109
Chicken Scotch Eggs 34
Chicken Shawarma Bites 15

Ninja Foodi 2-Basket Air Fryer

Chicken Skewers 86
Chicken Spiedies 108
Chicken&Rice Sautée 87
Chile Con Carne Galette 58
Chili Cheese Dogs 109
Chili Hash Browns 28
Chinese Fish Noodle Bowls 70
Chinese-style Lamb Chops 52
Chocolate Chip Banana Muffins 34
Christmas Eggnog Bread 26
Cinnamon Banana Bread With Pecans 34
Cinnamon Biscuit Rolls 27
Cinnamon Canned Biscuit Donuts 117
Citrusy Brussels Sprouts 43
Classic Chicken Wings 16
Classic Potato Chips 12
Coconut Shrimp With Plum Sauce 65
Coconut-custard Pie 116
Coconut-shrimp Po'Boys 72
Coffee Cake 31
Coffee-rubbed Pork Tenderloin 48
Corn And Pepper Jack Chile Rellenos With Roasted Tomato Sauce 105
Corn On The Cob 42
Cornflake Chicken Nuggets 82
Country Gravy 25
Country-style Pork Ribs(2) 46
Crab Cakes On A Budget 72
Crispy Brussels Sprouts 41
Crispy Chicken Bites With Gorgonzola Sauce 12
Crispy Chicken Parmesan 82
Crispy Cordon Bleu 79
Crispy Herbed Potatoes 36
Crispy Lamb Shoulder Chops 51
Crispy Smelts 66
Crispy Smoked Pork Chops 46
Crunchy Falafel Balls 109
Crunchy Parmesan Edamame 22
Crunchy Rice Paper Samosas 99
Crunchy Veal Cutlets 55
Curried Cauliflower With Cashews And Yogurt 42
Curried Potato,Cauliflower And Pea Turnovers 92
Curried Sweet-and-spicy Scallops 66
Curried Veggie Samosas 21

D

Daadi Chicken Salad 85
Dark Chokolate Cookies 121
Delicious Juicy Pork Meatballs 50
Dijon Artichoke Hearts 38
Dijon Chicken Wings 17
Dijon Thyme Burgers 110
Dill Fried Pickles With Light Ranch Dip 16
Dilly Red Snapper 68
Dilly Sesame Roasted Asparagus 37

E

Easy Asian-style Tuna 68
Easy Carnitas 51
Easy Cheese&Spinach Lasagna 98
Easy Scallops With Lemon Butter 75
Easy Zucchini Lasagna Roll-ups 97
Easy-peasy Beef Sliders 60
Easy-peasy Shrimp 73
Effortless Mac`n´Cheese 93
Effortless Toffee Zucchini Bread 31
Egg&Bacon Toasts 32
Eggplant Parmesan Subs 109
English Breakfast 33

F

Falafels 99
Fall Pumpkin Cake 119
Family Fish Nuggets With Tartar Sauce 75
Fancy Chicken Piccata 86
Farmer´s Fried Chicken 89
Farmers Market Quiche 28
Fast Brownies 115
Fiery Sweet Chicken Wings 13
Fiesta Chicken Plate 89
Fish Cakes 77
Fish Goujons With Tartar Sauce 75
Fish Nuggets With Broccoli Dip 71
Fish Piccata With Crispy Potatoes 68
Fish Sticks With Tartar Sauce 71
Fish Tacos With Jalapeño-lime Sauce 71
Five Spice Red Snapper With Green Onions And Orange Salsa 70
Flounder Fillets 73
Fluffy Orange Cake 124
Fluffy Vegetable Strata 30
French Fries 37
French-style Pork Medallions 47
Fried Bananas 22
Fried Cannoli Wontons 119
Fried Cheese Ravioli With Marinara Sauce 22
Fried Green Tomatoes 17
Fried Gyoza 24
Fried Pearl Onions With Balsamic Vinegar And Basil 38
Friendly Bbq Baby Back Ribs 58
Fruity Oatmeal Crisp 118
Fry Bread 31
Fusion Tender Flank Steak 59

G

Garlic And Oregano Lamb Chops 61
Garlic Bread Knots 30
Garlic Chicken 86
Garlic Wings 21
Garlicky Brussel Sprouts With Saffron Aioli 95
General Tso's Cauliflower 101
German Chicken Frikadellen 89
Giant Buttery Oatmeal Cookie 122
Giant Vegan Chocolate Chip Cookie 123
Gingerbread 113
Gluten-free Nutty Chicken Fingers 83
Golden Pork Quesadillas 47
Greek Pork Chops 57
Green Beans 43
Green Dip With Pine Nuts 40
Green Olive And Mushroom Tapenade 18
Grits Casserole 41

H

Ham And Cheddar Gritters 33

Harissa Veggie Fries 94
Hasselback Garlic-and-butter Potatoes 36
Hawaiian Brown Rice 39
Hellenic Zucchini Bites 94
Herb-crusted Sole 72
Herbed Baby Red Potato Hasselback 40
Holiday Shrimp Scampi 69
Homemade Pork Gyoza 57
Homemade Potato Puffs 45
Home-style Buffalo Chicken Wings 14
Home-style Pumpkin Pie Pudding 118
Honey Brussels Sprouts 42
Honey Donuts 32
Honey Mesquite Pork Chops 60
Honey Pear Chips 104
Honey Tater Tots With Bacon 24
Honeyed Tortilla Fritters 120
Honey-mustard Asparagus Puffs 39
Honey-mustard Roasted Cabbage 39
Honey-roasted Mixed Nuts 123
Honey-roasted Parsnips 38
Horseradish Tuna Croquettes 69
Horseradish-crusted Salmon Fillets 78
Hot Avocado Fries 20
Hot Calamari Rings 63
Hot Cheese Bites 23
Hush Puffins 25

I

Indian Cauliflower Tikka Bites 20
Indian-inspired Chicken Skewers 80
Inside Out Cheeseburgers 107
Inside-out Cheeseburgers 110
Irresistible Cheesy Chicken Sticks 90
Italian Roasted Chicken Thighs 81

J

Jalapeño Poppers 24
Jerk Chicken Drumsticks 90

K

Katsu Chicken Thighs 82
Kentucky-style Pork Tenderloin 52
King Prawns Al Ajillo 69
Korean Brussels Sprouts 23
Korean-style Fried Calamari 78

L

Lamb Koftas Meatballs 48
Lamb Meatballs With Quick Tomato Sauce 54
Lemon Monkey Bread 26
Lemon Sage Roast Chicken 83
Lemon&Herb Crusted Salmon 77
Lemon-dill Salmon Burgers 68
Lentil Burritos With Cilantro Chutney 96
Lime Halibut Parcels 65

M

Maewoon Chicken Legs 89
Mango Cobbler With Raspberries 114
Maple Bacon Wrapped Chicken Breasts 81

Maple Balsamic Glazed Salmon 65
Masala Chicken With Charred Vegetables 84
Masala Fish`n´Chips 64
Matcha Granola 26
Mediterranean Potato Skins 16
Mediterranean Salmon Cakes 65
Mexican Cheeseburgers 111
Mexican Twice Air-fried Sweet Potatoes 98
Mini Everything Bagels 33
Mini Meatloaves With Pancetta 57
Mixed Berry Hand Pies 120
Mixed Berry Pie 117
Mojito Fish Tacos 66
Mojo Sea Bass 67
Morning Apple Biscuits 29
Morning Burrito 31
Morning Loaded Potato Skins 28
Moroccan Cauliflower 43
Mouth-watering Provençal Mushrooms 45
Mushroom&Quinoa-stuffed Pork Loins 52
Mushroom&Turkey Bread Pizza 81
Mushrooms 42
Mustardy Chicken Bites 83

N

Natchitoches Meat Pies 53
Nicoise Deviled Eggs 18
Nutty Banana Bread 118
Nutty Cookies 117
Nutty Shrimp With Amaretto Glaze 76
Nutty Whole Wheat Muffins 33

O

Oat&Nut Granola 29
Oktoberfest Bratwursts 50
Old Bay Crab Cake Burgers 76
Old Bay Fish`n´Chips 70
Old Bay Lobster Tails 63
Orange-chocolate Cake 123
Oreo-coated Peanut Butter Cups 116
Original Köttbullar 50
Oyster Shrimp With Fried Rice 67
Oyster Spring Rolls 17

P

Panko-breaded Onion Rings 14
Panko-crusted Zucchini Fries 40
Paprika Chicken Drumettes 89
Paprika Fried Beef 58
Parmesan Crusted Chicken Cordon Bleu 87
Parsnip Fries With Romesco Sauce 37
Patatas Bravas 45
Peach Cobbler 115
Peachy Pork Chops 46
Peanut Butter-barbeque Chicken 91
Pecan Turkey Cutlets 86
Peppered Maple Bacon Knots 31
Peppered Steak Bites 60
Pepperoni Bagel Pizzas 59
Pepperoni Pockets 51
Perfect Burgers 108
Perfect French Fries 35

Ninja Foodi 2-Basket Air Fryer

Perfect Soft-shelled Crabs	66
Pesto Egg&Ham Sandwiches	30
Philly Cheesesteak Sandwiches	107
Piña Colada Shrimp	69
Pine Nut Eggplant Dip	93
Pineapple&Veggie Souvlaki	103
Pizza Portobello Mushrooms	96
Poblano Bake	88
Polenta	43
Popcorn Chicken Bites	18
Popcorn Chicken Tenders With Vegetables	80
Popcorn Crawfish	65
Pork Loin	60
Powerful Jackfruit Fritters	105
Prosciutto Polenta Rounds	18
Puff Pastry Apples	114
Pumpkin Bread With Walnuts	26
Pumpkin Brownies	119
Pumpkin Empanadas	34

Q

Quick Tuna Tacos	77
Quinoa Burgers With Feta Cheese And Dill	102
Quinoa Green Pizza	105
Quinoa&Black Bean Stuffed Peppers	102

R

Ranch Chicken Tortillas	88
Raspberry Empanada	115
Restaurant-style Breaded Shrimp	73
Rib Eye Bites With Mushrooms	46
Rice&Bean Burritos	106
Rich Salmon Burgers With Broccoli Slaw	73
Rich Turkey Burgers	86
Ricotta Stuffed Apples	116
Ricotta Veggie Potpie	98
Roasted Belgian Endive With Pistachios And Lemon	44
Roasted Broccoli And Red Bean Salad	35
Roasted Brussels Sprouts With Bacon	40
Roasted Fennel Salad	39
Roasted Pears	121
Roasted Ratatouille Vegetables	37
Roasted Thyme Asparagus	41
Roasted Vegetable Pita Pizza	100
Roasted Vegetable Thai Green Curry	101
Roasted Vegetable,Brown Rice And Black Bean Burrito	100
Russian Pierogi With Cheese Dip	14

S

S'mores Pockets	115
Sage Pork With Potatoes	49
Sage&Paprika Turkey Cutlets	85
Sage&Thyme Potatoes	38
Salmon Croquettes	71
Salmon Puttanesca En Papillotte With Zucchini	74
Salmon	75
Salty German-style Shrimp Pancakes	66
Salty Pita Crackers	23
Satay Chicken Skewers	80
Saucy Chicken Thighs	88
Saucy Shrimp	76
Sea Bass With Fruit Salsa	73

Sea Salt Radishes	40
Sea-salted Caramel Cookie Cups	116
Shakshuka Cups	25
Shrimp Al Pesto	77
Shrimp Patties	75
Shrimp Toasts	15
Shrimp,Chorizo And Fingerling Potatoes	76
Shrimp-jalapeño Poppers In Prosciutto	63
Simple Green Bake	42
Simple Peppared Carrot Chips	43
Simple Salsa Chicken Thighs	80
Sinaloa Fish Fajitas	72
Sirloin Steak Bites With Gravy	55
Skirt Steak Fajitas	59
Sloppy Joes	50
Smoked Paprika Sweet Potato Fries	103
Smoked Salmon Croissant Sandwich	31
Smokehouse-style Beef Ribs	47
Smoky Chicken Fajita Bowl	79
Southeast Asian-style Tuna Steaks	68
Southern-fried Chicken Livers	85
Spanakopita Spinach,Feta And Pine Nut Phyllo Bites	19
Spanish Fried Baby Squid	17
Speedy Baked Caprese With Avocado	35
Speedy Shrimp Paella	63
Spiced Fruit Skewers	117
Spiced Nuts	21
Spiced Parsnip Chips	18
Spicy Bean Patties	104
Spicy Chicken And Pepper Jack Cheese Bites	13
Spicy Hoisin Bbq Pork Chops	47
Spicy Vegetable And Tofu Shake Fry	99
Spinach And Cheese Calzone	100
Spinach And Feta Stuffed Chicken Breasts	84
Spinach-bacon Rollups	27
Sriracha Green Beans	35
Sriracha Pork Strips With Rice	57
Steak Fries	41
Steamboat Shrimp Salad	44
Sticky Broccoli Florets	43
Strawberry Donuts	114
Strawberry Pastry Rolls	113
String Bean Fries	23
Stuffed Baby Bella Caps	22
Stuffed Portobellos	97
Stuffed Prunes In Bacon	23
Stuffed Zucchini Boats	97
Stunning Apples&Onions	35
Succulent Roasted Peppers	41
Sunday Chicken Skewers	82
Super-simple Herby Turkey	79
Sushi-style Deviled Eggs	94
Suwon Pork Meatballs	49
Sweet Apple Fries	23
Sweet Corn Bread	95
Sweet Potato Chips	19
Sweet Potato Fries	44
Sweet Potato-cinnamon Toast	27
Sweet Potato–wrapped Shrimp	64
Sweet&Spicy Swordfish Kebabs	67
Sweet-and-sour Chicken	85

T

Tacos Norteños	58

Tamari-seasoned Pork Strips	58
Tasty Filet Mignon	55
Tasty Roasted Black Olives&Tomatoes	15
T-bone Steak With Roasted Tomato,Corn And Asparagus Salsa	62
Tempura Fried Veggies	21
Teriyaki Chicken Drumsticks	84
Teriyaki Chicken Legs	83
Teriyaki Country-style Pork Ribs	48
Teriyaki Tofu With Spicy Mayo	44
Tex-mex Fish Tacos	69
Thai Peanut Veggie Burgers	102
Thai-style Pork Sliders	110
Thanksgiving Turkey Sandwiches	107
The Ultimate Chicken Bulgogi	90
Thyme Lentil Patties	95
Tofu&Broccoli Salad	43
Tomato Candy	37
Tomato&Halloumi Bruschetta	24
Tomato&Squash Stuffed Mushrooms	99
Tonkatsu	54
Tortilla Fried Pies	118
Traditional Italian Beef Meatballs	52
Traditional Moo Shu Pork Lettuce Wraps	49
Tropical Salsa	96
Tuna Nuggets In Hoisin Sauce	64
Tuna Platter	36
Turkey Burger Sliders	18
Turkey Scotch Eggs	90
Turkey&Rice Frittata	81
Tuscan Chimichangas	50
Tuscan Toast	25

V

Vanilla-strawberry Muffins	122
Vegan Buddha Bowls(2)	94
Vegetable Couscous	92
Vegetable Hand Pies	95
Vegetable Spring Rolls	13
Vegetarian Eggplant"pizzas"	98
Vegetarian Paella	95
Vegetarian Shepherd´s Pie	102
Veggie Chips	20
Veggie Fried Rice	93
Veggie&Feta Scramble Bowls	32
Vietnamese Gingered Tofu	101
Vietnamese Shaking Beef	48
Vip´s Club Sandwiches	84

W

Wasabi Pork Medallions	56
Wasabi-coated Pork Loin Chops	57
Western Omelet	30
White Bean Veggie Burgers	110
Wild Blueberry Lemon Chia Bread	27
Wild Blueberry Sweet Empanadas	113
Windsor´s Chicken Salad	89
Wrapped Shrimp Bites	12

Y

Yellow Squash	38
Yummy Salmon Burgers With Salsa Rosa	74

Z

Zesty London Broil	46
Zucchini Boats With Bacon	16
Zucchini Tacos	100
Zucchini Tamale Pie	93

Ninja Foodi 2-Basket Air Fryer

Manufactured by Amazon.ca
Acheson, AB